W9-CSU-764

IMPORTANT

HERE IS YOUR REGISTRATION CODE TO ACCESS MCGRAW-HILL PREMIUM CONTENT AND MCGRAW-HILL ONLINE RESOURCES

For key premium online resources you need THIS CODE to gain access. Once the code is entered, you will be able to use the web resources for the length of your course.

Access is provided only if you have purchased a new book.

If the registration code is missing from this book, the registration screen on our website, and within your WebCT or Blackboard course will tell you how to obtain your new code. Your registration code can be used only once to establish access. It is not transferable.

To gain access to these online resources

1. **USE** your web browser to go to: **http://www.mhhe.com/walker2e**

2. **CLICK** on "First Time User"

3. **ENTER** the Registration Code printed on the tear-off bookmark on the right

4. After you have entered your registration code, click on "Register"

5. **FOLLOW** the instructions to setup your personal UserID and Password

6. **WRITE** your UserID and Password down for future reference. Keep it in a safe place.

If your course is using WebCT or Blackboard, you'll be able to use this code to access the McGraw-Hill content within your instructor's online course.

To gain access to the McGraw-Hill content in your instructor's WebCT or Blackboard course simply log into the course with the user ID and Password provided by your instructor. Enter the registration code exactly as it appears to the right when prompted by the system. You will only need to use this code the first time you click on McGraw-Hill content.

These instructions are specifically for student access. Instructors are not required to register via the above instructions.

The McGraw·Hill Companies

McGraw-Hill Irwin

Thank you, and welcome to your McGraw-Hill/Irwin Online Resources.

Walker
Modern Competitive Strategy, 2/e
ISBN-13: 978-0-07-327762-2
ISBN-10: 0-07-327762-2

BKTT-YXDV-YAQK-TAVY-PYAD

REGISTRATION CODE
REGISTRATION CODE

The McGraw·Hill Companies

McGraw-Hill Irwin

Modern Competitive Strategy

second edition

Gordon Walker
Southern Methodist University

**McGraw-Hill
Irwin**

Boston   Burr Ridge, IL   Dubuque, IA   Madison, WI   New York   San Francisco   St. Louis
Bangkok   Bogotá   Caracas   Kuala Lumpur   Lisbon   London   Madrid   Mexico City
Milan   Montreal   New Delhi   Santiago   Seoul   Singapore   Sydney   Taipei   Toronto

McGraw-Hill Irwin

MODERN COMPETITIVE STRATEGY

Published by McGraw-Hill/Irwin, a business unit of The McGraw-Hill Companies, Inc., 1221 Avenue of the Americas, New York, NY, 10020. Copyright © 2007 by The McGraw-Hill Companies, Inc. All rights reserved. No part of this publication may be reproduced or distributed in any form or by any means, or stored in a database or retrieval system, without the prior written consent of The McGraw-Hill Companies, Inc., including, but not limited to, in any network or other electronic storage or transmission, or broadcast for distance learning.

Some ancillaries, including electronic and print components, may not be available to customers outside the United States.

This book is printed on acid-free paper.

1 2 3 4 5 6 7 8 9 0 DOC/DOC 0 9 8 7 6

ISBN-13: 978-0-07-310284-9
ISBN-10: 0-07-310284-9

Editorial director: *John E. Biernat*
Senior sponsoring editor: *Ryan Blankenship*
Editorial coordinator: *Allison J. Belda*
Marketing manager: *Sarah Reed*
Senior media producer: *Damian Moshak*
Project manager: *Dana M. Pauley*
Senior production supervisor: *Sesha Bolisetty*
Senior designer: *Kami Carter*
Senior media project manager: *Susan Lombardi*
Cover design: *Kami Carter*
Typeface: *10.5/12 Times New Roman*
Compositor: *International Typesetting and Composition*
Printer: *R. R. Donnelley*

Library of Congress Cataloging-in-Publication Data

Walker, Gordon, 1944–
    Modern competitive strategy / Gordon Walker.—2nd ed.
        p. cm.
    Includes index.
    ISBN-13: 978-0-07-310284-9 (alk. paper)
    ISBN-10: 0-07-310284-9 (alk. paper)
    1. Strategic planning. 2. Industrial management. I. Title.
HD30.28.W3349 2007
658.4'012—dc22
                                                                2006041984

www.mhhe.com

To Nancy, Emma, Curran, and Ian

About the Author

Gordon Walker is Professor and Chairman of the Strategy and Entrepreneurship Department at the Edwin L. Cox School of Business at Southern Methodist University. He received his BA from Yale University and an MBA and PhD from the Wharton School, University of Pennsylvania. Dr. Walker has previously taught at the Sloan School, MIT; at the Wharton School, University of Pennsylvania; and at Yale University. The author of numerous articles, he is on the editorial boards of *Administrative Science Quarterly, Strategic Organization,* and *Organization Science.* He has received several grants from the National Science Foundation.

Dr. Walker has consulted and performed contract research for a number of organizations, including Chaparral Steel, Sprint, Xerox, General Motors, Johnson & Johnson, Carlson Restaurants, Texas Instruments, The Associates, Halliburton, UICI, and EDS, as well as numerous smaller firms. His executive training programs include senior management seminars at Southern Methodist University, the Wharton School, Yale University, and INSEAD. He was named among the best business policy teachers in the United States in 1994 and 1998 by *BusinessWeek* magazine and received the President's University Teaching Award in 1999 at SMU. He is listed in *Who's Who in America* and *Who's Who in the World.* He serves on the board of directors of Alico, Inc. (NASDAQ), where he chairs the Strategic Planning and the Nominating and Governance Committees. Professor Walker was an infantry officer in the Marine Corps from 1967 to 1970 and was awarded the Bronze Star.

The genesis of this book lies in my experience as a strategy professor. Over the past 24 years, I have taught the core strategic management course in some very good MBA programs. When I began as an assistant professor, Michael Porter's book, *Competitive Strategy,* had recently been published, and I adopted it. The book brought the concepts and observations of industrial economists into the realm of business policy in a way that students and practitioners could comprehend and appreciate. At the time Porter's book was introduced, there was little research in strategic management, and his book presented the most rigorously developed set of frameworks available to academics teaching and doing research in strategy.

Over the past two decades, however, the strategy field has developed into a robust discipline with its own interests and research topics. Many of these topics build on the original synthesis of industrial economics in early strategy texts. However, many current ideas, concepts, and theories are only loosely related to traditional industry analysis. Practitioners, moreover, have continuously innovated to solve strategic problems in ways that the frameworks of industry analysis do not address. Its major points remain essential, but these points do not cover as much of the territory of strategy as they once did.

As the field developed, I moved more to teaching with readings, a shift that I believe has been fairly common for strategy courses in many business schools. But because many effective readings were (and are) written in practitioner journals, they were often oriented primarily toward application. This emphasis was beneficial for some topics, but the course was often perceived as lacking sufficient theoretical content or coherence.

What was needed then was a book founded on disciplinary research which at the same time included the concepts and topics of strategy that have been developed over the past 20 years. Moreover, since I teach at all levels—undergraduate, MBA, and EMBA—the book had to be understandable to students who had never been in business and yet offer immediate practical benefits to line managers and executives. And it had to be readable and fit within the confines of a module or quarter (7 to 10 weeks) or a semester-long course.

This is the book I have tried to write.

The organization of the book in this edition is unchanged from the first. The book has five parts:

- Introduction
- Building Competitive Advantage
- Managing the Boundaries of the Firm
- Expanding the Scope of the Firm
- Governing the Firm

Each part deals with a separate set of strategic issues as the firm grows from one to multiple lines of business.

Part I lays out the concept of strategy and argues that strategy is about achieving superior performance over time. Companies can accomplish this goal in ways that look very different across industries. But a single theme underlies these differences: The superior firm produces more value for the customer at a lower cost than competitors and defends the sources of this advantage—the firm's resources and capabilities—from imitation. This traditional but robust approach to defining competitive advantage pervades the book.

The chapters in Part II describe how successful firms build competitive advantage within the constraints of industry forces as they evolve over time, with a separate discussion of strategy execution within the organization. Part III focuses on how the firm executes its strategy by managing its boundaries through vertical integration and outsourcing and takes a separate look at partnerships. Part IV expands the scope of the firm to global markets and multiple businesses. Last, Part V outlines in detail the major issues of corporate governance, including its legal and institutional frameworks, and of strategic planning, the practical tool that brings the logic of strategy systematically to the whole organization.

I believe this approach has three main advantages:

- It provides a relevant, discipline-based underpinning to the discussion of important strategy topics and allows the student to make connections among these topics as the course proceeds. By the end of the course, the student should see that many strategic problems can be understood as elaborations of a small number of theoretical frameworks. Thus, the course is an integrated experience.

- It provides a clear way to understand the similarities and differences between single and multibusiness strategic issues. Identifying how a business can be improved as part of a multibusiness enterprise is a central management task. However, this task cannot be accomplished if the business and its parent organization are not understood through common strategic frameworks. In other words, there can be no concept of corporate strategy without a clear and practical concept of business strategy.

- The text covers a wide range of current strategy topics and links current theory to management practice. My experience with the frameworks in the book is that they are especially well suited for teaching cases, from any era currently in the case archives—Head Ski to Blockbuster and Microsoft 2002, Crown Cork and Seal to Merck and Zara. Further, when students read the business press, they will be able to see the applicability of what they're being taught. Also, it has been my experience that senior executives resonate with the approach taken in the book and relate its frameworks in their own decision making.

These benefits can be realized at any level of instruction. It can be gratifying to see undergraduates respond appropriately and enthusiastically to almost the same material that executive MBAs appreciate for somewhat different reasons. The undergrads like the clarity, coherence, and consistency of the approach to strategy, while EMBAs can take much of the material and apply it directly to their work. Needless to say, regular MBAs can experience the material in both ways.

Several teaching supplements are available to adopters of this text: an instructor's manual, including lecture notes, multiple-choice questions, and suggested cases for each chapter; a computerized test bank; and PowerPoint slides with key figures from the book and other lecture materials. Select supplements and additional resources are available from the book website at www.mhhe.com/walker2e.

What Is New in This Edition?

In this edition I have tried to deepen and broaden the content of the earlier book in those places where I felt something was obviously missing. It is certain, however, that strategy specialists will still see areas that could be developed more effectively, and students will inevitably want more examples and tools for practice. These additions will have to wait until the next time around. Also, I have tried to keep the book grounded in research or, when research was lacking, in the most reasonable logic available.

The book needed a better introduction, and so I have rewritten the first chapter almost completely, with many new examples and concepts. The goal in this new chapter is to introduce the concept of strategy in its multiple forms without losing the central point that strategy defines how the firm makes money. Moving away from this definition only muddies the waters and creates trouble for both researchers and managers. The chapter ends with a section on the financial performance measures used by Standard & Poors. This part shows how S&P uses assessments of competitive advantage in rating companies. The point is that a firm's creditworthiness is a function not only of financial outcomes, but also of the strategy that produces them.

I have also substantially revamped Chapter 2, "Building Competitive Advantage." Chapter 2 contains a new section on "willingness-to-pay," with methods and examples. As a concept, willingness-to-pay underlies the notion of customer value, a key construct in this book without which strategy has no grounding in practice. There is also an extended section on Target Corporation, an exemplar of the successful firm that is "stuck in the middle." Consistent with the first edition, this version of the book strongly advocates focusing on superior productivity, in terms of offering customers more value at a lower cost, the so-called V minus C paradigm. Chapter 2 lays out this model, which is then used in every chapter that follows to synthesize the material.

Chapter 3, "Industry Analysis," has also been rewritten extensively. The key addition here is a section on competing in an oligopoly. The new material contains examples of two rivals that are price takers (Cournot competition) or price makers (Bertrand competition) and an extended discussion of tacit collusion and cartels. The point of this section is that interfirm coordination on price or other variables is hard to establish and, even when it is legal, hard to maintain. Although it is essential to be knowledgeable about strategic interaction and its consequences, becoming more productive is a more robust path to strong performance.

In the rest of the chapters, I have tried to update examples and insert material that would increase the reader's appreciation of the concepts. For example, Chapter 4 now includes a chart on Samsung's dynamic growth cycle and on the substitution of DVDs for VCRs; Chapters 6 and 8 have sidebars on China; Chapter 10 has a new section on divisional performance metrics, based on residual income; and Chapter 11 has a new sidebar on Sarbanes-Oxley (SOX) Rule 404 and a section on the consequences of board practices for the firm's share price. These additions are meant to complement and expand the existing text, which in almost all cases has itself been revised to improve readability.

At the end of each chapter I've appended "Questions for Practice" in order to stimulate the reader to imagine how the chapter's concepts would apply to the situations that companies face.

Many people have helped in preparing this version of the book. Without their assistance, it could not have been accomplished. Steve Postrel has been remarkably helpful in commenting on the material. His input has been critical for choosing and organizing content throughout the book, but especially Chapter 3. Jon O'Brien was also very helpful in his comments on that chapter. Tammy Madsen's thoughts on many aspects of the book have been consistently useful and penetrating. I have benefited from conversations with Nick Argyres, Jackson Nickerson, Russ Coff, Anita McGahan, Marvin Lieberman, Rich Makadok, Bruce Kogut, Margie Peteraf, David Hoopes, David and Rachel Croson, Gary Moskowitz, Michael Jacobides, Ron Adner, Tim Folta, Javier Gimeno, Tom Moliterno, Ed Zajac, Andy Spicer, Jordan Siegel, Pankaj Ghemawat, Gautam Ahuja, Asli Arikan, and Robert Burgelman. I have appreciated the perspectives and insights of the executives who have discussed aspects of the book with me. I have had helpful conversations with Paul Passmore, Greg Mutz, John Alexander, Charles Palmer, Jack McCarty, Raymond Herpers, Chuck Armstrong, and Atul Vohra.

The following reviewers of the book were very helpful in keeping my language and concepts straight: Raja Roy, Tulane University; Michael Pitts, Virginia Commonwealth University; Glen Hoetker, University of Illinois; Roy Suddaby, University of Iowa; Will Mitchell, Duke University; Richard Spinnello, Boston College; William Bogner, Georgia State University; Susan McEvily, University of Pittsburgh; Jonathan O'Brien, University of Notre Dame; Lyda Bigelow, Washington University.

I don't think I have done justice to the excellent comments of these reviewers. But without them the task of steering this material through the shoals of the strategy field would have been impossible.

I am indebted to my students who allowed me to experiment with the book's concepts as they applied to a wide range of teaching cases. This experience was essential for helping me appreciate how the book's ideas worked in the classroom. In many cases, the linkages between the ideas and their range of applicability were not clear until the ideas were taught.

My publisher has provided invaluable assistance in putting this book together. My editors at McGraw-Hill/Irwin—Ryan Blankenship and Allison Belda, and especially my developmental editor, Judith Gallagher—have been constantly supportive of this project and remarkably patient about its development. Thanks also to Dana Pauley, my project manager, who kept me on schedule.

Finally, my family deserves the greatest thanks. It will take me a long time to repay their kindness and generosity.

Gordon Walker

Brief Contents

Contents

Managing the Boundaries of the Firm

CHAPTER 6

Expanding the Scope of the Firm
CHAPTER 8
Competing in Global Markets   211

CHAPTER 9
New Business Development   239

CHAPTER 10
Managing the Multibusiness Firm   255

5
Governing the Firm
CHAPTER 11
Corporate Governance   279

CHAPTER 12
Strategic Planning and Decision Making   307

Introduction

What Is Strategy?

Roadmap

The concept of strategy helps us grasp why some firms succeed and others fail. In simple terms, since failure is typically driven by economic factors, strategy explains how a firm makes money. Good strategies produce higher profits, and bad ones threaten the firm's existence.

Although a clear game plan is important for major investments, such as a new technology or a new plant, strategy also refers to the broad swath of routines, policies, and decisions that occur throughout an organization. Together these determine the firm's position in its product market and to some degree its vulnerability to competition. A strong, defendable market position is the essence of an enduring competitive advantage.

In this chapter, we introduce strategy as a concept and discuss its significance for company performance. The chapter is structured as follows:

- Why Do We Study Business Strategy?

- How Important Is Strategy, Really?

- The Origins of Strategy.

- Strategy over Time: Growth and Innovation.

- Strategy Execution and Strategic Planning.

- Strategy in Single and Multibusiness Firms.

- Definitions of Business Performance.

- Summary

Why Do We Study Business Strategy?

The concept of **business strategy** fills a need in management thinking in three ways. First, it describes how the resources and capabilities of a business relate to its markets—the better the match, the better the firm's performance. Second, it provides a framework for integrating the firm's activities, such as marketing and operations, so that they reinforce each other to produce stronger outcomes. Last, knowledge of business strategy disciplines decision making, focusing attention on more valuable investments and reducing the number of missteps.

It is common to put the word *competitive* before strategy in order to highlight the persistent rivalry firms face in their markets. Because this competition is often intense, business strategy is seen as analogous to the strategy of an army at war. It is misleading, however, to take the martial analogy too far. It is true that when firms compete head to head, they view each other as the enemy (e.g., Coke versus Pepsi, Intel versus AMD, Boeing versus Airbus), especially in sales. But firms have customers, whereas armies do not. Because they compete for customer accounts, firms act differently from soldiers fighting in battle. For example, firms do not confront each other directly, which means that there is no face-to-face conflict where one tries to kill the other. Customer purchasing decisions, not arms, determine success and failure. *In fact, without customers, a firm's produces nothing of value at all.* This fundamental difference between warfare and competition in business means that we should not overgeneralize military metaphors (e.g., Sun Tzu's teachings, the OODA loop), however interesting and motivating they may be.[1,2] It is important to know the competition very well, but attention to the customer comes first.

Businesses clearly differ in how they become successful. Some, like the Apple iPod (see the sidebar), provide superior value to the customer through a more appealing design, greater functionality, or other characteristics. Others, like Dell in PCs and Nucor in steel, become number one in their industries because of low cost. High value and low cost are two ends of the market spectrum. Can a firm succeed in the middle? The answer is yes. A good illustration is Dannon Yogurt, the worldwide market share leader. Dannon offers the best value-price combination even as it is flanked on each side of the market by more upscale and lower cost competitors.[3] In a final example, some firms succeed by swamping the competition early in the stages of industry development and then by defending their dominant positions aggressively as the industry matures. This is Microsoft's story.

These examples of successful companies lead to a fundamental premise of this book: An effective framework for understanding business strategy has to start with an emphasis on the transaction with the customer. The transaction can be broken down into two parts. The first part has to do with inducing customers to buy the product. No business can succeed without delivering enough value so that buyers make a purchase. This statement is so basic as to be almost folk wisdom. But achieving dominance in an industry by following this fundamental idea is neither simple nor easy. The iPod example clearly shows that customers received significant value from using the product (basically the fun of listening to a massive amount of their own music on a cool, portable device) even when its price was rather high. Also, Apple understood that the number of buyers would grow substantially as the price went down and the firm enhanced the customer's experience with the product (e.g., more storage, more accessories, more tunes to play).

Apple iPod

In October 2001, Apple Computer introduced a portable MP3 player called the iPod, a product that almost immediately dominated its market. What has made the iPod so successful? How does Apple maintain its dominance over its competitors in this market?

Apple did not invent MP3 technology, nor was the iPod the first MP3 player. In fact, the idea for the iPod did not even originate at Apple. The concept of a player coupled with an online source for music was developed by an independent consultant. Apple hired him and then built a design team around him. Steve Jobs, Apple's CEO, was deeply involved in the iPod's design, much of which was coordinated with a suite of vendors. These included PortalPlayer, which provided the system-on-a-chip core processing unit; Toshiba, which produced the product's original tiny hard drive; and Samsung, which manufactured the memory chip that protects against skips. Apple does not even assemble the iPod; it is put together by Inventec, a Taiwanese firm. So Apple really doesn't do much more than design and market the product, along with managing the whole value chain of partners.

Compared to other MP3 players, the first iPod could play more songs, was smaller and lighter—and cost much more: $399 for a 5G disk drive. The iPod's major innovations were its cool design, a 1.8-inch hard drive that held roughly 1,000 songs, and a scroll wheel that allowed the user to choose and manipulate the playlist more effectively than competing machines. The iPod also could download songs from multiple online sources, such as Napster and iTunes.

After the iPod's initial success, Apple moved quickly to expand and improve the product line. A second generation of iPods was introduced in 2002 at lower prices. The scroll wheel technology was enhanced, and the iPod could now link to both Apple computers and Windows-based PCs. Apple launched a third generation in April 2003, and a fourth generation appeared in 2004 with greater disk capacity and extended battery life. Apple also expanded the product line with the iPod mini, the iPod U2, the iPod shuffle, and the iPod Photo. Apple's product variations covered the product space almost completely.

To broaden its distribution channels, in January 2004 Apple formed a partnership with HP to sell HP iPods through retail electronics stores. Further, many companies had introduced products to support the iPod, such as docking stations for cars, hookups with home audio systems, microphones for voice recording, holders for bicycles, and upscale speaker systems.

In late 2004, the iPod commanded over 80 percent of the market. Dell, Sony, iRiver, Rio, and Creative introduced competing players, each with innovative features. But none of these could overcome Apple's dominant position.

What were the key elements of the iPod's successful strategy? Obviously Apple pursued the high end of the market, emphasizing value and not price. Apple bet rightly that the look and feel of the iPod plus its larger storage capacity would overcome any sticker shock. The product's value lay in its aesthetics, its technology (disk storage capacity, scroll wheel), the presence of complementary products (music download sites, speaker systems, docking stations) that enhanced the iPod's usefulness, and probably Apple's brand.

Also, the time was ripe for a new consumer electronics innovation. Stereo music systems were long past their prime, and PCs were getting old.

Finally, Apple's innovations—expanding the product line and adding more value at each price point—undoubtedly attracted more customers and kept competitors off guard. This ongoing cycle of growth and innovation was essential in Apple's effort to make the iPod the market standard.

The chart below shows the iPod's remarkable rise from early 2003 until the end of 2004. The break between spring and summer of 2004 was obviously an inflection point. In the last quarter of 2004, the iPod accounted for roughly 46 percent of Apple's revenues.

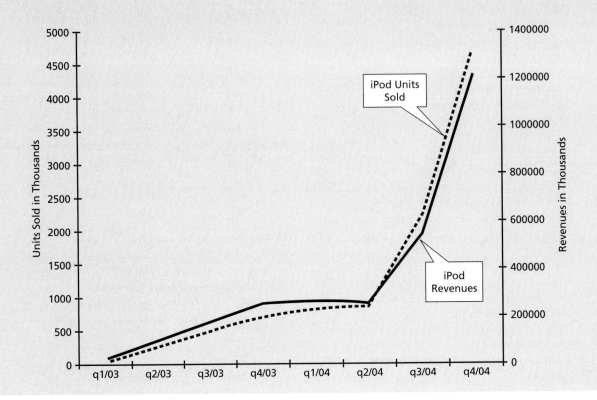

Value and price are critical, but they are only half of the equation. The second part is how much money the firm makes in the transaction—the difference between the product's price and the cost to the firm of making or delivering the product. This is obviously the firm's profit. The money the firm makes can be used to reinvest in improving the product so that the firm grows further, as happened rather rapidly in the case of the iPod. Obviously, the firm can do other things with profits such as distribute them to shareholders in the form of dividends, buy back stock, or pay down debt.

Thus, we can think of the transaction as the sum of two parts: value to the customer less the price of the product (the bigger the difference, the more customers buy the product) and price minus cost to the firm (the bigger the difference, the more money the firm makes). Every successful strategy focuses on both of these parts, some firms emphasizing value first (Apple Computer), some cost first (Nucor), and some the combination of value and cost (Dannon Yogurt). This focus on the transaction with the customer is the beginning, but far from the end, of how to think about business strategy.

So what about Microsoft? A lot has been written about how Microsoft came to dominate PC operating systems, much of it based on U.S. and European antitrust cases that began in 1994 and 2000, respectively. These cases focused more on how the company defended its dominant market position than on whether the position was superior to competitors. It is safe to say that for Microsoft, defense has been very important. To understand how Microsoft sustained its dominance, we therefore need to lay out how firms protect their market positions from competitors.

There are two ways to defend a market position. The first is keeping customers from defecting to rivals. The simple way to do this is to make defection expensive. The higher the **switching costs,** the longer a customer is likely to stay with the current product. The second way is making certain that competition for customers is low. This can be accomplished by ensuring that (1) there are severe difficulties associated with copying the dominant firm's technology or practices and (2) the costs of entry into the market are high. Microsoft used both of these defenses—higher switching costs and higher copying/entry costs—as it became dominant in PC operating systems and applications software.

We study strategy to learn both how businesses become dominant and how they defend their superior positions. As we will see later, these two pillars of sustainable competitive advantage—offense and defense—are the goal of strategic thinking in any ambitious company. Their combination is a formidable managerial tool for improving financial performance over the long haul.

How Important Is Strategy, Really?

To get a sense of the importance of business strategy, we need to understand the full range of factors that affect a firm's profitability. There are three major categories: (1) macroeconomic forces, such as exchange rates, tax policy, and regulation; (2) **industry forces,** such as competition and buyer and supplier power; and finally (3) characteristics of the business itself, like its strategy. Of these three types, research has shown that the firm's unique characteristics are frequently the most important.[4]

It would be foolish to ignore the effect that the macroeconomy has on business profits. When global markets are growing, as they were in the 1990s, firms in many industries make more money simply because demand is strong and products can be sold at higher prices. Sometimes single countries can affect the fortunes of an entire region. The rise of China, for example, has been a boon to many companies in Korea, Japan, Taiwan, and the rest of Asia. In contrast, when global markets are weak, prices drop and profits fall. Within nations, profits rise and fall with the state of the economy. Regulation and taxes also limit how much money firms can make.

Industry conditions also have an obvious influence on profits. Some industries grow quickly (MP3 players, video games) as others grow slowly (toasters, lawnmowers). Likewise, customers will buy everything firms can produce in one industry, while companies in other industries struggle to sell their products. Some industries can be relatively cheap to enter and are over-run with competition (cattle ranching, money market funds), while the cost of entering other industries is prohibitive (automobiles, aluminum). Even within industries that are hard to enter, firms can fight each other fiercely for a share of the market (Coke versus Pepsi) or live and let live (the global cement indus-try). The strength of buyers and suppliers also affects firm performance. The more powerful they are, the more they limit how much money firms can make. In combination, then, these industry forces—competition, entry, buyers and suppliers—as well as other factors such as substitute products (skis versus snowboards) constrain profits.

Third, and most important, economic performance is determined by how the firm is positioned in its market and how well the firm defends itself from com-petition. As the examples above showed (Apple, Nucor) establishing a successful **market position** is essential for **competitive advantage.** Successful positioning is based on assets and activities that offer customers value at a price that gives the firm a superior return. Once established, the position must be defended from other firms to prevent price competition. Firms in the same industry can differ substantially in their resources and activities, leading to wide variation in prof-itability independent of macroeconomic and industry factors.

The Origins of Strategy

Where did strategy come from as a field of study? Although military theo-rists, such as von Clausewitz, and political philosophers, such as Machiavelli, offer interesting insights about stratagems and power, many other sources of models and frameworks are also useful. The six basic origins of strategy are the following:

- Industrial and evolutionary economics.
- Case studies of exemplary companies.
- Business and industry history.
- Economic and organizational sociology.
- Strategic planning tools.
- Institutional economics.

Each of these touches on the question of why some firms are more successful than others. But none provides a wholly satisfying answer. Only viewed as a whole can they give us a reasonable framework for understanding competitive advantage.

The most salient discipline underlying the field of strategy is industrial economics.[5] Industry forces constrain what a firm can do (see Chapter 3), especially as they shift over time (see Chapter 4).[6] But analyzing the industry falls short because it does not get at the heart of the entrepreneurial activity that makes firms profitable. Examining how innovative routines develop over time, as evolutionary economists have done, gets closer to this critical entrepreneurial function (see Chapter 5).

The second building block of strategy consists of in-depth case studies of exemplary companies.[7] Cases capture the challenges behind the investment decisions that create successful market positions and protect them from competition. Although cases cannot completely explain how a company competes, they provide important insights, especially by showing how firms develop innovations that competitors can't imitate. The concept of a distinctive competence or capability has been derived from case studies and is critical for understanding competitive advantage (see Chapter 2).

Business and industry histories have also added significantly to strategy.[8] Because of their scope and detail, firm histories deepen the empirical base from which strategic concepts are formed. By describing competitive behavior over time, historians show how successful market positions have emerged.[9]

The contributions of economic and organizational sociology to strategy are found in five areas.[10] First, analyses of industry trends, especially rates of firm failure, have shown the relative importance of firm size and age for survival (see Chapter 4). Second, the internal structures and processes of firms have been analyzed for their relative efficiency and potential for generating innovations (see Chapter 5). Third, the development of networks of organizations has been analyzed as a strategic resource (see Chapter 7). Fourth, advantages associated with geographical location have been identified (see Chapter 8). Last, trends in corporate governance, including top management compensation and practices of boards of directors, have been examined systematically (see Chapter 11). These contributions are important pieces of the strategy puzzle.

Strategy has also evolved from planning tools for top managers.[11] Although strategic planning can improve performance markedly, it does not actually determine the array of investments managers choose from (see Chapter 12). Indeed planning is neither necessary nor sufficient for higher performance, since as long as a firm invests in projects that have a higher value than those of competitors, it need not have a formal strategic plan to be successful. However, planning models frequently capture key challenges and therefore can be very useful in identifying strategic problems (see Chapter 12). Without effective planning, a successful firm in a changing market can lose its advantage very quickly.

The final building block of strategy is institutional economics, which focuses on the effective governance of the firm's boundaries.[12] Governing the firm's boundary through vertical integration, outsourcing, and partnering is critical for strategy execution (see Chapters 6 and 7) and has become important in global industries over the past 30 years (see Chapter 8). Boundary decisions and the firm's market position are closely tied to each other since where the firm places its boundaries depends crucially on what activities it needs to control in order to succeed with customers.

Toyota

Toyota has risen from the ravages of postwar Japan in the late 1940s to the most successful auto company in the world today. The accompanying figure shows the extent to which Toyota has come to dominate its competitors in terms of productivity over the 30-year period from the late 1960s to the late 1990s.[13] For comparison purposes, the technical efficiency trend for General Motors, the worst performer in the industry, is shown. Other firms fall in between Toyota and GM.

What made Toyota such a formidable competitor? Obviously, autos are a relatively mature industry and have not changed much in basic design for roughly 50 years. So Toyota could not have prospered through a design breakthrough. Rather, Toyota is able to design and produce more attractive and higher quality cars at a lower cost than anyone else. The chart shows that Toyota has done this steadily over 40 years. What is Toyota's secret?

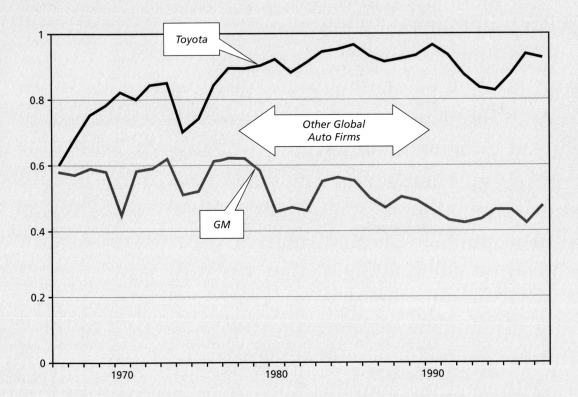

A large part of the answer is the Toyota production system. Developed by Taichi Ohno, Toyota's chief of production after World War II, this system evolved through trial and error by following a number of basic principles. Primary among these were just-in-time production processes, so that inventory within the plant was cut to the barest minimum, and the willingness to stop the assembly line whenever a worker made or found an error (a rule called *jidoka*). The goals of the system, pursued relentlessly, were highest quality, lowest cost, and shortest lead time. Toyota's suppliers integrated their production processes and logistics into the system and adopted its principles. A fundamental tenet underlying Toyota's method was a focus on solving problems scientifically so that they stayed solved. By following these principles, the production system evolved into the most powerful and widely adopted manufacturing model in the late 20th century.

At the same time that Toyota has improved its technical efficiency, it seems clear that General Motors' ability to produce high-quality cars at low cost has declined. GM's example shows that a firm can destroy its capabilities as well as build them. The key to understanding the changing fortunes of car companies is therefore how well they manage their investments in growth and innovation: Those that understand the importance of these investments succeed and those that seem to disinvest in innovation become weaker.

While none of these building blocks alone is enough to encompass the discipline of strategy, each makes critical contributions. In this book they are combined with mainstream strategic analysis to cover the key topics for understanding competitive advantage.

Strategy over Time: Growth and Innovation

As new challenges emerge, a firm's strategy must shift to meet them. To compete successfully, a firm must change its size and shape by adding or eliminating products, activities, and people. Without adaptation, profitability declines as new products invade the market with higher value or competitors invest in new processes that allow lower prices. Consequently, successful firms grow over the industry life cycle by maintaining a high level of productivity through innovation in resources and capabilities. These innovations involve changes in both value and cost drivers as the industry matures. The sidebar on Toyota on page 10 clearly shows how focusing on capability development leads to superior productivity.

Strategy Execution and Strategic Planning

How do firms decide what strategy to pursue and how do they implement the strategy once they've identified it? These questions are typically thought of as pertaining to **strategy formulation** and **strategy implementation,** respectively.[14] During strategy formulation, managers gather information about the firm's markets and competitors and identify its resources and capabilities. They then make careful decisions about what strategy the firm should follow to achieve its financial goals. Subsequently, in the implementation stage, managers invest in projects to build or buy the assets that are necessary for the strategy to be successful.

In this book, instead of discussing formulation and implementation, we focus on the concepts of strategic planning and strategy execution. The reason is that planning and execution, together or independently, are closer to what firms actually do. Not all businesses "formulate" a strategy per se; that is, their managers do not necessarily sit down and decide period after period what resources and capabilities the firm should have to achieve and then defend a specific market position in order to meet targeted financial goals. But even in the absence of a formulation process, the business still has a strategy. Although managers may not articulate what determines their firm's cash flows, the factors that underlie the firm's profitability can still be identified, even if they are quite complex or unusual. As these factors surface, the strategy of the business becomes apparent. Strategy execution therefore is ongoing, necessary, and in fact inevitable. Every business executes whatever strategy it has, whether goals are met or not. In fact, in many businesses it is only through execution that the strategy itself can be identified.[15]

Strategy execution essentially entails the continuous development, maintenance, and improvement of the resources and capabilities that are central to the business's market position. In this book (see Chapter 5), we will look at four elements of execution:

- Incentives and compensation.
- Control and coordination systems.
- The degree of consistency among the firm's activities.
- The firm's culture and human resource systems.

Each of these contributes in a particular way towards building the capabilities necessary for achieving a competitive advantage. Furthermore, effective strategy execution requires that each of these elements reinforce the others. For example, as the three largest major U.S. airlines—American, United, and Delta—attempt to reposition themselves in the market to compete with low-cost carriers such as Southwest and JetBlue, they face challenges in each of the elements of strategy execution. Compensation contracts must be changed; coordination systems must be altered to promote efficiency; the airline's policies and activities must be continually redesigned to lower costs; and a host of cultural and human resource issues must be confronted as traditional practices are eliminated. As these airlines shift their market positions, strategy execution along the dimensions outlined above is paramount.

As a management practice, strategic planning is more specific than strategy formulation (see Chapter 12). Planning models describe in detail the process for developing a business strategy and linking it to operational programs and investments. Strategic planning overlays and informs the financial reporting system by detailing the logic behind cash flow forecasts. Moreover, an effective plan moves the business closer to choosing the best set of projects for improving performance, given the business's current market position and the constraints of competition. The following sidebar presents a representative planning format and its purposes.

One can think of the firm's strategic initiatives, when developed effectively through a planning process, as linking functional activities together in

The Strategic Planning Format

A strategic plan at the business level typically has the following elements:

- A mission statement that defines the business's scope of business and strategic intent.

- An analysis of the business's industry and market position relative to competitors and a statement of assumptions regarding the competitive environment.

- A statement of the business's financial and operating goals.

- The strategic initiatives necessary to achieve these goals.

- The specific programs necessary to achieve each strategic initiative.

As a practice the strategic planning process should also do the following:

- Act as a tool for management decision making.

- Communicate the organization's strategy without jargon and in a format that is conceptually coherent.

- Generate commitment from employees and motivate their actions.

- Motivate the organization's systems of financial and operating control, including its metrics.

- Be reviewed regularly and in response to unexpected and significant market changes.

a single, coherent framework that leads to stronger business performance (see Figure 1.1).

Not uncommonly, this framework emerges as the strategic planning process uncovers or articulates the strategy the firm is following. Some firms, but certainly not all, go through a strategic planning process carefully in order to gain more control over their investment decisions. This was a major motivation behind the implementation of strategic planning methods at General Electric in the late 1960s. In fact, in a way, because strategic planning increases control, planning can be thought of as part of strategy execution, turning the sequential process of formulation and implementation on its head.

A second important benefit from a strategic planning process arises from its potential to solve problems and develop innovations. In the process, participants commonly raise a range of strategic and operating issues, some of which are new to other managers. The exposure of these issues in the planning forum

FIGURE 1.1

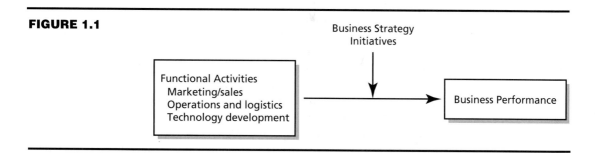

often stimulates the development of creative ways to resolve them. Planning sessions are also sometimes useful for generating innovative ideas to move the firm in a new strategic direction, whether it is a novel technology, market, or way of organizing. For example, when Royal Dutch Shell used scenarios in its strategic planning, it uncovered a radically new approach to predicting market trends. This lesson led to a change in the company's investments in refinery capacity, greatly reducing exposure to shifts in demand.[16]

Strategy in Single and Multibusiness Firms

The strategies of single and multibusiness firms require different types of analysis. Companies like Dell Computer, a firm engaged almost exclusively in the assembly and sale of personal computers and therefore a single business, obviously face quite different challenges than diversified firms like GE, one of the largest companies in the world. Dell has one business model. But GE is composed of six major segments, each of which contains a range of businesses. The GE spectrum stretches from aircraft engines to a major media unit (NBC/Universal) to engineered plastics to financial services. In general, single businesses make money by making and selling goods and services in one industry. On the other hand, multibusiness firms are composed by definition of more than one business and make money by supporting these units effectively.

Single businesses compete by building superior market positions. A business also acts to lower the effect of market competition on its profits in part by discouraging other firms from entering the industry. Implementing a strategy successfully entails organizing the business's activities to support its goals.

In contrast, the strategy of a multibusiness firm involves managing a portfolio of businesses. Business units within the firm may provide inputs to each other, including capital, technology, materials, and know-how. These inputs substitute for goods and services available in markets outside the firm. Multibusiness organizations may also provide their businesses with management skills that help them compete more effectively, such as general management or entrepreneurial practices.

A multibusiness firm continuously faces the question of why its business units are better off under its ownership than being managed together by some other multibusiness firm or separately and independently. A well-articulated strategy that indicates how the businesses gain from being managed together in the same organization helps to answer this question. Such a strategy may also point to how the business mix should evolve to improve the corporation's economic performance, thus guiding resource allocation decisions. Moreover, if the businesses benefit from being together in the same institution because they share specific resources or capabilities, strategic thinking can have a positive effect on how the firm is managed and organized to create these valuable interunit connections.

To get a comprehensive view of strategy in organizations, we must start with how the business unit competes and how industry forces affect economic performance. Then we can examine how multibusiness organizations come about and how they are continually reconstituted through the addition of new businesses and elimination of old ones. We must also address the important problems of how the firm, single or multibusiness, governs itself, especially with respect to the board of directors and the top management team. These topics are discussed at length in Chapters 10 through 12.

Definitions of Business Performance

Two types of performance measure are common. The first is based solely on accounting data taken from the firm's financial statements, such as ratios comparing the firm's net income after tax to sales or to invested capital. The second combines accounting data with information from the firm's capital markets in an attempt to correct for the opportunity costs of investing in the firm.

Investors have long used **accounting measures of performance** to evaluate a firm's potential, and rating agencies have used them to assess its creditworthiness. The primary reasons for the wide acceptance of these measures are their availability and the development of systems for interpreting them. However, they have been frequently criticized for two major reasons.

First, management has some control over accounting policy, leading to variation across firms in the reporting of the same items. In response to the accounting scandals of the early 2000s, the Sarbanes-Oxley Act of 2002 markedly increased public regulation of firms' internal financial controls and the responsibility of corporate leadership for the accuracy of financial statements. Firms are therefore under much greater public scrutiny regarding their financial reporting practices. However, in industries where these practices vary depending on how rules are interpreted, legitimate managerial discretion remains, complicating the evaluation of performance across firms.

Second, accounting measures do a poor job of capturing the firm's "secret sauce." The **intangible assets**—product quality, customer service, technological functionality—that lead customers to buy a firm's product consistently are not reflected directly in financial statements. These assets are only loosely observed through their effects on accounting outcomes. However, they can be highly predictive of the firm's success in the market. The vagueness with which intangible assets are measured makes it more difficult to use financial statements to forecast how well the firm will do in the future. Debt rating agencies therefore take a broader view of a firm's value than simply its accounting numbers. The sidebar that follows on Standard and Poor's methods spells out how financial performance measures are used to assess company creditworthiness.

Measures of **economic performance** partially adjust for the deficiencies of accounting metrics through the use of capital market variables, particularly the firm's **market value** and its **cost of capital.** Both of these variables capture investors' expectations of the firm's performance in different ways.

S & P Key Financial Ratios and Bond Ratings

One of the best-known debt rating companies is Standard & Poors. S & P rates company debt from AAA to below BBB- or junk status when the bond is issued. The higher the rating of a bond, the lower the company's predicted risk of default, and so the lower the interest rate. A lower interest rate reduces the firm's cost of capital.

To assign a rating to a bond, S & P looks at a company's business position and financial statements. Business position is defined by characteristics of the company's industry, the company's market position within the industry, and aspects of the firm's organization and management. These characteristics vary by industry. For example, when it rates the debt of an airline, in addition to industry attributes, S & P collects data on the firm's market share and market share trend, its membership in a global alliance, utilization of capacity, pricing, aircraft fleet characteristics, labor costs, service reputation, and many other

factors. The key *general* financial ratios used by S & P are shown in Table 1.1.

S & P issues a set of guidelines to firms in each industry as targets for specific bond ratings. For example, the guidelines for the ratio of Funds from Operations/Total Debt—for firms in service, transportation, and manufacturing businesses—are shown in Table 1.2. This table conveys several interesting bits of information. Note first that no firm with a poor business position can get a debt rating over BBB, no matter how low its funds to debt ratio may be. Second, as the business position of the firm worsens, its financial statements must get better and better to receive a positive judgment from S & P. The guidelines for other ratios show a similar pattern. Having strong financial statements is therefore not at all sufficient to produce good debt ratings.

Even so, the firm's accounting data generally reflect the strength of its business position.

TABLE 1.1 | S & P Formulas for Key Financial Ratios

1. **EBIT interest coverage**—Earnings from continuing operations before interest and taxes (EBIT)/Gross interest incurred before subtracting capitalized interest and interest income.
2. **EBITDA interest coverage**—Earnings from continuing operations before interest, taxes, depreciation, and amortization (EBITDA)/Gross interest incurred before subtracting capitalized interest and interest income.
3. **Funds from operations/total debt**—Net income from continuing operations plus depreciation, amortization, deferred income taxes and other noncash items/Long-term debt plus current maturities, commercial paper, and other short-term borrowings.
4. **Free operating cash flow/total debt**—Funds from operations minus capital expenditures, minus (plus) the increase (decrease) in working capital, excluding changes in cash, marketable securities, and short-term debt/Long-term debt plus current maturities, commercial paper, and other short-term borrowings.
5. **Return on capital**—EBIT/Average of beginning of year and end of year capital, including short-term debt, current maturities, long-term debt, noncurrent deferred taxes, and equity.
6. **Operating income/sales**—Sales minus cost of goods manufactured (before depreciation and amortization), selling, general and administrative, and research and development costs/Sales.
7. **Long-term debt/capital**—Long-term debt/Long-term debt + shareholders equity, including preferred stock, plus minority interest.
8. **Total debt/capital**—Long-term debt plus current maturities, commercial paper, and other short-term borrowings/Long-term debt plus current maturities, commercial paper, and other short-term borrowings + shareholders equity, including preferred stock, plus minority interest

Stronger financial results will typically correlate strongly with higher ratings by S & P. Table 1.3 shows the median values across the S & P ratings for long-term debt for industrial firms. These values form two obvious and intuitively understandable patterns: (1) when some form of income is in the numerator, the highest percentages are associated with high ratings; and (2) when some form of debt is in the numerator, the lowest percentages are aligned with high ratings. To get a superior debt rating from S & P, therefore, a firm should make much more than it owes, a logical, reasonable rule to follow.

TABLE 1.2 | S & P Guidelines for Funds from Operations/ Total Debt

| Company Business Position | S & P Rating Category | | | | |
	AAA	AA	A	BBB	BB
Well above Average	80%	60%	40%	25%	10%
Above Average	150	80	50	30	15
Average	—	105	60	35	20
Below Average	—	—	85	40	25
Well below Average	—	—	—	65	45

TABLE 1.3 | Median Financial Ratios for Industrial Firms

| Financial Ratios | Debt Rating | | | | | | |
	AAA	AA	A	BBB	BB	B	CCC
EBIT interest coverage	21.4%	10.1%	6.1%	3.7%	2.1%	0.8%	0.1%
EBITDA interest coverage	26.5	12.9	9.1	5.8	3.4	1.8	1.3
Free op. flow/total debt	84.2	25.2	15.0	8.5	2.6	(3.2)	(12.9)
FFO/ total debt	128.8	55.4	43.2	30.8	18.8	7.8	1.6
Return on capital	34.9	21.7	19.4	13.6	11.6	6.6	1.0
Operating Income/Sales	27.0	22.1	18.6	15.4	15.9	11.9	11.9
Long-term debt/capital	13.3	28.2	33.9	42.5	57.2	69.7	68.8
Total debt/capital	22.9	37.7	42.5	48.2	62.6	74.8	87.7
No. of companies	8	29	136	218	273	281	22

A firm's market value (the sum of the market value of its equity and the book value of its debt) is often compared to the replacement value of the firm's assets. This ratio is called **Tobin's q,** after James Tobin, the Nobel Prize winner who developed it. When Tobin's q is high, the firm is more valuable to investors than the assets under its control, suggesting that it has used and promises to use these assets productively. When Tobin's q is low, or even negative, investors believe the firm's assets have a weak future under current management.

The firm's cost of capital is the weighted sum of its cost of equity and its tax-adjusted cost of debt. The cost of equity is commonly calculated using the

capital asset pricing model or CAPM, which combines (1) the rate of return from investing in a risk-free security like a short-term government bond, (2) the rate of return on a diversified portfolio of securities like the S & P 500, and (3) the association of the firm's share price with this diversified portfolio, called the firm's **beta.** The relationship among these variables, according to CAPM, is:

$$\text{expected return on equity} = \text{the risk-free rate} + \text{beta}^* \text{(a diversified portfolio's return minus the risk free rate)}$$

Obviously, the lower the beta, the closer the expected return on equity to the risk-free rate.

The cost of capital indicates investors' expected return from the firm. If the firm's return on invested capital is greater then the cost of capital, then we can say the firm is exceeding market expectations. On the contrary, if the return on capital is lower than its cost, then the firm is doing badly. The cost of capital has been used for many years as a means to evaluate units within the firm. An internal performance metric that includes the cost of capital is called **residual income** (see Chapter 10) and is a precursor to the more sophisticated methodologies used today to evaluate the firm overall.[17]

Summary

In this chapter we have covered the basic motivations for studying business strategy. A range of firms with superior strategies was discussed and analyzed, along with the origins of strategy as a field of study. Two important perspectives on strategy were introduced: (1) growth and innovation, and (2) execution and planning. We also examined the difference between strategy in single business and multibusiness firms. Finally, the chapter laid out the basic approaches to measuring firm performance with special emphasis on the valuation methodology used by the credit rating firm, Standard & Poors. Most of the topics discussed here will be dealt with in greater depth later in this book.

End Notes

1. See Sun Tzu, *The Art of War,* trans. Thomas Cleary (Boston: Shambhala, 1988).

2. See John Boyd, *Patterns of Conflict,* mimeo, 1986.

3. See David Besanko, Sachin Gupta, and Dipak Jain, "Logit Demand Estimation under Competitive Pricing Behavior: An Equilibrium Framework," *Management Science* 44 (1998), pp. 1533–1547.

4. See Richard Rumelt, "How Much Does Industry Matter?" *Strategic Management Journal* 12 (1991), pp. 167–185; and Anita McGahan and Michael Porter, "How Much Does Industry Matter, Really?" *Strategic Management Journal* 18 (1997), pp. 15–30.

5. For summaries see Jean Tirole, *The Theory of Industrial Organization* (Cambridge, MA: MIT Press, 1988); F. Michael Scherer and David Ross, *Industrial Market Structure and Economic Performance* (Boston: Houghton Mifflin, 1990); Michael E. Porter, *Competitive Strategy: Techniques for Analyzing Industries and Competitors* (New York: Free Press, 1980); Adam Brandenburger and Barry Nalebuff, *Co-opetition* (New York: Doubleday, 1996); and Pankaj Ghemawat, *Games Businesses Play: Cases and Models* (Cambridge, MA: MIT Press, 1997).

6. See Richard Nelson and Sidney Winter, *An Evolutionary Theory of Economic Change* (Cambridge MA: Harvard University Press, 1982).

7. See Joseph Bower, *Business Policy: Text and Cases,* 8th ed. (Burr Ridge, IL: McGraw-Hill-Irwin, 1995).

8. See Alfred D. Chandler, *Strategy and Structure* (Cambridge, MA: MIT Press, 1962).

9. See Robert Burgelman, *Strategy Is Destiny* (New York: Free Press, 2002).

10. For example, Glenn Carroll and Michael Hannan, *The Demography of Corporations and Industries* (Princeton, NJ: Princeton University Press, 1999); and Jay Galbraith, *Organization Design* (Reading, MA: Addison-Wesley, 1977).

11. Arnaldo Hax and Nicolas Majluf, *The Strategy Concept and Process: A Pragmatic Approach* (Englewood Cliffs, NJ: Prentice Hall, 1995); and Charles Hofer and Dan Schendel, *Strategy Formulation: Analytical Concepts* (St. Paul, MN: West, 1978).

12. See Oliver Williamson, *The Economic Institutions of Capitalism* (New York: Free Press, 1985).

13. This chart is adapted from Marvin Lieberman and Rajeev Dhawan, "Assessing the Resource Base of Japanese and U.S. Auto Producers: A Stochastic Frontier Production Function Approach," *Management Science* 51 (2005), pp. 1060–1075.

14. See Hofer and Schendel, *Strategy Formulation;* J. Galbraith and R. Kazanjian, *Strategy Implementation: Structure, Systems and Process,* 2nd ed. (St. Paul, MN: West, 1986); and Lawrence Hrebiniak, *Making Strategy Work* (Philadelphia, PA; Wharton School, 2005).

15. See Jack Welch, *Winning* (New York: HarperCollins, 2005).

16. Pierre Wack, "Scenarios: Uncharted Waters Ahead," *Harvard Business Review* 5 (1985), pp. 73–89; Pierre Wack, "Scenarios: Shooting the Rapids," *Harvard Business Review* 6 (1985), pp. 139–150.

17. David Solomons, *Divisional Performance: Measurement and Control,* 2nd ed. (New York: Markus Weiner, 1985); and Joel Stern and John Shiely, *The EVA Challenge; Implementing Value-added Change in an Organization* (New York: John Wiley, 2001).

Building Competitive Advantage

CHAPTER 2

Building Competitive Advantage

Roadmap

The aim of this chapter is to present the fundamentals of the key concept underlying business strategy: *sustainable competitive advantage*. Its elements are discussed as follows:

- Introduction
- Competitive Positioning with Customers
  - The Value-Cost Framework
  - Generic Strategies
  - Value versus Cost Advantage
  - Value and Cost Drivers
  - Value Drivers
  - Cost Drivers
- Defending against Competitors
  - Preventing the Imitation of Resources and Capabilities
  - Increasing Customer Retention
- Summary
- Questions for Practice

Introduction

Leadership and organization are sometimes viewed as the key elements of strategy. All a firm needs is strong senior management and a compelling sense of forward direction. Certainly, these can help a company achieve high performance and in many cases are essential. However, they work *only* if they are guided by the economic fundamentals of the business. When management is guided by these fundamentals, the company is more likely to attain sustainable competitive advantage.

By definition, competitive advantage produces superior economic performance. Sometimes, however, strong macroeconomic and industry forces may mask its power. For example, in a growing industry with high average profitability competitive advantage may not affect a firm's performance as much as industry trends. For example, many firms entered the IT consulting business in the late 1990s, and their performance was buoyed by the industry's strong growth rate. However, when the market declined after 2001, weaker firms began to suffer and firms with stronger market positions, such as Accenture, began to stand out. So over time, firms that have built a competitive advantage always win. Those who expect that industry factors will be enough for strong long-term performance are always disappointed.

To achieve a **sustainable competitive advantage,** a company must do two things. First, it must have a strong offense. It must set an objective to attain a dominant market position. Market superiority and competitive advantage are virtually synonymous.[1] But just achieving market dominance is not enough. The second task is to develop a strong defense in order to protect the firm's returns from the effects of competition. Without an offense and a defense that are both creative and aggressive, no firm can have above-average performance or maintain it for long.

What do we mean by a firm's *market position*? Basically, it is the difference between the value the firm offers its customers and the firm's cost to produce that value. The higher the value or benefit customers get from a product, at a given price, the more satisfied they are and the more they buy. For example, when you're shopping for a new cell phone and are looking at several that have the same price, you'll probably buy the one that has more of the features you want (e.g., photo or e-mail capability). Your preference for enhanced technology might lead you to buy one cell phone over another, even though their prices are the same. But adding more features is likely to cost the cell phone company more money, and while having satisfied customers is important, the firm must also make a profit. If the firm offers a lot of technology, it may end up making no money at all. In other words, the firm must be productive in offering value to the customer. So the higher the value delivered to the customer and the lower the cost it takes to produce that value, the stronger the firm's market position.

But the firm must also defend its market position from the competition. Competitors are always interested in stealing each other's buyers and in copying successful strategies. Because copycats typically crowd the market and force prices down, successful innovators must erect barriers around their customers and key assets. If the successful firm can't protect itself from rivals, its advantage slowly disappears. For example, Xerox, once the dominant firm in copiers worldwide, has been barely able to withstand an onslaught of Asian competitors over the past 30 years, and Microsoft Windows today is facing increasing pressure from Linux, a nonproprietary operating system.

Both a superior market position, in terms of a high customer benefit produced at a low cost to the firm, and an effective defense against competitors are necessary for achieving a sustainable competitive advantage. Neither alone is sufficient. Examples of successful firms that have followed this logic are many. Intel's success in the microprocessor industry and Toyota's increasing dominance in automobiles are due in large part to the abilities of these firms to provide products and services that offer value to customers at a level of efficiency rival firms cannot imitate. Other businesses with strong defendable market positions are Nucor in steel and Southwest Airlines in the U.S. airline industry.

Competitive Positioning with Customers

The Value-Cost Framework[2]

Effective **competitive positioning** means first offering a product whose characteristics match buyer preferences. We can think of the product's value to the customer as the highest price he or she is willing to pay in the absence of a competing product and in the context of other items to buy. This price is called **willingness to pay.** Any higher price means that the customer simply refuses to purchase the product. A key point then is that in the absence of fraud or extortion, the customer, not the seller, always determines the product's value.

Customers rarely pay for the value they receive from the product because competition drives the market price down. Returning to the cell phone example above, consider how much you would be willing to pay for your current cell phone service, assuming you already had a phone. A few customers might not pay a nickel more. But my guess is that many would be willing to pay another $10, perhaps $20 or more, for the many conveniences cell phones offer, especially as the number of places we can use them expands around the world. The price for cell phone service is less than our willingness to pay because companies selling the service compete on price to induce us to buy from them.

Another example: Imagine a manufacturing firm that is thinking about reducing its costs by buying a new machine. If there is only one supplier selling the machine, with no threat of entry, the supplier might ask the manufacturer to pay a price quite close to the amount its costs are reduced, since this price reflects the machine's value. In a competitive market, however, where more than one supplier offer comparable machines, prices are likely to decline as the suppliers compete to get the customer's business. The more prices go down, the more money the customer makes from the transaction and the less the supplier makes. Note that even as prices are reduced, the value of the machine to the manufacturer, in terms of reducing its production costs, remains the same. The sidebar, on page 26, presents a range of ways to estimate willingness to pay.

Effective market positioning obviously involves more than just satisfying customers: They must be satisfied efficiently. Within an industry, firms vary not only on the kind and amount of value they offer but also on the costs they incur to produce that value. The simple rule is that companies that have achieved enduring success in their industries offer more value per unit cost than their competitors, consistently over time.

Estimating Customer Willingness to Pay[3]

A customer's willingness to pay can be measured in several ways, whether as a specific dollar amount or more generally as the lowest value a product must have to induce a customer to buy it. Three conventional measurement methods are internal engineering, customer perceptions of willingness to pay, and quantitative analysis of product attributes and purchase behavior.

Internal Engineering

In many cases, the economic benefit provided by the product can be assessed by direct inspection. A new software product, for example, may reduce manufacturing costs by a certain amount compared to an existing system. Such an amount is typically measurable and, in conjunction with the costs of switching from the old to the new product, sets an upper bound on how much the company will pay for the new software.

Customer Perceptions of Product Value

A second way to determine willingness to pay is simply to ask the customer his or her perception of the maximum price he or she would be willing to pay before ruling out a purchase decision. Here the buyer simply states the benefit in dollar terms. Although this method seems reasonable on its face, potential customers do not always state the value they would actually use in purchase decisions.[4] To solve this problem, several techniques have been developed to raise the buyer's incentive to expose his or her real willingness to pay.[5] It is important that the context be realistic and specific to the situation in which the product is expected to be purchased, since the price a buyer is willing to pay can vary over different settings. In one classic example, customers may pay a high price for a beer in a fancy restaurant and a low price for the same beer bought in a run-down grocery store.[6]

A simple example of the importance of context is shown in Table 2.1. In this case, a random sample of shoppers was asked whether they were willing to pay more than the market price for goods sold in different convenience stores in Guangzhou, China in 2004. Roughly 40 percent said their willingness to pay exceeded the market price for 7 Eleven stores. Competing stores received much less favorable assessments. Willingness to pay was thus clearly related to the store in which the product was bought, a testimony to 7 Eleven, whose stronger reputation allowed it to charge higher prices.

Quantitative Analysis

The third method for determining willingness to pay involves the complex statistical analysis of data from customer surveys or purchase decisions. In this approach the analyst first puts together a list of product attributes—such as quality, functionality, service, geographical location, ease of use, and breadth of line—that might influence willingness to pay. Then the effects of these attributes on real or projected customer purchase decisions are estimated in conjunction with the product's market price. If the willingness to pay above the market price is zero, then these factors will have no effect at all. If on the other hand the customer values these factors, then they will have some effect on his or her purchase decision and willingness to pay will exceed the market price.[7]

Let's look at an application of this method to how much customers are willing to pay for energy efficiency and easy credit terms in appliances.[8] It would be normal to assume that both of these attributes would lead customers to pay more for an appliance, and in fact this has been found to be true. The following figure shows how much an average customer would be willing

TABLE 2.1 | Customer Willingness to Pay for Convenience Store Goods in Guangzhou, China—2004

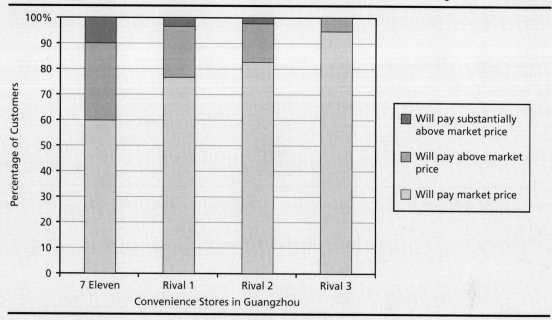

to pay over the market price for these attributes when purchasing a refrigerator:

Types of Value Offered to the Customer (value drivers)	Willingness to Pay (purchase price over the market price)
$1 savings from energy conservation	$2.45
$1 additional amount available to be borrowed to pay for the refrigerator	$0.32
1 percent lower interest rate of the loan	$39.43

The table shows that customers are willing to pay an extra $2.45 for every energy conservation dollar the refrigerator saves them, a remarkable premium. Customers also value debt and are quite sensitive to the interest rate on the loan. Note that all three of these types of value to the customer—the degree of energy efficiency, the amount the customer can borrow to finance the purchase, and the interest rate—are under the control of the supplier and can be manipulated to increase demand. We will call them and other ways the firm contributes value to the customer *value drivers*. They are a crucial way of understanding how firms establish their market positions.

The difference between a product's value and its cost is the **economic contribution** produced by the firm. The larger the economic contribution, the stronger the firm's market position. In competitive markets, buyers capture part of the overall economic contribution the firm produces. The part the buyer captures—called the **buyer surplus**—is the difference between the product's

FIGURE 2.1 |

The Value Minus
Cost (V – C)
Framework

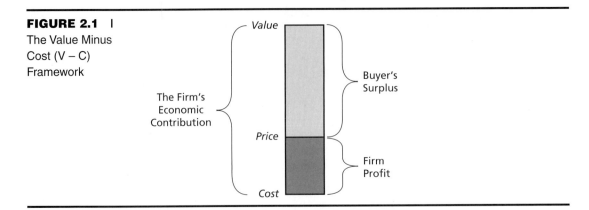

value to the buyer and its market price. The firm captures the rest, which is its **profit**—the difference between the price and unit cost (see Figure 2.1).

Generic Strategies

It has been argued that a successful firm must have one of two generic strategies—differentiation or cost leadership.[9] A **differentiator** invests in offering high value, and the **cost leader** has the lowest costs compared to the competition. These strategies apply to the market overall or to a market niche. In the case of a niche, the strategy is called "focus." If a firm is neither a differentiator nor the cost leader, it is often called "stuck in the middle."

There are many examples of apparently successful firms at one end of the market or the other. Rolex and Philippe Patek are obvious differentiators in the watch industry. Both brands are noted for their high price and cachet and are sold primarily through jewelers as opposed to department stores. Hyundai in contrast is clearly a cost leader in automobiles. The Korean firm has made a mark in American and European markets selling sedans and minivans at very low prices and with a notable 100,000 mile warranty to assure customers that low price does not necessarily mean low quality. Cars made in China (e.g., Chery) where labor costs are low may soon occupy the low-cost position of the world market.

From this perspective, a firm must make an essential trade-off: It must choose between investing in higher value *or* investing in lower cost; it can't do both and be successful. The differentiator's investments in producing value cost money, raising costs. In turn, the cost leader emphasizes lowering costs by reducing investments in value.

Figure 2.2a shows this trade-off in a simple way for three firms: D for differentiator, LC for low cost, and SIM for stuck in the middle. SIM lies between D and LC on the high-value–low-cost continuum. The figure also shows the

FIGURE 2.2 | Value and Cost as Substitutes or Complements

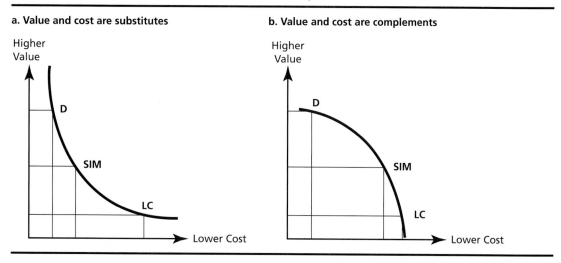

a. Value and cost are substitutes

Higher
Value

D

SIM

LC

Lower Cost

b. Value and cost are complements

Higher
Value

D

SIM

LC

Lower Cost

economic contributions of each type of firm. These contributions are simply the level of value the firm offers compared to the cost it incurs to produce this value. SIM provides more value than LC, the cost leader, but has higher costs; the firm also has lower costs than D, the differentiator, but produces less value. It is important to note that the trade-off SIM makes between value and cost produces a smaller economic contribution than either D or LC. Therefore SIM is at a competitive disadvantage.

Two assumptions lie behind the argument that firms in the middle do poorly. First, because the resources and capabilities of a firm like SIM are not dedicated to achieving either high value or low cost, the firm cannot compete effectively on value with the differentiator or on cost with the cost leader. So when a company tries to pursue both higher value and lower cost at the same time, it suffers. The problem of the firm in the middle is thus one of strategy execution. The second assumption is that the customer base of the firm in the middle isn't large enough to allow it to improve its abilities, given competition with the other firms. That is, customers gravitate toward the higher value of the differentiator and are willing to pay the price it charges, or they buy the lower value product at the cost leader's lower price. There is little market opportunity for a firm in the middle to improve its position.

An instructive example of the stuck in the middle phenomenon is the domestic U.S. airline industry at the end of 2004. The airlines are divided into three groups—Network, Regional, and Low-Cost—following the U.S. Department of Transportation categories (see Figure 2.3). As the chart shows, only two groups have any profitable airlines: Low-Cost (Southwest, JetBlue, Airtran,

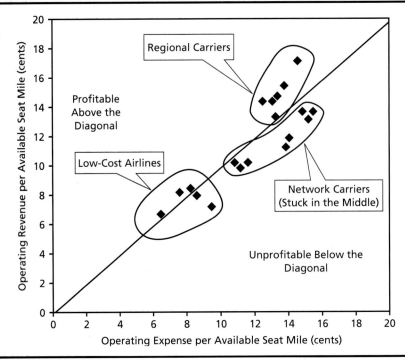

FIGURE 2.3 |

U.S. Domestic Airline Revenues and Costs, 4th Quarter 2004

and others) and Regional (American Eagle, Pinnacle, ExpressJet, and others). None of the legacy Network carriers (United, Delta, American, Northwest, and others), which are stuck in the middle between the Regionals and the Low-Cost firms, are profitable. These airlines have been unable to lower costs sufficiently to compensate for the price reductions they have had to make in order to compete with Southwest and the other Low-Cost firms. The Regional airlines, interestingly, have higher costs than the other groups; but they also have much higher revenues per seat mile because of their fewer empty seats and special route structures, in some cases linked to the hubs of Network carriers. In fact, a number of the regional carriers are subsidiaries of the parent companies that own the Network airlines. Not all the Low-Cost airlines are profitable, indicating that just because an airline is efficient does not mean it attracts enough customers to make money.

But wait! Let's stop and think for a moment. Before we accept that stuck in the middle is always bad, let's consider a well-known firm like Target, the U.S. discount retailer. Target sells products that are generally more upscale than Wal-Mart, the low-cost giant. At the same time, Target's products are not as upscale as conventional U.S. department stores like JCPenney, Macy's, Dillards, and Foleys. Target is "in the middle." Can it make any money, squeezed between the two ends of the market? So far the answer is a resounding

FIGURE 2.4

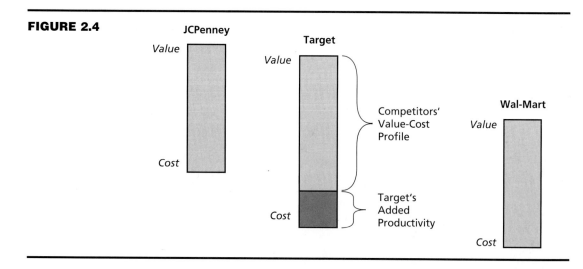

yes! In fact, it makes more money, in terms of return on sales, than both Wal-Mart and the bevy of department stores Target competes with. Its superior returns can be shown in two simple comparisons. First, Target's gross margin (the difference between revenues and cost of goods sold) over revenues is close to that of department stores. Second, its operating costs per revenue dollar are closer to Wal-Mart. Thus, Target sells higher value goods at lower costs than its immediate competitors. To understand Target's market position, then, we thus need to look at both the value a firm offers customers, which determines the demand for its products and consequently its revenues, and the cost the firm incurs to deliver that value. The sidebar on page 32 details how well Target performs in the middle.

Target's higher performance is clearly inconsistent with the airline industry example. Target succeeds in the middle (see Figure 2.4), where the Network carriers in the airline industry struggle. How can these two competitive situations be reconciled?

The solution is to focus on what drives a firm's value and cost, not on whether the firm is at the high or low end of the market. Industry structure is based on relative abilities of firms to build more or less effective cost positions in the context of what customers are willing to pay for the product. Cost drivers may be powerful at high levels of value, and value drivers powerful for low levels of cost. Thus, a more innovative firm, like Target, may be able to achieve higher margins in the middle, even though the firm's value to the customer is not the highest, and its costs are not the lowest. Figure 2.2b shows this relationship, where value and cost complement rather than substitute for each other.[10]

Ultimately, the difference between value and cost, not their levels, relative to competitors determines superior market positioning. Competitive advantage is not about differentiation or cost leadership. It is about producing and then protecting a greater economic contribution than rivals.

Target

The Target Corporation began as a new line of stores for the Minnesota-based Dayton company, which became Dayton-Hudson, and then eventually assumed the Target name in 2000. The first Target was opened near Minneapolis in 1962 as a discount operation, designed to compete with Kmart and other growing low-cost retailers. Sam Walton started Wal-Mart at roughly the same time.

Target's growth over the past 10 years has been remarkable. Ten thousand dollars invested in Target in June, 1995, would be worth $89,610 10 years later, a return of almost 800 percent. How did the company achieve this astounding record?

From the beginning, Target emphasized style at a very reasonable price. The company has partnered with well-known designers, including Michael Graves and Isaac Mizrahi, to develop and brand its products. At the same time, its cost structure looks more like Wal-Mart than a full-line department store. The ability to offer customers affordable chic and keep costs low is the key to Target's success.

Table 2.2 shows Target's quarterly return on sales (ROS) in 2003 and 2004, which is defined as operating income over revenues. Target's ROS is compared to two competitors: Wal-Mart at the low-cost, lower value end of the market and JCPenney, the full-line department store at the higher cost, higher value end. During this period JCPenney experienced a successful turnaround, which is visible in the table. Target's ROS exceeds those of both firms in every quarter and is consistently about twice that of Wal-Mart.

Tables 2.3 and 2.4 show how Target manages to achieve such high relative performance. Table 2.3 compares the firms' gross margin over revenues. Gross margin is the difference between a firm's revenues and the cost of goods sold. A high gross margin means that the firm has managed to buy goods cheap and sell them dear,

TABLE 2.2 I Return on Sales (ROS)

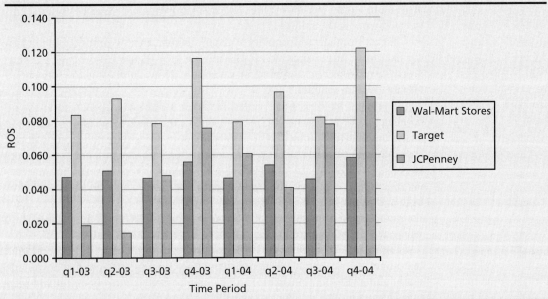

TABLE 2.3 | Gross Margin/Revenues

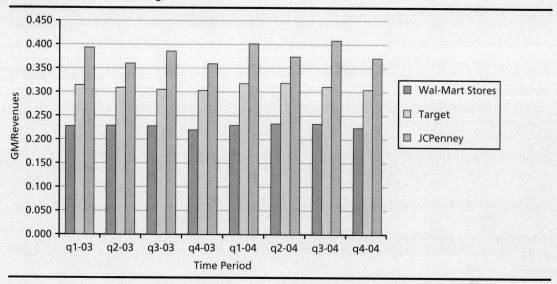

TABLE 2.4 | SGA Expense/Revenues

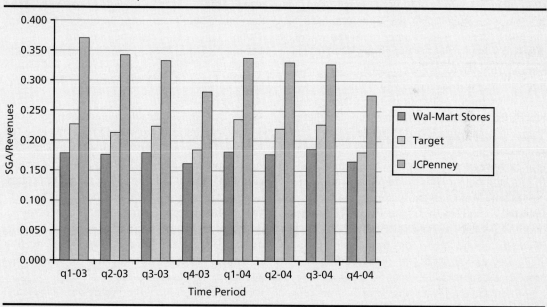

which is typical of products that have a higher value to the customer; and dividing a firm's gross margin by its revenues shows how much of it is produced by a dollar of sales. The higher this ratio, the more differentiated the store. For example, Tiffany's ratio in 2004 was .54. Since JCPenney is the fanciest of the three stores, it makes sense that it has the highest ratio of gross margin to revenues (average .38), followed by Target (average .31) then by Wal-Mart (average .23). So Target is just a little closer to JCPenney than to Wal-Mart.

Table 2.4 shows how much it costs the firm to convince customers they should shop and buy at its stores. This selling, general and administrative expense (SGA) covers marketing, in-store operations, administrative overhead, and so on. Dividing this expense by revenues indicates how much a dollar of sales costs the firm. The higher this ratio, the more it costs the firm to sell a dollar of merchandise; the lower the ratio, the less a sale costs the company. So it makes sense that Wal-Mart, a low-cost firm, should have the lowest ratio (average 0.18), and JCPenney (average 0.33), the higher value firm, the highest ratio. Target again is in the middle (average .22). Here Target is much closer to Wal-Mart than to JCPenney. This fact, combined with the information in Table 2.3, indicates that Target sells its differentiated goods more efficiently than either of its rivals. That is, Target has the greatest difference between its gross margin ratio and the SGA ratio, so it makes more money on every sales dollar.

In addition to return on sales, Target surpasses both Wal-Mart and JCPenney in return on invested capital (ROIC). Target's ROIC is a little over 28 percent in both 2003 and 2004. Wal-Mart's is around 15 percent for both years, and JCPenney has an ROIC of 16 percent in 2003 and 24 percent in 2004.

Interestingly, Target was not only more profitable than Wal-Mart and JCPenney in 2003 and 2004; it also grew faster in what are called comparable store sales. This measure captures how much the firm is increasing revenues in stores that have been around for a year or more, as opposed to growing through building new stores. It therefore suggests how well the firm is retaining customers. The following table shows the comparable store sales for the three firms in 2003 and 2004:

Comparable Store Sales Growth

	2003	2004
Target	4.4%	5.3%
Wal-Mart Stores (excluding Sam's Club and International)	3.9	2.8
JCPenney	0.9	5.0

Target's growth has not always been so robust against Wal-Mart. In the previous four years (1999–2002), Wal-Mart grew faster. Why then has Target emerged so strongly as a market leader? One reason may be that consumer confidence in the United States is sufficiently strong that families are willing to spend a little more on their daily purchases in a store that is more appealing aesthetically. If this is so, then Target may be vulnerable to an economic slowdown that reduces the average family income. Another possibility is that the company has slowly perfected its retailing practices, especially in merchandising, and is now executing well enough to attract customers that used to shop at full-line department stores. A slowdown in the economy might increase the size of this market segment, helping Target and hurting JCPenney and stores like it. Whatever the answer, it is clear that Target succeeds because it offers customers higher value at a lower cost than its competitors.

Value versus Cost Advantage

Even though being a product differentiator is not sufficient for competitive advantage, the concept does highlight one way firms can compete. Differentiation focuses on increasing customer value rather than reducing costs. When are investments in value justified? An obvious answer is: when a high proportion of potential customers are value sensitive. The more sensitive to value improvements customers are, and the less entrenched with competitors, the more increased value induces them to buy the firm's product. Investing in value is common in an emerging market composed of early adopters who are highly attuned to product technology (a valued product attribute). Here competitors invest repeatedly in technology enhancements to attract more customers, while cost improvement is less of an issue. Investing in higher value can also lead to competitive advantage in *mature* markets as the case of Target shows.

More generally pursuing a value advantage also is preferred when it produces a higher return than opportunities to reduce costs. Cost reduction is less attractive when all firms in an industry have access to the same processes and practices and to the same sources of lower cost inputs. In this case, although a firm must lower costs to remain competitive, it cannot improve its market position since all firms reduce their costs together.

Alternatively, cost reduction provides a greater return when the marginal customer is price-sensitive, and the cost improvement can be protected from competitors. In this case, the firm can lower its price and still maintain its margin. Price sensitivity is common in economies with low growth rates where customers have diminished expectations regarding future income. For example, Japanese buyers in the late 1990s became markedly more oriented toward price, as their economy continued to stagnate, allowing low-cost retailers such as Costco to enter the market successfully.

Cost-reduction programs are also more likely to be initiated when improvements in value are difficult or increasingly expensive. For example, major enhancements in value often become more expensive in the later stages of a technology's life cycle, as Intel found in the development of its 8086/8 microprocessor platform. As this platform matured, efficiency became more important for Intel both to maintain low prices and to develop the financial resources necessary for the costly iterations of technological innovation.

Value and Cost Drivers

What should firms focus on to improve productivity compared to competitors? The obvious answer is anything that raises value to the customer or lowers cost with a net increase in the firm's market position. We will call the factors that determine customer value, **value drivers,** and those that determine the firm's costs, **cost drivers.** The reason we are interested in value and cost drivers is that they have a direct influence on the firm's market position and therefore its degree of competitive advantage as Figure 2.5 shows:

FIGURE 2.5 |

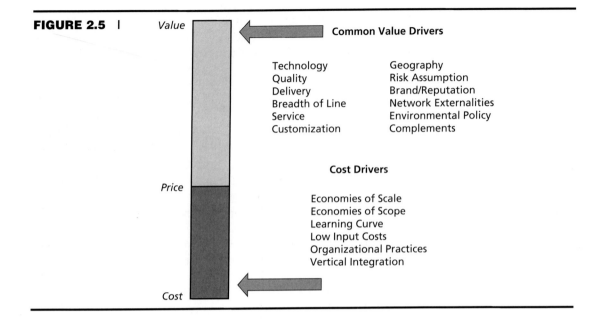

Value Drivers

In all markets, firms compete on the value their products provide to customers. An example of how value drivers play a role in competition was given earlier in the chapter in the box titled "Estimating Customer Willingness to Pay." There we looked at three factors that drove the purchase of refrigerators. These value drivers were: (1) energy efficiency, a feature of the product's technology; (2) the amount a customer could borrow to make a purchase, a feature of the vendor's consumer financing policy; and (3) the interest rate on the customer's loan, another financing variable. Firms that sold more efficient appliances, allowed consumers to borrow more money, and charged a lower interest rate on the loan sold more than their competitors, even when the price of the refrigerator was considered. So why weren't all refrigerator producers investing heavily in each factor? Simply put, some firms could invest in these value drivers more cheaply than others. It is also likely that the competitors assessed the effectiveness and the costs of each value driver differently.

Value drivers are thus an essential bridge between the firm's investment decisions and the benefit customers receive from the product. Investment decisions constitute wagers on what customers want, and competitors make them continuously. Controlling for cost, successful firms by definition make better bets. The value drivers these firms invest in attract more buyers than their rivals or they attract buyers who are willing to pay more money.

There is no complete list of value drivers to cover all transactions, nor should there be. All markets have idiosyncrasies that need to be defined in the light of how customers perceive the product they are offered. An effective definition of value drivers in specific markets will take these special conditions into account. Nonetheless, a common set of value drivers can be identified across a wide range of markets and discussed in general terms. The twelve described below constitute such a list.

Technology   Positioning the product with superior technology implies better design, features, or functionality than competitors. We live in a technologically intensive society, but this does not mean that investing in more technology is always value producing. Although some buyers require higher functionality and features, others trade off better technology for a lower price. In the latter case, the customer's tasks are likely to be less technically demanding. Further, the interplay between technological innovation and customer buying patterns is central to competition in technology-intensive industries. For example, when technological change is rapid, some customers will avoid investing in the most advanced technology in the expectation that it will soon be supplanted.

Quality   A product's quality entails its durability and reliability, as well as its aesthetic effect. In many industries, customers will not accept quality below a relatively high level, either because of safety concerns, as in automobiles and airplanes, or the high cost of downtime, as in telecommunications equipment. In other industries, there is significant room for a moderate quality producer. The quality of wines varies substantially, for example.[11]

Delivery   The delivery of the product within a specified time frame can be a key performance attribute. The diffusion of just-in-time logistics procedures has increased expectations about delivery times in many industries, especially durable goods. Customers in growing industries value a firm's ability to deliver goods or complete a project within a specified time frame. Without on-time delivery, downstream market share may be lost to faster competitors.

Breadth of Line   A firm may offer a broad product line for several reasons. First, a broader line provides customers with one-stop shopping to fill a variety of needs. Second, some firms, such as Ryobi in garden appliances, sell modular products with interchangeable parts, lowering the customers' costs. Third, buying from one supplier ensures better compatibility at the interfaces between products when they are used as an ensemble as, for example, in telecommunications. Fourth, demand for the product line may increase through cross-selling or through trading up by customers.[12]

Service   Many customers want ancillary services to provide information and solve unexpected problems. The value some products offer customers can decline quickly if service is not effective. Service expertise can also compensate for poor customer experience with a product early in its life cycle, as bugs are identified and fixed. Further, an enhanced service capability can build customer loyalty. A good example of a firm that has built a

Cisco Systems

Since its inception in 1984, Cisco Systems has been one of the clearest examples of strong market positioning based on two major value drivers: *customer service* and *breadth of product line.* Cisco sells telecommunications equipment to four types of customer—telecommunications companies, large businesses (over 500 employees), small businesses, and consumers. Its product line consists of four segments or types of product: (1) *routers,* which move digital voice, data, and video transmissions from one network to another across the Internet; (2) *switches,* which are used to send transmissions in local networks (e.g., LANs); (3) *access devices,* which allow remote users, such as home workers, to connect effectively with the Internet; and (4) *other products* such as services and network management software.

Cisco has focused on providing outstanding customer service and a very broad line of compatible products. John Chambers, Cisco's CEO, demands excellent customer service from his employees. Service increases customer value since downtime in telecommunications equipment causes an immediate economic loss. Cisco's service processes are driven by its use of information technology, especially the Internet. Significantly, not only is the Internet an efficient means of solving customer problems, it is also Cisco's core business. So Cisco's use of the Internet in providing customer service is both a key capability supporting its market position and a demonstration of why the Internet is so useful, which is why customers should buy Cisco's products.

Through the Internet Cisco connects its customers with the companies that manufacture its products. (Cisco is a devout outsourcer of manufacturing.) Customers are also connected directly to any Cisco unit that can help solve problems. And Cisco units are connected to each other. To the extent Cisco can assure customers that their needs will be met quickly and effectively with up-to-date technology, Cisco is well positioned to increase demand for its products, relative to competitors whose promises of better service may not be as credible.

Given its dominant market share in the core router market, Cisco has been able to introduce a range of compatible products that together bind customers to Cisco's technology. Cisco has been vigorous in licensing and promoting the technical standards underlying these products so that its customers benefit from a larger market of firms selling compatible technology. Breadth of line increases value to the customer by providing an integrated system of telecommunications hardware and reducing problems of communication at the interface between system components.

But by far the most important capability contributing to Cisco's broad product line is the company's expertise in acquiring and integrating other firms. In an industry with a very high rate of innovation, Cisco has developed a marked skill in identifying, acquiring, and integrating start-up firms whose technology is at the leading edge of an emerging subfield, such as optical switching equipment and wireless technologies, and whose management and culture fit well with Cisco's organization.

strong value driver in service and breadth of line is Cisco Systems, as described in the sidebar above.[13]

Customization Customized products frequently provide the buyer with greater value since they are tailored to the buyer's needs. However, custom goods typically command a higher price reflecting their higher costs. With the advent of mass customization, driven by process innovations originating in Japan, the prices of customized products in durable goods industries, such as personal computers, have declined. Dell is the worldwide leader here. But standardized goods can sometimes outcompete custom products, as has happened in applications computer software. In this case, custom solutions have typically not been designed according to best practice, which standard software purports to embody. Standardized software is therefore cheaper and more current than older specialized solutions.

Geography   There are two types of customer value based on geography: location and scope. Location adds value when the firm is close enough to its customers to lower the cost of coordination in handling logistics or other activities. Large durable goods assemblers—for example, Ford, General Motors, DaimlerChrysler, Toyota, and Nissan—frequently encourage their parts suppliers to set up factories near assembly plants in order to lower coordination costs. In turn, geographic scope extends location advantage to multiple regions. In this case, firms with facilities in multiple locations are better positioned to serve customers with a comparable geographic reach. For instance, large multinational customers benefit substantially from Citibank's extensive global banking network.

Risk Assumption   A firm may signal the quality or performance level of its product by assuming a large part of the risk of product failure. Warranties regarding product failure are common for durable goods—for instance, automobiles or stereo equipment. Here the more extensive the guarantee, the higher quality the product is assumed to be. Thus, top-line car producers, such as Mercedes and BMW, offer more extensive warranties on their automobiles than midrange car companies. Hyundai's 100,000 mile warranty is an example of a lesser automobile brand signaling unexpectedly high quality.

Brand/Reputation   Brand and reputation both signal the level of product quality or performance. In some cases, such as Wal-Mart, the brand indicates adequate quality and low price, attracting price-sensitive buyers. In other cases, the brand signals high quality or cachet, for example, Tiffany or Rolex. Reputation also pertains to the execution of cooperative agreements. Firms with strong reputations—for example, Intel in semiconductors and Amgen in biotechnology—are better positioned in markets involving interfirm cooperation than firms with histories of failed partnerships.[14]

Network Externalities   Many markets exhibit **economies of scale in demand,** which means that the benefit each customer receives increases as new customers are added. These economies are typically based on the adoption of a standard communication technology, as in telephone switches, word processing programs, or more generally, spoken and written languages. In the market's early stages, many standards typically compete. Eventually, one becomes dominant, like Microsoft's Office Suite. More users of a standard indicate a greater network externality, which means a higher benefit to new users when they adopt the technology.[15]

Environmental Policies   Some buyers prefer to purchase from firms with progressive environmental policies. Although customers receive an indirect rather than direct benefit from social and environmental programs, the effect these programs have on buying behavior can be significant. Interface, a Georgia carpet company, has built a strong image as a developer of operating practices linked to the concept of sustainability, that is, not harming the natural environment. The company initiated this program because customers were concerned about the company's environmental policies and because the CEO had developed strong environmental beliefs. BP and GE are also industry leaders in improving the environmental impact of company products and operations.

Complements   The value of many products increases with the availability of complements. Two products are complements when they functionally enhance each other and their demand curves are therefore positively correlated. There is a host of examples: The value of DVD players rose as more movies and other types of entertainment became available on DVD disks. Extensive road systems made motor vehicles more useful. Sailboats need sails, and so on. In some cases, complements are produced by the same firm. But this need not be so since the resources and capabilities required to compete in complementary industries can be quite different. For example, Intel does not write operating system software, and Microsoft does not make semiconductors. Yet the Intel Pentium chip and Microsoft's Windows software are highly complementary.[16]

Cost Drivers

Firms compete on cost as well as value. Opportunities to improve costs relative to competitors are present whether firms differ widely or narrowly in efficiency. The major cost drivers are described below.

Scale Economies   **Scale economies** are related to the decline in a firm's average costs with higher volume over the long term, as fixed costs are spread across a larger number of units produced. Firms with high fixed costs cannot be profitable unless they produce above breakeven. How average costs decline with increases in volume depends on whether fixed costs are recurring or non-recurring. Firms with recurring fixed costs must reinvest in new capacity in a stepwise fashion as volume grows. Here the average cost curve rises and falls as new facilities are added. In contrast, for many firms—for example, those producing information goods such as movies or software—the cost of developing and producing the product is a large up-front investment that is nonrecurring and cannot be recovered (i.e., the process invested in cannot be sold to another firm). Further, this investment can often dwarf other costs. In these

Vanguard Group

An interesting example of a cost leader is the Vanguard Group, a mutual fund company. One of Vanguard's product lines is money market mutual funds, a type of fund that invests in short-term securities and therefore has a low yield but also low risk. Because of their low risk, these funds are often seen as a substitute for cash. The main component of value to the buyer is the net yield on the fund, which is determined by both the ability of the fund to forecast government interest rates, which drive the returns on the securities the fund invests in, and the costs the fund incurs to administer its operations. It turns out that although funds differ in their forecasting ability, on average they do not pass along their forecasting earnings to customers. So, net yields differ across funds primarily because of variation in their expenses, and Vanguard has low costs compared with other firms. The company's cost structure thus allows it to have higher profitability in a very competitive market and greater flexibility to provide higher yields to customers through charging them less for administrative expenses. Higher yields in its money funds attract more customers, which increases the size of Vanguard's assets. Greater size reduces costs further through economies of scale. So Vanguard's competitive advantage due to its superior cost structure can endure.

industries, the average cost curve declines steadily with higher volume, and the profits made on sales beyond the break-even point can be substantial.

A common assumption is that larger scale allows the firm to invest in more efficient processes so that variable costs per unit are lower. Higher volume enables more standardized, usually automated procedures. One of the most famous examples of this phenomenon is Ford's assembly line, which revolutionized competition in the automobile industry in 1908. Ford's innovation was enabled by higher car sales and wiped out many higher-cost competitors. Scale efficiencies are thus tied to ongoing process innovation as a firm grows.

While it is common to identify a minimum efficient size in an industry at which firms begin to achieve economies of scale, competitors typically vary in the volumes at which these economies are reached. The reason is that the technologies of firms, although similar, vary sufficiently to create different cost structures. This variation is driven by unique cost-reducing capabilities and by differences among firms in the implementation of standard practices. These differences create an opportunity for more efficient firms to achieve a competitive advantage. But this advantage may not be sustainable since as the firm grows, it may not be able to apply its cost-reducing capabilities beyond a certain size.[17]

Scope Economies   Another source of lower costs is **economies of scope.** A firm achieves economies of scope when the cost of producing two products using shared assets and practices is less than the costs of producing the products separately. The concept also applies to lowering costs through sharing assets across geographical locations. For example, a firm may enter a new geographical market by investing in an infrastructure that supports several regional facilities, but open these facilities sequentially, as Wal-Mart typically does. The firm begins to achieve economies of scope in the regional system when there are enough facilities to cover the costs of the shared infrastructure.

A cost advantage over competitors through economies of scope can be achieved in two ways. First, two products may share a specialized resource that is more efficient than competitors. For example, Nucor has developed highly efficient minimills, each of which manufactures many steel products. These are produced at low cost in part because they share the common production system. Second, the practices a firm uses to coordinate asset sharing may be superior to competitors' practices. More efficient coordination practices, relative to competitors, contribute to a cost advantage for each product.[18]

The Learning Curve   A third source of lower costs is the refinement of practices due to learning within and across activities. Originally observed in aircraft assembly, the learning curve has long been recognized as a key contributor to making production systems more efficient, especially in technically complex processes such as semiconductor manufacturing. Complex processes have more steps and are more complicated within each step. Initial production designs are never the most efficient. So, as products are made, line workers and engineers experiment with new practices directed at reducing costs.

Most learning curves are quite steep, with the major improvements occurring early in the life of the process. The effect of cumulative volume on costs is thus commonly represented by an exponential function. As the amount produced doubles, cost declines by a fixed percentage. This percentage, and therefore the shape of the learning curve, varies according to the activity involved.

To achieve a cost advantage through the learning curve, a firm must learn faster and longer than rivals, typically through producing more volume first. Differences in learning rates across firms in an industry are determined by their capabilities, which are based on investments in employee expertise and training. Companies also invest in organizational policies to exploit learning benefits once they are identified. For example, Intel has a policy, called Copy Exactly, of building virtually identical manufacturing facilities so that process innovations, once discovered, can be diffused to all plants with a minimum of trouble.[19]

Low Input Costs   A firm can also have lower costs than its rivals because its inputs—materials, labor, capital, information, and technology—are cheaper. In global markets, cheaper manufactured inputs are available from low-cost operations in developing or newly developed nations, such as China and India. If this opportunity expands and becomes available to all firms, then the firms that move early to exploit it will experience only a temporary cost advantage. Thus, the source of low input costs must thus be protected from competition for an enduring advantage to be achieved.

A firm may also benefit from lower capital costs. Larger firms with strong balance sheets typically have a lower cost of capital than smaller independent competitors, allowing the larger company to invest in more opportunities for growth. A smaller business that is part of a diversified corporation may thus benefit from its parent's superior financing costs.

Partnerships between firms can also be a source of lower-cost inputs, especially information and technology. Reciprocal agreements between companies lower transaction costs and smooth the transfer of proprietary assets that would be costly to acquire in the open market. Partners may provide each other with information on common customers, for example, and cross-licensing agreements can lower technology acquisition costs.

Vertical Integration   In many circumstances, vertical integration can lower the cost of coordinating transactions between adjacent activities in the design and commercialization of the firm's product. Transaction costs in the market are higher than comparable in-house costs when the adjacent activities are specialized to each other.[20] However, achieving lower transaction costs within the firm depends critically on how the firm is organized. The more centralized the control over the interface between activities, the more efficient coordination is likely to be. Likewise, the more control over the interface is decentralized, the more the interface resembles a market and the less the firm benefits from vertical integration. The coordination benefits from vertical integration may lower costs, improve value, or both.[21]

Organizational Practices   Firm-specific process innovations, based in organizational practices, are a major source of lower costs relative to competitors. Firms that focus on lowering costs tend to develop a range of efficiencies in all activities, especially operations and logistics. To provide a persistent cost advantage, these programs must be resistant to imitation. An excellent example of a firm that continuously innovates to lower costs is Southwest Airlines, which has pursued cost-reduction programs since its inception. Also, Japanese automobile manufacturers, such as Toyota, are legendary for their ability to reduce costs in operations.

Defending against Competitors

To defend its superior market position from erosion by industry forces, a firm must prevent rivals from copying its core assets and practices and must induce customers not to switch to comparable or substitute products. Firms employ a variety of means to protect their resources, capabilities, and customers from competitors. These **isolating mechanisms** range from exercising property rights to maintaining a high rate of innovation to increasing customer costs in searching for new products (see Figure 2.6).[22]

To understand how firms protect their market positions, it is useful to introduce the concepts of resource and capability. A **resource** is a relatively

FIGURE 2.6 I
Isolating
Mechanisms

Increasing Customer Retention	Preventing Imitation
Search costs	Property rights
Transition costs	Dedicated assets
Learning costs	Causal ambiguity
	Development costs

stable, observable asset, such as a brand or geographical location, that contributes to the firm's value or cost drivers. Resources can usually be valued in a market and traded by their owners. A **capability,** on the other hand, denotes the firm's ability, using its organization and people, to accomplish tasks at a high level of expertise continuously over time. One example of a capability is continuous cost reduction through superior learning as volume increases; another example is shortening the design-to-production cycle for each new product. Capabilities are developed and maintained through the coordinated efforts of the firm's employees and are impossible to trade without selling the whole company or, at a minimum, the units containing the capability.[23]

Resources and capabilities are developed over time within the firm or bought with more or less accurate foresight for their strategic value.[24] They define the kind and amount of value the firm offers as well as the cost at which this value is produced. They thus determine the firm's market position and must be defended from competitors.

To defend its market position, the firm must align its value and cost drivers, and the resources and capabilities that produce these drivers, with the factors that reduce imitation and increase customer switching costs. Without these isolating mechanisms competitive forces would quickly eat up the firm's profit.

Preventing the Imitation of Resources and Capabilities

Because a valuable resource generally can be observed, the firm must shield it from being copied by competitors. There are two ways to prevent imitation. First, if the firm owns the resource, such as a technology, it can establish and enforce **property rights** regarding how the resource is used.[25] Second, if the resource is external to the firm, the firm can turn the resource into a **dedicated asset** by absorbing its capacity, thereby excluding competitors from using it.

A resource that can be protected through rights of ownership is among the most durable sources of a superior market position. Trademarks and patents, for example, are crucial legal safeguards against the imitation of brands and technologies, respectively. Without these protections, the returns from investing in these assets would be significantly lower.

Resources vary in terms of how well they can be legally protected. Patented biotechnology innovations, for example, can usually be copied—competitors can create new compounds that mimic the function of the patented substance but not closely enough to constitute an infringement of the innovator's rights. In some cases, firms avoid patenting a core resource because the process would expose details about its design, thus making it easier to imitate.

In addition, property rights are especially hard to enforce across borders. Many countries, such as China before its entry into the World Trade Organization, have legal systems that do not impose strict, consistent sanctions on copying technologies, brands, or other strategic assets. This inattention to property rights can weaken the motivation of firms within the country to innovate as well as the incentive of foreign firms to compete in the country's markets.

Another way to protect a strategically important asset from competitors is to tie up its capacity. To use up the capacity of an asset—for example, a dedicated distribution channel or supplier of specialized inputs—a firm must effectively absorb its output of goods or services. Firms can also tie up assets through partnerships and long-term contracts. Rupert Murdoch's expansion of Fox's global media franchise is based on locking in key communications channels, especially satellite systems, early in the development of a market, as in the United Kingdom and Australia.

The economic benefit of a dedicated asset depends on its contribution to a firm's value and cost drivers. For instance, tying up suppliers of low-cost inputs helps a firm protect its cost advantage. Similarly, locking in a supplier of advanced technology can help sustain a value advantage.

A dedicated asset preserves a firm's market position only as long as the returns to building an alternative are so low that entry is deterred. When the market growth rate is high and the expected size of the market is large, absorbing the capacity of a critical asset is typically not sufficient to protect the firm's competitive advantage. In this case, rivals may invest in new assets that compete with the firm's dedicated source. For example, new distribution channels may be built or new sources of specialized inputs developed.

Dedicated assets are also vulnerable to self-interested behavior by the asset owner. When the asset's owner attempts to capture more profit by raising the price or lowering value, the firm's market position is threatened. Potential solutions are to acquire the asset from the owner, develop a proprietary alternative to the asset in-house, or change the firm's strategy to remove its dependence on the asset.

Unlike a resource, which can generally be observed, valued, and traded, a capability is typically based in organization-specific routines that cannot be separated from the firm itself. To the extent competitors can't understand how a firm's capability works, the capability is protected from imitation. Its causes are hidden from view and so cannot be replicated by rivals. For example, when Southwest Airlines found in the early 1970s that it was possible to turn a plane around at the gate in less than 20 minutes, thereby increasing the number of short-haul flights the plane could make each day, many competitors rushed to Houston to see the company's employees in action. But, even though the practices could be observed, they were based on a set of conditions the other airlines could not replicate: flexible labor rules, employee commitment, the absence of baggage transfers, no assigned seating, and standardized boarding passes. Beneath the observable procedures were hidden rules among pilots, baggage handlers, ground crew, and others that speeded up the process. So, even if a competitor were able to organize its personnel along the lines of Southwest, the interactions of the rival's employees would not be as effective.

There are therefore two major impediments to copying capabilities. The first is **causal ambiguity** regarding how the capability is executed.[26] In many instances, it is simply not feasible for an outsider to model the procedures that underlie a capability. The second impediment is the **development costs** a rival must incur to replicate the capability. In the absence of a well-defined model, a rival may attempt to learn the capability through experimentation. However, when the capability is complex or its execution requires knowledge that can only be developed over time, the costs of developing a comparable alternative may be prohibitive.

Causal ambiguity forces firms to develop capabilities that are approximations of each other, leading to different performance levels across firms. Moreover, these differences in performance will persist over time as each firm develops its practices along a relatively unique path. Causal ambiguity therefore acts as both a barrier to improvement for the poor-performing firm and a shield against imitation for the firm with a superior market position.

Causal ambiguity is prevalent in the capabilities that underlie value drivers such as delivery, quality, service, and customization. These value drivers are almost always based on organizational practices that evolve through process innovations that rivals find it hard to model effectively. However, when powerful buyers insist on adherence to industry performance standards, such as the ISO series of quality certification protocols, the ability of any firm to achieve a value advantage on the basis of these drivers is reduced. An exception may be customization, for which standardized metrics are hard to create.

Two cost drivers for which causal ambiguity is strong are the learning curve and organization-specific practices. Although many industries have established tacit benchmarks for the benefits of the learning curve in a specific activity, competitors vary systematically around them. Causal ambiguity about capabilities protects them from imitation and thus allows more able firms to sustain their cost advantage. More generally, causal ambiguity protects firms that have established a cost advantage because of superior coordination practices or continuous cost-based process innovation, as the example of Southwest Airlines shows.

There is an obvious relationship between causal ambiguity and a rival's costs in learning a capability. The greater the ambiguity, the higher the costs. But even when ambiguity is not high, development costs may be substantial for some firms.

Dierickx and Cool have called the cost of trying to develop a capability in less time than the original firm a **time-compression diseconomy**.[27] Diseconomies are greater when the stock of knowledge enabling the capability is organization-specific. They are also larger when the capability's contribution to value or cost drivers is dependent on characteristics of its developmental path.

If the stock of knowledge resides in an individual, not the organization, then it would be possible simply to hire him or her to capture it. For example, Amazon tried to capture Wal-Mart's expertise in logistics by hiring Wal-Mart's senior logistics executive. Unfortunately, it is rarely the case that one individual or even a group of managers can quickly replicate in a new firm a valuable capability that existed at an earlier employer, even when there is little ambiguity regarding execution. More often, building the key organizational assets that support the original capability takes time, as Amazon found out. How long this process takes obviously depends on the size of the task. The larger the task and the more resources required, the higher the costs of development.

Development costs are also high when a capability is tied to complementary practices within an organization. For example, the effectiveness of Lincoln Electric's piece-rate compensation system, which is a key contributor to the firm's low cost structure, is tied to human resource, marketing, and production policies. It would be difficult for a competitor to copy Lincoln's system and receive the same benefit from it without also adopting the policies that support it. But adopting these complementary policies and practices increases the cost of imitation.

History-dependent capabilities are also expensive for a rival to develop. A capability is history-dependent when it is based on unique practices developed over time. A useful analogy is the scaffolding used to construct a building and then removed.[28] The scaffolding, like earlier practices, is gone, but the building, or capability, that could not have been built without it, remains. To replicate the capability, each firm must somehow simulate the effects of the scaffolding-like practices, which increases its costs. This problem is endemic in benchmarking exercises between intense competitors, such as Bao Steel (China) and Posco (Korea) in sheet steel, which have different manufacturing histories but attempt to match value and cost in the present.

Learning and development costs are always considered sunk, since the learning process is irreversible. The costs are recouped only through the returns that are produced by what has been learned. Since these returns are uncertain, the higher the costs, the less likely are rivals to attempt imitation, especially against a firm that has already developed the value driver. Citibank's broad geographical scope in global commercial banking and Intel's position as the dominant standard in PC microprocessors are examples of value drivers based on sunk cost investments that are formidably expensive for rivals to replicate.

Increasing Customer Retention[29]

Firms are threatened by substitution as well as imitation. Substitute products have value-cost profiles based on resources and capabilities that differ substantially from those of the products that are substituted for. For example, different modes of transportation—car, train, airplane—are obvious substitutes, each requiring very different resources and capabilities to provide value to the customer. To prevent the erosion of its competitive advantage by substitutes and by new products produced by competitors, a firm can either (1) increase the customer's surplus relative to substitutes by raising the value offered or lowering price or (2) raise the costs of switching.[30]

Switching costs are based on three types of cost. First, the more a buyer must search for an alternative to its current product, the higher its **search costs** and the more expensive it is to switch to a new supplier. Second, the more extensive and complex the process of switching from one product to another, the higher the **transition costs.** Last, the more new information and skills the buyer must learn in adopting a new product, the greater the **learning costs.** These three components of switching costs—search, transition, and learning—are a function of the supplier's value drivers and so can be manipulated to increase customer retention. In addition, search costs are determined by inherent characteristics of the product, specifically whether its value can be assessed without the product actually being used.

A product whose value cannot be measured accurately without a trial is called an *experience good*. Experience goods have higher switching costs because the buyer must try them out to find out what they are worth. A new bottle of wine is an example of an experience good since its value cannot be assessed until the wine is drunk. A veteran wine drinker will have less uncertainty regarding the wine, however, since he or she can calibrate the year, winery, appellation, and so on. Ultimately, however, the proof is in the tasting. A branded soft drink, such a Coca-Cola or Pepsi-Cola, is not an experience good, simply because these vendors strive to produce a uniform product in every bottle or can, no matter where it is produced worldwide. So, once a buyer has tasted the soft drink, there should be no uncertainty regarding the value of any bottle in the future. Thus, a product is more or less an experience good depending on buyer experience and product standardization, both of which affect the level of uncertainty regarding its value.

Many value drivers are directly related to increasing switching costs. Customization locks buyers in by providing the firm with deep knowledge of the customer's business. This knowledge reduces communication costs in the supply relationship and perhaps increases flexibility, as long as the firm does not exploit the buyer's dependence on it by reducing service levels or raising prices. The customer's transition costs are raised when it shifts to a new product since it must throw out the old customized protocols.

Reputation and brand also contribute significantly to customer retention. Reputation acts as a signal of performance that reduces the buyer's uncertainty. Switching away from a major brand entails high search costs since it takes time to validate a new supplier's promises. IBM, in its prime period of selling mainframes to large corporations, understood very well that its brand offered a certification of quality and service.

Firms competing on service expertise can create high switching costs since service performance is inherently an experience good. It is difficult for a buyer to assess the level of service without directly observing it in the context of specific problems. We need only think about our aversion to switching from suppliers of good service to understand how costly searching for alternatives can be.

Network externalities also increase switching costs, as the recent antitrust suits against Microsoft argue. These costs are caused by the time and expense of making a transition from the protocols of one standard to those of another. Adopting the new standard also creates learning costs.

In some industries, product line breadth may allow the customer to communicate seamlessly across products through standard interfaces, as in the example of Cisco's switches and routers. The benefit of interoperability increases the cost of switching to a competing supplier. The cost is associated with the difficulty of designing a compatible interface between the products of the old supplier and the products of the new. The buyer is more likely to replace the entire product line, which is much more expensive.

A similar argument can be made regarding the costs of switching from a supplier with an extensive geographical scope that matches the buyer's operations. In this instance, there need be no firm-specific technology that ties regions together. However, communication and coordination across regions are likely to be more efficient within a single firm than in a coalition of several firms that are geographically fragmented.

The combination of a superior market position and defense against competitors is shown below in Figure 2.7.

FIGURE 2.7 I Building Sustainable Competitive Advantage

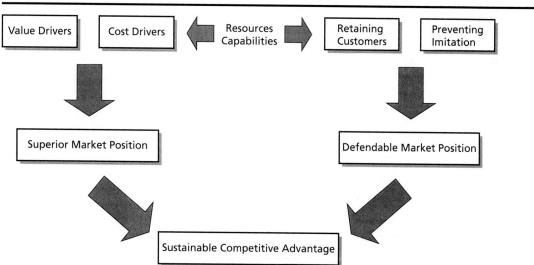

Summary

In this chapter, we have discussed how competitive advantage is built and sustained. At its core, competitive advantage means producing a larger economic contribution than competitors and defending the sources of that contribution from rivalry. To establish a dominant market position, a firm must invest in resources and capabilities that determine value and cost drivers. It is the difference between value and cost, not their absolute value relative to competitors, that determines the firm's advantage. The larger this difference, the more productive the firm and the stronger its position in the market.

Protecting a firm's economic contribution from competitors produces a larger and longer-lived financial return. By retaining customers and preventing the imitation of important resources and capabilities, a firm can reduce price competition and sustain margins. Without a defense against rivals, competitive advantage is either short-lived or cannot be achieved at all.

But no advantage is permanent. Ultimately, increased rivalry is inevitable. As competition beats down market prices, buyers capture more surplus, reducing the firm's profits. Further, innovation by entrants and shifts in customer perceptions of value will eventually erode any market position.

Summary Points

- Competitive advantage is a combination of effective market positioning and defense against competitors.
- Market position is characterized by the difference between the value the customer receives from a product and the cost the firm incurs in producing this level of value.
- The firm's resources and capabilities determine the value and cost drivers on which it competes.
- The customer, not the seller, always determines the value of the product.
- The value of a product is the price at which a buyer would purchase it in the absence of alternatives or close substitutes and given the buyer's other purchasing opportunities.
- Competition and bargaining with customers drive the market price below the product's value.
- Two generic strategies, differentiation and cost leadership, are related to achieving higher value and lower cost, respectively.
- Generic strategies do not explain superior market positioning.
- A firm can occupy a superior market position without having the lowest cost or highest value.

- Defending against competitors is necessary to sustain a superior market position.
- Defense against rivals entails establishing isolating mechanisms to prevent imitation and retain customers.
- Imitation is reduced by strong property rights, dedicated assets, high causal ambiguity, and high development costs.
- Customers are more likely to stick with the firm's product when their search costs, learning costs, and transition costs are high.

Questions for Practice

Think how you would answer these questions for your current company, your previous place of work, or a business you are studying.

1. What are the key drivers of customer value for your business?
2. What are your business's key cost drivers?
3. What is the marginal cost of increasing customer value for each of your value drivers?
4. How is your business positioned in terms of value and cost against your competitors?
5. What market position consistently produces the most profit in your industry?
6. How sustainable is the success of that market position?
7. How successfully do you retain customers?
8. What are the factors that determine customer retention in your industry?
9. What important barriers to imitation do you use to protect your critical resources and capabilities against imitation by competitors?
10. What barriers to imitation have your competitors erected to protect their key assets from imitation by your company?

End Notes

1. See Steven Postrel, " What Is Competitive Advantage?" working paper, Cox School of Business, Southern Methodist University, 2005.
2. This approach is based on Pankaj Ghemawat, *Commitment: The Dynamic of Strategy* (New York: Free Press, 1991), and Steven Postrel, "Notes on Strategic Advantage," mimeo, Cox School of Business, Southern Methodist University, 2000; see also Jean Tirole, *The Theory of Industrial Organization* (Cambridge, MA: MIT Press, 1988), pp. 22–27.

3. This section draws in part from James C. Anderson, Dipak Jain, and Pradeep Chintagunta, "Customer Value Assessment in Business Markets: A State of Practice Study," *Journal of Business-to-Business Marketing* 1 (1993), pp. 1–29.

4. One of the most widely used methods is called contingent valuation (CV). CV involves asking respondents how much they would be willing to pay for a particular program, such as a pollution control initiative, given explicit costs and benefits that the program would produce. A comprehensive critique of this technique is given by Kenneth Arrow, Robert Solow, Paul R. Portney, Edward E. Leamer, Roy Radner, and Howard Schuman, *Report of the NOAA Panel on Contingent Valuation,* May 9, 2001.

5. Two notable techniques have been proposed to induce the respondent to reveal his or her true preferences. The first is called a Vickrey auction, which uses multiperson lotteries to elicit willingness to pay. The second, developed by Becker, DeGroot, and Marschak, asks respondents their willingness to pay and then sets the product price from a random distribution. In both cases, the respondent is required to buy the product at the market price. For a discussion of these methods, see Klaus Wertenbroch and Bernt Skiera, "Measuring the Consumer's Willingness to Pay at the Point of Purchase," *Journal of Marketing Research* 39 (2002), pp. 228–41.

6. See Richard Thaler, "Mental Accounting and Consumer Choice," *Marketing Science* 4 (1985), pp. 199–214.

7. The preferred method for estimating willingness to pay using quantitative analysis is called the random effects logit demand technique. See Kenneth Train, *Discrete Choice Models with Simulation* (New York: Cambridge University Press 2003), Chapter 6.

8. This example is taken from David Revelt and Kenneth Train, "Mixed Logit with Repeated Choices: Households' Choices of Appliance Efficiency Level," *Review of Economics and Statistics* 80 (1998), pp. 647–67.

9. For the seminal statement on generic strategies see Michael Porter, *Competitive Strategy* (New York: Free Press, 1980).

10. For an analytical approach to this distinction see Ron Adner and Peter Zemsky, "A Demand-Based Perspective on Sustainable Competitive Advantage," working paper, INSEAD, 2005.

11. The wave of quality improvement in goods and services worldwide in the last 20 years, due initially to superior Japanese durable goods, represents a more pervasive sensitivity to product quality as a significant value driver. Among the seminal works of W. Edwards Deming, see *Quality, Productivity and Competitive Position* (Cambridge, MA: MIT, Center for Advanced Engineering Study, 1982).

12. See Kelvin Lancaster, "The Economics of Product Variety: A Survey," *Marketing Science* 9 (1990), pp. 189–207; Ruth Raubitschek, "A Model of Product Proliferation," *Journal of Industrial Economics* 35 (1987), pp. 269–79.

13. See Leonard L. Berry, *Discovering the Soul of Service: Nine Drivers of Sustainable Business Success* (New York: Free Press, 1999).

14. The value of a brand is represented in the product's brand equity; see David Aaker, *Managing Brand Equity* (New York: Free Press, 1991).

15. See Michael Katz and Carl Shapiro, "Network Externalities, Competition, and Compatibility," *American Economic Review* 75 (1985), pp. 424–40; Neil Gandal, "Competing Compatibility Standards and Network Externalities in the PC Software

Market," *Review of Economics and Statistics* 77 (1995), pp. 599–608; Joseph Farrell and Garth Saloner, "Standardization, Compatibility, and Innovation," *RAND Journal of Economics* 16 (1985), pp. 70–83.

16. For a comprehensive essay on product complements, see Paul Samuelson, "Complementarity: An Essay on the 40th Anniversary of the Hicks-Allen Revolution in Demand Theory," *Journal of Economic Literature* 12 (1974), pp. 1255–89.

17. See Marvin B. Lieberman, "Market Growth, Economies of Scale, and Plant Size in the Chemical Processing Industries," *Journal of Industrial Economics* 36 (1987), pp. 175–91; Zvi Griliches and Vidar Ringstad, *Economies of Scale and the Form of the Production Function* (Amsterdam: North Holland, 1971); C. F. Pratten, "Economies of Scale for Machine Tool Production," *Journal of Industrial Economics* 19 (1971), pp. 148–65; Richard Makadok, "Interfirm Differences in Scale Economies and the Evolution of Market Shares," *Strategic Management Journal* 20 (1999), pp. 935–52.

18. See John Panzar and Robert Willig, "Economies of Scope," *American Economic Review* 71 (1981), pp. 268–72; David Teece, "Economies of Scope and the Scope of the Enterprise," *Journal of Economic Behavior and Organization* 1 (1980), pp. 223–27.

19. See A. Michael Spence, "The Learning Curve and Competition," *Bell Journal of Economics* 12 (1981), pp. 49–70; Werner Z. Hirsch, "Firm Progress Ratios," *Econometrica* 24 (1956), pp. 136–43; Marvin B. Lieberman, "The Learning Curve and Pricing in the Chemical Processing Industries," *RAND Journal of Economics* 15 (1984), pp. 213–28.

20. See Oliver Williamson, *The Economic Institutions of Capitalism* (New York: Free Press, 1985).

21. Chapter 6 in this book, "Vertical Integration and Outsourcing," is dedicated to the costs and benefits of vertical integration.

22. The concept of isolating mechanisms comes from Richard Rumelt, "Towards a Strategic Theory of the Firm," in *Competitive Strategic Management,* Robert Lamb, ed. (Englewood Cliffs, NJ: Prentice Hall, 1984), pp. 557–70.

23. The concepts of resources and capabilities as critical for competitive advantage are based on Jay Barney, "Firm Resources and Sustained Competitive Advantage," *Journal of Management* 17 (1991), pp. 99–120; Raphael Amit and Paul Schoemaker, "Strategic Assets and Organizational Rent," *Strategic Management Journal* 1 (1993), pp. 33–36; Ingemar Dierickx and Karel Cool, "Asset Stock Accumulation and Sustainability of Competitive Advantage," *Management Science* 35, no. 12 (1989), pp. 1504–14; and Margaret Peteraf, "The Cornerstones of Competitive Advantage: A Resource-Based View," *Strategic Management Journal* 14, no. 3 (1993), pp. 179–91.

24. See Jay Barney, "Strategic Factor Markets: Expectations, Luck and Business Strategy," *Management Science* 32 (1986), pp. 1231–41; Richard Makadok, "Toward a Synthesis of the Resource-Based and Dynamic Capability Views of Rent Creation," *Strategic Management Journal* 22 (2001), pp. 387–401.

25. See David Teece, "Profiting from Technological Innovation," *Research Policy* 15 (1986), pp. 285–305.

26. The idea of causal ambiguity comes from Steven Lippman and Richard P. Rumelt, "Uncertain Imitability: An Analysis of Interfirm Differences in Efficiency under Competition," *Bell Journal of Economics* 13 (1982), pp. 418–38.

27. See Dierickx and Cool, "Asset Stock Accumulation and Sustainability of Competitive Advantage," pp. 1504–14.

28. I am indebted to Steve Postrel for this analogy.

29. See Anita McGahan and Pankaj Ghemahat, "Competition to Retain Customers," *Marketing Science* 13 (1994), pp. 165–76.

30. For a review of the current approaches to switching costs, see Paul Klemperer, "Competition When Consumers Have Switching Costs: An Overview with Applications to Industrial Organization, Macroeconomics, and International Trade," *Review of Economic Studies* 62 (1995), pp. 515–39.

Industry Analysis

Roadmap

This chapter focuses on *industry analysis,* an important task for understanding the causes of firm performance. We will examine the range of industry forces that make firms in different industries more or less profitable. The sequence of topics as follows is:

- Introduction
- Defining Industry Boundaries
- How Industry Forces Influence Profitability
- Industry Forces That Drive Profits Down: The Five Forces
  - Competition
  - Entrants and Entry Barriers
  - Buyers
  - Suppliers
  - Substitutes
- Industry Forces Driving Profits Up: The Value Net
  - Complementary Products
  - Cooperation with Buyers and Suppliers
  - Coordination among Competitors
- Strategic Groups
- Summary
- Questions for Practice

Introduction

Ultimately, firms create industries, not the reverse. As firms compete over time, they influence each other through shifts in product value and price. With experience, firms' costs become better defined, and common supplier markets emerge. Through increasing strategic interaction, the companies begin to recognize their mutual dependence, and their behavior and performance become subject to a set of common industry forces. How these forces affect the firms in the industry and how the firms respond is the focus of industry analysis.

Industry forces are important because they affect how much money a firm makes. They influence product price as well as the conditions for competing on cost and customer value. Forces such as *buyers* and *substitutes* determine the lower bound of the value a product must offer. These factors also influence the market price at which the offer is made. Firms whose products are too low in value or too high in price simply can't compete and must shape up or leave the industry. Another industry force, *suppliers,* plays a strong role in determining both product value and cost. By reducing the benefit their products provide, powerful suppliers push down the amount of value firms in the industry can offer their customers; and by raising prices, dominant suppliers push up industry costs. Further, the threat of *entry* can cause firms in the industry to lower their prices or make commitments to keep potential competitors out. The irony is that these defensive moves can ruin profits in the industry even as they keep it safe from entrants. Finally, products that are *complements* (e.g., TV programming and TV sets) can raise the value of the industry's product to its customers. To emphasize how each of these forces affects the firm's market position (value, price, and cost), we will diagram the relationship as we discuss each one of them.

Industry forces can be strong and enduring or weak and transient, and along with the macroeconomic environment (e.g., regulation, interest rates), determine a level of performance around which firms in the industry vary, based on their different strategies. The sidebar on the next page shows how much variance in firm performance is due to (1) the firm in an industry, (2) factors (e.g., buyers, suppliers, competition) that are common to the industry, (3) the year of performance measurement, and (4) unspecified, random influences. Although the effect of a firm's industry on performance varies by economic sector (e.g., transportation, manufacturing), in general, it appears to be quite significant. The table thus shows how important it is to understand the influence of industry forces on firm strategy.

Defining Industry Boundaries

Before we can analyze the forces in an industry, we must first define its boundaries. Which firms belong in an industry and which do not? No industry definition is absolute. However, a reliable rule of thumb is to identify firms whose products do the same thing in the same way (e.g., air conditioners) and that compete with each other through changes in price and value.[1] *Technological similarity* is needed to separate an industry from substitutes (e.g., air conditioners versus fans). *Market interdependence* among firms forms the basis for strategic interaction.

Relative Contributions of Industry and Business Unit to Economic Performance

How much do macroeconomic, industry, and firm factors contribute to a firm's performance? The answer depends on which sector of the national economy the industry belongs to. The pie charts below show the relative contributions to business unit performance of year, industry, and the business units themselves, along with other factors.[2]

The year in which business performance is measured represents the general contribution of macroeconomic factors. Although these factors varied substantially from 1980 to 1994—there were three recessions and one stock market crash, for example—it appears that they have very little influence on economic returns in any of the sectors. However, the sectors differ quite a bit in the effects of industries and firms. In the manufacturing sector, industry forces explain about 11 percent of a business's performance, which is less than one-third what the businesses themselves explain (35 percent). But in the transportation sector, this proportion is more than reversed: Industry factors contribute 40 percent to business unit performance, but the units determine only 10 percent. The relative percentages for services lies between the other two sectors—the business unit contributes 33 percent to performance and industry 46 percent.

Although the contributions of the business unit and its industry vary, they are important in all sectors. So it pays to analyze both these factors carefully. The last chapter looked at businesses. This chapter looks at industries.

Percentage Contribution of Business Segment, Industry, and Other Factors to Business Return on Assets 1980–1994 (U.S. data)

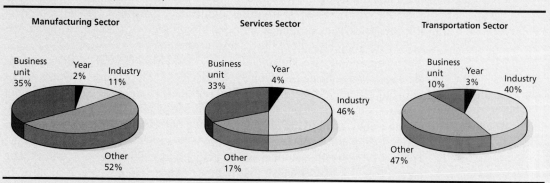

By interdependence we mean that a change in the value or price of one firm's product affects demand for the product of a competitor. For example, a rise in value, holding price constant, increases the buyer surplus, which raises demand for the product at the expense of rivals. Typically, demand also increases when the price is lowered.

Identifying strategic interaction among firms is more difficult when firms compete across geographic regions and customer segments. To analyze geographic competition, for example, we might clump together firms that produce the same products in different parts of the world, but only if they have a common competitor that competes in both regions. For example, we might say that

Kelon, a Chinese producer of air conditioners, is in the same global industry as Lennox, a U.S. air conditioner manufacturer, even though they sell only to customers in domestic markets. Kelon and Lennox can be linked because they both compete with Haier, the giant Chinese appliance company, which sells air conditioners in both China and the United States.

As for *market segmentation,* firms in an industry typically align their product lines with one or more customer segments, but these segments can often overlap. A segment consists primarily of buyers with common preferences, but it also typically contains some buyers whose preferences blend into neighboring segments. For example, some of us are very particular about the restaurants we like—say, fast food, casual dining, or upscale restaurants—while others of us will eat anywhere. The restaurant industry therefore has a fast food segment, a casual dining segment, an upscale dining segment, and so on. Obviously, these segments are distributed along the dimensions of value and price. Fast food is lower value and lower price; upscale, higher value and higher price.

Some firms choose to compete in a single segment and tailor their products to it. These firms are specialists. Other firms, called generalists, offer one product for all segments or a line of products each tailored to a specific segment. A generalist offering one product is typically positioned in the middle of the market, drawing price sensitive customers up from the low end and value sensitive customers down from the high end. A generalist offering a product line competes by exploiting economies of scope across products to lower costs or by exploiting breadth of line as a value driver.[3]

Two examples are McDonalds and General Motors. McDonalds is a classic specialist dedicated, obviously, to fast food. McDonalds makes a lot of effort to serve Big Mac diehards and a little effort to serve those who might eat fast food some of the time. Does McDonalds compete with Chili's, a casual dining chain? Yes, but only barely, since the number of people who would eat lunch or dinner at both restaurants is probably rather small. In fact, restaurant businesses generally see themselves competing within segments rather than across them. A classic generalist with a product line is General Motors. In 1927, Alfred P. Sloan reorganized the company's car lines into divisions that were directed at specific customer segments. Each segment had a unique market position. Chevrolet was the cheapest car with the lowest value and Cadillac was the most expensive and luxurious; Pontiac, Oldsmobile, and Buick fell in between. Sloan's idea was that a customer would buy a Chevy when he or she was young and poor and then with age and more income migrate up the product line, eventually to a Cadillac. GM developed economies of scope in producing components and in marketing and distribution. Other car companies, such as Toyota, Nissan, Ford, and DaimlerChrysler, are organized similarly. Automobile firms thus compete against each other as multisegment generalists. But they may also be rivals with specialist firms in particular segments; for example, Cadillac (GM), Lexus (Toyota), Infiniti (Nissan), and Mercedes (DaimlerChrysler) all compete with BMW, a specialist luxury car company. In general, then, auto firms see themselves as competing both across segments and within them.

An industry's boundary is affected by its stage of development. Early in an industry's history, products may be similar only in what they are called. But over time the boundaries of the industry become clearer. For example, the first personal computers in the late 1970s and early 1980s differed remarkably in their technology and in the way they were produced and sold. Yet they performed roughly the same functions. The PC market was highly segmented and segment boundaries were unclear, since buyer preferences were vague. As the industry grew, standards in hardware and software were adopted (i.e., Microsoft/Intel on the one hand and Apple's proprietary systems on the other) and customer expectations began to gel. As value and price began to converge across products, the industry's boundaries became better defined.

How Industry Forces Influence Profitability

Industry forces may either decrease average firm profitability or increase it. From one point of view, firms are essentially contentious; they fight over customers or over the spoils in a transaction. This perspective has substantial face validity since markets are generally organized as competitions. In fact, without rivalry, the basic notion of competitive advantage would have little meaning. Boeing battles Airbus, HP and Lenovo go after Dell, Target fights Wal-Mart, and so on. This is the traditional view of industrial economics.[4] But from a second perspective, there is much to learn from approaching industry forces as sources of potential cooperation or coordination. The point of this approach is that overall returns can be increased as firms benefit from cooperative practices such as setting standards, sharing information, and coordinating investments with companies whose products are complementary to the industry. This view is less conventional and is captured by Brandenberger and Nalebuff's concept of the value net.[5]

Both the competitive and cooperative perspectives are useful. Industry forces act as powerful constraints on performance and must be addressed by every firm. At the same time, there are typically many opportunities for increasing average profitability through (legal) coordinated action. In this chapter, we will address both views.

Industry Forces That Drive Profits Down: The Five Forces

In his seminal book on business strategy, Michael Porter argued that five industry forces affect the average profitability of firms (see Figure 3.1). These forces are

- The strength of competition.
- The potential for entry into the industry.

FIGURE 3.1 |

Porter's Five Forces
Framework

Source: Michael Porter,
Competitive Strategy (New
York: Free Press,
1980), p. 4.

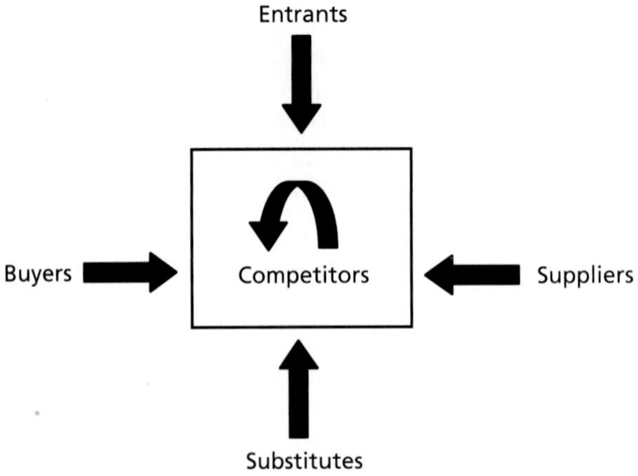

- The power of buyers.
- The power of suppliers.
- The strength of substitutes for the industry's products.[6]

When these five forces are strong, average profits in the industry go down. Conversely, when the forces are weak, the firms in the industry make more money. For example, strong competition and easy entry reduce product price, decreasing the firm's margins. Powerful customers also push down prices and may require higher value, which leads to higher costs in most cases. Likewise, a firm's powerful suppliers can decrease the value they provide and increase their prices, lowering the value the firm provides to customers and driving up its costs. Finally, the availability of strong substitutes, such as snowboards for skis or DVDs for VCRs, puts pressure on the value offered by the firm and on its prices.

Competition

Competition is the most obvious industry force that influences firm performance. Holding value and cost constant, strong competition can drive prices down so that customers do not pay full value for the products they purchase. In the absence of competition, we would all be forced to make very severe choices in the products we buy because they would all cost us so much. Strong competitors may also increase the value they offer customers but not charge more for it. But higher value is likely to lead to higher costs. In this case, then, price is held constant but value and costs rise and profits decrease. So competition reduces profits, either by lowering prices but not costs, or by raising costs but not prices (see Figure 3.2).

Monopoly   In order to understand the power of competition, we first need to understand its opposite, **monopoly.** A monopoly exists when only one firm serves the market. According to United States law, it is not illegal to be

FIGURE 3.2 ।
How Competition
Affects the
Transaction with
the Customer

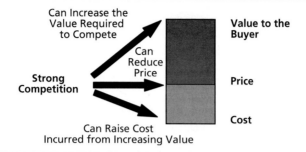

or even to price like a monopolist, but it is a crime to act in a way that perpetuates or improves your position—a fine distinction. Thus, the Department of Justice sued Microsoft in 1998 not because it had a monopoly in personal computer operating systems, but because it exploited and tried to defend its monopoly position. Compared to firms in a competitive market, monopolists produce less and charge more. They make as much money as their customers and suppliers will let them, given the substitute products available. The returns to a monopoly serve as the benchmark for the highest profits possible in an industry.

Perfect Competition   At the other end of the spectrum is **perfect competition,** when competition is strongest. Here many firms produce very similar products. The value and cost drivers of these competitors are roughly the same, and so are their market positions. For there to be many such firms, they should be able to enter the industry easily, suggesting that the market must be quite large compared to the average firm size. Further, no firm should be able to protect its innovations from diffusing to competitors. In perfect competition, firms may assume that they can sell as much as they want without influencing the market price. However, this assumption is unfortunately false: Additional industry volume drives the market price down to marginal cost. So no firm makes a profit over the long run.[7]

What industries might approximate this state? One possibility is money market mutual funds (see sidebar). This industry almost meets the conditions of perfect competition, but not quite. For one thing, the costs and value offered by fund families differ substantially. These differences are due to variation in fund capabilities regarding scale economies and forecasting ability, neither of which is easily copied. The money market mutual fund industry is thus an example where managers have established capabilities that cannot be imitated in order to avoid the poor returns of perfect competition.

Which of the conditions of perfect competition is most important for driving prices down? For example, if the number of rivals in an industry is small but the other conditions are met, are firms' profits still reduced to zero? Or if there are many firms but their value-cost profiles are quite different, do the

The Money Market Fund Industry

A money market fund is a type of mutual fund that invests its shareholders' money in low-risk debt securities with a maturity of one year or less. The short maturity of money market funds provides a degree of downside risk low enough to be comparable to a bank account. A fund's total return to its customer is reflected in its dividend yield, which, combined with the very low level of risk associated with it, is the value the customer receives from the fund. Since their inception in 1971, money market funds have grown rapidly in popularity as a substitute for bank savings accounts. A fund can be part of a mutual fund company, such as Fidelity; an investment bank, such as Salomon Brothers; a commercial bank, such as Citicorp; or even a nonfinancial corporation, such as American Airlines.

The operational innovations in the industry have been a steady stream of incremental improvements in information technology used for back-office transaction processing. These innovations are available to all firms through competing suppliers. Also, although new types of money funds have proliferated, the vast majority of fund families compete directly with each other through overlapping product lines.

It would appear that the money fund industry offers an almost ideal situation to observe perfect competition: easy entry, easy exit, many firms, observable and available production processes, and a common set of buyers. So, one would expect the returns to money funds to be roughly the same and close to cost. But this is not the case for several reasons.

Money funds differ in a number of ways. First, they vary in their abilities to forecast interest rates, and these differences have an impact on how much money the funds make. Better forecasters keep more of the income they receive from their investments, which allows the fund families to invest more in growth. Second, the fund families differ in how aggressively they subsidize their expenses. Expense subsidization increases the yield to shareholders and thereby attracts new business. Third, fund families vary systematically in their scale economies. This means that at any particular size, the costs of fund families are different.

It seems clear then that even in an industry that on the surface has excellent potential to represent perfect competition, there are many important differences among firms that have a significant influence on their growth and profitability. Yields vary, costs vary, and consequently growth rates vary. There is thus a role for strategic thinking even in the simplest industries.

firms make more money? There are no simple answers to these questions. With only a few firms in the industry, firms may control output or collude to raise prices and therefore profits, or price competition may drive profits to zero. A rise in barriers to entry also implies either a rise in profits or the same return as perfect competition, depending on how much the firms in the industry discourage entrants.[8] However, when the market positions of firms deviate, as we see in the money fund industry, the likelihood that some firms will make superior profits goes up, as long as these firms can protect the factors that make them more productive.

Competing in an Oligopoly   An **oligopoly** is a small group of firms that compete with each other and dominate rivalry in an industry. Firms in an oligopoly are aware that their actions affect market price and that aggressive actions by

TABLE 3.1 | Four- and Eight-Firm Concentration Ratios for a Sample of U.S. Service Industries in 2002

Industry	Four-Firm Concentration Ratio	Eight-Firm Concentration Ratio
Hardware and Plumbing Wholesalers	.115	.162
Books, Periodicals, and Newspaper Wholesalers	.300	.453
Investment Advice	.248	.328
Portfolio Management	.161	.237
Commercial Banking	.299	.424
Credit Unions	.072	.098
Trucking	.095	.139
Natural Gas Pipelines	.633	.785
Couriers	.914	.926
Newspaper Publishers	.322	.446
Software Publishers	.394	.455
Internet Service Providers and Portals	.493	.593
Sporting Event Promoters	.269	.375
Gasoline Stations	.880	.153
Electronics and Appliances Stores	.439	.509

one firm affect the returns of the others. When such a group emerges, competition is said to be concentrated. Table 3.1 shows the **concentration ratios** (total sales for the top four or top eight firms over the total sales of the industry) for a range of U.S. service industries in 2002. These ratios range from .914 for couriers (e.g., FedEx, UPS) to .072 for credit unions.

Why are some of these industries highly concentrated and others not? There are, in general, two key factors. The first is the ratio of market size to the minimum setup costs necessary to compete. The larger the size of the market relative to the average firm size, the lower the level of concentration, simply because more firms can compete at or above their break-even volumes. For example, as Table 3.1 shows, the credit union industry is not at all concentrated, reflecting the low level of fixed costs these institutions incur compared to the overall market size. In contrast, the courier business is highly concentrated. We need only think about the massive, ongoing investments in aircraft and logistics facilities that FedEx and UPS make to see why there can be only a few players in this business. The second factor inhibiting entry is the level of sunk cost investment made by incumbent companies in activities such as advertising, research and development, and the development of network externalities. The costs associated with these value drivers are mostly nonrecurring, but the benefits from them, such as an established brand, can endure. So to get up to speed in the industry, entrants must spend money to catch up with incumbents. This puts new firms at a relative cost disadvantage, making the industry less attractive to enter.[9]

Why do we care about concentration? The answer is that in many industries concentration is related in a small but significant way to the average level of profitability.[10] Why is this so? More importantly for managers, what does this relationship between concentration and profitability imply for decision making?

The answers to these questions depend on the underlying causes of the concentration-profitability relationship. There are three possibilities:

- Larger firms are more efficient.
- Large firms interact strategically, but without cooperating, to increase profits.
- Large firms collude to increase profits.

We will deal with each of these below.

Efficiency Differences among Firms   Concentrated industries may be more profitable because larger firms are more productive. In this view, some firms succeed and grow in size by being more efficient than rivals.[11] Each firm invests according to its experience with customers and its expectations of improving these relationships with both enhanced value to the customer and lower prices based on lower costs. Firms that do not invest in cost-saving innovations, whether through learning or scale, remain small and have lower profits.

According to this view, interaction with competitors is not necessary to increase profits. It is not necessary for a firm to know exactly what rivals are doing. A company need not take into account possible rival responses to its investments and may not even perceive the real responses of rivals after the investments are made.[12] The perceived relationship between industry concentration and average industry profitability emerges as growing firms become more efficient and stronger performers.

Noncooperative Strategic Interaction: Reata and the Ponderosa   Another possible reason concentrated industries are slightly more profitable is that firms in an oligopoly interact by observing each other and make decisions based on what the others do. This approach is the province of noncooperative *game theory*.[13] The idea here is that firms in an oligopoly act as if they were playing a game with each other, taking each other's moves into account, just as if they were playing checkers, chess, or poker. It is crucial that in playing the game, the firms only observe and predict each others' behavior, like jet fighters in a dog fight; they do not communicate directly to each other what they are going to do.

In many situations, thinking of rivalry as a game can be useful simply as an analytical exercise. Laying out how competitors will react may be valuable for understanding how much money a firm can make. For example, in closely knit

The Battle Over the Repeal of the Wright Amendment

One instance of reactive competition that can be understood as a game is the fight between American Airlines and Southwest Airlines over local airport regulation in Dallas. Until early 2005, American Airlines, a network carrier, and Southwest Airlines, a low-cost carrier, had a détente regarding their rivalry in North Texas. This mutually accommodative position was based in part on a collective understanding of their very different market positions, the returns to which each airline could accurately estimate. Southwest flew only out of Love Field, a low-cost airport in Dallas; and its flights were mostly to states that were geographically contiguous to Texas because of federal legislation called the Wright Amendment. American flew out of DFW airport, a higher-cost airport, to anywhere it wanted. The arrangement suited the strategies of each airline. Until early 2005, given their very different market positions, the two airlines had no reason to change the status quo. However, increased costs due to higher fuel prices changed the landscape. Southwest began to lobby for the repeal of the restrictive legislation so that the airline could fly to states not adjacent to Texas. However, it refused to agree to fly from DFW airport since it was too expensive. In turn, American fought to keep the regulation in place in order to protect important routes from Southwest's low fares and to force Southwest to fly from DFW if it wanted to fly outside the region. It is safe to say that each airline knows the important stakes of this conflict with accuracy. Furthermore, there is no apparent outcome that represents a compromise. American and Southwest are like two fighters, staking out their ground and developing alternative actions to improve or protect their positions. Treating the conflict as a game helps to understand why each airline makes its decisions and perhaps what decisions each will make as the battle continues.

industries, such as airlines, where good operating and financial data on competitors are publicly available, strategic interaction can be intense. Airlines can be very knowledgeable about how other companies in the industry operate and even predict each other's cash flows with precision (see the sidebar above).

Can a firm make money in a noncooperative game? Interestingly, the answer is yes. There are two possibilities. To explore these possibilities, let's imagine that there are two ranches, Reata and the Ponderosa, that deliver heifers (young cows) to a town. (We call two firms that dominate a market in this way a **duopoly**.) Both ranches have enough cows and bulls to produce all the heifers the town needs. Further, let's assume, quite reasonably, that the marginal cost to produce and sell each additional heifer is constant and is about zero. To understand how both ranches can make money, we first need to ask: Are the ranches "price takers" or "price makers"? By **price takers** we mean that there is a market price that the cattlemen respond to when selling their young cows to the town. Here the ranchers engage in *quantity competition;* that is, they adjust the number of cows they sell in order to make the most money. By **price makers** we mean that Reata and the Ponderosa offer their own prices to the town in order to win the cattle contract. In this case, the ranchers are involved in *price competition* and assume that whoever wins the contract can deliver all the cattle the town needs.

This distinction is important because it determines whether the two ranches will make a profit. Interestingly, even though their cattle are commodities, the ranchers can make profits as price takers but not as price makers. As price makers, the cattlemen just cover their costs.

Let's look first at why Reata and the Ponderosa can make money as price takers. In this case, the ranchers must decide how many cows to breed, given the price customers will pay for the total number of heifers both ranchers will deliver. For example, if the ranches deliver only a few heifers, the price will be quite high, since beef will be scarce and the townspeople who crave it will pay more for it. But if the ranchers flood the market, beef will be plentiful and the price will drop. There is therefore an obvious problem. When Reata and the Ponderosa together sell *too few* heifers, they lose potential revenues because their volume is too low, even though the price is high; and when they jointly sell *too many* heifers, they lose potential revenues because the price is too low, even though their total volume is high. What is the best solution? As the sidebar "Quantity Competition" shows, the key to understanding this form of competition is to look at how much money a ranch makes for each number of heifers, *given the number of heifers brought to market by its competitor*. When the problem is examined in this way, a target number of heifers can be identified for each ranch. At this volume, neither ranch has an incentive to change how many heifers to produce, since a change would lead to lower revenues as long as heifer production by the other ranch stays the same. In Table 3.2 in the sidebar, this number is 70 heifers (seven lots) for both Reata and the Ponderosa. At this amount each ranch makes $4,900.

It is important to note that the profits Reata and the Ponderosa make at this target level are not as good as if the ranches were allowed to coordinate their heifer production directly. If Reata and the Ponderosa used the outcomes in Table 3.2 to coordinate their production, each ranch would clearly choose to produce 50 heifers and not 70. At 50 heifers, the ranches receive $5,500 apiece, $600 more than the $4,900 they each receive from planning heifer production without communicating. So even though two firms in a duopoly can make money without communicating their decisions, they don't make as much as if they colluded. We will deal with this issue when we discuss collusion below.

Because firms make money without colluding when they compete on *how much* to sell, this framework is frequently used to find out whether the profits of firms in real industries are due to simple quantity competition or to something more nefarious. Among the industries where this framework has been used to sleuth for real or potential collusion are electric power, radio broadcasting, sugar, and corporate and retail banking.[14] When firms make more money than the framework would predict, analysts look more closely at where the profits come from.

Now let's look at why Reata and the Ponderosa can't make any money as *price makers*. In this case, both ranches drive each other to reduce their prices

Quantity Competition

In the case of quantity competition, the market sets the price for the total production of both firms.[15] Given this pricing scheme, each firm decides how much to produce by projecting the other's choice and identifying the level of production that leads to the best response for both. It assumes that its rival does the same. Alternatively, if the firms are less imaginative, they could slowly move towards that level of production as they compete over time.

Let's imagine that the ranches—Reata and the Ponderosa—sell heifers in lots of 10. Assume also that the town is willing to pay $2,000 if the supply of heifers is only 10 cows (the town has some very devoted beef lovers), but then the price drops by $100 with each additional lot brought to market. Table 3.2 shows the revenues for various joint ranch outputs. For example, when both Reata and the Ponderosa bring one lot to the market, there are 20 heifers for sale and the price drops by $100 to $1,900 per lot. Both firms receive this amount for their 10 cows, as shown in the upper left cell in the table. If Reata decides to sell one more lot, the number of heifers for sale increases to 30, and the price drops by $100 to $1,800. Here Reata receives $3,600 for its two lots (two times $1,800), and the Ponderosa gets $1,800 for the one lot it sells. The revenues in all the cells can be calculated

in this way. Reata's revenues (in hundreds) are the left number in each cell, and the Ponderosa's revenues (in hundreds) are the right number.

The table also shows something else: It illustrates the best response of each ranch to the other's output decisions. These responses are contained in the cells with the revenue numbers that are in bold. For example, if Reata decided to produce three lots (30 heifers), the Ponderosa's best production level is nine lots (90 heifers). The reason is that the Ponderosa cannot make more than $8,100 when its competitor delivers three lots. At both 8 and 10 lots, the Ponderosa makes $8,000, $100 less than it makes at nine lots. We can track these "best responses" through the table for each level of production of the two firms.

Tracing the best responses through the table (note that the paths are symmetric), we can see that at one point (70, 70), the shifting stops and each firm makes $4,900. At this point, neither ranch has an incentive to change how many heifers it sends to market, given the number chosen by its competitor. No other point in the table has this stability. The seven lot choice by both firms is therefore an equilibrium, a kind of target solution which neither firm wants to leave unilaterally, since if it did, it would make less money.[16]

TABLE 3.2 | Revenues for Each Ranch (in hundreds of dollars)

		Number of Heifers Delivered by the Ponderosa									
		10	20	30	40	50	60	70	80	90	100
	10	19, 19	18, 36	17, 51	16, 64	15, 75	14, 84	13, 91	12, 96	11, 99	10, **100**
	20	36, 18	34, 34	32, 48	30, 60	28, 70	26, 78	24, 84	22, 88	20, **90**	18, 90
	30	51, 17	48, 32	45, 45	42, 56	39, 65	36, 72	33, 77	30, 80	27, **81**	24, 80
Number	40	64, 16	60, 30	56, 42	52, 52	48, 60	44, 66	40, 70	36, **72**	32, 72	28, 70
of Heifers	50	75, 15	70, 28	65, 39	60, 48	55, 55	50, 60	45, 63	40, **64**	35, 63	**30**, 60
Delivered	60	84, 14	78, 26	72, 36	66, 44	60, 50	54, 54	48, **56**	**42**, 56	**36**, 54	30, 50
by	70	91, 13	84, 24	77, 33	70, 40	63, 45	**56**, 48	*49, 49*	42, 48	35, 45	38, 40
Reata	80	96, 12	88, 22	80, 30	**72**, 36	**64**, 40	56, **42**	48, 42	40, 40	32, 36	24, 30
	90	99, 11	**90**, 20	**81**, 27	72, 32	63, 35	54, **36**	45, 35	36, 32	27, 27	18, 20
	100	**100**, 10	90, 18	80, 24	70, 28	60, **30**	50, 30	40, 38	30, 24	20, 18	10, 10

Best Response

Price Competition

There are two quite distinct situations where firms compete as price makers. In the first situation, each ranch can deliver enough heifers to cover the town's desire for beef. Imagine that the town gathers in the square to hear the ranchers' offers in a kind of reverse auction. First Reata shouts, "$2,000 for one lot." What happens? There is silence. Why? Because the market is waiting to hear from the Ponderosa, which logically says, "$1,900 a lot." Again there is silence. And so on, until the price goes down to the ranches' break-even amount. Neither ranch will rationally shout out a price below this amount, so the auction stops. Why doesn't Reata or the Ponderosa simply stop lowering its price before it reaches its breakeven point? The reason is that neither ranch has an interest in stopping the bidding as long as it has a chance of getting the whole job. In this case, greed (and rational decision making) propel both ranches to reduce their offers until there is no profit left.[17]

In the second situation, neither ranch has enough heifers to satisfy the town's beef needs. So there is a kind of rationing of demand between Reata and the Ponderosa, even as they compete on price. Here, interestingly, they don't beat each other up quite so badly, and the result ends up looking more like quantity competition than bare-knuckled price competition. So when neither firm can satisfy the whole market, the destruction wrought by competing on price is moderated.[18]

until they make no money above their costs, just as in perfect competition. The winner then delivers heifers to the town, to cover all its demand. The details are shown in the sidebar, "Price Competition."

How does this type of competition compare to monopoly and perfect competition? Clearly, since in this case no firm earns a profit, competing on price produces results that are identical to perfect competition. So when competitors have the same market positions and compete only on price, it only takes two rivals to mimic the zero-profit conditions of perfect competition.

How much higher are the profits from the quantity game over the price game? The answer depends on the number of competing ranches. Imagine that several other large ranches are established near the town in order to benefit from its desire for beef. Or suppose instead that the patriarchs of Reata and the Ponderosa decide to split their ranches up and give the pieces to their children. In either case, as the number of competitors goes up, the profits associated with quantity competition go down.

What can managers do about the destructive results (for the ranches, but not for the beef lovers in the town) of competing on price? The most obvious answer is that the cattlemen should differentiate their beef. For example, Reata might sell heifers that were low in fat to townspeople concerned about their cholesterol, while the Ponderosa might specialize in somewhat fatter heifers for traditional beef lovers. Some townspeople might like both kinds of beef and straddle these two market segments so that the sales of the two ranches remained interdependent. However, because each rancher has a unique customer base, the differentiation between the ranches would allow them to make more money, while acting as price makers, than if they were competing head-to-head with the same product.

The price competition framework can be readily used to estimate the expected profits of differentiated price makers in a market. This is useful because we are often forced to ask: Why are firms in an industry making money? Is it because they are differentiated or because they are somehow colluding? In many industries, we can find the answer to this question because the price maker framework is so successful at determining the level of profits that are due just to competition. This sets the bar for profits and anything beyond this level must be due to some form of coordination among the firms.

Collusion   The third reason that oligopolies may make more money is that the firms collude. **Collusion** may be either indirect or direct. Indirect or **tacit collusion** occurs through a system of public, unstated, informal rules and roles to follow, such as a leader-follower setup for setting industry prices, or through signaling among firms, such as announcing product plans or investment decisions. In contrast, direct or **explicit collusion** happens when the firms actually discuss together what they will do. This type of communication is against antitrust laws in the United States and Europe but can be found in other parts of the world. Direct collusion often leads to the formation of cartels, such as OPEC, which in 2005 was composed of 11 of the world's largest oil-producing countries.

Tacit Collusion   Tacit collusion works when firms can establish and maintain strategies that produce profits above the competitive outcome. A classic example of the difficulties in making this happen is the Prisoner's Dilemma game. Here two players must choose, without communicating, between two courses of action: One, when jointly chosen, leads to a moderately good outcome for both players, and the other, when jointly chosen, leads to a moderately bad outcome for the players (see Table 3.3). The problem is that, if the players choose what's best for them individually, paradoxically they always lose out collectively.

As an example, let's return to the choices Reata and Ponderosa had to make in delivering beef to the local town. In this case, let's focus only on two choices, 50 lots of cattle and 70 lots, and assume, for the sake of argument, that these are the only quantities the ranches can deliver. The payoffs to these choices are shown in Table 3.3.

TABLE 3.3 I The Prisoner's Dilemma

		The Ponderosa	
		50 lots	70 lots
Reata	**50 lots**	$55K, $55K	$45K, $63K
	70 lots	$63K, $45K	$49K, $49K

Looking at the table, we can see that Reata has higher profits at 70 lots, no matter what the Ponderosa does. If the Ponderosa sells 50 lots of cattle, Reata should choose 70 lots ($63K over $55K), and if the Ponderosa sells 70 lots, Reata does better if it matches this move ($49K over $45K). The same pattern is true for the Ponderosa—under all circumstances, its profits are higher when it chooses 70 lots. The paradox here is that when both ranches choose 70 lots, they receive lower profits than they would have if they had jointly chosen 50. This is the classic problem of the Prisoner's Dilemma: The dominant strategies of the firms—70 lots—lead to a worse outcome for both.

In order to achieve the best outcome, both firms must coordinate their decisions and choose 50 lots together. How can they achieve this without communicating directly? What factors enable tacit collusion? Pankaj Ghemawat has identified four conditions:[19]

- *Mutual Familiarity.* The firms must be familiar with each other. Without familiarity they would have poor information on each other's activities and motivations, leading to misinterpretation. Such information is critical for assuming that the firms have enough knowledge of each others' investment decisions and the outcomes associated with them. Two examples: First, airlines whose routes overlap substantially are less likely to engage in destructive fare wars; second, early providers of cellular service that were rivals in more than one market were more likely to charge noncompetitive prices.[20]

- *Repeated Interaction.* The firms should compete repeatedly with each other. Repetition typically improves management's understanding of the outcomes associated with each decision. Firms therefore try out alternative courses of action and converge on the game's best combination of outcomes. It has been suggested that repeated interaction led to the dramatic exercise of market power by electricity firms in California at the beginning of deregulation in 2000.[21] Because the companies had a long experience of competing against each other, they were able to coordinate pricing decisions rather than compete head on as regulators had expected.

   Repeated interaction is one answer to the problem of the Prisoner's Dilemma. In fact, there is a long history of research on how two players, facing the kinds of payoffs shown in Table 3.3, can figure out how to cooperate without communicating. Learning through repeated interaction seems to be crucial in this process.[22]

- *Consistent Roles.* Firms should have consistent roles in competing with each other, as American and Southwest did until 2005 when Southwest went on the attack and destroyed the existing equilibrium in North Texas. If one or more firms decide to change their roles, as might happen for example if price leaders or followers behave inconsistently, the model of interaction as a game loses predictability.

One potentially important role a firm can play is price leadership. When an industry has a **price leader,** the process of achieving consensus is simplified since all firms agree that a single firm, the price leader, will set the common price and that the others will follow, as Nucor does for example in structural steel. In the absence of such a role, to collude firms must be able to converge on a common price and adjust it in unison as market conditions change. Since this process of convergence is a behavioral minefield, even among long-lived competitors, price leadership can be an attractive means of achieving and maintaining tacit collusion.

- *Strategic Complementarity.* For tacit collusion to be effective, the payoffs to it must be stable. One source of stability, according to Ghemawat, is strategic complementarity. This means that rivals benefit more at the margin when they follow the same strategy. Imagine, for example, a situation where firms can behave either aggressively or meekly, say by increasing or reducing their investments in advertising. Let's assume further that when they are both meek, and invest in fewer ads, they make more money. In this case, the firms would be very interested in being meek together. The meek-meek combination is therefore stable since the firms have an interest in perpetuating it. Their actions are therefore strategic complements.

  A clear example of an industry where strategic complementarity is absent is U.S. automobiles. Throughout 2005, U.S. car manufacturers, led by GM, reduced prices drastically and successfully to induce demand. At the same time, Toyota, Nissan, and Honda kept prices high and actually increased them, relying on their superior brands and quality. Rather than losing market share, the three Japanese automobile companies actually gained it and made more money as well. So even though the U.S. companies increased their volume by lowering prices, they still lost ground against more expensive Japanese models.

Another mechanism for coordinating decisions that occurs in the context of Ghemawat's conditions is **information signaling.** Signaling within an industry typically involves the announcement of new products and production plans. For example, in many commodity industries, such as steel and lumber, prices and output are regularly reported publicly, which helps competitors to forecast industry volume and demand. Another example is the auto industry. Automobile companies regularly announce their capacity expansion intentions, enabling the entire industry to plan more effectively. In fact, information sharing in the U.S. auto industry has been shown to help firms achieve better profits.[23]

Explicit or Formal Collusion: Cartels   Explicit collusion in an industry means that firms coordinate their major decisions through ongoing face-to-face communication. How easy is it to put together and sustain these kinds of arrangements? One way to answer this question is to look at the problems firms have had in forming and running cartels.[24]

A **cartel** is an extreme case of collusion. Firms in a cartel organize and communicate directly to raise profits through noncompetitive behavior, such as price fixing, capacity constraints, coordinated investments, and entry deterrence. The firms also decide on cartel administration and policies, for example, the penalties for cheating. Given the financial benefits of colluding and the communication benefits of face-to-face interaction, cartels might seem to be highly stable and enduring. The facts show, however, that this is far from true.

Cartels are illegal now in the United States and in Europe, but they haven't always been; at times, moreover, they've been encouraged (e.g., the beer cartel after Prohibition ended in the United States in 1932). Most of the cartels we know about are the ones that have been caught. We need to be a little careful in generalizing from this group. Even so, they show some important regularities in duration, profitability, and tendency to fail.

In what kind of industries do cartels emerge? Generally, they occur among firms that sell standard products. There are a few exceptions to this pattern—electrical equipment, for example—but generally the list of cartels over the past two centuries reads like a who's who of commodities—sugar, tea, bromine, oil, cement, potash, steel, shipping, and mercury. One likely reason for cartelization in commodity industries is that the firms in them have relatively homogeneous market positions, which simplifies mutual understanding and the coordination of prices and output.[25] A second reason may be that the firms have been competing against each other for a long time, leading to mutual familiarity, which makes getting together to control competition somewhat easier. But also, as we have argued, commodity industries are vulnerable to destructive price competition, which firms want to avoid, and forming a cartel is a solution.

Several other possible conditions for the creation of cartels are the lack of viable substitutes and the degree of industry concentration. When substitutes are lacking (for example, try to imagine an alternative to cement), industrywide prices can be raised without a significant drop in total demand. This condition is important since increasing prices is typically what cartels are all about. How concentration affects cartel formation is a little more complicated. Concentration per se is less the issue than the aggregate market shares of the colluding firms. These shares should be high for the cartel to succeed, since cartels must effectively control the market. Further, the number of firms in a cartel is less important than the number of decision makers. Many successful cartels have been organized hierarchically, with a policy-making group on top and underlings below. Trade associations have also played a role in organizing cartels in less concentrated industries.[26]

Although a few cartels can last for decades, the average length is around five years, and many barely get off the ground. Even when the necessary conditions for effective collusion are present, cartels still fail at a remarkable rate. Why is this so? There appear to be four major reasons:

- An inability to prevent entry into the industry.
- Uncontrolled cheating or defection from the cartel (think of the Prisoner's Dilemma).

- Fluctuations in demand.
- Bargaining problems among the cartel members.

The first two reasons cause a breakdown because the cartel loses control over the industry. Without effective entry deterrents, new firms can sap the cartel's power. So can cheaters that are not penalized. The second two reasons have to do with the ability of the cartel to manage itself. When demand fluctuates, the firms in a cartel must reset its target price and guess whether any member has decided to cheat by undercutting the cartel price.[27] Market instability thus raises the costs of coordinating prices effectively, threatening the cartel's viability. Bargaining problems may also arise for other reasons such as cost differences among the firms, cultural differences (in international cartels), and conflicts over how the cartel should be organized.

Ultimately, a cartel's ability to manage itself, as it develops over time, determines to a large degree its long-term success. The firms must overcome a host of challenges early in the cartel's history to figure out how to govern their collusive relationship effectively. Only the cartel with the most promising initial conditions can build the capabilities necessary for weathering the threats to its existence.

Summary of Competition in an Oligopoly   What can we take away from this discussion of competition in oligopolies? Or more generally, what can managers learn from the analysis of concentrated industries? Some of these conclusions are obvious, but others are not.

- In general, fewer competitors are better for profits, but even two rivals can drive profits to zero when competing on price.

- It is better to compete on how much to produce, taking market prices as given, than on how much to charge.

- Competing on how much to produce leads to profits, but not as much as the firms could make if they colluded.

- Product differentiation leads to higher profits, assuming of course that customers want the product.

- Firms must know a lot about each other to engage in tacit collusion effectively.

- Explicit collusion appears mostly in commodity industries.

- In general, it is difficult to establish and maintain collusion, even when the firms are communicating directly with each other.

Entrants and Entry Barriers

In general, the higher the entry barriers to an industry, the lower the competitive pressure on incumbent firms. But protecting the industry from entrants can come at a significant cost.[28] To prevent entry incumbent firms

FIGURE 3.3 |
How Entry Barriers
Affect the
Transaction with
the Customer

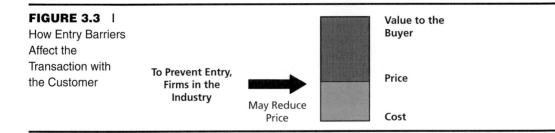

may lower prices and therefore profits, as Figure 3.3 shows. Incumbent firms
may reduce prices to a point where no new firms have an incentive to enter,
a practice called **limit pricing.** Obviously the viability of limit pricing
depends on the relative cost structures of incumbents and potential entrants.
In order to make the limit price credible, incumbents need to have costs that
are low enough that entrants will not be able to match them without losing
money. If incumbent costs are relatively high compared to entrants, as can
be the case for example in deregulating industries, then limit pricing is infeasible. Only if incumbent costs are lower than expected entrant costs does
limit pricing allow a positive return.

Industries that have high fixed costs, especially those with large economies
of scale in operations, are much more expensive to enter. Also, as we argued
above, high sunk costs by incumbent firms in activities such as branding and
research and development also deter entry. Those industries where fixed costs
and sunk costs are both substantial tend to have very high barriers to entry.[29]

High entry barriers are also erected when incumbents are able to protect critical resources and capabilities from imitation. There are four means
of slowing the pace of imitation: property rights over key resources, absorbing the capacity of a key external resource such as a distribution channel,
causal ambiguity regarding the execution of capabilities, and high costs in
developing the capability. All these factors increase the costs of entry and
preserve the firm's market position. In general, existing assets in an industry impede entry when they are specialized to incumbents and contribute to
value or cost drivers.

In addition, high customer switching costs deter entry. A market position
built around investments in network externalities, customization, service,
quality, and delivery is much harder to penetrate, since the customer incurs
substantial search and transition costs in switching to a new firm.

Buyers

Buyer power both drives industry prices down and establishes a baseline for
the value firms must offer in order to compete, as Figure 3.4 illustrates. Buyers are powerful when they can force a firm to increase the value it provides
without increasing its price or to decrease the price it charges at the same value

FIGURE 3.4 |
How Buyer Power
Affects the
Transaction with
the Customer

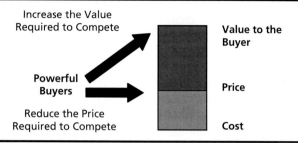

offered. In the first case, as price goes down, the firm's profit obviously decreases. In the second case, higher value may increase cost, which lowers the profits of the firm.

A good example of buyer power in action occurred in the transformation of durable goods industries in Europe and the United States, such as automobiles and copiers, in the 1980s and 1990s. These buyer industries were highly concentrated with few firms and at the same time received inputs from highly competitive component markets. The transformation occurred as many large firms in the buyer industries (e.g., Ford in autos, Xerox in copiers), under pressure from low-cost Asian competitors, reduced the number of their component firms to gain greater control over price and quality. Attrition in the component industries was whopping, with usually only 10 percent of the firms surviving. The buyers asked that the remaining component firms agree to reduce their prices every year by a target amount and at the same time introduce significant changes in their operations to increase quality. Those that were unwilling were removed from the selected supplier list. These mandates increased the buyers' surplus by raising value and lowering price.

Buyer power arises when competing suppliers offer roughly the same value and price. Given this condition, seven factors determine how much power buyers have:

- Buyer concentration.
- Market growth rate.
- Percentage of product sold to the buyer.
- Strategic importance of the buyer to the firm.
- Strategic importance of the product to the buyer.
- Firm's need to fill capacity.
- Buyer's credible threat of vertical integration.

Some or all of these factors may be present in a buyer-supplier relationship.

Buyer Concentration   Buyers are more powerful when there are only a few of them. The reason is that the firms that supply them have little flexibility to shift to another customer if the terms of trade become onerous. Even if the few buyers are fierce competitors, their rivalry may be translated into intense bargaining pressure on their suppliers, as in the example of the durable goods assemblers above.[30]

Market Growth Rate A slower market growth rate shifts the balance of bargaining power toward buyers and away from firms in the supplying industry. As these firms struggle to maintain their rates of expansion, battles for market share break out. This increased competition leads to a focus on retaining current customers and attracting the customers of competitors, putting buyers in a position of greater power. Buyers leverage their stronger position by demanding either higher value or lower prices, or both. For example, the worldwide PC industry in 2001 and 2002 faced increasingly powerful customers due to a reduced market growth rate.

Percentage of Product Sold to the Buyer When a firm sells a large percentage of its business to one customer, this buyer de facto has significant leverage in setting the terms of trade. This is likely to be the case for smaller firms in any industry that build their businesses selling to a few customers. However, for this effect to be prevalent in an industry, so that average profitability is lowered by buyer power, the *average* firm must have concentrated its sales with several buyers. For instance, Microsoft is well known for its market power over software firms developing specialized products for the Windows platform.

Strategic Importance of the Buyer to the Firm A firm may be dependent on a buyer in ways other than selling a large percentage of output to it. For example, a buyer may have a strong reputation for purchasing only from highly competent firms. A firm selling to this buyer may use the supply relationship to increase its own reputation in selling to other customers. Consultants, for example, trade on their relationships with high-profile clients. Other types of non-volume-related strategic importance may involve geographic location, location in a network of partnerships, and access to key technologies.

Strategic Importance of the Firm to the Buyer The flip side of a buyer's strategic importance to a firm is the firm's strategic importance to the buyer, which may mitigate substantially the buyer's power in the relationship. A firm selling critical inputs will be less vulnerable to pressure on pricing simply because buyer switching costs are higher. If the firm can sell its product to other buyers, its ability to neutralize buyer power increases markedly.[31]

Firm's Need to Fill Capacity In many industries, such as steel, oil refining, and chemicals, capacity is added in large increments. Expanding volume in order to break even is critical when a new facility is brought on board. Buyers may be able to exploit this situation by forcing a firm to reduce prices.

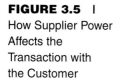

FIGURE 3.5 |
How Supplier Power
Affects the
Transaction with
the Customer

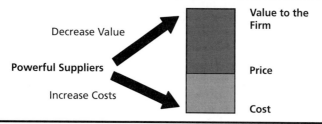

Buyer's Credible Threat of Vertical Integration   When a firm has strategically important inputs and resists improving its value or reducing its price in response to pressure from a buyer, the buyer may choose to vertically integrate the production of the product. In this sense the buyer is both the firm's customer and, through the threat of vertical integration, its competitor. However, when the buyer cannot credibly pose this threat, its power to negotiate more favorable terms in the supply relationship is reduced. Semiconductor firms, for example, frequently will make their own testers rather than buy them from test equipment suppliers. This puts pressure on the suppliers to increase the value of their products and lower their price.

Suppliers

Supplier power is the flip side of buyer power. The firm is now the buyer and wants to be powerful over its own suppliers as a customer (see Figure 3.5). The ideal situation for the firm is to have weak buyers, so that it can charge higher prices, and weak suppliers, so that its input costs are low. This is the classic situation of buy low–sell high.[32]

Suppliers set the baseline for the input costs of firms in an industry. If input prices increase above the price a firm can charge its customers, the firm goes out of business. Alternatively, if the firm's customer demands a lower price, and suppliers will not lower their prices, the firm fails.

Also, relationships with suppliers can affect the value the firm offers its customers. This influence can be important when an input's value is based on technology, quality, delivery, or service. Powerful suppliers can lower the value they provide, for example, by lowering service levels, stretching out delivery times, or reducing the performance of the product.

Supplier Concentration   Weak supplier competition gives a firm in the buyer industry fewer options in choosing a source of inputs and raises a supplier's ability to increase its profits, either by raising prices or lowering value. One notable instance of supplier power is Microsoft. Microsoft's abuse of its significant power in selling Windows to PC original equipment manufacturers (OEMs) led to antitrust suits in the United States and Europe. Another example is the newsprint industry where consolidation has led to higher prices and therefore higher costs and lower profits for newspaper companies.

Percentage Volume Sold to the Firm   A supplier that sells a substantial percentage of its volume to a firm has lower bargaining power. This type of supplier weakness is common in the relationships of start-ups in emerging industries to more established firms, such as the ties of biotechnology ventures to pharmaceutical and chemical companies.

Strategic Importance of the Supplier to the Firm   The more strategically important a supplier is to a firm, the greater the supplier's bargaining power. Strategic importance is evident in the firm's need to control aspects of the supplier's investment behavior—for example, its investments in quality improvement or cost reduction. Alternatively, a supplier may be powerful when it provides a firm with critical resources such as specialized access to end users.

Strategic Importance of the Firm to the Supplier   The reverse of a supplier's strategic importance is the firm's strategic importance to the supplier. For example, the firm may have resources, such as a brand or distribution channel, that are critical for the supplier's business. In this case, the supplier is weakened in negotiations and can't lower value or raise its price easily.

Substitutes

Substitutes compete with the products in an industry without belonging to the industry itself. For example, snowboards are a substitute for skis. Both are used to glide downhill on snow with energy and grace, most of the time. But the athletic experience of snowboarding is different from skiing, so much so that many snowboarders stop skiing entirely. Skis and snowboards perform the same function but not at all in the same way. Likewise, e-mail substitutes for regular mail, fax, and telephone conversation, each of which also substitutes for the others as means of communication.

The analysis of substitutes involves comparing the substitute's buyer surplus to that of the product. The result of this comparison determines in part the range of value and price that products in each industry must offer to compete. Because they are outside the industry, substitutes are part of the framework within which customers assign value to the industry's product. So for those customers who believe they can be active in either sport, the value of skiing is appraised within the context of snowboarding. This means that as substitutes improve their value so must the firm increases the value it offers in order not to lose customers (see Figure 3.6). Thus, if snowboards became easier and more fun to ride, more skiers would switch to them. Likewise, if snowboards declined in price, relative to skis, it is possible that price-sensitive skiers would switch.

How should firms in an industry defend against substitutes? There are two ways. First, firms compete against substitutes just as they do against rivals in their own industry: through innovation. Improving value to the customer and reducing the cost to produce that value keep old customers and attract new

FIGURE 3.6 |
How Substitutes
Affect the
Transaction with the
Customer

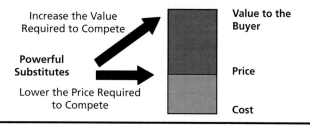

ones. Ski designs have become much more innovative since snowboards were introduced, making skiing both a more extreme sport for experts and an easier sport to learn for novices. A second means of defending against substitutes is to increase customer switching costs. Buyers will remain loyal to a product when their costs of adopting a substitute exceed the benefits they could receive from it. Even when the buyer surplus offered by a product is lower than that of its substitute, high customer transition and learning costs will impede switching. No matter how much fun snowboarding appears to be, many older skiers have not switched because of the learning costs involved.

Industry Forces Driving Profits Up: The Value Net

Overview

Industry forces may also *increase* firm performance. Brandenburger and Nalebuff's **value net** (see Figure 3.7) captures the potentially positive effects of industry forces on average firm profits.[33] The value net is similar to the five forces model, except that it focuses on (legal) overt cooperation for mutual gain rather than competition for dominance. The most intuitive element in the value net is the complementary product. Complements are sold by firms outside an industry but increase demand for the industry's product, as, for example,

FIGURE 3.7 |
The Value Net

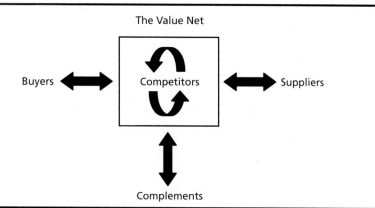

the erection of towers for transmitting wireless telephone signals increases the demand for cell phones. Another source of mutual gain is cooperation between the firms in an industry and their buyers or suppliers, either to lower costs or raise value. Increasing the economic surplus through cooperation can produce economic benefits for both parties. Finally, competitors within an industry may also cooperate, although obviously within the guidelines of antitrust law. Cooperation of this kind may take the form of industry associations and research and development joint ventures.

Complementary Products

Just as some products in other industries may act as substitutes for a firm's product, others may serve as complements. Complementary products, such as high definition televisions and HDTV transmission equipment, have a positive influence on each other's demand. In fact, almost all products are embedded in systems of complements.[34]

A good example of a firm that understands the value of complements is Intel. Intel's internal venture capital unit, called Intel Capital, invests in technology start-ups that not only are promising as businesses but also have products that are complementary to Intel's product lines. Because of Intel's superior technological expertise, the due diligence performed on these start-ups before they are financed is deep and comprehensive. Thus, Intel rarely makes a poor investment. However, by far the most important result of funding the start-ups is the support they give Intel's products in their markets. Intel calls the range of complements in which it invests a "market ecosystem."

Cooperation with Buyers and Suppliers

A major type of cooperation to increase profitability, either by increasing value or lowering costs, occurs between firms and their buyers and suppliers. Just as the firm and its buyers bargain over the distribution of the economic contribution, so too are there inducements to increase this contribution to benefit both firms. This form of interfirm coordination can take the form of sharing information or transferring resources and capabilities.

Sharing Information In many supply relationships, sharing knowledge about strategic routines and plans can lower cost and improve value. For example, if delivery is a key value driver for the buyer, greater information flow between the firms concerning logistics routines is likely to shorten shipping times, which increases the value provided. Procter & Gamble, for example, has substantially raised its value to Wal-Mart by lowering delivery time through coordinating logistics processes.

Strategically important information may also be shared between firms, typically when they have formed an alliance for the supply of a critical component. This form of cooperation increases the value offered as the supplying firm is able to direct its investments to meet future needs of the buyer.

However, the buyer may face a significant trade-off between the benefits of sharing information and the risk of having it exposed to competitors.

Sharing Resources and Capabilities   Buyers that have developed state-of-the-art capabilities may transfer them to firms supplying critical inputs in order to improve value, lower costs, or both. For example, Toyota built its supplier base after World War II by transferring quality-control techniques to component manufacturing firms in Japan. Also, there is evidence that quality-control methodologies, such as ISO 9001, diffused from large assembly firms in the United States to component firms to suppliers of materials within a very short time frame.

Interestingly, the more standardized these practices, the easier they are to transfer, but also the more readily they can be copied by competitors. Therefore, for cooperation between a buyer and its suppliers to improve the buyer's competitive advantage, part of the transfer process should be nonstandard and proprietary. This tension between standardization and uniqueness in the capabilities that are transferred is central to how firms can improve their performance through cooperating with their suppliers.

Coordination among Competitors

In a variety of circumstances, rivals may be able to join together to cooperate on specific industry problems, such as lobbying for favorable legislation or developing technology for broad industry application. Sematech, a research and development consortium of U.S. semiconductor companies organized in 1987 to respond to Japanese advances, spurred many other such arrangements in the U.S. economy. Partnerships and cooperative networks of rivals will be discussed in detail in Chapter 7.

Throughout our discussion of competition and cooperation we have noted how industry forces influence the value offered, price, and cost of firms. Table 3.4 summarizes these effects.

Strategic Groups

As discussed above, industries are commonly divided into more than one customer segment, and firms may compete by specializing in serving the needs of one segment alone. Firms serving a distinct segment typically have developed relatively similar value and cost drivers. Firms that share a market position in this way are frequently called a **"strategic group."** In some industries, these groups are quite distinct, almost composing separate industries. In other industries, the groups overlap as numerous firms compete across customer segments. In either case, building an industry map of strategic groups can provide important information on firm strategies and how they influence performance.[35]

Strategic groups represent a level of analysis between the industry and the firm. Firms within a group have similar value and cost drivers compared to firms in other groups. This is so because each group of firms develops comparable

TABLE 3.4 I   The Effect of Industry Forces on Value, Cost, and Price

Industry Force	Effect on:		
	Value	Cost	Price
Stronger Rivalry	May raise value required to compete in the industry	May increase cost associated with higher value	Lowers the price required to compete in industry
Stronger Buyers	Raise the value required to compete in industry		Lower the price required to compete in industry
Stronger Suppliers	Lower the value to firms in the industry	Raise the costs of firms in industry	
Lower Entry Costs			Lower the price to keep entrants out of industry
More Powerful Substitutes	Raise the value required to compete in industry		Lower the price required to compete in industry
Industry Cooperation			
Between Firm and Buyers	Raises the value to buyers without comparable rise in firm costs	Lowers firm costs without comparable drop in buyer value	
Between Firm and Suppliers	Raises the value to firm without comparable rise in supplier costs	Lowers supplier costs without comparable drop in firm value	
Between Firm and Competitors	Raises the value to industry buyers without comparable rise in industry costs (shared innovation)	Lowers the costs in industry without comparable drop in value to industry buyers (shared innovation)	Raises the potential price necessary to compete (cooperative pricing)
Complements			
Effective Complements	Raises the value to industry buyers without comparable rise in industry costs		

resources and capabilities to serve the particular preferences of its customer segment. For example, customers in many durable goods industries (e.g., cars, PCs, and fax machines) are segmented according to their price sensitivity and their sensitivity to different types of value, such as quality, technology, and service. Correspondingly, the resources and capabilities of the firms aligned with each segment are markedly different.

The airline industry provides a graphical example, shown in Figure 3.8. Firms that are above the main diagonal of the chart had operating profits in the quarter, and firms below the diagonal had operating losses. The industry is split into three groups of airlines—Low-Cost, Network, and Regional—as defined by the Bureau of Transportation Statistics of the U.S. Department of Transportation. Low-Cost firms generally focus on low costs to compete; the

FIGURE 3.8 I Strategic Groups—U.S. Domestic Airline Industry, 4th Quarter 2004

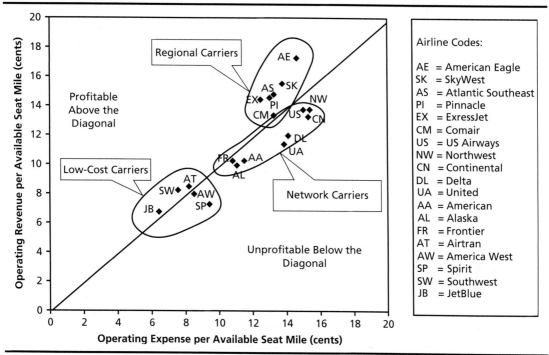

Network carriers are the traditional incumbents that built hub and spoke systems in order to compete after the industry deregulated in 1978 (Frontier is the exception); and the Regional airlines are smaller carriers that mostly operate flights that feed the Network carrier hubs. So the market positions of the three strategic groups vary substantially. Further, the groups clearly differ in their profitability, from uniformly positive returns among the Regional carriers to mixed profitability in the Low-Cost group to uniformly negative returns in the Network group.

More generally, since strategic groups are relatively distinct in terms of their value and cost drivers, they are likely to be affected differently by the power of buyers and suppliers, substitutes, and potential entry. Further, they may have different opportunities for cooperation and for supporting complements. In addition, the customer segments of the groups may vary in size and growth rate.

Because of this variation among groups in profit potential, firms within a more profitable group are likely to defend their shared strategic position against encroachment from other firms in the industry, much as firms within the overall industry raise barriers to keep outside firms from entering. These impediments to large shifts in market position within the industry are called **mobility barriers.**[36] Without strong barriers to mobility across groups, more profitable groups would slowly lose their advantage as other firms in the industry enter them.

The three strategic groups in the airline industry shown above manifest significant mobility barriers. Perhaps the most challenging mobility barrier lies between the Network and Low-Cost airlines. Both United and Continental have tried to build low-cost operations to compete primarily with Southwest. But their efforts have failed. American has reduced its costs substantially so that it butts up against the Low-Cost group. Yet the members of this group remain more efficient.

How do strategic groups emerge? One standard explanation is that experimentation in value and cost drivers by start-ups in the early stages of industry development produces a range of market positions that vary in their potential profitability due to differences in customer characteristics. Firms in more profitable positions attract imitation, and the less profitable firms fail. The industry thus converges on more effective combinations of resources and capabilities. Over time, due to differences in innovation and in the ability to protect market positions though mobility barriers, the groups begin to vary in their average performance, and the industry becomes stratified.

In some industries, however, disruptions can create opportunities that reshape the competitive landscape and lead to new strategic groups. This is what happened in the U.S. airline industry to produce the strategic groups discussed above. The disruptive event was the deregulation of the industry. Smaller, more efficient carriers such as Southwest moved into the national market, and entry into the Low-Cost group was strong. Incumbent firms became the Network group as they built hub and spoke systems in the expectation of economies of scale, and the Regional airlines emerged to service the hubs. The three distinct groups were defined therefore primarily in response to a shift in the rules governing competition in the industry.

Summary

In this chapter we have examined the industry forces that determine firm profitability. These forces—competition, buyer and supplier power, substitutes, and potential entry—may drive profits down by forcing prices down or costs up. We examined the various forms of competition, especially in concentrated industries. We looked in detail at how firms compete on quantities or prices and at the conditions under which collusion, both tacit and explicit, might emerge. We also examined how buyers and suppliers try to gain an advantage over the firms in the industry. Then we turned to other industry forces that involve cooperation and complements so that profits are increased rather than eroded.

Last, we discussed strategic groups. These groups constitute a separate layer of competition within the industry that influences firm performance. A strategic group is typically dedicated to a specific customer segment, and the performance of firms in the group depends on their ability to produce a superior economic contribution and to protect the sources of this contribution from imitation by other firms, both within and outside the industry.

Summary Points

- Industry and firm factors differ in their contributions to firm performance according to the industry's sector.
- Industry forces may decrease or increase profitability.
- Five forces that drive down profitability are rivalry, buyer power, supplier power, potential entry, and substitutes.
- Perfect competition is never found in reality, but it is useful to highlight the importance of rivalry in reducing prices to marginal cost.
- There are three rationales for the finding that the average profitability in more concentrated industries is frequently a little higher.
  - Larger firms are more efficient.
  - Firms in an oligopoly are price takers and engage in quantity competition or are price makers and sell differentiated products.
  - Firms in the oligopoly collude.
- The basic conditions for collusion in a concentrated industry are mutual familiarity, repeated interaction, consistent roles, and strategic complementarity.
- The four factors that threaten cartel stability are:
  - An inability to prevent entry into the industry.
  - Uncontrolled cheating or defection from the cartel.
  - Fluctuations in demand.
  - Bargaining problems among the cartel members.
- When firms in an industry offer roughly the same economic contribution, high buyer power drives average industry profits down.
- Supplier power sets the baseline for the costs firms in an industry incur in producing value for their customers.
- In general, the higher the entry barriers to an industry, the lower the competitive pressure on incumbent firms.
- Substitutes determine in part the range of value and price that products in each industry must offer.
- Complementary products have a positive influence on each other's demand.
- An industry is commonly composed of groups of firms, called "strategic groups," each of which is aligned with a particular customer segment and thus has a relatively distinct approach to competition.

- The average performance of strategic groups may vary substantially.
- Impediments to large shifts in market position within the industry are called mobility barriers.

Questions for Practice

Think how you would answer these questions for your current company, your previous place of work, or a business you are studying.

1. How is your industry defined? What are the key dimensions your firm uses to identify competitors?
2. What are the key forces limiting profits in your industry?
3. How concentrated is your industry? What factors have led to concentration or are preventing it?
4. If your industry is concentrated, how efficient or productive are the largest firms in your industry compared to the second and lower tiers? If it is not concentrated, are there opportunities to consolidate activities that would lead to greater efficiency with an increase in size?
5. To what extent do firms in your industry engage in strategic interaction? Are they price takers or price makers?
6. How differentiated are the products in your industry? What effect does the degree of differentiation have on firm profitability?
7. How powerful are buyers in your industry? How powerful are suppliers?
8. What entry barriers does your industry pose to possible entrants?
9. What are the major substitutes your industry confronts?
10. In what ways do firms in your industry cooperate—with each other and with buyers and suppliers—in order to improve profitability?
11. What are the key complements to your industry and how does your industry support their expansion?
12. What are the key strategic groups in your industry? What are the key mobility barriers that keep firms from moving from one group to another?

End Notes

1. See John Nightingale, "On the Definition of 'Industry' and 'Market,'" *Journal of Industrial Economics* 27 (1978), pp. 31–40.
2. The data in this section are taken from Anita M. McGahan and Michael Porter, "How Much Does Industry Matter, Really?" *Strategic Management Journal* 18 (1997), pp. 15–30.

3. See George Day, "Strategic Market Identification and Analysis: An Integrated Approach," *Strategic Management Journal* 2 (1981), pp. 281–99.

4. See Michael Porter, *Competitive Strategy* (New York: Free Press, 1980), chap. 1.

5. See Adam Brandenburger and Barry Nalebuff, *Co-opetition* (New York: Doubleday, 1996).

6. See Michael Porter, *Competitive Strategy* (New York: Free Press, 1980).

7. See Joan Robinson, "What Is Perfect Competition?" *Quarterly Journal of Economics* 49 (1934), pp. 104–20.

8. See Richard Gilbert, "Mobility Barriers and the Value of Incumbency," in R.Willig and R. Schmalensee, eds., *Handbook of Industrial Organization* (Amsterdam: North Holland, 1990).

9. See John Sutton, *Sunk Costs and Market Structure* (Cambridge, MA: MIT Press,1990).

10. See Richard Schmalensee, "Interindustry Studies of Structure and Performance," in R.Willig and R. Schmalensee, eds., *Handbook of Industrial Organization* (Amsterdam: North Holland, 1990), chap. 1.

11. See Harold Demsetz, "Industry Structure, Market Rivalry and Public Policy," *Journal of Law and Economics* 16 (1973), pp. 1–4; Steven Klepper, " Entry, Exit, Growth and Innovation over the Product Life Cycle," *American Economic Review* 86 (1996), pp. 562–83; and Richard Nelson and Sidney Winter, *An Evolutionary Theory of Economic Change* (Cambridge, MA: Harvard University Press, 1982).

12. See Richard Cyert and James March, *The Behavioral Theory of the Firm* (Englewood Cliffs, NJ: Prentice Hall, 1963).

13. James Friedman, *Oligopoly Theory* (New York: Cambridge University Press, 1983); Jean Tirole, *The Theory of Industrial Organization* (Cambridge, MA: MIT Press, 1988).

14. See Severin Borenstein, J. Bushnell, and J. Wolak, "Measuring Market Inefficiencies in California's Restructured Wholesale Electricity Market," *American Economic Review* 92 (2002); Severin Borenstein, "On the Efficiency of Competitive Markets for Operating Licenses," *Quarterly Review of Economics* 103 (1988), pp. 357–85; David Genesove and Wallace Mullin, "Testing Static Oligopoly Models: Conduct and Cost in the Sugar Industry, 1890–1914," *Rand Journal of Economics* 29 (1998), pp. 355–77; Sigbjorn Berg and Moshe Kim, "Oligopolistic Interdependence and the Structure of Production in Banking: An Empirical Investigation," *Journal of Money, Credit and Banking* 26 (1994), pp. 309–22.

15. For a discussion of quantity (Cournot) competition, see Tirole, *Theory of Industrial Organization,* chap. 5.

16. This equilibrium found by Cournot in 1835 has been shown to follow the mathematical principle developed by John Nash, a mathematician who published his work in the early 1950s and who won the Nobel Prize in 1994 for his work on game theory. Nash proved that this equilibrium will always exist in this kind of game.

17. For a discussion of price (Bertrand) competition, see Carl Shapiro, "Theories of Oligopoly Behavior," in R. Willig and R. Schmalensee, eds., *Handbook of Industrial Organization* (Amsterdam: North Holland, 1990), chap. 6; and Tirole, *Theory of Industrial Organization,* chap. 5.

18. D. Kreps and J. Scheinkman, "Quantity Precommitment and Bertrand Competition Yield Cournot Outcomes," *Bell Journal of Economics* 14 (1983), pp. 326–37.

19. Pankaj Ghemawat, *Games Businesses Play* (Cambridge, MA: MIT Press, 1997).

20. See Gary Fournier and Thomas Zuehlke, "Airline Price Wars with Multi-market Carrier Contacts and Low-Cost Carrier Entrants," working paper, Department of Economics, Florida State University; and Meghan Busse, "Multi-market Contact and Price Coordination in the Cellular Phone Industry," *Journal of Economics and Management Strategy* 9 (2000), pp. 287–320.

21. Severin Borenstein, J. Bushnell, and J. Wolak, "Measuring Market Inefficiencies."

22. See Robert Axelrod, *The Evolution of Cooperation* (New York: Basic Books, 1984).

23. Maura P. Doyle and Christopher M. Snyder,"Information Sharing and Competition in the American Automobile Industry," *Journal of Political Economy* 107 (1999), pp. 1326–64.

24. Margaret Levenstein and Valerie Suslow, "What Determines Cartel Success," *Journal of Economic Literature*, forthcoming.

25. Rhee, Ki-Eun and Raphael Thomadsen, "Costly Collusion in Differentiated Industries," working paper, Columbia University, 2004.

26. George Symeonidis, "In Which Industries Is Collusion More Likely? Evidence from the U.K." *Journal of Industrial Economics* 51, no. 1 (2003), pp. 45–74.

27. Edward J. Green and Robert H. Porter, "Noncooperative Collusion under Imperfect Price Information," *Econometrica* 52, no. 1 (1984), pp. 87–100.

28. See Tirole, *Theory of Industrial Organization,* chap. 8; Dale Orr, "An Index of Entry Barriers and Its Application to the Market Structure Performance Relationship," *Journal of Industrial Economics* 23 (1974), pp. 39–49.

29. See Tirole, *Theory of Industrial Organization,* chap. 6.

30. See Ute Schumacher, "Buyer Structure and Seller Performance in U.S. Manufacturing Industries," *Review of Economics and Statistics* 73 (1991), pp. 277–84.

31. See Ralph M. Bradburd, "Price-Cost Margins in Producer Goods Industries and the Importance of Being Unimportant," *Review of Economics and Statistics* 64 (1982), pp. 405–12.

32. For a comparison of relative buyer and seller concentration, see Vincent A. LaFrance, "The Impact of Buyer Concentration—An Extension," *Review of Economics and Statistics* 61 (1979), pp. 475–76, Notes.

33. See Adam Brandenburger and Barry Nalebuff, *Co-opetition* (New York: Doubleday 1996).

34. See Paul A. Samuelson, "Complementarity: An Essay on the 40th Anniversary of the Hicks-Allen Revolution in Demand Theory," *Journal of Economic Literature* 12 (1974), pp. 1255–89.

35. See Avi Fiegenbaum and Howard Thomas, "Strategic Groups and Performance: The U.S. Insurance Industry, 1970–1984," *Strategic Management Journal* 12 (1990), pp. 197–215.

36. See Richard Caves and Michael Porter, "From Entry Barriers to Mobility Barriers," *Quarterly Journal of Economics* 91 (1977), pp. 241–61.

CHAPTER 4

Competing over Time: Industry and Firm Evolution

Roadmap

Creating competitive advantage always occurs in the context of shifting industry forces. Most industries follow a life cycle from growth to maturity and then through rejuvenation back to growth again. In this chapter we will examine this complex and periodically harrowing process and its effect on how firms compete. These are the topics that guide our discussion:

- Introduction
- The Stages of Industry Evolution
- Stage One—Growth
  - Dynamic Capabilities and the Growth of the Firm
  - Developing Scalable Value and Cost Drivers
  - Early Mover Advantage
  - Strategic Pricing
- Stage Two—Shakeout
  - The Maturation of the Product Life Cycle
  - The Emergence of a Dominant Design
  - Shakeout Duration and Severity
- Stage Three—Maturity
  - The Decline in the Market Growth Rate
  - An Increase in Buyer Experience
  - The Concentration of Market Share among Similar Large Firms
  - The Persistence of Niche Markets

Introduction

When we look at the large, successful companies that make the goods we buy, we tend to see them only as they are now, without histories. Yet every one of them started out small and grew through competition. Usually, as these firms grew, their industries developed over time as well. How did this happen? Amazingly, many industries share a common pattern of development that has important implications for how companies compete over time. This pattern is the subject of this chapter.

All industries evolve over time as new firms enter and failing firms exit. Entry is driven by expectations of profitable sales, and exit by the failure to achieve them. Start-ups bet that their initial value and cost drivers will be effective. Incumbents bet on their abilities to improve their market positions in a context of shifting technologies and customer preferences. Good bets help firms survive and poor bets lead to failure.

The more a firm resists evolutionary change, the less likely it is to endure. Early market leaders frequently lose their dominant positions as the industry matures (e.g., Apple Computer in personal computers), and only a few of the firms that survive to maturity manage to remain successful when their industries are disrupted by technological or institutional change. Some firms, such as Digital Equipment, fail to manage the transition to new product technologies. Others, such as Eastern Airlines, go bankrupt because they cannot take advantage of industry deregulation. IBM, Johnson & Johnson, and Sony are among the rare examples of firms that have survived multiple industry life cycles in their core businesses with relatively strong economic performance.

Industry evolution threatens all types of competitive advantage. Each firm develops its value and cost drivers within historically determined market constraints. As these constraints change, keeping a superior market position depends on meeting the challenges of competing over time.

The Stages of Industry Evolution

No two industries have the same evolutionary path. However, most paths, as captured by the entry and exit rates of firms, are quite similar. The typical pattern of industry evolution has three major stages:[1]

- *Stage One—Growth:* new product commercialization and industry expansion as the entry rate exceeds the exit rate.

- *Stage Two—Shakeout:* a systematic drop in the rate of entry and rise in the rate of exit, decreasing the number of firms in the industry.
- *Stage Three—Maturity:* industry stabilization as entry and exit rates converge.

Many industries in the mature stage also experience technological or regulatory shocks that threaten the market positions of established firms. In this potential fourth stage, which we will call **industry disruption,** industry practices are rejuvenated as start-ups enter and incumbents adapt to the new rules of competition.

Closely tied to industry evolution is the concept of the **product life cycle.** The life of every product follows a cyclical pattern, just like an industry. When new products are introduced, they appeal to just a few buyers. Then, if the product provides a significant buyer surplus, volume grows. But at some point, the number of buyers who want the product levels off, and the product life cycle enters the mature phase. Ultimately, most products die and are replaced.

Over the course of industry evolution, companies are likely to introduce many products, each following its own trajectory of shifting volume over time. For example, think of how many different kinds of cell phone Nokia, Motorola, Samsung, and Ericsson have introduced since they began competing against each other. This kind of repeated new product introduction is often a force that drives industry development.

It should be clear, however, that the industry life cycle subsumes the life cycles of individual products. Both the growth and the mature stages of an industry can last much longer than the life cycles of the products introduced within them. A classic example of an industry that has progressed from growth through shakeout to maturity and that shows the tie between new products and this evolutionary process is U.S. automobiles (see the sidebar).

Industries differ in their progress through the first three stages of industry evolution. Table 4.1 shows the results from a study of the years selected industries have spent in each stage. The time span runs from industry inception to 1981, the last years the count of firms was measured. Some industries remain in Stage 1 for a long time as entrepreneurs struggle to find the right combination of value drivers. Other industries, such as fluorescent lights, accelerate and mature quickly. If entry barriers are low, new firms start up in the expectation that they can solve the productivity challenges incumbents are facing. But the costs of entry rise once these challenges are solved and surviving incumbents improve their market positions. Table 4.2 shows the rates of attrition in Stages 2 and 3, during and after the shakeout. Clearly, industries vary in the number of firms that exit during the shakeout and therefore in the number that survives into maturity.

Stage One—Growth

All new industries start with a product innovation that offers a superior buyer surplus compared to substitutes. This surplus is typically based on a novel design, innovative product features, and the availability of new complements.

The U.S. Automobile Industry

Automobiles are so pervasive and taken for granted in the modern era that we almost assume that the companies and brands we know were born successful and that the industry's current structure has always been in existence. These assumptions are simply not valid. The auto industry in the United States emerged slowly and has had an amazing number of competitors (roughly 2,350) over its history. The first graph below shows the trend from 1880 to 1975 in the number of companies founded, the number of companies that exited, and the total number of firms in the industry in each year.[2] Consistent with the three stages of industry evolution, the total number of firms rises sharply, then drops and levels off.

The second graph shows that the production of automobiles generally rises with the growth of the U.S. economy. The drop in sales to zero in the early 1940s reflects the radical shift from consumer to military spending during World War II. It is interesting that after the war, production resumed at about the prewar level.

The production trend shows that the evolution of the auto industry does not map onto a product life cycle in which demand flattens out in the later stages. Rather, the auto industry's evolution has more to do with the introduction of the Model T by Ford Motor Company in 1908. The Model T offered sufficient value at a very low price to generate wide acceptance (see the

Entries, Exits, and Total Firms in the U.S. Automobile Industry, 1880–1974

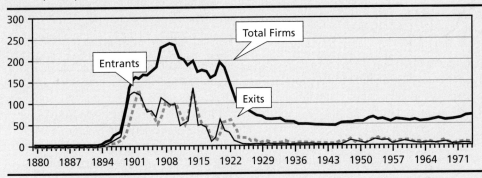

Total Production of U.S. Automobile Firms (in millions)

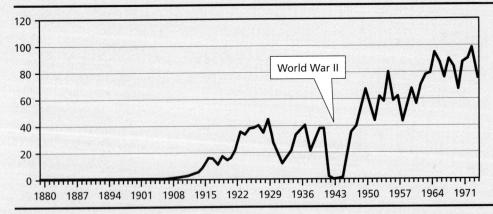

third graph). Consequently, it drove many firms out of the market. The rise of the automobile industry from roughly 1913 until 1923 reflects the increase in demand for the Model T.

Ford discontinued the Model T in 1926, however. In the early 1920s Alfred P. Sloan had successfully turned General Motors around with a strategy based on a broad product line of cars that had improved comfort and aesthetics. These GM cars were priced low enough to neutralize Ford's advantage and push the Model T from the market.

Total Automobile and Model T Production, 1909–1927

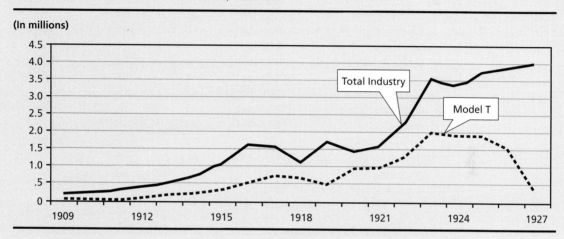

For example, the first automobiles competed with trains, trolleys, horses, and horse-driven carriages as modes of transportation. Early cars were composed of an innovative power train and engine, among other components, and required better roads and gas stations as complements for travel over long distances. Another example is personal computers. PCs have become widely accepted as a replacement for the typewriter and simple computer terminal, but their expansion required the development of new software and hardware, including operating systems, applications, storage devices, and semiconductors. Similarly, as a form of mass communication, television has become a substitute for radio in the home. But frequent television broadcasts became feasible only with the development of complements such as programming, cameras, transmission stations, and other specialized equipment.

Early in a new industry's history, entrants differ widely in their resources and capabilities, reflecting different bets on what buyers want in the market.[3] Experimentation by entrants creates a range of market positions based on variation in value and cost drivers.[4] At this stage, the evolutionary path of the market is highly uncertain. There are no rules of the game, and the ultimate

TABLE 4.1 | Number of Years in Each Developmental Stage for Selected Industries from the Inception of the Industry

Product	Period	Stage 1 Growth	Stage 2 Shakeout	Stage 3 Maturity
Freon compressors	1935–1981	45	1	
Piezo crystals	1936–1981	31	4	10
DDT	1943–1981	9	22	7
Electrocardiographs	1914–1981	50	17	
Electric blankets	1911–1981	51	13	6
Fluorescent lamps	1938–1981	2	1	40
Gyroscopes	1911–1981	55	15	
Outboard motors	1908–1981	9	6	58
Penicillin	1943–1981	7	23	8
Radar	1940–1981	22	19	
Radio transmitters	1922–1981	40	13	6
Styrene	1935–1981	45	1	
Cryogenic tanks	1959–1981	8	1	13
Oxygen tents	1926–1981	32	23	
Automobile tires	1896–1981	26	10	49
Artificial Christmas trees	1912–1981	52	17	
Windshield wipers	1914–1981	11	9	47
Zippers	1904–1981	55	13	9

Source: Adapted from Steven Klepper and Elizabeth Graddy, "The Evolution of New Industries and the Determinants of Market Structure," *Rand Journal of Economics* 21, no.1 (1990).

TABLE 4.2 | Number of Firms Remaining at the End of Stages 1 and 2 for Selected Industries

Product	Number of Firms at End of Stage 1	Number of Firms Exiting During Stage 2	% Decrease in Firms from the Number at the Peak
Piezo crystals	45	17	38%
DDT	38	33	87
Electric blankets	17	11	65
Fluorescent lamps	34	14	41
Outboard motors	21	8	38
Penicillin	30	24	80
Radio transmitters	76	55	72
Cryogenic tanks	84	29	35
Automobile tires	275	211	77
Windshield wipers	51	30	59
Zippers	49	9	18

Source: Adapted from Steven Klepper and Elizabeth Graddy, "The Evolution of New Industries and the Determinants of Market Structure," *Rand Journal of Economics* 21, no.1 (1990).

characteristics of the market cannot be predicted. Nor can the trajectory of the product's technology be forecasted with any accuracy.

Dynamic Capabilities and the Growth of the Firm

As an industry develops in the growth stage, firms enter and customers choose among the products offered, favoring those with higher value-price differentials. As firms observe buying behavior, they adjust their market positions to increase demand for their products, shifting toward more successful combinations of value and cost and reducing the heterogeneity in the industry. At the same time, new firms enter with innovations, some of which increase the level of competition while others fall by the wayside. As more productive entrants survive and grow, the level of heterogeneity increases. These trends in imitation and innovation by both incumbent and entering firms determine the range of market positions in the industry.

As the industry grows, firms improve their market positions through a process we can call the **dynamic growth cycle.**[5] Companies begin this process by investing in product or process innovations to increase value and lower cost. Assuming positive returns to scale, these innovations improve productivity and thereby raise the firm's margins. Higher margins increase profitability, which provides cash for capacity expansion. In turn, the size of the firm increases. Greater size means more resources for innovation, and this cycle relating size, innovation, profitability, and growth repeats itself (see Figure 4.1).

More productive firms are able to attract buyers through higher value at a given price or a lower price at a given value, forcing weaker firms out of the market and increasing the exit rate. Potential entrants observe the steadily improving productivity of successful incumbents and are deterred from competing in the industry. At the point when the rising exit rate exceeds the entry rate, a shakeout begins.[6]

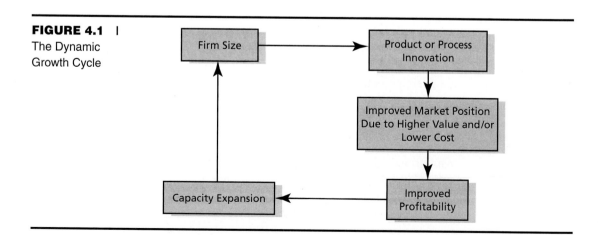

FIGURE 4.1 |

The Dynamic Growth Cycle

The dynamic growth cycle implies that firms in Stage 1 of industry evolution grow through two types of investment: (1) innovations that increase productivity and (2) capacity expansion that increases firm size. Each of these is necessary for the other. The resources gained through productivity improvements are required to expand the organization's scale of operations. At the same time, the resources associated with larger size are needed to develop or adopt the innovations that improve productivity.

How is this process initiated? Obviously it begins when a new firm develops or adopts a successful innovation, which then leads to growth in size. But this is only the start. The key part of the cycle involves the entrepreneur's ability to exploit the firm's larger scale so that investment in innovation continues and improves the firm's market position as the industry expands. Enacting this part of the growth cycle repeatedly—from size through innovation to an improved market position—requires a **dynamic capability.**[7] It is located in those activities and business processes where key innovations improve a firm's value or lower its cost. Without this capability, enacted over and over, a firm cannot neutralize and overcome the onslaught of start-up innovations.

For example, the features and manufacturing processes that defined the Model T were the culmination of a continuing effort by Ford to improve the cars he sold. Before the Model T, there was the Fordmobile, the (original) Model A, the Model C, and the Model N, each an advance on its predecessor. Ford also borrowed many innovations from other automakers, such as the assembly line itself, which was introduced to the industry by Ransom Olds. Olds had used an assembly line to produce the Oldsmobile starting in 1901 before he sold his company to General Motors. With each new car, Ford moved closer to the combination of value and cost that defined the market position of the Model T. This path of iterative innovation reflects Ford's dynamic capability.

Ford's path of innovation was not completely opportunistic. Every investment decision channeled organizational resources along a particular technological path that opened the firm to new opportunities for innovation and closed it to others. Potential innovations were more or less compatible with existing technology and practices. Those that were more compatible were adopted because they were easier to design and cheaper to implement, and led ultimately to the breakthrough product—the Model T—that revolutionized the industry.

Taking Ford as a representative case, we can say that each company progresses technologically and organizationally along a relatively unique path for developing new techniques. These successive innovations build on each other and can be seen as stages in a single developmental process, each stage compatible with the next. This phenomenon of historical investments guiding future innovation is called **path dependence.**[8]

A modern example of path dependence is the development of Intel's microprocessor platform. The microprocessor chip is the guts of a personal computer, and Intel was an early innovator. The company's first micro-processor was the 4004, developed in 1971. In 1978, Intel got the contract to supply IBM with microprocessors for its PC and over the next 26 years created 13 enhancements to the basic design of this chip, ending with the Pentium M. Each new chip in this progression was more powerful and more expensive to design and build and was technologically reliant on the one before, suggesting that Intel's innovations had a path dependent pattern.

Path dependence is relevant not only to innovations developed inter-nally but to those adopted from other firms. A firm's historical investment behavior determines the range and types of ideas and techniques a firm is open to adopting and forms the basis of its **absorptive capacity.**[9] Absorp-tive capacity is a firm's ability to adopt innovations developed by other organizations.

Consider again Ford's assembly line innovations as an example. First, he adopted the Olds mass production process in 1903 and refined it over time to produce the first Model T in 1908. Using this "push" assembly line, with interchangeable parts, he produced one car for every 12.5 man-hours. In 1913 Ford made a trip to a hog slaughterhouse and observed an early instance of a "pull" assembly line using conveyor belts. He adopted the technique and increased line productivity to one car for every 1.5 man-hours. Ford's early investment in assembly line techniques sensitized him to the potential benefit of the pull system in the slaughterhouse, even though it was carrying pigs, not automobiles.

It should be noted that Ford's commitment to the assembly line eventually caused the firm to decline. The company's tendency to explore only innova-tions consistent with mass production led to decisions that ultimately reduced customer value, such as painting cars only in black (because black paint dried faster) and bringing out new models every two or three years instead of annu-ally. Alfred Sloan at General Motors understood that cars in different colors and more frequent model changes would increase demand. GM implemented these innovations in the early 1920s, causing Ford's market share to drop. Ford's powerful path of innovative designs and production techniques had become a **core rigidity.**[10]

The concept of core rigidity indicates that it is not enough just to inno-vate as the industry grows; rather, each innovation must improve the firm's market position. The challenge is to recognize when the marginal returns to a firm's innovative activity are decreasing and then to redirect investments to a more productive path of innovation. Whether a firm can make such a change before its market position erodes significantly is a key question. Ford's switch was clearly too late to prevent General Motors from surpass-ing it in market share, just as General Motors' innovations did not kept pace with Toyota later in the century. The concepts underlying the dynamic growth cycle are shown in Table 4.3.

A recent example of a firm that explicitly follows a dynamic growth cycle is Samsung. Samsung's "virtuous cycle" emphasizes financial resources rather

TABLE 4.3 | Key Concepts in Developing and Maintaining Dynamic Capability

- Dynamic growth cycle

  The cycle of firm growth linking size, innovation, productivity, profitability, and capacity expansion.

- Dynamic capability

  The ability of a firm, as it grows, to build its innovative potential and exploit it effectively.

- Path dependence

  The tendency of a firm over time to invest in innovations that are upwardly compatible with each other, thereby creating a relatively unique path of product and process development.

- Absorptive capacity

  The ability of the firm to adopt innovations developed by other organizations based on its prior experience with similar or related practices or technologies.

- Core rigidity

  The inability of a firm to adapt to changing market or technological conditions because of its attachment to its core practices and customers.

than size per se (see Figure 4.2). The key similarities to the dynamic growth process (shown in Figure 4.1) are an emphasis on investment ahead of the competition (innovation), market leadership (improvement in the firm's market position), and high profits. These three parts of the process capture the essence of the ongoing dynamic capability that is central to the firm's repeated success in its product markets. Samsung spreads its innovations over a diversified portfolio of products, capturing economies of scope in technology platforms such as LCD technology for both cell phones and large screen televisions.

FIGURE 4.2 |
Samsung's Virtuous
Cycle in 2003

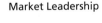

Investment Ahead of Competition

Cash Flows and
Balance Sheet Flexibility

Market Leadership

High Profits

Developing Scalable Value and Cost Drivers

In a new industry, firms focus on building dominant market positions through investing repeatedly in innovative value and cost drivers. Repeated investment is necessary since the contributions of early innovations in value and cost are likely to erode as the industry evolves. The erosion is caused by changes in demand and by decreasing returns to scale in the firm's initial cost drivers. These shifts in the focus of innovation are a major challenge for entrepreneurs as the firm grows.

Scale-Driven Value Drivers   Market penetration in Stage 1 requires a broader set of value drivers than technology alone. A start-up's initial value driver is commonly an advanced product technology with which the firm competes against substitutes. Early adopters are interested primarily in technological advances and weight functionality strongly. But later adopters want additional value drivers, especially those related to wide market acceptance, as well as lower price.[11] The shift from the early market of technophiles to mainstream adopters is a major strategic hurdle in Stage 1 (see Figure 4.3). To expand beyond early adopters—called *crossing the chasm*—the firm must develop other sources of value that lead to broader acceptance.[12]

Which value drivers a firm invests in depends on what the majority of buyers want. For example, Dell discovered that commercial customers benefited from customized PCs since they lowered the costs of shifting old software to the new machines. Likewise, because we value wide geographical scope for cell phone service, wireless phone companies have expanded their services across regions. And when network externalities reduce customer costs, firms attempt to increase the installed base of their standards through licensing and investing in complements, as Intel and Microsoft did to dominate the market in PCs.

FIGURE 4.3 | Customer Segmentation over the Product Life Cycle

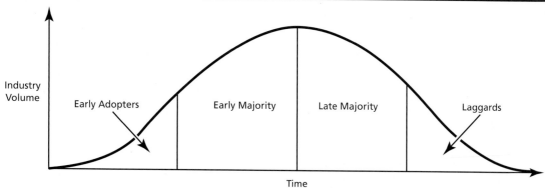

Firms are often challenged by how to time the trade-off between investing in technology and investing in other value drivers. Overinvesting in technology after the product has begun to diffuse to the early majority can stall market growth. Early majority customers are simply less sensitive to technology than early adopters and won't switch from substitutes without other sources of value. But underinvesting in technology before the product diffuses to the majority reduces sales to early market technophiles. To be successful firms must time their investments to match the segment served. The growth of many new industries is limited because entrepreneurs are unable to make this important transition.

Scale-Driven Cost Drivers   Like value drivers, cost drivers vary in their effectiveness over the course of firm and industry evolution. A young firm must rely on practices and low-cost inputs to increase productivity, since at low volumes these are the only cost drivers available. As the firm grows, these drivers may be preserved if decreasing returns to scale can be prevented. For example, as it grew in Internet brokerage, Charles Schwab continually increased productivity through innovation in its information technology practices, prolonging their contribution to the firm's low costs. Southwest Airlines is another example of a firm that grew by modifying its practices to work in larger-scale operations. It is more common, however, for practices developed at low volumes to become less efficient as the firm grows.

To overcome declining efficiency with greater size, firms typically invest in new processes that lower costs with higher volume and a broader product line. These processes are based on economies of scale, the learning curve, and economies of scope. A classic example of scale and learning—one more time—is Ford's assembly line. A notable instance of scope economies is the set of practices developed by Vanguard, the mutual fund company, to lower expenses by sharing highly efficient activities among its products.

However, the development of scale and scope economies may cause a firm to trade off cost reductions against value. Scale-based cost drivers can lead to lower value as inputs and processes become more standardized. For example, financial service firms frequently trade off high customer service levels, based on customer-specific knowledge and procedures, against low-cost service operations, based on standard protocols more amenable to large-scale automation.

The key question for a firm developing scale-based cost drivers is whether the drop in value is more than offset by the reduction in cost. The answer in many industries has generally favored scale and standardization. A notable example is retail banking. In some industries, however, scale-based cost drivers decrease value so much that they hurt firm performance. If entry barriers are low enough, these industries remain fragmented as smaller firms develop market positions that are at least as competitive as firms attempting to become more efficient through scale and scope economies.

An equally important question is how much investing in higher value forces a firm to incur higher costs. For example, the emergence of large global firms in professional service industries, such as advertising and legal services, has been driven by value-oriented investments in broad product lines and geographical scope. The competitive strength of these larger firms depends on their abilities to make these investments productive, so that margins can be maintained. If costs rise more than increases in value, growth degrades the firm's market position.

Therefore as the industry develops, firms compete both by offering buyers new sources of value and by investing in new cost drivers. During stage 1 one firm's practices may be countered by a rival's economies of scale. Who wins this competition depends on the relative effectiveness of the capabilities that produce each firm's levels of value and cost.

The viability of these capabilities varies across industries. In automobiles, for example, Ford's scale economies devastated craft-based rivals. But in the U.S. airline industry, which has been rejuvenated by deregulation, the story is different. As a low cost firm, Southwest has been consistently profitable using scalable practices focused on increasing efficiency. However, major airlines, such as Delta and United, have not been as successful. Their performance has been more variable than Southwest in part because they have not realized significant scale-based efficiencies from their investments in hub and spoke route systems. In autos, scale-based economies won, but in airlines the competition is still raging. Every industry's development depends on how this classic contest plays out.

Early Mover Advantage[13]

We often hear about the perils or rewards of being a "first mover" in an industry. The first mover is either the pioneer with arrows in its back or the first firm to arrive at a new territory and stake out a valuable claim. However, since firms typically enter an industry as cohorts, it is more appropriate to analyze early movers as a group rather than as individual first movers per se.

In many industries there is a benefit to being an early mover for two reasons. First, an early entrant may establish and defend a strong, enduring market position. Its value and cost drivers may be scalable as the market matures, and its position protected effectively by isolating mechanisms. The second reason is that the earlier the entrant, the longer it is exposed to opportunities for growth and innovation. If the early mover does not seize these opportunities and develop a dynamic capability, it is just as likely to fail as a later entrant whose options may be fewer. Research shows that over the long term, survival over the industry life cycle is related less to a firm's age than to its size, which is determined by the company's ability to grow.[14]

Only those entrants that can establish and defend superior market positions—as well as adapt continuously to shifts in demand and supply—will survive the course of industry evolution. We usually don't remember the early movers that failed since their brands have been overpowered by the survivors. For example, old personal computer hands know that both Radio Shack and Digital Equipment once had a reasonable share of the PC market, but these businesses were washed away by Dell, Compaq, and IBM, early movers whose growth dynamics were more powerful. In the end, it is the combination of competitive advantage in the short term and dynamic capability in the long term that determines early mover advantage. Both are necessary and neither is sufficient.

Strategic Pricing[15]

During the growth phase of the industry, a firm may try lower prices in order to expand more rapidly but without reducing costs, thus squeezing margins. This practice, called strategic pricing, is based on two assumptions: (1) customer switching costs are high enough to ensure a reasonable retention rate; and (2) scale-based cost drivers are currently in place or can be developed. For example, strategic pricing is endemic in many industries with strong learning curves, such as aircraft and semiconductor manufacturing, and in industries with strong scale economies, such as money market funds. In these industries, as firms grow, they reduce their costs and increase their profitability, even as the product's low price is maintained. The strategic benefit of this policy is that the firm has achieved its profit target based on lower costs due to the learning curve or scale economies, while growing larger and establishing a sustainable market position.

The risks of strategic pricing are, however, substantial. First, and most obvious, is the possibility that the decline in cost due to learning or scale does not match the profits forgone from setting a lower price. A common cause of such a shortfall is a poor understanding of the activities whose costs are expected to decline over time. Also, poor forecasting may lead to ineffective production planning and costly periods of excess capacity. Another important risk is that the firm may be unable to protect its cost advantage. When cost-reducing innovations based on the learning curve can be imitated by other firms, all firms can price strategically and offer the buyer the same deal. So no firm gains. If a company can't protect its learning curve from competitors, it has less incentive to expand volume through lower prices.

Stage Two—Shakeout

Stage 1 continues until the industry loses its attractiveness to potential entrants and weaker firms exit at the same or a greater rate, producing a shakeout. The shakeout occurs when the rate of exit exceeds the rate of entry, and the number of firms in the industry begins to drop. What causes this transition?

The trigger point is when one or more firms achieve a level of productivity that neither weaker rivals nor potential entrants can match.[16] Thus, the shift in entry and exit rates is ultimately caused by successful and sustainable growth strategies. Only the presence of one or more firms whose dynamic capabilities create dominant, defendable market positions can deter entrants and force weak competitors to leave the industry.

The emergence of dominant competitors based on their capabilities may be associated with a maturing of the product life cycle, or with a shift in technology to an industrywide dominant design. In the absence of strong competitors, neither of these factors alone can push the industry into a shakeout. But when they are present, they can strengthen the effect of superior dynamic capabilities on the pattern of entry and exit.

The Maturation of the Product Life Cycle

As the rate of growth in demand begins to decrease, the product life cycle begins to mature. The industry then looks much less promising as an opportunity to build a new business. Slowing demand also increases the pressure on firms to retain current customers, either through raising the value offered or by lowering prices; and because there are fewer new customers, firms must fight more intensely for them. These forces ultimately drive weaker firms from the market. The combination of slowing entry, due to lower long-term growth, and rising exit rates, due to greater competition, raises the potential for a shakeout.

The television receiver industry in the early 1950s is an interesting example of this pattern. The industry began in the early 1930s but was slow to expand until after World War II. Sales then slowed in the early 1950s, stabilizing at around seven million sets a year. Volume was relatively flat thereafter until the rise of color television in the mid-1960s. Correspondingly, the number of producers peaked in 1951 at 92 and then declined substantially. Thirty eight firms remained in the industry in 1958. This reduction in the number of firms closely matches the drop in the growth rate, so a maturing product life cycle is a logical explanation for the shakeout.

But the life cycle concept does not provide a complete answer to questions about industry evolution. It does not explain why some firms survive a shakeout and others do not. Further, in some industries, a shakeout can occur even when the growth rate in the number of customers remains strong and relatively steady as a replacement market develops, as in the U.S. auto industry described earlier. Only the presence of firms with superior dynamic capabilities is sufficient to cause the shift to Stage 2 competition.

The Emergence of a Dominant Design[17]

A **dominant design** is the culmination of a series of innovations in a product's components and architecture and in related value drivers, such as service, network externalities, complements, or breadth of line. At some point late in Stage 1, buyer preferences converge on a specific configuration of technological features that have been introduced independently at different times throughout the industry's history. These features, together with associated value drivers, improve the buyer's surplus significantly over previous versions of the product.

The evolution toward a dominant design commonly involves many competitors, each firm introducing products with specific features and the last firm combining these innovations into a whole. As competitors invest in the

FIGURE 4.4 |

Rates of Product
and Process
Innovation over the
History of the
Industry

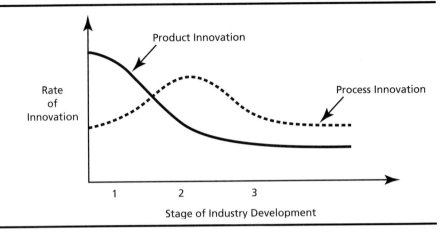

dominant design, variance in their market positions is reduced. Companies that can copy the dominant design survive while those that cannot fail. The design typically remains the standard product model for many years. During this time firms compete on lowering costs through process innovation. A useful example is the general purpose tractor (see the sidebar).

A key corollary to the idea of a dominant design is that firms in an industry shift their focus from product to process innovation, from value to cost advantage, as the industry shifts from Stage 1 to Stage 2 to Stage 3. Companies make this change because the wide acceptance of the dominant design reduces opportunities for developing a major new product architecture or new product components. Figure 4.4 shows the shift between product and process innovation over an industry's history.

A good example of this trend is the personal computer industry, which converged on a standard design with the introduction of the IBM PC in 1982. Improvements in component technology, driven by Intel and Microsoft, stimulated repeat purchases throughout the 1980s and 1990s without changing the product's basic configuration. These innovations were available to all PC manufacturers, making it difficult for them to compete on differences in functionality. During this period, Dell's continuing innovations in operations and logistics processes gave the firm a cost advantage across its markets, allowing the company to expand its market share among large customers. These innovations were difficult to imitate, forcing competitors to lag behind Dell in their process improvements.

Although the emergence of a dominant design may play a role in industry evolution, it is neither necessary nor sufficient as the cause of a shakeout. Shakeouts can occur in the presence of more than one product standard. And by reducing technological uncertainty, the success of a single design may encourage new firms to enter, prolonging the industry's growth stage. Further, the existence of a dominant design does not explain how some firms grow and

The General Purpose Tractor

The dominant design for the general purpose tractor took 36 years to emerge. The innovations started in 1902, when the first tractors were sold, and ended in 1938, when Ford-Ferguson introduced the final invention—the "three-point hitch." The original tractor, introduced before World War I, had low clearance and steel wheels, making it suitable for plowing and mowing, but not for cultivating crops. Competition between Ford and International Harvester produced a number of innovations, the first of which was the power takeoff, allowing attachments to be powered by the tractor engine rather than by a wheel rolling on the ground. In 1925 International Harvester introduced the Farm-all, a smaller, lighter general purpose tractor with a higher clearance. This design could be used for cultivation in addition to plowing, mowing, and reaping and was superior to Ford's product. Deere, Massey-Harris, and Case quickly copied International Harvester's concept. Over the next 10 years, three more innovations, rounded out the tractor's dominant design. These were the power lift, introduced by Deere in 1927, rubber tires in 1932, and diesel engines in the mid-1930s. In 1934 International Harvester produced a small "one-plow" tractor with a high clearance and adjustable front wheels. This machine was cheaper and so could be sold to small farms, especially in the southern part of the United States. It therefore diffused rapidly. Larger tractors eventually followed a similar design. After 1938 no major changes occurred in the tractor's design. The basic tractor in a farmer's barn today is almost the same as it was in the late 1930s, a remarkable case of technological longevity.[18]

The general purpose tractor emerged over time through a long process of innovation involving many competitors. But once the pieces were in place, virtually no changes were made for two generations. The design succeeded because it provided a greater surplus to the customer at a cost that was sustainable as volume increased. Before the dominant design became established, competitors' market positions differed widely in value and cost, as each firm experimented in an effort to find the one product that would capture and keep the preponderance of customers. Once this design emerged and was established, these firms—Deere, Case, International Harvester, and others—stopped investing in major product innovations and competed on marketing, distribution, service, and price.

innovate. Again, it is the presence of dominant competitors with strong isolating mechanisms that determines the onset of the shakeout.

Shakeout Duration and Severity

Industries differ substantially in the duration of the shakeout. As Tables 4.1 and 4.2 show, the shakeout may be as short as 1 year or endure for more than 20 years. However, there is a strong correlation between the duration of the shakeout and the percentage of incumbents left when the industry stabilizes. The shakeout in zippers lasted 13 years and only 18 percent of the incumbents exited, whereas after 23 years of decline in penicillin, 80 percent of the firms left the industry. Excluding extreme industries like fluorescent lamps where stage 2 lasted only one year, the average percentage decline during the shakeout is around 6 percent of the number of firms per year.

What determines the severity of the shakeout? There are three factors:

1. Expectations about future market demand and the degree of sunk costs.
2. The imitability of the dominant firms' resources and capabilities.
3. The presence of defendable niche markets.

Exit is slowed when weaker firms have sunk investments in resources, such as brand equity, and expect demand to grow beyond the production capacity of the dominant firms. Sunk costs create a drag on exit if the investments would be more expensive to rebuild upon reentry. So firms remain in the industry longer, hoping that future demand will produce a return to profitability. A second reason to postpone exit is based on the possibility that the firm can improve its poor market position by imitating some or all of the industry leaders. When the isolating mechanisms of dominant firms can be attacked, less advantaged firms will tend to remain in the industry longer. Third, the shakeout may be slowed when weaker competitors can avoid direct rivalry with the dominant firms by competing in niche markets. Niche markets allow firms to avoid exit by building defendable market positions, albeit with fewer customers. This puts a drag on the shakeout.

Stage Three—Maturity

At the end of the shakeout, weaker firms have exited the industry in the face of competition from firms with stronger market positions. These dominant firms have also raised the bar for start-ups seeking to enter the industry, causing the entry rate to drop substantially. Entry and exit continue, but at roughly equal rates that are much lower than in earlier stages, and without significant upward or downward trends. The number of firms in the industry remains about the same over time, and the industry has reached the maturity stage.

This does not mean, however, that only large firms survive. The typical distribution of firm sizes is highly skewed with many small firms, fewer firms of moderate size, and even fewer large firms. This skewed distribution in the mature stage indicates that firms remain somewhat heterogeneous in their market positions, although less so than in Stage 1. The industry structure therefore remains complex.

How long does Stage 3 last? It lasts until a new, viable substitute technology appears. Substitution can occur rapidly and repeatedly, as it did in the shift of tire cord material from cotton to rayon to nylon to polyester in the 20th century. In other industries the period of maturity lasts for some time. For example, since the shakeout ended in 1923, there has been little change in the entry and exit rates in outboard motors for a very long time (see Table 4.1).

Competition in the mature stage differs markedly from earlier periods. Firms continue to compete through the dynamic growth cycle, since both innovation and growth remain strategically important. However, firms must adapt to four new industry conditions:

1. A decline in the market growth rate.
2. A rise in buyer experience.
3. The concentration of market share among relatively similar large firms.
4. The persistence of niche markets.

Decline in the Market Growth Rate

During Stage 1, the market growth rate is based on the increasing number of buyers switching from substitutes to the industry's product. But as the shake-out ends and industry maturity begins, this type of customer becomes scarce. Demand is no longer driven by an expanding number of buyers but by replacement purchases and population demographics. The growth rate is therefore substantially lower. This reduced rate of market growth determines which kinds of innovation will produce higher returns. With lower growth, projects requiring an increase in capacity (e.g., those based on the learning curve) are more expensive since higher volume is harder to achieve. There are few new buyers coming into the market in the mature stage, so firms must fight each other for customers, increasing the costs of acquiring them. Under these circumstances, it is more efficient for firms to keep their customers, through tactics such as price reductions and value enhancements, than to lose them and then try to win them back. These retention tactics by competitors lower firm growth rates across the industry and make investing in new projects based on the learning curve less attractive.[19]

However, innovations that replace current processes can be powerful sources of improved market positioning. Process redesign can lead to significantly higher value and lower cost, if the implementation is well planned and executed as Dell's innovations in manufacturing and logistics have been. The adoption of new practices, such as total quality management (TQM) in operations and just-in-time (JIT) in logistics, has led to lower costs and improved customer value in mature industries. Also, Internet-based innovations have led to substantial cost reductions in almost all industries.

Firms may also lower costs by investing in innovations based on economies of scope. Combining activities, either across products or geographical regions, generally increases efficiency. However, it may also reduce value as differences among customers are ignored. The key question is whether this trade-off between cost and value improves the firm's overall market position. The early battle in interstate banking between Bank One (now part of JPMorganChase) and Nationsbank (now Bank of America) reflects two different views on this question. Bank of America's more centralized approach, favoring lower costs, appears to have been more successful as the race to acquire customers through acquisition has slowed.

An Increase in Buyer Experience

Experienced buyers have more clearly defined preferences and have lower search costs. They are therefore harder to retain. To counter buyer experience, firms develop value drivers, such as service, quality, breadth of line, and customization that increase customer switching costs. Lower prices also defend against the power of more experienced buyers. Innovations in practices and scope economies that raise productivity allow lower prices without lowering margins. Assuming the innovations can be protected, the improved buyer surplus leads to higher retention rates and steals customers from competitors.

The Concentration of Market Share among Similar Large Firms

An industry is much more concentrated at the beginning of the mature stage than at the end of the growth stage. During the shakeout, large firms absorb the customers of weaker firms that have exited. But the degree of concentration can vary widely across industries.

Industry concentration depends on three factors:

1. Market size.
2. The minimum scale required to compete.
3. Sunk cost investments in value drivers that have increasing returns to scale.

When the minimum scale to compete is large relative to market size, the concentration ratio is high, as in large-scale processing industries like aluminum or gypsum production. In contrast, if the minimum scale is small relative to market size, concentration will be lower, as in retail bakeries. How low depends on the presence of increasing returns to scale in value drivers. In industries where the minimum scale is relatively low but the effects on market share of value drivers such as brand and technology are significant (e.g., personal computers and beer), concentration ratios are higher.[20]

In concentrated industries, larger firms have typically invested in similar cost and value drivers, so their market positions resemble each other. These firms are typically older and belong to the same cohort of firms that entered the industry in the growth stage. For example, Coca-Cola, Pepsi-Cola, and Dr Pepper all started up between 1885 and 1898. Because large firms have been competing with each other for many years, they have observed each other's innovations and when possible absorbed those that were effective. This long process of innovation, competition, and imitation makes the large firms more similar in their practices and product lines. Because of their age and size, the largest firms compete with each other differently than other firms in the industry.

It is common for the dominant firms to face off against each other with broad product lines across geographical regions or market segments. This form of complex rivalry is called **multipoint competition.**[21] Multipoint competition takes place in closely fought skirmishes along many fronts. The deterioration of these skirmishes into total war, through price decreases or overinvestment, pushes profitability down. One key to avoiding this outcome is a series of footholds by each firm in the core markets of its rivals. Mutual footholds create the potential for competitive stability since each firm can attack its rivals in their home markets and is vulnerable to attack from them. The pattern of footholds across markets represents a series of threats whose credibility is crucial for the system's stability. Competition in the U.S. airline industry has shown this pattern of strategic behavior.[22]

The relative similarity of large firms also affects the direction and rewards these firms receive from innovation. Together, innovations by these firms in both value and cost constitute an **arms race,** in which no firm benefits for long from its improved market position.[23] Firms observe each other competing for a common customer base and innovate in the same direction at roughly the same pace to satisfy the same buyer preferences. Even though there are no enduring isolating mechanisms, each firm must invest in innovation to stay abreast of the others. Any misstep in this competition can be damaging as customers, who are the winners in this game, switch to more productive rivals.

The combination of multipoint competition and an arms race is sometimes called **hypercompetition.**[24] Hypercompetition is a dynamic growth cycle in which increments to profitability and capacity are low, even as firms innovate repeatedly. Profitability is lower because innovations are difficult to protect from rivals that have developed comparable absorptive capacities for new product or process technologies. Capacity expansion is limited since market growth is lower and competitors vigorously defend their customer bases. In spite of these constraints, firms must continue to innovate to keep up with industrywide productivity levels. The destructive effect of hypercompetition on firm profitability can be moderated by informal price coordination. Although short-term prices are determined by supply and demand, the long-term trend in industry prices is generally downward, with a leveling off in industry maturity. One explanation of this flattening out of prices is that most process innovations leading to greater efficiency have been discovered. For example, standard DVD players have reached this stage, unlike HD-DVD players, which have a way to go since major process innovations are still ahead. But a second explanation is that competitors have learned how to coordinate prices based on their long experience with each other's strategies and reactions to changing industry conditions. This is the realm of tacit collusion in which firms producing highly similar products, such as aluminum or structural steel, develop ways, such as price leadership, to prevent price wars.

The Persistence of Niche Markets

In many large mature industries, even those that are highly concentrated, small firms thrive in low-volume **niche markets** that larger firms are either unable or unwilling to serve. Buyers in a niche have relatively unique preferences. For example, many small applications software firms have focused on industry niches—so-called vertical markets (e.g., construction or trucking) that require specialized products—or on local small business customers that can be offered superior service. In each niche, smaller firms have been able to thrive by providing a higher economic contribution than their larger rivals, which are focused more on building dominant market positions in the core market.

Niche markets may emerge during the growth or mature stages of the industry life cycle. They may be based on old customer segments formed in the growth stage but separated from the mainstream as the industry developed, as in the case of Apple Computer customers. These mature niches are served by older small firms that have survived by investing repeatedly in practices that increase productivity. A niche may also emerge in the mature stage when a group of customers changes its preferences and creates a new segment, like the adopters of the Linux operating system. Demand in newer niches typically grows at a faster rate than the overall industry and attracts entrants. The ability of these emergent niches to threaten the core market depends on the evolution of customer preferences and the dynamic capabilities of the new firms, leading possibly to industry disruption.

Niche characteristics also affect how many small firms will remain viable in the industry. Small firms can compete in a niche when they are able to build market positions without investing in scale. Thus, how many small firms a niche can support depends on the minimum scale necessary to compete in it. The lower the minimum scale relative to the size of the niche, the more small firms the niche can contain. When there are many niches of this type in an industry, there are many small firms.

Small firms are threatened when they can no longer defend against the economies of scope and core market value drivers of larger firms. The benefits from value drivers tailored to a niche drop as customer preferences become more similar to the market as a whole. To protect its market position in this case, a small firm can invest in improving value and increase buyer switching costs. Small firms must also repeatedly improve nonscale-based cost drivers to remain viable.

Industry Disruption

Stage 3 is not the end of industry evolution. Every industry in its maturity is vulnerable to radical innovations that create new market positions threatening incumbent firms. When incumbents cannot adapt, innovative entrants replace them. More frequently, however, many incumbents find ways to adjust to the shift in competition. The industry then evolves as entrants grow larger and incumbents develop the resources and capabilities necessary to compete in the new market. Cars were a radical innovation that slowly replaced earlier forms of private transportation, such as horse-driven carriages. Many early auto companies were in fact offshoots of older industries, such as gasoline engine companies, carriage makers, bicycle manufacturers, and machine shops (in the case of Henry Ford).[25] These offshoots had a better chance of surviving industry evolution than those firms that had no obvious industrial background.

What are the chances incumbents will be able to adapt to industry disruption? The answer depends on three factors: [26]

1. The degree of incumbent control over complementary assets providing access to customers.
2. The strength of isolating mechanisms protecting the new technology.
3. The magnitude of short-term opportunity costs incumbents incur in adopting the new technology.

When all of these factors are against them, incumbents are unlikely to survive. In this case, how fast incumbents die depends on how fast start-ups can expand. However, when any of these factors favors incumbents, the rate of start-up penetration can be slowed.

Control over the assets needed to commercialize an innovation gives incumbents time to learn about the new product, especially through alliances with start-ups. A good example is the pervasive partnering that has occurred between new biotechnology companies and established pharmaceutical firms. Big pharmaceutical companies have large marketing, sales and distribution capabilities that biotech start-ups lack. The start-ups in turn have the newest product development skills. So the alliances between these two groups represent a good match of complementary assets.

Also, when the isolating mechanisms, especially property rights, protecting the innovation are weak, incumbents may be able to imitate the technology and compete directly with start-ups. But even when copying the new technology is easy, incumbents may still be slow to adopt the innovation. The reason is that they can be intensely focused on competing effectively in the mature, hypercompetitive industry and not on radical product innovation. In effect, because the short-term opportunity costs to incumbents of new technology adoption are high, they might wait too long to innovate and thus give the attackers an irreversible advantage.

These three factors pertain to the three major types of industry disruption:

1. *Technological substitution.* The introduction of a radically new technology that has a higher rate of return on investment in R&D than the current technology in the industry.[27]
2. *Disruptive innovation.* The introduction of a new product based on standard technologies that has a stronger long-term market position than the industry's current product.[28]
3. *Radical institutional change.* A radical shift in the institutional environment of the industry—for example, the deregulation of entry and prices—that opens the market to firms with innovative capabilities.

In all three types, incumbents may control complementary assets yet delay adapting to avoid short-term opportunity costs with core customers. When the

FIGURE 4.5 I
Industry Disruption
from Technological
Innovation

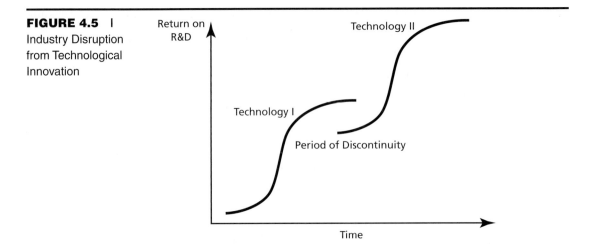

disruption involves a technological substitute, strong isolating mechanisms around the innovation may slow incumbent adaptation even further.

Technological Substitution

All technologies are subject to an eventual flattening of research and development productivity. As a technology matures, it becomes vulnerable to alternatives whose life cycles are just beginning. For example, jet engines replaced gasoline engines in commercial aircraft; CDs have largely eliminated LPs; and digital cameras have substantially reduced the sales of analog cameras.

Industries frequently experience periods of discontinuity as they shift from one technology, whose productive history is ending, to another, whose productive history is just beginning (see Figure 4.5). Since investments in the new technology bring higher benefits, the technology attracts entrants that use it to build their market positions. As investment in the older technology begins to decline, so do the market positions of firms that cannot make the transition to the innovation.

A recent and compelling example of technological substitution is the rise of DVD players and the corresponding decline of VCRs. Figure 4.6 shows how VCR sales declined as DVD players grew to dominate the market for recorded video content. The spikes for DVD players occur at the end of the year during the Christmas buying season.[29] In addition, again we have an example of how complements influence each other's growth rates. DVD players obviously need DVDs to play. Blockbuster, the United States video rental firm, began to actively support DVDs in April, 1999. The growth in DVD players accelerated soon thereafter.

FIGURE 4.6 | Trends in VCR and DVD Sales in the United States by Quarter, 1998–2003

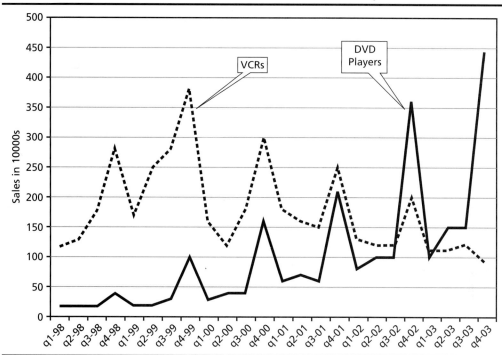

A **technological substitute** may come from within or outside an industry. In many instances, a major firm within the industry may develop the new technology, which then spreads to competitors. The diffusion of the technology separates incumbent firms into early and late adopters (see Figure 4.2), a rift that can have significant consequences for long-term market positioning. But when start-ups introduce the innovation, the potential for larger-scale industry disruption emerges, especially if no incumbent can match the dynamic capabilities of the new firms.

Incumbents delay in adopting a technological substitute, even when the technology is legally available, for three reasons. First, when an incumbent assesses its R&D projects, it emphasizes the total return on investment in an innovation based on spreading the gain over the firm's customer base. Although technical improvements are typically small late in a technology's life cycle, sales based on them can be large. But opportunities for these kinds of incremental innovations cannot last forever. When the current technology dries up, competitors investing in the new technology may have moved far ahead and started pulling the incumbent's customers away.

Second, the introduction of a new technology cannibalizes the profits of an incumbent's traditional business. Profitability goes down because the firm must pay for new capacity to commercialize the innovation. However, a competitor with no capacity in the traditional market has no trade-off with an existing business and so makes no immediate sacrifice to innovate.

Third, incumbents may have poor absorptive capacities to adopt the new technology. Switching to the new technology may require a major overhaul of the firm's research infrastructure, as many pharmaceutical companies have found in trying to start up biotechnology units. The costs of such a transition can slow down the timing of adoption.

Sustaining and Disruptive Technologies

In his analysis of how incumbents can be replaced by aggressive entrants, Clayton Christensen makes the distinction between sustaining and disruptive technologies. A **sustaining technology** is a technological substitute that is compatible with the way incumbents understand their existing business. Even though these innovations may be quite expensive to develop or adopt, they increase customer value as incumbents currently understand it. In contrast, a **disruptive technology** adds very little to current customer value, so an incumbent has little incentive to adopt it or even to pay attention to it. However, as time progresses, customer preferences shift towards it, blindsiding incumbents. Their market share is eroded and they are ultimately forced from the industry.

Disruptive technologies cause the demise of incumbents under the following conditions:

1. The technology is initially introduced by one or more start-ups into a niche market that is too small to attract incumbents' attention.

2. Compared to incumbents' products, the product based on the technology has lower initial functionality but also has a lower cost, perhaps determined by cheaper standardized inputs.

3. The price and type of value offered by the new product does not initially attract customers in the industry's core market, inhibiting incumbent adoption.

4. Over time, the preferences of incumbents' customers shift toward the value-price profile of the new product.

5. Incumbents do not control complementary assets, such as distribution, necessary for the market penetration of the disruptive technology.

6. Start-ups selling the new product develop a dynamic growth cycle that allows them to penetrate the core market rapidly through scale-based cost drivers.

These conditions together present a formidable challenge to incumbent firms, so much so that when all conditions are met, most and perhaps all incumbents will fail. The vulnerability of incumbents arises from their resistance to investing in a product that does not match their customers' current preferences.

As customer preferences shift toward the new technology, the combination of entrant growth capabilities and weak entry barriers is fatal for the incumbents' market positions. The threat of low-cost competition that can expand rapidly from the periphery of the industry as customers become oriented less toward performance and more towards price is extremely important for incumbents to recognize early.

For this reason, the concept of a disruptive technology has received wide attention and spurred companies to analyze competitors, technological trends, and customer preferences more broadly. Also, even if incumbents control customer access and slow the market penetration of a disruptive innovation, the rise of a new technology forces these firms to change their strategies.

Disruption by Regulatory Change

Competition over the industry life cycle occurs within a specific regulatory context. When this context shifts, so do the forces influencing rivalry. For example, a change in industry subsidies and tariffs can alter entry and especially exit rates almost immediately for firms at the margin of the industry. In extreme cases, **industry deregulation** can induce massive change in industry structure and practices, as the U.S. telecommunications industry experienced starting in 1984 with the breakup of AT&T.

Since 1978 six major industries in the United States have experienced price and entry deregulation: airlines, trucking, railroads, commercial banking, natural gas, and telecommunications. Some of these industries (e.g., airlines, railroads, and trucking) were opened to competition almost all at once, while others were opened gradually (e.g., telecommunications). In all cases, however, new entrants or revamped incumbents put significant pressure on competitors to change their strategies. Table 4.4 shows the attrition rates of incumbents in four of these industries roughly 10 years after deregulation.

Like a radical technological innovation, a major institutional change—such as deregulation—induces a wave of entry by new firms with different value and cost drivers from incumbents. Typically, entrants have much lower costs than incumbents and offer lower service levels, similar to the start-ups in

TABLE 4.4 | Incumbent Survival in Four U.S. Industries after Price and Entry Deregulation

Industry	Incumbents Surviving (%)
Airlines, 1978–1988	32
Banking, 1985–1994	71
Railroads, 1980–1994	37
Trucking, 1980–1993	59

Christensen's model of disruptive technology. As they grow by attracting early adopters, entrants invest in value drivers to attract customers in the core market, following the pattern of expansion in Stage 1 of industry evolution.

As Table 4.4 shows, the rise of entrants can induce a shakeout among incumbents, so that the net effect of deregulation is a decrease in the number of firms in an industry. This effect varies by industry, depending on the number of incumbents—in telecommunications, there was only one—and the vulnerability of incumbents to entrant strategies. Because of their control over the industry's basic infrastructure, incumbents in railroads and natural gas remained strong and took advantage of deregulation to consolidate the industry through acquisition. Likewise, deregulation in interstate banking spurred a massive wave of acquisition, creating multistate bank holding companies, such as Bank of America and Bank One. Entry and consolidation also occurred in airlines and trucking.

Summary

In this chapter we have examined how firms compete over the industry life cycle, including its rejuvenation through disruptive innovation, whether technological or regulatory. Each phase of competition presents a new strategic challenge, which many firms fail to meet successfully. Early in the history of the industry, start-ups must develop dynamic capabilities to improve their market positions. New value and cost drivers are required to compete as firms grow and penetrate the core of the market. As the industry matures, however, the reduced market growth rate forces larger firms to compete head-to-head through innovations that are more difficult to protect. At the same time, on the periphery of the market, niches persist for smaller firms whose profitability may equal or exceed that of the large competitors at the market's core. In this mature state, the industry is continually vulnerable to the emergence of technological substitutes with higher value or lower price and to the shift of customer preferences toward these substitutes. Given the rigors of strategic change over the life cycle, few firms survive with their identities intact. Fewer still endure this challenge repeatedly.

Summary Points

- All industries evolve over time as new firms enter and failing firms exit.
- Industry evolution threatens all sources of competitive advantage.
- Each firm develops its value and cost drivers within market constraints that are historically determined.

- The more a firm resists evolutionary change, the less likely it is to survive.
- The prototypical pattern of industry evolution has three major stages: growth, shakeout, and maturity.
- All new industries start with a product innovation that offers a superior buyer surplus compared to substitutes.
- Early in a new industry's history, entrants differ widely in their resources and capabilities, reflecting different bets on what buyers want in the market.
- In the growth stage, the trajectory of a product's technology cannot be forecast with any accuracy.
- Firms can improve their market positions over time through both innovation and imitation in a growth process called the *dynamic growth cycle.*
- A *dynamic capability* is the ability of a firm to innovate to improve its market position at larger scale.
- Historical investments can also guide future innovation, a process called *path dependence.*
- *Absorptive capacity* is a firm's ability to adopt innovations developed by other organizations, including sources of technology such as universities and government agencies.
- The shift from the early market of technophiles to mainstream adopters is the major strategic hurdle in stage 1.
- The combination of competitive advantage in the short term and dynamic capability in the long term determines early mover advantage.
- A shakeout occurs as the rate of exit exceeds the rate of entry and the number of firms in an industry begins to drop.
- Only the presence of one or more firms whose dynamic capabilities lead to dominant market positions and are protected from imitation can deter entrants and force weak competitors to exit.
- Although the emergence of a dominant design may play a role in industry evolution, it is neither necessary nor sufficient as the cause of a shakeout.
- Once the shakeout begins, its duration and the percentage of incumbents left when the industry stabilizes are strongly correlated.
- The average percentage decline during a shakeout is around 6 percent of the number of firms in an industry each year.
- Three factors determine the severity of the shakeout: (1) expectations about future market demand and the degree of sunk costs, (2) the imitability of the dominant firms' resources and capabilities, and (3) the presence of defendable niche markets.
- At the end of the shakeout, entry and exit continue, but at roughly equal rates that are much lower than in earlier stages, and without significant upward or downward trends.

- The duration of industry maturity depends on how short a time it takes for a new and viable substitute technology to appear.

- In the mature stage, firms must adapt how they innovate and grow to four new industry conditions: (1) a decline in the market growth rate, (2) a rise in buyer experience, (3) the concentration of market share among relatively similar large firms, and (4) the persistence of niche markets.

- Industry concentration at maturity depends on three factors: (1) market size, (2) the minimum scale required to compete, and (3) the extent of sunk cost investments in value drivers, such as advertising (brand) and research and development (technology) that have increasing returns to scale.

- It is common for the dominant firms to face off against each other with broad product lines across geographical regions for consumer market share or, if their customers are other businesses rather than consumers, for the dominant share of large accounts. This form of complex rivalry is called *multipoint competition.*

- The large firms that engage in multipoint competition sometimes compete with innovations in both value and cost. In this situation, called an *arms race,* no firm benefits from its improved market position for long.

- The combination of multipoint competition and an arms race is sometimes called *hypercompetition.*

- Many large mature industries, even those that are highly concentrated, however, retain a place for small firms, which thrive in low-volume niche markets that larger firms are either unable or unwilling to serve.

- Both large and small firms in a mature industry are vulnerable to radical innovations that create new market positions threatening incumbent firms.

- Industry disruption can arise from technological substitution, disruptive innovation, or radical institutional change.

- Incumbents can adapt to industry disruption when (1) they control complementary assets necessary for new product commercialization, (2) they can imitate the disrupting innovation, and (3) they overcome short-term opportunity costs associated with disinvesting in their traditional businesses.

Questions for Practice

Think how you would answer these questions for your current company, your previous place of work, or a business you are studying.

1. What stage of development is your industry in?

2. If your industry is in the growth stage, can you forecast the shakeout? If so, when it occurs, how will your firm be positioned?

3. What are your firm's key technology platforms? Its central paths of innovation? Its core rigidities?

4. How well does your firm execute a dynamic growth cycle? Do you have a strong dynamic capability?

5. How well has your firm developed scale-based value and cost drivers?

6. If your industry is in the mature stage, how is your firm positioned? In the core market or in peripheral niche markets?

7. If you compete in niche markets, how vulnerable are they to rivalry with large incumbents?

8. If you compete in the core market, how effectively does your firm compete against rivals across products and market segments?

9. How attuned is your firm to major technological disruptions?

10. Can your firm identify and neutralize major internal impediments to technological change?

End Notes

1. The most current empirical articles that describe the three-stage model of industry evolution are Steven Klepper and Elizabeth Graddy, "The Evolution of New Industries and the Determinants of Market Structure," *RAND Journal of Economics* 21, no. 1 (1990), pp. 27–44; Steven Klepper and Kenneth Simons, "Technological Extinctions of Industrial Firms: An Inquiry into their Nature and Causes," *Industrial and Corporate Change* 6, no. 2 (1997), pp. 379–460; Steven Klepper and Kenneth Simons, "The Making of an Oligopoly: Firm Survival and Technological Change in the Evolution of the U.S. Tire Industry," *Journal of Political Economy* 108, no. 4 (2000), pp. 728–60.

2. I am indebted to Glenn Carroll and Stanislav Dobrev for the use of these data; for a paper which examines why firms survive in the automobile industry, see Glenn Carroll, Lyda Bigelow, Marc-David Seidel, and Lucia Tsai, "The Fates of De Novo and De Alio Producers in the American Automobile Industry, 1885–1981," *Strategic Management Journal* 17 (1996), pp. 117–38.

3. See Steven Lippman and Richard Rumelt, "Uncertain Imitability: An Analysis of Interfirm Differences in Efficiency under Competition," *Bell Journal of Economics* 13 (1982), pp. 418–38.

4. For an alternative model of a differentiated industry in which firms learn their costs over time, see Boyan Jovanovic, "Selection and the Evolution of Industry," *Econometrica,* 1982.

5. For a broad description of this dynamic process focusing on investments in research and development, see Richard Nelson and Sidney Winter, *An Evolutionary Theory of Economic Change* (Cambridge, MA: Harvard University Press, 1982), chap. 12.

6. See Steven Klepper, "Entry, Exit, Growth and Innovation over the Product Life Cycle," *American Economic Review* 86 (1996), pp. 562–83.

7. See David Teece, Gary Pisano, and Amy Shuen, "Dynamic Capabilities and Strategic Management," *Strategic Management Journal* 18 (1997), pp. 509–33; Kathleen Eisenhardt and Jeffrey Martin, "Dynamic Capabilities: What Are They?" *Strategic Management Journal* 21 (2000), pp. 1105–21.

8. For important arguments on path dependence, see Brian Arthur, "Competing Technologies, Increasing Returns, and Lock-In by Historical Events," *Economic Journal* 99 (1989), pp. 116–31; for an empirical demonstration of how investments in innovation are highly correlated over time, see Constance Helfat, "Evolutionary Trajectories in Petroleum Firm R&D," *Management Science* 40 (1994), pp. 1720–47.

9. The seminal article in strategy on absorptive capacity is Wesley Cohen and Dan Levinthal, "Absorptive Capacity: A New Perspective on Learning and Innovation," *Administrative Science Quarterly* 35 (1990), pp. 128–52.

10. The seminal reference for core rigidities is Dorothy Leonard-Barton, "Core Capabilities and Core Rigidities," *Strategic Management Journal* 13 (1992), pp. 111–25.

11. For a recent reference on this model, which was developed by Frank Bass, see Vijay Mahajan, Eitan Muller, and Frank Bass, "Diffusion of New Products: Empirical Generalizations and Managerial Uses," *Marketing Science* 14 (1995), pp. 79–88.

12. Geoffrey Moore's two books, *Crossing the Chasm* (New York: HarperBusiness, 1999) and *Inside the Tornado* (New York: HarperBusiness, 1995) develop in detail the challenges start-ups face when they move from the periphery to the center of the market during the growth stage of the industry.

13. For an extensive discussion of first mover advantage, see Marvin Lieberman and David Montgomery, "First-Mover Advantages," *Strategic Management Journal* 9 (1988), pp. 41–58.

14. For an extensive discussion of this issue, see Michael Hannan, "Rethinking Age Dependence in Organizational Mortality: Logical Formalizations," *American Journal of Sociology* 104 (1988), pp. 1126–64.

15. See Birger Wernerfelt, "Brand Loyalty and Market Equilibrium," *Marketing Science* 10 (1991), pp. 229–45.

16. For an analytical model of this argument, see Steven Klepper, "Entry, Exit, Growth and Innovation over the Product Life Cycle," *American Economic Review* 86, no. 3 (1996), pp. 562–83.

17. For a useful presentation of the role of dominant designs in industry evolution, see James Utterback, *Mastering the Dynamics of Innovation* (Cambridge, MA: Harvard Business School Press, 1994); Fernando Suarez and James Utterback, "Dominant Designs and the Survival of Firms," *Strategic Management Journal* 16, no. 5 (1995), pp. 415–30; Michael Tushman and Philip Anderson, "Technological Discontinuities and Dominant Designs: A Cyclical Model of Technological Change," *Administrative Science Quarterly* 35 (1990), pp. 604–33.

18. See William J. White, "Economic History of Tractors in the United States," *EH. Net Encyclopedia,* ed. Robert Whaples, August 5, 2001.

19. Michael Spence makes this point in his seminal analytical paper on the learning curve, "The Learning Curve and Competition," *Bell Journal of Economics* 12 (1981), pp. 49–70.

20. See John Sutton, *Sunk Costs and Market Structure* (Cambridge, MA: MIT Press, 1990).

21. For an interesting game theoretic view of multipoint competition, see Aneel Karnani and Birger Wernerfelt, "Multiple Point Competition," *Strategic Management Journal* 6 (1985), pp. 87–96.

22. See Javier Gimeno, "Reciprocal Threats in Multimarket Rivalry: Staking out 'Spheres of Influence' in the U.S. Airline Industry," *Strategic Management Journal* 20 (1999), pp. 101–28.

23. The notion of an arms race has often been compared to Alice's confrontation with the Red Queen in Lewis Carroll's *Through the Looking Glass.* No matter how fast Alice walks, she never moves forward since the landscape is moving at her speed in the same direction. For a study of the Red Queen phenomenon in the commercial banking industry, see William Barnett and Morten Hansen, "The Red Queen in Organizational Evolution," *Strategic Management Journal* 17 (1996), pp. 139–57. For a discussion of how arms races figure in evolutionary theory, see Richard Dawkins, *The Blind Watchmaker* (New York: W. W. Norton, 1996), chap. 7.

24. For the key text on hypercompetition, see Richard D'Aveni, *Hypercompetition: Managing the Dynamics of Strategic Maneuvering* (New York: Free Press, 1994).

25. For a careful study of entrants that came from a prior industry, see again Glenn Carroll et al., "The Fates of De Novo and De Alio Producers."

26. See Mary Tripsas, "Unraveling the Process of Creative Destruction: Complementary Assets and Incumbent Survival in the Typesetter Industry," *Strategic Management Journal* 18 (1997), pp. 119–42; and Will Mitchell, "Whether and When? Probability and Timing of Incumbents' Entry into Emerging Industrial Subfields," *Administrative Science Quarterly* 34 (1989), pp. 208–30.

27. See Richard Foster, *Innovation: The Attackers Advantage* (New York: Summit Books, 1985).

28. See Clayton Christensen, *The Innovators Dilemma* (Cambridge, MA: Harvard Business School Press, 1997).

29. Firat Inceoglu and Minsoo Park, "Diffusion of a New Product Under Network Effects: The Case of U.S. DVD Players," working paper, Department of Economics, Boston University, 2003.

CHAPTER 5

Strategy Execution

Roadmap

This chapter covers the important topic of **strategy execution.** Effective execution means getting to the head of the pack, ahead of those firms competing in the same market position. The best executor develops and then repeatedly improves the resources and capabilities underlying critical value and cost drivers. With each step forward in execution, the firm's market position becomes stronger. In fact, without effective execution, a strategy is just an idea waiting to happen. The chapter proceeds as follows:

- Introduction
- The Basic Elements of Strategy Execution: Resources and Capabilities
  - Resources
  - Capabilities
- Relating Resources and Capabilities
- Building Capabilities
  - The Value Chain
  - Activity Systems
- The Organizational Dimensions of Capability Development
  - Complementarity and Consistency
  - Control and Coordination Systems
  - Compensation and Incentive Systems
  - Culture and Learning
- Summary
- Questions for Practice

Introduction

No firm can succeed for long without an intense focus on execution. Average executors are average performers, and poor executors constantly risk failing. Sometimes a successful company's market position is given to it as events unfold, as Microsoft gained share in operating systems with the success of the IBM standard in the early 1980s. But even lucky firms need deliberate execution to sustain their superiority.[1, 2] The less fortunate have to build their strategies from scratch. Here, detailed, persistent attention to execution is essential. Superior executors that have emerged to dominate their industries—such as Dell, Wal-Mart, Toyota—know this rule by heart.

Execution must always be tied to the firm's value and cost drivers. Companies can compete on the same value and cost drivers but differ in how well they achieve them. Two firms competing on quality and service, for example, can vary substantially in how effectively they execute the activities that produce these types of value. Likewise, companies that compete on price can have different levels of efficiency. For example, using its low-cost model, Southwest Airlines succeeded in California's airline market first by shutting out PSA and then dominating United Airlines Shuttle. United Airlines developed the Shuttle as a low-cost competitor but has been unable to develop the capabilities to match Southwest's efficient practices. So Southwest remains the superior executor.

It is important to note that execution may include, but is not the same as, strategic planning. Execution is the substance of strategic action, while strategic planning is the process of articulating the firm's strategy and the programs that implement it. Although effective execution is always necessary for competitive advantage, planning may not be. For example, a relatively simple firm, whose competitive advantage depends solely on a key resource such as a patent or geographical location (or a gold mine) must be operationally efficient to realize the resource's value. But as long as the firm's competitive situation is relatively simple and stable, strategic planning probably produces little incremental benefit (in contrast to operational planning, which is always required). The contribution of strategic planning increases dramatically, however, as the firm's competitive situation and strategic decisions become more complex.

The Basic Elements of Strategy Execution: Resources and Capabilities

Resources

A **resource** is a relatively observable, tradable asset that contributes to a firm's market position by improving customer value or lowering cost (or both). The classic example is geographic location, the retail competitor's mantra (location, location, location). Other examples of resources are the following:

- A patent or combination of patents on a product (think of the patent on the original microprocessor or on the original television picture tube).

- A proprietary process (for example, the process Illinois Tool Works has developed for producing screws specialized to plastic and concrete).

- Ownership of an abundant or especially valuable natural resource (e.g., a mine).

- An established brand (IBM, Porsche).

- A dedicated distribution network (Caterpillar Tractor's dealers).

Some resources, such as a patent or geographical location, keep their value with only a little husbanding. But other resources, like a brand or distribution channel, need to be nurtured continuously. For example, a brand's value depends on effective product design and marketing decisions, as Reebok and Adidas have discovered in competing against Nike in athletic shoes.

To produce an economic advantage, a resource must be difficult for competitors to imitate or for substitutes to neutralize. Coca-Cola has built a large global presence in soft drinks on the basis of Coke's taste, which comes from the special syrup that goes into each can or bottle and whose formula the company owns. The firm closely guards the syrup's secret ingredients to prevent competitors from imitating it. Without this syrup, it is inconceivable that Coca-Cola could have achieved such a wide acceptance of its product.

Resources are typically tradable in the sense that they can be put up for sale by the firm and valued by potential buyers. However, as we will see below, a resource's value depends in part on how much its contribution to performance is independent of the rest of the firm. In the case of Coca-Cola, the value of Coke's syrup may be amplified by the company's capabilities in operations, logistics, distribution, and especially marketing. (Think about how many times you've seen an ad for Coca-Cola.)

Capabilities

Resources can be sufficient for competitive advantage but they are not necessary. Many firms succeed on the basis of their superior capabilities. A **capability** denotes a firm's ability to accomplish tasks that are linked to performance by increasing value, decreasing cost, or both.[3] These tasks are performed over time through the coordinated efforts of teams within the organization, whose members may change even as the practices involved persist and improve. These practices are specific to the firm. They are also difficult to describe in detail. But in many cases, their contribution to the firm's economic performance is clear. For example, Intel's superior ability to innovate within its microprocessor platform is widely seen as critical for the company's continued market dominance. To stay afloat, Intel's major rival, AMD, has had to develop a comparable expertise in innovation. The process Intel uses to develop new products involves extensive interunit coordination, especially between R&D and manufacturing, and is not separable from Intel as an organization. The firm's capability therefore cannot be bought and sold as one might buy and sell the patents Intel holds on its microprocessor designs.

Forecasting Ability as a Capability

Every function in a firm, from marketing research to human resources to technology development to the controller's office, requires a forecast of the future. But if forecasting is to be a capability, it must contribute to how much money the firm makes. Moreover, the firm should be able to appropriate this portion rather than pass it on to customers as a result of price competition in the product market. Also, this benefit should lead to firm growth so that the capability can be developed further through reinvestment. All these characteristics can be found when we analyze how well financial institutions forecast interest rates.

The industry where we observe this forecasting capability is money market funds, which try to forecast short-term interest rates. The reason is that interest rates affect the value of the securities in the money fund's investment portfolio. When interest rates go up, the value of debt securities goes down; when interest rates go down, the value of debt securities goes up. Since short-term debt is generally less sensitive to interest rate movements than long-term debt, the trick is to structure the money fund portfolio with short- and long-term securities to make the most money as interest rates change. Therefore, if a money market fund could forecast interest rates accurately, its best policy would be to invest in short-term maturity debt when interest rates were about to rise and long-term maturity debt when rates were about to fall.

Each money fund family (e.g., Fidelity, Vanguard, Federated) forecasts interest rates using a team of professionals. On average, however, these professionals do not forecast interest rates very well. But are some fund families better forecasters than others? The answer is yes. Some funds beat the average by a wide margin, *systematically*.

The more accurate a fund's forecasting, the more money it makes. Does it keep this money? The answer again is yes. Funds that forecast effectively tend to keep the economic rents better forecasting gives them. If a fund could forecast rates perfectly, its gross yield would increase 25 basis points. How much money are we talking about? For example, a money fund with 50 billion in assets, somewhat smaller than Fidelity Cash Reserves, would make an extra $125 million.

Forecasting accuracy in money market funds is a capability since it is

1. Specific to each organization.
2. Predictive of economic returns that the organization keeps.
3. Related to organizational growth, both as a cause and a consequence.

We can speculate that other types of forecasting are also capabilities. For example, most firms need accurate estimates of future demand and costs in order to make reasonable budgeting decisions. To show that one of these types of forecasting, or any other activity for that matter, is indeed a capability, one would want to be able to measure it and relate it to performance over time, just as has been done for money market funds. However, this can be hard to do. So, in practice, we typically make sensible guesses about which activities define capabilities and how strongly they are related to performance.[4]

A capability is likely to be both less stable and less easily traded than a resource. It is less stable because it is developed and sustained through the coordinated efforts of individuals who may come and go over time. Capabilities are thus dynamic. They improve or decline as a firm grows, reorganizes, and gains or loses key personnel. A capability cannot be traded like a resource, since it is embedded in the firm's decision-making processes and operating activities. If another organization wanted to buy the capability, it would have to buy the organization or at least the operating unit where the capability was located.

Many capabilities contribute to firm performance without being linked to a resource. The development of several value drivers—especially service, quality, and customization—depends only on how employees design and execute their tasks. For example, as discussed in the sidebar, a deceptively simple activity such as forecasting can be an important capability that determines how much money a firm makes.

Relating Resources and Capabilities

Capabilities often contribute to performance by supporting resources, as in the case of Coca-Cola above. Another example is a company that markets fashion goods, such as Esprit or Polo. Such companies are managed to build and maintain their brands. These firms have developed highly effective marketing techniques and constantly fine tune their methods of selecting and monitoring suppliers. Their supplier-oriented practices are directed at maintaining high quality in the firm's branded goods at an appropriate cost. Without the capability in supplier management, variance in product quality would be higher and the brand's value would decline.

Caterpillar's distribution network is another instance of a crucial resource supported by a key capability. The company's dealers are a central part of the company's sales and service activities. Many dealers have been in place since World War II, building their franchises as the global postwar economy grew. They provide fast, expert service to contractors working under deadlines. Without this rich and highly competent network, it is not clear that Cat would be able to withstand the competitive pressure of Komatsu, its major rival. Cat's management therefore has developed extensive capabilities to support the dealers through programs in logistics and marketing.

Thus, a firm's expertise in exploiting a resource strongly influences how much it is worth to the company. When a resource is auctioned, a firm's bid for it is determined in large part by how effectively the resource will interact with the firm's existing mix of assets and skills. The sidebar on Makadok's model gives a deeper look at the logic of **resource complementarity.**

In addition to the American Airlines–TWA example in the sidebar, there are many other cases of acquisition behavior that reflect the importance of resource complementarity and the relationship between resources and capabilities. Successful U.S. bank holding companies, such as Banc One (now part of JPMorgan-Chase), Nationsbank (now Bank of America), and First Union (now merged with Wachovia) grew during the 1980s and 1990s by developing methods for turning around small- to medium-sized local banks. The premiums paid for these targets reflected how much the acquiring banks expected to gain over the long term based on their capabilities in integrating the targets and improving their performance. Telecommunications companies, especially Cisco Systems, pursued a similar

Makadok's Model

Richard Makadok has explored the ways a firm can become more profitable than its competitors.[5] His framework is based on two firms bidding for a resource, such as a plot of land or piece of machinery, in an auction. He identifies three kinds of difference between the bidders.

- The asset complements the resources of one firm more than the resources of the other.
- One firm has a greater ability to forecast the value of the asset after it is acquired.
- The capabilities of one firm contribute more strongly to the asset's postacquisition performance than its competitor's capabilities.

We will discuss each of these in turn.

Resource Complementarity

The complementarity between the asset being auctioned and the existing resources of the bidding firms determines the least amount each will bid. A higher level of complementarity produces a higher expected value of the asset to the firm and therefore a higher bid. For example, when American Airlines bought TWA's assets in a bankruptcy sale in 2001, its bid exceeded (and had more credibility than) those of other airlines largely because TWA's hub cities and route structure complemented American's routes very nicely. TWA's St. Louis hub was geographically well placed between the American hubs in Chicago and Dallas. Also, the overlap between the routes of the two airlines was quite small, only about 12 percent. The acquisition did not cannibalize American's current routes, so there was little basis for an antitrust suit. American's expected profit from TWA was therefore simply higher than that of Continental or Northwest, who were interested in some of TWA's assets.

Forecasting

Makadok calls this factor "resource picking." The idea is that better forecasting—based on the firm's more reliable information sources—produces a more accurate expected value of the asset.[6] More accurate valuation leads to a more effective bid. If the firm buys the asset and doesn't overbid, it makes more money since its acquisition cost is lower. On the other hand, if the firm bids accurately but loses the auction, no profits are forgone. In the American–TWA acquisition, American had extensive knowledge of TWA's assets based on a long history of previous transactions between the two airlines and on a detailed due diligence beginning three months before TWA filed for bankruptcy. This information sharpened American's estimate of TWA's value.

Capabilities

The higher the contribution of the firm's capabilities to the value of a resource, the more the resource is worth to the firm. Let's look again at the American–TWA acquisition as an example. American had developed a very strong expertise—called yield management—in achieving a high average revenue per seat. Because TWA's revenue per seat was substantially lower than American's, one of American's motivations for acquiring TWA was to apply its yield management capability to TWA's routes, thereby increasing their profitability. Interestingly, the costs of the two airlines were about the same, so there was little American could do to improve TWA's efficiency after the acquisition.

Which Factor Is More Important?

It is obviously best to be strong in all three factors: high resource complementarity with the target, powerful capabilities that improve its value, and accurate forecasts of its worth. But what if the firm has to make trade-offs among these factors? In Makadok's approach, a firm's resource complementarity with the target asset always establishes the baseline price the firm is willing to pay for it. The relative benefit of investing in forecasting or capabilities depends on how different the bidders for the asset are.

When one firm has a stronger resource complementarity with the target, forecasting ability is not very important. This is so because, holding capabilities constant, the firm with the stronger complementarity will buy the asset anyway. On the other hand, when neither firm has a distinct edge, it is a good idea to invest in forecasting since it increases the chances that whatever bid is made will be the most profitable.

Now let the firms invest in capabilities as well. The implications of unequal resource complements are somewhat different. The weaker firm now can invest in capabilities to raise the asset's value, bringing it closer to that of the other bidder. As the value of the asset rises for the weaker firm through its enhanced capabilities, so does the importance of investing in forecasting. Improved forecasting may increase the likelihood that the asset will be bought, which would justify the investment in capabilities.

These are not simple relationships. But they highlight how important the trade-off among these important factors can be.

acquisition strategy during the 1990s to broaden and refresh their product lines. For the banks, the primary resources acquired were the target firm's book of business and relationships with customers. For Cisco and its competitors, the resources were the target firms' technologies and people. In both cases, the firm's ability to benefit by integrating the resource with existing systems had a significant effect on the acquisition price.

Building Capabilities

Capabilities are produced by specific activities and policies. For example, superior customer service on the telephone requires careful personnel selection, well-designed training and recognition programs, and effective information systems. Each of these is necessary for fast and effective solutions to customer problems.

How should management think about designing and implementing such an integrated set of programs? First, it needs to have a clear picture of their economic value. But second, managers need a way of mapping them to facilitate program development and allow comparisons with competitors. The value chain and activity system frameworks described below are useful tools for this purpose.

The Value Chain

One way to identify capabilities in activities is Michael Porter's **value chain** diagram.[7] As Figure 5.1 shows, the value chain breaks a firm down into nine activities. Five of these—inbound logistics, operations, outbound logistics, marketing (which includes distribution and sales), and service—are primary in the sense that they represent a flow of goods and services from inputs (inbound logistics) to the sale and service of final outputs (marketing and service). The remaining four activities—technology development (in products and processes), procurement, human resource management, and infrastructure (which includes the organization's reporting structure and its accounting and control systems)—are secondary in that they support or are found in each of the

FIGURE 5.1 |
The Value Chain

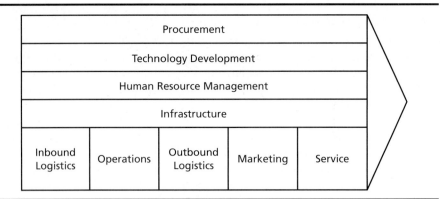

primary activities. For example, technology development, when viewed as process innovation, can be found in logistics, operations, marketing, and service. Technology development as product innovation is located in research and development or product engineering.

A firm's value chain is likely to be broader and more detailed than Porter's framework. For example, the distribution function in many service firms includes fulfillment, a key subactivity for communicating with customers. Also, the infrastructure of a large manufacturing firm is likely to include ERP software, an important control system. As a general rubric, however, the value chain shown in Figure 5.1 is a useful starting point for representing a single business.

The value chain is also helpful for analyzing competitors that share a market position based on similar value and cost drivers. Rivals will almost always differ in their investments in value chain activities. Competitors can also vary in whether they perform an activity inside the company or outsource it to a supplier.

For example, compared to other major pharmaceutical firms, Merck has been slow to outsource a major part of R&D to small bioscience firms. A value chain chart of Merck's technology development activity would therefore look quite different from its competitors, say Pfizer and Eli Lilly. This difference represents a fundamental divide in the approaches of these firms to research. Which view is correct—Merck's or its rivals'—will depend on their success in drug development.

Activity Systems

A broader framework than the value chain is an **activity system.**[8] Activity systems are composed of organizational components that contribute to the firm's key value and cost drivers. Such a system can contain the policies and behavior of specific activities in the firm's value chain, general characteristics of the firm's structure and culture, product attributes, and key resources such as technologies and brands.

The benefit of mapping a firm's activity system is that it shows how these components relate to and reinforce each other. At the core of the system are key activities that have a major impact on the firm's market position. These core components are supported by ancillary, secondary activities.

For example, Figure 5.2 shows the activity system of Vanguard, the mutual fund company, in 1997. [9] The system shows how Vanguard achieved a significant cost advantage over its competitors coupled with high-quality service to ensure reasonable rates of customer retention. The system has seven **core elements:** (1) the fund family's governance structure—mutual not stock; (2) the distribution of the product—direct rather than brokers; (3) conservatively managed funds— low rather than high risk; (4) low cost; (5) candid communication; (6) focus on long-term performance; and (7) high-quality service. The **supporting elements** include value chain activities, such as service (high quality), investment manage- ment (outsourced at low fees), human resource management (college graduates, no Wall Street veterans, no perks for management), and infrastructure (in-house fund administration). Vanguard was very careful how it handled or outsourced each activity in order to achieve higher value at lower cost. In addition to candid communication, the activity system included other cultural attributes, such as the zeal to restructure the industry through Vanguard's innovations, high esprit de corps, and the significant influence of John Bogle, Vanguard's chief executive. All of these elements reinforce each other to produce a powerful market position, pri- marily driven by low costs.

How did Vanguard's system evolve? The evolution of an activity system involves four distinct processes: patching, thickening, coasting, and trimming. **Patching** involves the addition of a new core element to the system. In the 1970s, for example, Vanguard brought distribution in-house to lower costs and added an emphasis on high-quality service to improve its market position. **Thickening** occurs when a firm adds activities around a core element. For example, to remain faithful to its focus on low cost, Vanguard instituted a "partnership plan" for employees, rewarding them for improvements in the company's expense ratio relative to the industry average. **Coasting** entails the continuation of the activity system without changes. And **trimming** means the deletion of a core element and the elements attached to it when they fail to fit into the rest of the activity system. At Vanguard, no core element ever became inconsistent with the others, so trimming was not observed.

The Organizational Dimensions of Capability Development

But focusing on activities individually misses how organizationwide practices contribute to economic performance. The major organizational dimensions of capability development can be summarized as follows (see Figure 5.3):

- **Complementarity and consistency** among a firm's resources, tasks, and policies is achieved when they are jointly aligned with the firm's market position and reinforce each other's contributions to it.

FIGURE 5.2 | Vanguard's Activity System at the Beginning of 1997

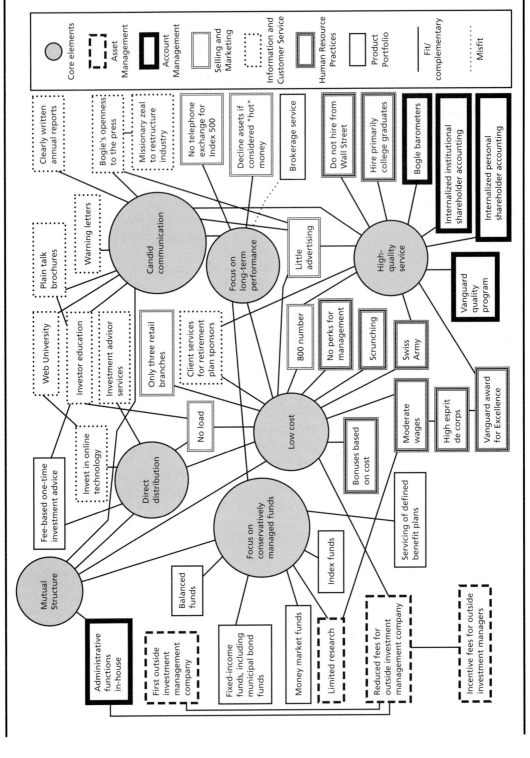

FIGURE 5.3 | The Organizational Dimensions of Capability Development

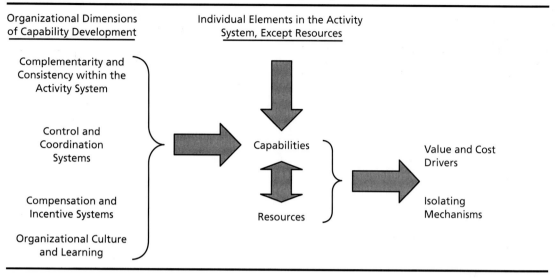

Organizational Dimensions
of Capability Development

Individual Elements in the Activity
System, Except Resources

Complementarity and
Consistency within the
Activity System

Control and
Coordination
Systems

Capabilities

Value and Cost
Drivers

Compensation and
Incentive Systems

Resources

Isolating
Mechanisms

Organizational Culture
and Learning

- **Control and coordination systems** are the infrastructure through which tasks, transactions, and decisions within the firm are governed.
- The firm's **compensation and incentive systems** determine the rewards and punishments associated with task outcomes, from the highest to the lowest levels of the organization.
- The **culture and learning behavior** of the firm shape capability development through their influence on decision making and task performance.

No firm can succeed over time without focusing intensely on these four elements and synchronizing their planning and execution.

Complementarity and Consistency

Complementarity and consistency are similar but not identical. As discussed above, two or more resources or capabilities may be **complementary** when they produce a more effective outcome together than either produces independently.[10] Complementary resources and capabilities reinforce each other in support of achieving the same goals (see the following sidebar on Internet retailing).

Activities are consistent when they are jointly in tune with the firm's strategy even if they don't interact directly with each other. **Consistency** or *fit* implies that the firm's policies and practices are aligned with its market position.[11] Vanguard's activity system, shown in Figure 5.2, demonstrates how tightly strung a firm can be to support its strategy (basically, low cost, high customer service).

Channel Complementarity

The rise of Internet retailing provides an interesting case for examining the complementarity between types of marketing channel. In the 1990s many traditional retailers began to adopt e-commerce as they watched the rise of Internet start-ups. The incumbents came in three varieties. One group, like Lands' End, sold through catalogs. A second group, like The Gap, sold through stores. Finally, a third group, like JCPenney, sold through both a catalog and stores.

As the start-ups began to fail from 2000 through 2002, a growing consensus emerged that multichannel retailers would dominate the Internet. One rationale for this assertion was that, unlike the start-ups, these retailers had established brands, which allowed them to earn higher margins on more frequent purchases. A second argument for the success of multichannel retailers was that they could leverage their existing infrastructure to enable order fulfillment and processing in their online businesses.

However, catalog and store operations contributed different kinds of capability to the online business. Catalog operations typically managed a larger number of products and a more extensive order-processing system, including a network of distribution centers. They also developed an ability to forecast sales for catalog items, many of which were also sold on the firm's Web site. Store operations, in contrast, only had a transportation network for carrying goods.

Not surprisingly, an analysis of Internet sales for incumbent retailers shows that those firms with catalog operations experienced significantly greater growth than firms with only stores. But, interestingly, the companies that had both catalog and stores did better than companies with a catalog alone. These findings hold up even when the size of the firm is included in the analysis. The implication is that the catalog channel for a retailer was an important complement to the online business and that stores added value to Internet sales only in the presence of catalog operations.[12]

Consistency, Value Advantage, and Cost Advantage   Successful cost and value leaders endure because their policies are designed and executed within a single strategic framework. It is in these generic market positions that consistency makes the most sense. Exemplary *cost leaders,* such as Vanguard and Southwest Airlines, set policies and design their activities to keep expenses low while providing customers with sufficient value to create an adequate buyer surplus. *Value leaders,* such as Mercedes-Benz, continually emphasize the key factors that make their products or services worth the premium customers pay for them. The Mercedes unit of DaimlerChrysler has built an organization of skilled workers for making and installing a wide variety of high-grade materials and components, using robots for only 30 percent of the fabrication and assembly. In comparison, the Chrysler unit of DaimlerChrysler uses 70 percent robots in its plants to produce lower-cost cars.

The internal consistency of firms with successful value or cost-based market positions constitutes a formidable barrier to imitation by less developed organizations. The major airlines in the United States (American, United, Delta, Continental, Northwest) are experiencing this barrier in competing against Southwest, JetBlue, and Airtran, the dominant low-cost airlines. The alignment of policies and activities within highly consistent firms is typically the result of extensive learning, as the history of Vanguard shows. In fact, the ability of a firm to build and maintain fit among activities over time is a capability in itself.

The Pitfall of High Consistency   A high level of consistency provides superior economic returns for well-positioned firms in stable industries. However, the more consistent an organization's activities, the more difficult they are to change. The reason is that consistency is driven by and fosters an adherence to a few decision rules that together define the organizing principles of the firm. When the market shifts, new organizing principles are typically required, challenging deeply held assumptions systemwide. A less consistent company would be able to adopt new decision rules more easily. For example, Kodak, a classic value leader in the film industry, suffered extensively over time when Fuji aggressively entered the U.S. market with low prices, drawing customers away from Kodak's traditional brand. Kodak's transformation into a lower-cost firm took many years as its commitments to differentiation were slowly broken. Johnson & Johnson, a highly consistent differentiator in health care products, faced similar challenges when its market shifted toward lower-priced goods in the 1980s and 1990s.

Control and Coordination Systems

Building capabilities requires the development of **control and coordination systems.** These systems should focus on the specific capabilities the firm needs to succeed within its market position. When this focus is strong, the firm will execute its strategy effectively. Where the focus is weak, execution will be less effective, and competitors will have higher performance.

A firm's financial and operational control systems are central for deciding which investments the company will make and therefore which capabilities developed. Without conventional financial control and budgeting protocols, it is obvious that any firm would quickly lose control over its capital resources and begin to fail. Operational control processes are also critical for the firm's viability, since they direct attention to strategic outcomes.

For example, in a host of service businesses, such as insurance, investment advising, transportation, and telecommunications, managing the frequently complex interface with customers is necessary for reaching a high level of customer retention. Higher retention on average lowers the cost per customer, smoothes cash flows, and in many businesses increases revenues through cross-selling. But the interface typically stretches across many functions including sales, marketing, and operations, with support from information systems. Unless retention is measured in the operational control system, managers in these functions will subordinate it to other goals, such as increasing market penetration or cost reduction. Putting customer retention in the control system is therefore a key part of strategy execution.

Coordination systems determine how projects will be executed across the units in the organization. Without effective coordination, no market position can be sustained for long. Coordination aligns transactions between units through shared information and influence and through the exercise of management authority.

Jay Galbraith presents five mechanisms, in addition to management authority, for coordinating interunit relationships.

1. Standardized procedures.
2. Joint planning.
3. Liaison personnel.
4. Task forces with members from multiple activities.
5. Teams that institutionalize the task forces.[13]

These are added, one after the other, as the complexity and rate of change in an interunit relationship increase. When the relationship is simple and stable, basic procedures are effective. These break down, however, when the relationship becomes complex or changes frequently. To get the relationship back on track, the units introduce planning processes. The combination of procedures and planning is effective until uncertainty increases further and some goals lose their currency. In response to these changes, liaison personnel are put in place. Then, when new coordination problems swamp the liaisons, temporary task forces are instituted, followed if necessary by teams, which have greater permanence and depth. Thus, as the interface between activities becomes increasingly complex and fluid, the number of coordination mechanisms expands to keep the project moving forward.

Galbraith's framework contains one more coordination mechanism: **hierarchical referral**—which means sending the problem up the chain of command. Managers resort to this mechanism last. The reason is that referring problems upward is usually politically charged and expensive. It exposes conflicts that lower-level managers cannot resolve and thus shows the limits of their competence, and it uses up the more expensive time of senior executives.

Management hierarchies in a single business are typically organized along one or more of the following dimensions: *function, geographic region, customer,* and perhaps to a small degree, *product* (see Figure 5.4). A function is simply an activity in the value chain such as research and development (R&D), operations, marketing, or service. A functional organization is therefore one in which the direct reports of the CEO are functional managers—vice presidents of R&D, of operations, of marketing, and others. In a similar vein, the direct reports of the CEO of a firm organized primarily by

FIGURE 5.4 | Types of Organizational Structure

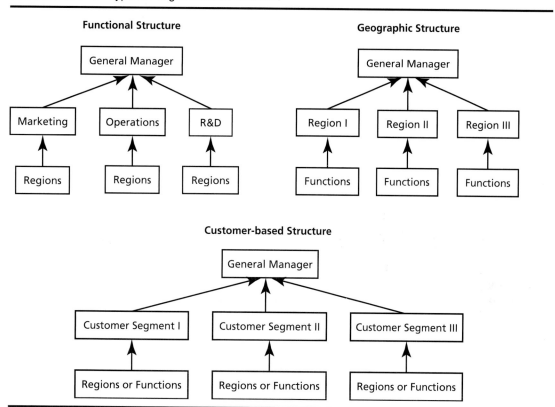

geography are the vice presidents of the eastern region, the southern region, the western region, and so on. Likewise, in a customer-based organization, CEO direct reports are associated with types of customer as defined for example by specific industries or size classes.

The structure of a firm's reporting hierarchy contains important information about how conflicts are resolved and therefore which capabilities the firm is developing. The higher in the hierarchy a mode of organizing (function, geography, customer), the more important it is in making decisions. Why is this so? The reason is that a manager's primary responsibility determines his or her priorities regarding how and which capabilities are built. For example, an engineering manager focuses on developing and implementing engineering programs, marketing managers design and execute marketing programs, and so on. Regional managers in turn are concerned with the special characteristics of their geographic territories. Likewise, customer account managers are responsible for programs that serve the needs of specific customers. So, how the reporting hierarchy is structured signals the types of program the firm considers more important. Functional organizations put functions above geography and customers; geographically organized firms put geographical differences above functions and customers; and firms organized by customer put customer segments first.

For example, until 1999 Cisco was organized by customer segments: Enterprise, Small/Medium Business, and Service Provider. The company then shifted to a three-division worldwide geographic organization. This change indicates that Cisco perceived that the differences among its global regional markets were more important for performance improvement than differences among its types of customer. So geography now dominates customer segment in decision making. This does not mean that segments and functions (R&D, marketing, operations) are not important. Rather, they are coordinated across geographic divisions, which is inherently more difficult than within their own centralized units.

Rivals with different hierarchical structures build different kinds of capability. In one firm the CEO's direct reports might be in charge of functions, such as marketing, operations, and research and development. These managers develop capabilities in the functions first and then generalize them across regions and customers. In the other company, the CEO's direct reports could administer geographic regions. Here, regional capabilities are dominant and generalize across functions and customers. These two firms thus execute their strategies along distinct paths, by developing different capabilities, one set dominated by functional concerns, the other emphasizing regional markets.

Functional Organizations   In companies organized by function, coordination among activities is ultimately guided by the aims of the functions themselves. Building capabilities within R&D, marketing, or operations has priority over projects related to a specific geographical region or type of customer. The types of capability that can be built within functional structures are numerous and important.

First, organizing by function enables a firm to reduce costs through economies of scale and learning within each function. Lower costs are achieved by

1. Reduced overhead from combining functional tasks across regions or customers.
2. Standardization of procedures within functions.
3. Process innovation specific to each function.
4. Greater power over suppliers due to increased scale in purchasing.

Second, a functional organization allows a firm to invest in function-specific expertise that may increase value to the customer, such as

1. Technology development programs within R&D.
2. Skills in sales and marketing research.
3. Quality improvements in operations, logistics, and service.

Third, a functional structure provides a mechanism for firm growth through

1. Centralized functions that facilitate the continuous introduction of new products.
2. Investment in stronger technology platforms for future product development.

Geographic Organizations   Organizing by geography makes sense when regions are markedly different strategically. Customer preferences may differ so much by region that competing with local firms requires specialized capabilities. For example, in Texas Coca-Cola competes strongly against Dr Pepper which Texans perceive as a kind of fruit drink. If Texas were an independent country, it would be Coke's sixth largest national market. But Coke does not decentralize operations to its Texas franchise, preferring instead to run Texas policy from Atlanta, which designates Dr Pepper as a root beer. As a result, Coke does not achieve its potential in the Texas market.

Also, regional suppliers may require unique policies and procedures that are best managed locally. Local suppliers may have lower prices and better delivery times than large-scale vendors selected by corporate purchasing. Attempts to exploit these regional benefits often create conflict between local and corporate management, exposing unresolved inconsistencies in strategy of the firm.

Finally, the conditions of local competition may be unique. Large centralized firms frequently have difficulty penetrating a local market because of their inability to align with local business practices. Management may therefore be required to develop a specialized regional market position in order to compete effectively.

Customer-based Organization   Firms organized around customers deliver products specialized to well-defined customer segments. These segments must be unique enough in their requirements to warrant this heightened attention. Customer-based structures are frequently found in firms that compete in professional service industries, such as consulting or accounting. These firms are typically organized by industry sector, such as telecommunications, financial services, transportation, and energy. The client needs in each sector are sufficiently distinct that special industry knowledge has substantial value and trumps the benefit a generalist might provide.

The Matrix Form[14]   Firms often face a trade-off between two organizing dimensions (say function and geography), both of which are critical strategically. To avoid the problems of favoring one mode of organizing over the other, a company may structure itself on both dimensions simultaneously. Such a structure is called a **matrix.**

In a matrix structure, some managers report along two hierarchies instead of one. So, for example, a marketing manager in the United States would have a U.S. regional boss and at the same time a global marketing boss. The company benefits since specific U.S. market needs are attended to and global scale in marketing is achieved.

Matrix structures emerged in the defense industry in the 1960s and became quite popular among technology firms in the 1970s and 1980s. Rapidly changing customer segments and technologies both required significant attention and could not be short-changed. The matrix gave these dimensions joint power over projects. The structure continues to be used in companies such as Agilent, Novartis, and Acer to address complex organizational demands for strategy execution.

The major problem with a matrix structure is its complexity. The managers with dual reporting relationships are torn between the demands of the two sides of the company and frequently burn out after several years. Similarly, the tension between the two reporting hierarchies produces battles over resource allocation and policy formulation. Matrix structures are also more expensive to manage than conventional one-hierarchy structures simply because the matrix requires greater administrative overhead to operate effectively.

Matrix structures are a sign that a firm has internalized competing forces in its market, such as the inconsistent demands of customer specialization and low costs. By choosing to organize on both dimensions, the firm is trying to satisfy both strategic requirements at the same time. How the industry evolves will ultimately determine the success of the firm's decision.

Compensation and Incentive Systems

Employees must be compensated and otherwise rewarded so that they can contribute effectively to their firm's strategy. The compensation system must (1) measure the task outcomes related to the firm's value and cost drivers, (2) set appropriate targets for each outcome, and (3) reward managers for achieving these targets. This is a tall order for any organization, but a useful aspiration.

Brian Hall identifies three types of problems inherent in designing incentive systems:[15]

1. *The controllability problem*—when managers are unable to identify how much performance is due to skill and effort, or to luck.

2. *The alignment problem*—when crucial tasks cannot be measured, leading to the overweighting of tasks that can be measured.

3. *The interdependency problem*—when performance depends on the efforts of a team, making it difficult to identify individual contributions.

These problems are to a degree unavoidable and create both noise and distortion in the compensation system. The controllability problem introduces **noise** by making it difficult to design rewards that encourage employee effort and skill independent of luck. Noise is compounded by the interdependency problem when performance depends on teamwork. The alignment problem adds **distortion** to the system since it underweights hard-to-measure activities and overweights those that are easy to measure.[16]

The best system has low levels of both noise and distortion. Unfortunately, this goal is rarely, if ever, achieved.[17] It turns out that noise and distortion must be traded off, as becomes apparent when a company is forced to choose between measures based on organizational or on individual performance.

Rewarding managers using firm-level metrics, such as overall profitability or growth in the firm's stock price, reduces distortion. These rewards are not attached to success on individual tasks, so the measurement of these tasks has no significance. Managers have no incentive to work harder on the tasks that can be measured at the expense of those that cannot. All employees are therefore motivated to work hard at whatever they are doing, assuming that it has been designed to contribute to the firm's performance. The alignment problem therefore disappears.

But the downside of emphasizing firm-level performance measures is that it increases problems of controllability and interdependency. The reward system does not differentiate between who is actively contributing and who is free riding. So noise in the compensation system increases. Compensation based on firm performance is thus a rather blunt instrument to induce managers to increase effort or ability in the absence of rewarding individual action.

Using individual performance measures creates the reverse problem. Noise is reduced, but distortion is increased. Tight coupling between rewards and individual task performance makes it easier to identify superior skill and effort, lowering the incidence of slacking off. But rewarding managers for their performance on measurable tasks skews attention toward then, to the detriment of less measurable but important activities such as interpersonal or interunit cooperation.

How do organizations deal with this dilemma? There is no consistent answer to this question. Each firm develops its own solutions over time, using a mix of firm-level and individual-level incentives to reduce the noise and distortion in the system. Two generic solutions discussed below are piece rate and the balanced scorecard. Each of these focuses first on lowering noise through task-based incentives and then on moderating the distorting effects of these incentives by adding firm-level rewards.

Piece Rate

The clearest, most direct policy for linking compensation to strategy execution is pay for performance. This compensation system, often called **piece rate,** focuses a worker's attention on his or her productivity over the pay period, since pay is directly related to how much is produced.[18] Higher productivity per worker translates into higher volume spread over the same fixed assets and results in lower costs. But cost need not be the only focus of pay for performance. The firm can reward any behavior that is tied to strategy execution—whether it

Conditions for the Effective Implementation of Pay for Performance Incentives

1. **Employees must be able to control the pace of production (controllability problem).** If parts of the production process, such as automated equipment, are programmed to override the discretion of employees in choosing their rates of productivity, then it makes little sense to reward workers on how much they have produced. Whatever their effort and ability, they have no control over the amount of work completed.

2. **The standard rate of production assigned to a job must be perceived as fair and not adjusted arbitrarily (controllability problem).** Standard setting is a critical part of any compensation system focused on individual accountability, and an effective standard requires experience with the job. This means that piece rate is difficult to apply when new jobs are introduced frequently or when a job is frequently redesigned. Further, employees may reduce their effort when rate changes cannot be justified on the basis of technology improvements, since management is perceived as exploiting the piece-rate system.

3. **If uncertainty is significant, piece rate alone becomes infeasible if the employee is risk averse (controllability problem).** Tying an employee's pay to performance is often complicated by factors that are outside his control, such as poor quality materials or late deliveries. When the effects of these factors are significant, the firm typically absorbs some of the risk by providing a base wage in addition to piece-rate compensation.

4. **Team members should have roughly the same preferences for expending effort (interdependency problem).** Conflict within the group about appropriate levels of effort can undermine the advantages of individual accountability. The selection of group members and the management of their relationships with each other are key elements in an effective piece-rate program.

5. **When cooperation is required to achieve productivity goals, a group bonus may be offered in addition to piece-rate compensation (interdependency problem).** This compensation scheme works better for small groups than large groups since small size improves the visibility of effort and reduces slacking. Moreover, rewarding cooperative effort requires that group members be carefully selected [see (4) above].

6. **Rewarding productivity requires an explicit lower bound on the quality of output (alignment problem).** Anyone getting paid according to his or her output alone will tend to lower the quality of the product in order to raise the amount produced. So careful monitoring of product quality is required coupled with a policy of no pay for substandard work.

is producing highly engineered widgets, developing large customer accounts, selling tract houses, or flying airplanes on long routes.

There are six conditions for implementing a piece-rate system effectively (see the sidebar). Each addresses one of the three problems (controllability, alignment, interdependency) in reducing noise and distortion in the incentive system.

Pay-for-performance systems are burdened by the problem of risk bearing. Typically, employees are less interested in taking risks than the firm simply because the firm has a larger portfolio of ventures. If the employee fails in his current job, his income may disappear, whereas the firm has other projects to fall back on. An obvious way to induce greater employee risk taking is to reward it. For example, if large customer accounts are more difficult to get but provide a disproportionately higher return, a salesperson might be rewarded extra for them.

Because of the factors discussed above, firms that have implemented the piece-rate system fine tune it continuously. The outstanding example of a firm that has committed itself over its history to making piece-rate work effectively is Lincoln Electric, a U.S. arc-welding equipment firm. Lincoln Electric's strategy centers on having the lowest costs and therefore the lowest prices in its markets, coupled with strong technical sales and service. Consequently, employee compensation focuses on productivity to keep costs low, with no pay for poor quality. The sidebar describes Lincoln Electric's development of administrative practices to support its piece-rate system as well as the company's recent problems in expanding globally.

The Balanced Scorecard

A recent innovation in compensation schemes linked to strategy is the **balanced scorecard,** a method of compensating managers based on achieving critical performance measures within four domains: financial outcomes, customer outcomes, internal process improvement, and learning and growth.[19] The scorecard thus links both financial and nonfinancial variables to the company's strategy. In a sense, the balanced scorecard is a kind of multiattribute compensation system in which rewards are integrated and tied to achieving a stronger and more sustainable market position.

The balanced scorecard has its drawbacks, and they are similar to the vulnerabilities of the piece-rate system. The following factors complicate implementation:

- Defining key metrics.
- Resolving conflicts over goal setting.
- Estimating team effects.
- Adjusting for noncontrollable factors.

Most vulnerable to these problems are performance variables in the domain of learning and growth. However, these difficulties should not dissuade a

Lincoln Electric

Lincoln Electric, a dominant firm in the global arc-welding equipment industry, is a classic example of a company run on the piece-rate incentive system to achieve sustainable low costs. Lincoln views itself as predominately a manufacturing firm. The company has endured for more than 100 years in a highly competitive industry by keeping prices low. It also provides excellent technical service. From its beginning, Lincoln has focused on developing administrative and operational procedures to achieve high efficiency without degrading quality. They are the following:

1. Compensation for piece work only, no hourly wages, except for those jobs where measuring output per employee has been shown to be infeasible.

2. A yearly bonus based on four factors: dependability, output, quality and ideas, and cooperation, each rated by a different department in the organization.

3. A very active stock purchase plan for employees.

4. Guaranteed employment after two years.

5. Continuous improvement in work methods by staff engineering and workers.

6. Employee guarantee of quality.

7. Price and volume targets to produce a planned financial return to the firm and to workers.

8. A policy of not hiring additional workers to increase production when demand increases.

9. Open discussion of job and employee ratings.

10. A system of consultation between workers and management, including an Advisory Board that meets twice a month, a top-management open-door policy, and extensive informal contact between management and workers on the shop floor.

11. A policy of promotion from within.

12. A flat hierarchy, giving workers easier access to top management.

13. A strenuous trial period for new employees which many do not pass.

The development of the company's routines was based on substantial practical knowledge about the details of effective interpersonal relationships in a piece-rate system. These aspects of the organization's culture are not easily replicable by other firms. For example, it would be difficult for another organization to replicate the cohort of senior workers that serve as role models for younger employees.

In the past several decades, Lincoln has expanded into international markets by establishing facilities in Europe, Asia, and Latin America. One reason for this expansion is to prevent ESAB, a large Swedish competitor, from dominating the global industry. ESAB has deep financial pockets and is able to penetrate new markets with low prices. Lincoln's global expansion has threatened its core compensation system in two ways. First, the company learned that what works in Cleveland, Ohio, its headquarters, does not work in Brazil, France, and other non-U.S. locations because of local laws and traditions. So Lincoln's top management had to be able to compete internationally with a variety of production and marketing systems, not just piece-rate compensation. Second, to expand into other countries Lincoln had to increase its debt, and the bankers who made loans to the company were not committed to maintaining its compensation system. This has meant that in some periods, workers have not gotten the bonus they expected because of payments to debt holders.

The point is that although Lincoln's piece-rate practices are an almost ideal compensation system for rewarding individual effort, it has been very challenging to sustain this system as the firm has grown in response to changes in the global industry. Intricate compensation systems based on piece-rate need to be buffered from environmental change. But even the most well designed buffers fail at some point. Lincoln continues to thrive with its piece-rate system intact, although it applies to a much reduced percentage of its workforce.

firm from rewarding employees on those performance metrics that are tightly linked to the firm's strategy.

Culture and Learning

Culture

A critical part of strategy execution is the firm's people and the culture they create and perpetuate.[20] Organizational culture is defined by the mores and expressive behavior of employees as they direct thought and activity toward or away from the organization's goals. Cultural content includes the official and unofficial values that individuals espouse and act on, the stories and anecdotes that employees hear and pass on as guides for appropriate or inappropriate behavior, the rules of thumb regarding decision making that are passed from one employee to another, and the resulting common understanding of a wide range of problems and tasks that pervade the organization over time.

David Kreps has argued that by creating focal points for decision making that are widely shared across a firm, organizational culture narrows the choices available to individuals, leading to commonly accepted decisions without extensive communication.[21] The development of focal points through organizational culture is especially valuable in a nonroutine decision context.[22] For example, when employees face an unusual and challenging customer problem, the implicit rule in one firm may be that they should go out of their way to help the customer, a practice for which Nordstrom, the upscale department store, is well known. If customer retention is a key component of a firm's competitive advantage, and the firm has developed a culture that perpetuates stories and rules of thumb that focus on high customer service, then the culture supports the strategy and will improve its execution. On the other hand, if customer retention is part of the strategy, but the firm has not developed a culture focused on solving difficult customer problems, then the culture and strategy are not synchronized. In this case, execution will be less effective.[23]

Learning

As a firm's culture provides a set of focal points for decision making, it also produces models for effective questioning and experimentation. Without inquiry, there is no initiative for enhancing strategy execution; without

Strong and Weak Cultures

Firms differ in their cultures, and cultures differ in their relative strength. Strong cultures are more enduring and create greater consistency in the behavior of employees. Weak cultures, on the other hand, are fragile and subject to fragmentation and violations of commonly understood rules of behavior.

Where does a strong culture come from? The standard explanation is that it is the product of the kinds of processes observed at Vanguard in the development of consistent activity systems. As managers try to build the capabilities that underlie effective value and cost drivers, the culture develops in response to feedback from the market. Given the frequently severe constraints markets can place on a firm to execute effectively, a strong culture is more likely to emerge in a firm that is performing at an increasingly high level. Research has shown in fact that firms with strong cultures tend to have higher economic performance over time, especially in markets that are highly competitive, where constraints on firm behavior are greater.[24]

Equally important is the effect of culture strength on performance variability.[25] In a firm with a strong culture, employees are more likely to conform more consistently with well-understood rules of behavior. Higher conformance leads to less deviation in the firm's performance with customers and suppliers, reinforcing the firm's reputation. More consistent performance also raises the credibility of the firm in the eyes of competitors.

experimentation, managers have little direction for improvement. Organizational learning is therefore necessary for adaptation to changing market conditions.

Learning within a firm typically is guided by established routines and subject to strong path dependence, as existing resources and capabilities provide the framework for future innovation. Within these constraints, managers set performance targets that direct the organization's pattern of experimentation.[26] This kind of inquiry is in many cases extremely effective. A process of directed trial and error creates a powerful dynamic capability to grow the firm.[27] For example, Southwest Airlines established its low-cost market position in Texas before deregulation in the U.S. airline industry in 1978 and was able to experiment with its practices in order to improve its economic contribution to its customers. After deregulation the airline continued to innovate within these constraints when it began to compete in other states.

However, effective adaptation sometimes requires investments that are inconsistent with the organization's traditional path of innovation. Chris Argyris and Donald Schon have made the distinction between single- and double-loop problem solving.[28] Single-loop problem solving entails working within the given parameters of a task to reach a solution. In this case, there is little or no questioning of the task as such; all search paths lie in well-understood and accepted territory as in the case of Southwest Airlines above. Double-loop problem solving, on the contrary, extends the problem-solving process outside the task's normal domain and raises questions about the task parameters themselves. Rather than finding ways to perform the task more effectively, double-loop thinking asks why it is configured as it is and even whether it is the correct task to be performed.

Effective strategy execution clearly requires the ability to engage in both types of problem solving. Single-loop learning is necessary and sufficient to solve routine problems. In these cases, it is simply not effective to explore outside the box. Double-loop learning becomes increasingly necessary, however, when the industry shifts from one growth stage to another, and especially when it is threatened by disruption due to technological or regulatory change. Developing effective double-loop learning in these circumstances can be a critical managerial task.

Double-loop learning means breaking down the cognitive barriers that surround a problem so that a new perspective can be adopted, even one that you can currently perceive but cannot seem to accept. For example, to shut down the company's DRAM business in 1984, two of Intel's top executives, Andy Grove and Gordon Moore, got up, mentally, out of their chairs, walked through the office door, and then walked back in with a new mind-set. In this cognitive exercise they fired themselves and then became new management. They were sure any new manager would get out of DRAMs, but they were so caught up in their own assumptions and commitments that they could make the decision they knew was right only by pretending to be someone else, someone more rational.

Summary

In this chapter we have examined how a firm executes its strategy. We distinguished between resources and capabilities and discussed how they are related. The key concepts of the value chain and activity systems were introduced as ways of analyzing what an organization does to deliver its goods or services. Finally, we discussed four elements of strategy execution that are critical for building capabilities: (1) complementarity and consistency among the firm's policies and activities, (2) the firm's control and coordination systems, (3) the firm's incentive systems, and (4) the culture and learning systems of the organization. The decisions managers make regarding each of these elements play a crucial role in developing the firm's value and cost drivers and therefore in determining its market position.

Summary Points

- The key to understanding strategy execution is how firms build and maintain resources and capabilities.

- To provide an economic advantage, a firm's resources must contribute to its value or cost drivers and be difficult for competitors to imitate or to neutralize through substitution.

- The ability of a firm to accomplish tasks that are linked to higher economic performance is called a capability. Capability-related tasks are performed over time through the coordinated efforts of teams whose memberships change even as the practices involved persist and improve.

- A capability must be associated with specific activities and programs within the organization.

- The major contributors to building and maintaining capabilities are consistency or complementarity among capabilities and resources, control and coordination systems, compensation and reward systems, and people and culture.

- Two or more resources may be complementary in that together they produce a more effective outcome than either produces independently.

- The concept of *consistency* or *fit* implies that the policies and practices of each activity are aligned with the demands of the firm's market position.

- A useful way to analyze a firm's consistency and examine the impact of activities on strategy execution is Porter's value chain diagram.

- Activity systems are composed of policies in value chain activities, general characteristics of the firm's structure and culture, product attributes, and key resources such as technologies and brands.

- The two end points of the spectrum of market positions in an industry—extreme value and cost advantage—require highly consistent execution.

- The more consistent an organization's activities, the more difficult they are to change.

- A firm's formal control systems for managing and allocating financial resources, such as its budgeting and financial reporting systems, determine which capabilities will be built and sustained.

- Galbraith presents five mechanisms for achieving interunit coordination, in addition to the use of hierarchical authority: (1) *standardized procedures,* (2) *joint planning,* (3) *liaison personnel,* (4) *task forces,* and (5) *teams.*

- Hierarchy is typically the last resort for managers unable to resolve their differences, no matter what other coordination mechanisms are in place.

- Management hierarchies in a single business are typically organized along one or more of the following dimensions: *function, geographical region, customer,* and perhaps to a small degree, *product.*

- Matrix structures are typically a sign that the firm has internalized competing forces in the market.

- Employees must be compensated and otherwise rewarded in such a way that they can exert and direct their activities towards the firm's strategic goals.

- As a firm's culture provides a set of focal points for decision making, it also needs to provide models for effective questioning and experimentation.

- Learning within a firm typically is guided by established routines and subject to strong path dependence, as existing resources and capabilities provide the framework within which innovations are developed.
- Effective strategy execution requires the ability to engage in both single- and double-loop problem solving.

Questions for Practice

Think how you would answer these questions for your current company, your previous place of work, or a business you are studying:

1. What are the key resources and capabilities underlying your value and cost drivers?

2. How well do these resources and capabilities complement each other? How could their complementarity be improved?

3. Can you map your firm's activity system? If you did so, how consistent do you think your activities would be?

4. How is your firm organized structurally? Does this structure support the development of your key capabilities?

5. What metrics does your organization use to measure financial and operating performance? How are they related to your business strategy?

6. How does your firm handle the trade-off between noise and distortion in its incentive system?

7. Does your company have a strong or weak culture? Do the characteristics of your culture contribute to your strategy?

8. What focal points does your firm use to make important decisions? Are they effective?

9. How do your company's policies regarding its people contribute to the development of key capabilities?

10. How effectively does your company engage in double-loop learning?

End Notes

1. For a broad look at how a firm's strategy and execution intersect, see Henry Mintzberg, Bruce Ahlstrand, and Joseph Lampel, *Strategy Safari, a Guided Tour through the Wilds of Strategic Management* (New York: Free Press, 1998).

2. For a clear statement on the importance of highly intentional strategic behavior by line management, see Larry Bossidy and Ram Charan, *Execution: The Discipline of Getting Things Done* (New York: Crown Business, 2002).

3. There is a large literature on capabilities that emphasizes their development, importance, and inertia, for example: Richard R. Nelson, "Why Do Firms Differ and How Does It Matter?" *Strategic Management Journal* 61(1991) pp. 61–74; Toby E. Stuart and Joel Podolny, "Local Search and the Evolution of Technological Capabilities," *Strategic Management Journal* 17 (1996) pp. 21–39; David Collis, "How Valuable Are Organizational Capabilities?" *Strategic Management Journal* 15 (1994) pp. 143–53; Daniel M. G. Raff, "Superstores and the Evolution of Firm Capabilities in American Bookselling," *Strategic Management Journal* 21 (2000) pp. 1043–60; Mary Tripsas and Giovanni Gavetti, "Capabilities, Cognition and Inertia: Evidence from Digital Imaging," *Strategic Management Journal* 21 (2000), pp. 1147–62; Rebecca Henderson and Kim Clark, "Architectural Innovation: The Reconfiguration of Existing Product Technologies and the Failure of Established Firms," *Administrative Science Quarterly* 35 (1990), pp. 9–31.

4. See Richard Makadok and Gordon Walker, "Identifying a Distinctive Competence: Forecasting Ability in Money Market Industry," *Strategic Management Journal* 20 (2000), pp. 853–64.

5. See Richard Makadok, "Toward a Synthesis of the Resource-Based and Dynamic Capability Views of Rent Creation," *Strategic Management Journal* 22 (2001), pp. 387–401.

6. See Jay Barney, "Strategic Factor Markets: Expectations, Luck and Business Strategy," *Management Science* 32, no. 10 (1986) pp. 1231–41.

7. See Michael Porter, *Competitive Advantage* (New York: Free Press, 1985).

8. Michael Porter, "What Is Strategy?" *Harvard Business Review* 74 (1996), pp. 61–78.

9. See Nicolaj Siggelkow, "Evolution Towards Fit," *Adminstrative Science Quarterly* 47 (2002), pp. 125–59.

10. See Paul Milgrom and John Roberts, "The Economics of Modern Manufacturing: Technology, Strategy and Organization," *American Economic Review* 80 (1990), pp. 511–28; Paul Milgrom, Y. Qian, and John Roberts, "Complementarities, Momentum and the Evolution of Modern Manufacturing," *American Economic Review* 81 (1997), pp. 84–88.

11. See N. Venkatraman, "The Concept of Fit in Strategy Research: Toward Verbal and Statistical Correspondence," *Academy of Management Review* 14 (1989), pp. 423–45.

12. See Edward Fox, Uday Apte, and Gordon Walker, "Channel Complementarity in Internet Retailing," working paper, Cox School of Business, Southern Methodist University, 2002.

13. See Jay Galbraith, *Competing with Flexible Lateral Organizations* (Reading, MA: Addison-Wesley, 1993).

14. See Stanley M. Davis, Paul R. Lawrence, and Michael Beer, *Matrix* (Reading, MA: Addison-Wesley, 1978); Christopher Bartlett and Sumantra Ghoshal, "Matrix Management: Not a Structure, a Frame of Mind," *Harvard Business Review* 68 (1990), pp. 138–45.

15. Brian J. Hall, "Incentive Strategy within Organizations," Harvard Business School, course note, 2002.

16. The concept of distortion here is similar to that made in Steve Kerr's classic article, "On the Folly of Rewarding A While Hoping for B," *Academy of Management Review* 18 (1975), pp. 769–83.

17. See George P. Baker, "The Use of Performance Measures in Incentive Contracting," *American Economic Review* 90 (2000), pp. 415–20.

18. See James Baron and David Kreps, *Strategic Human Resources: Frameworks for General Managers* (New York: John Wiley, 1999), chaps. 10–12.

19. See Robert S. Kaplan and David P. Norton, *The Balanced Scorecard: Translating Strategy into Action* (Boston: Harvard Business School Press, 1996).

20. For a comprehensive statement of the importance of organizational culture, see Edgar Schein, *Organizational Culture and Leadership,* 2nd ed. (San Francisco: Jossey-Bass, 1997).

21. See David Kreps, "Corporate Culture and Economic Theory," in James Alt and Kenneth Shepsle, eds., *Perspectives on Positive Political Economy* (New York: Cambridge University Press, 1990).

22. See Thomas Schelling, *A Theory of Conflict* (Cambridge, MA: Harvard University Press, 1960) for the original discussion of focal points.

23. For a discussion of how elements of a culture contribute to competitive advantage, see Jay Barney, "Organizational Culture: Can It Be a Source of Sustained Competitive Advantage," *Academy of Management Review* 11 (1986), pp. 656–65.

24. See John Kotter and James Heskett, *Corporate Culture and Performance* (New York: Free Press, 1992); Ronald Burt, S. M. Gabbay, G. Holt, and P. Moran, "Contingent Organization as a Network Theory: The Culture Performance Contingency Function," *Acta Sociologica* 37 (1994), pp. 345–70.

25. See Jesper Sorensen, "The Strength of Corporate Culture and the Reliability of Firm Performance," *Administrative Science Quarterly* 47 (2002), pp. 70–91.

26. For a comprehensive review on this topic, see Barbara Levitt and James March, "Organizational Learning," *Annual Review of Sociology* 14 (1988), pp. 319–40.

27. Maurizio Zollo and Sidney Winter, "Deliberate Learning and the Evolution of Dynamic Capabilities," *Organization Science* 13 (2002), pp. 339–551.

28. See Chris Argyris and Donald Schon, *Organizational Learning: A Theory of Action Perspective* (Reading, MA: Addison-Wesley, 1978).

Managing the Boundaries of the Firm

CHAPTER 6

Vertical Integration and Outsourcing

Roadmap

Every organization produces some goods and services and buys others as it needs them, frequently or infrequently. The line that separates the in-house and the external activities for each firm we will call the organization's boundary. As we will discuss below, decisions regarding the firm's boundaries can be critical to a firm's strategy and economic performance.

- Introduction
- The Employment Relationship
- Transaction Cost Theory
- The Property Rights Approach
- Strategy and Control
  - Control over Input Price
  - Control over Investment Decisions
  - Control over Access to Information
- Strategy and Relative Capability
- The Strategic Sourcing Framework
  - Explaining Vertical Integration
  - Explaining Outsourcing
  - Outsourcing in China
- Additional Issues
  - Differences among Types of Uncertainty
  - The Problem of Consistency
  - Industry Dynamics

Introduction

No organization performs all of the activities required to produce its product. For example, whole industries have emerged as single activities (e.g., transportation, distribution, engineering). The customers of the firms in these industries have decided to buy their goods or services rather than produce them in-house. For example, when Nike decides how to advertise a new running shoe, it may choose the services of an independent advertising company rather than the creative talent of Nike's own staff. In turn, the advertising company Nike hires may outsource a variety of functions such as media purchasing, Web site design, direct marketing, and collateral print material. The point is that any activity that occurs inside the firm can be also performed by an outside supplier. How can we explain a company's decisions to make or buy what it needs in order to compete effectively?

An example of a firm whose boundary decisions have been critical to its strategy is Dell Computer, the most successful personal computer firm in the world. Dell sells and distributes its own PCs; it does not sell through outside retailers. In contrast, Dell's major competitors, such as Toshiba, IBM (Lenovo), and Hewlett-Packard, continue to use independent retail channels to sell their products. The retail sales activity is performed completely inside Dell's boundary but mostly outside its major competitors' boundaries. Why is this so?

Dell's vertical integration of sales allows it greater control over how sales is designed and executed. Greater control allows Dell to coordinate sales and distribution with other activities such as logistics and operations so that the process of selling, producing, and delivering a computer can be streamlined with extremely low inventory at every stage. Less inventory not only reduces working capital requirements but also, given the rapid obsolescence of PC components, means more state-of-the-art machines can be sold at nondiscounted prices. This decision and the associated policy of custom-built personal computers was once seen as eccentric, against the industry trend; it is now seen as prophetic and a serious threat to PC retailers and other PC producers.

Why do organizations internalize some activities but not others? What are the strategic causes and consequences of where an organization draws its boundary? In today's fluid markets, it is often difficult to distinguish employees from suppliers, customers, or partners. Yet, one generally intuits that employees *are* different, especially when a firm wants extra creativity or effort on a project, special information for planning or decision making, or ongoing access to specific abilities. In this chapter we examine first the characteristics of the employment relationship and then a series of theories and frameworks that explain boundary decisions based on the ideas of ownership, control, and capability.

The Employment Relationship[1]

How is being an employee of the firm different from a market supplier? According to the U.S. legal system, employees have three duties to the firms they work in:

- **Duty of obedience:** Managers have the right to control both the process and outcomes of work, not just the outcomes alone. This often means that the employee must behave in a socially acceptable, respectful way with the employer. Of course, managers may encourage employees to be candid and open with their thoughts.

- **Duty of loyalty:** The employee should act in the interests of his employer and cannot benefit at the employer's expense. Self-dealing is inconsistent with the legal approach to the employee relationship.

- **Duty of disclosure:** The employee must disclose information that may benefit the employer. In fact, employees may be held legally accountable for losses that result from a failure to disclose critical information.

Suppliers have none of these duties, at least as recognized in the courts. It should be added that employers are accountable for their employees but not for suppliers. That is, an employer is liable for damage that his employee, but not his supplier, may do to a third party.[2]

The legal duties of employees highlight two important aspects of governance: (1) legitimate hierarchical authority and (2) the generation and use of strategically important information. The hierarchical authority of managers enables them to align incentives with the firm's market position, make the firm's activities more consistent with each other, and develop a culture that supports the firm's strategy. In turn, the more strategically useful information is available, the better strategic decision making should be.

Given these advantages of the employment relationship regarding execution, why don't firms always vertically integrate? The answer is that managers cost money, but markets are free. Under some conditions, the extra control that managers can exert may not be worth what the firm spends on them. What are these conditions and how can we use them to understand and make better vertical integration decisions? The following sections lay out the two theories—transaction costs and property rights—that focus on when firms are better than markets for governing transactions.

Transaction Cost Theory

Transaction cost theory focuses on the contracting difficulties between a firm and its supplier.[3] Under certain conditions, these problems can become so frustrating to the firm that the only option is to bring the activity in-house. Although in-house production is often more costly than sourcing the input in the market, the lower transaction costs of vertical integration can more than compensate for this disadvantage.

The theory specifies two basic conditions that in combination lead to vertical integration. The first condition is that the transaction between the firm and its supplier be exposed to a significant degree of uncertainty. Uncertainty here means that the contingencies that impinge on the supply relationship cannot be fully specified, so the firms must leave part of the transaction open for further discussion. For example, as we will see below, the firm may not be able to forecast perfectly how much of the supplier's product it will need in the future. In this case, the firm and the supplier experience **demand** or **volume uncertainty.** Or they may experience **technological uncertainty** because changes in product or process design are expected but cannot be specified. Another type of uncertainty can arise from volatility in input markets, such as labor and materials, which affect the supplier's costs and therefore future pricing.

When uncertainty exists, and there is always some, contracts are incomplete. **Incomplete contracting** thus occurs when part of the contract between the firm and the supplier remains unspecified. Because the future states of the supply relationship cannot be articulated effectively, the two firms must renegotiate the contract when changes need to be made.

According to transaction cost theory, uncertainty alone is not sufficient to lead to vertical integration; there must also be problems in renegotiating the contract. What might determine such problems? One possibility is that the buyer's costs of switching to another supplier are high and the current supplier exploits this situation. High switching costs occur when the supplier has invested in assets or activities that are specific to the firm. As the supplier makes these investments and its **asset specificity** rises, the firm may benefit because inputs are more customized to its requirements. This situation is an opportunity for the supplier to improve its profits in the relationship.

There are many types of specialization. For example, a supplier may locate its plant next to its customer to reduce transportation and inventory costs. When the customer is powerful, as Toyota is over its suppliers, colocation need not induce opportunistic behavior by the supplier. But when the power distribution in the supply relationship is more equal, as for instance between a coal mine and an electricity plant, contracting costs may increase when changes in the relationship need to be made.[4] Asset specificity may also involve specialized equipment or specialized skills, both of which may raise transaction costs over time.

For instance, when its own input prices decrease, the specialized supplier may not lower its price to the firm proportionately; or, to take advantage of its importance to the customer, the supplier may cut corners on quality, delivery, or other value drivers. Through these actions, the supplier decreases the surplus the customer receives. At some point, the customer becomes fed up with the supplier's uncooperative behavior and decides to perform the activity itself since cooperation is higher in-house due to the employment relationship.[5]

The Property Rights Approach

But why does a firm vertically integrate into the activity of its supplier, instead of the supplier vertically integrating into the activity of the firm? For example, in 1999, Viacom, the U.S. entertainment giant, bought CBS, the television network. A major argument for the acquisition was that coordinating the production of TV content (Viacom's Paramount studios produced TV shows such as *Frazier*) and content distribution (CBS had substantial broadcasting reach) would be more efficient in-house. But if this argument is valid, why didn't CBS buy Viacom? Viacom was not that much bigger, and a benefit from vertical integration would be achieved in any event. Why does one firm gain control over the other in vertical integration rather than the reverse?

The answer has to do with the relative benefit each firm receives from exercising control over the activity based on its complementarity with the firms' existing assets. The issue of relative gain from control is the foundation of the **property rights approach** to vertical integration.[6] In this approach, the asymmetry between firms in the benefits they receive is the key to understanding which firm should have control over the activity. The company that has more to profit from controlling investments in the activity is the one that internalizes it. An organization draws its boundaries around those activities that it can derive a higher value from controlling, compared to the firms that might supply it with the activity or its output.[7]

This approach sheds some light on an important aspect of the employment relation. Being an employee means giving up control over your work to a firm whose assets contribute more to the value of your work than your work contributes to the value of the assets. That is, the firm means more to your productivity than you do to the productivity of the firm.

In many cases, it is quite difficult to identify the contribution of the firm independent of employee activities. This is especially true as the firm's assets shift from being fungible (resources) to nonfungible (capabilities). Employees frequently exploit this difficulty by challenging management for control. Sometimes it is in fact the employee, not the organization, that has economic value.

There are many examples where the loss of key personnel has caused a firm to suffer a loss in performance. In these cases, the employees contributed more to the assets of the firm than the firm's assets contributed to the employees. But there are counterexamples as well, such as the defection of currency traders from Citibank to Deutsche Bank in 1997. Deutsche Bank hired the traders in the belief that their expertise was the primary reason Citibank's trading revenue had been so high. But it turned out that Deutsche Bank was wrong—these revenues were due to Citibank's prestige (and its massive distribution network), not to the traders themselves. How do we know this? After the traders left, Citibank suffered a small drop in trading volume and then regained its position in the market. However, the former Citibank currency traders could not expand the Deutsche Bank business as expected. In this case, Citibank owned critical assets—reputation and distribution—that the traders needed to attract customers. Citibank could replace the traders, but the traders could not replace Citibank.

Strategy and Control

It is a small but important shift in emphasis from the ownership of specialized assets to the strategy of the firm. Specialization is a necessary but not sufficient condition for higher economic value for the firm, relative to its competitors. It is necessary since a standard asset—for example, a generic database management system—is broadly available to all firms in an industry and so adds no incremental value to any firm in particular. However, it is not sufficient since specialization alone does not ensure that the asset will be aligned with the firm's market position. A unique asset that does not contribute to the firm's value and cost drivers is not strategically important.

Ideally, an organization has drawn its boundary around all the activities that are strategically valuable and left those activities that are strategically less important under the control of suppliers. If this were always the case, there would be almost no vertical integration or outsourcing events. But since strategies, markets, and capabilities change continually for a host of reasons, there are almost always nonstrategic activities inside the firm and strategic activities outside the firm.[8]

What types of control problem in a supply relationship might motivate a firm to consider vertically integrating an important activity? We can identify three:[9]

1. A problem in distributing the economic gain from the supply relationship, typically focused on price.

2. A problem in controlling the quality or quantity of supplier investments in assets, human resources, product design, management processes, and other activities that affect what it delivers to the firm.

3. A problem in the supplier's handling of information that is strategically sensitive to the buyer.

Conflict between the firm and the supplier over each of these can be significant and lead to the consideration of vertical integration.

Control over Input Price

Conflicts over pricing can emerge in two contexts. In one form, the problem appears when the supplier decides that it has sufficient leverage to raise its price without increasing the value it delivers. In essence, the supplier is saying "what we supply to you is special and we want more money for it." The reverse phenomenon occurs when the firm desires a lower price from its supplier that provides a specialized input, but the supplier is unwilling to comply. For example, many manufacturing firms, especially those with strategic sourcing relationships, have initiated target pricing programs with their suppliers to reduce purchasing costs. As long as the supplier is willing to go along with these programs, there is little reason to integrate vertically. However, when (1) a supplier balks at giving up its profits to the firm, (2) there are no alternatives to the supplier, and (3) the higher returns from a lower price are worth the firm's effort to self-manufacture, vertical integration might be considered.

Control over Investment Decisions

The second type of control problem concerns the supplier's investments in the assets or activities that produce the input. Critical investments might be the type of equipment bought, the quality and duration of worker and manager training, the qualifications of new workers and managers, and the quality and price of inputs to the supplier's processes—in short, anything that might affect a firm's value drivers.[10]

An interesting example of vertical integration to control investments in quality is Texas Land and Cattle, a classic Texas steak house chain with sawdust on the floor. The restaurant's steaks are unusually tender for a chain because the meat is very fresh. The freshness is due to the control the chain has over the butchering, packaging, and delivery of its meat. Each of these activities is performed by the organization itself. The restaurant butchers its own steaks in a single facility near downtown Dallas. The steaks are then vacuum packed, not frozen, in plastic bags and delivered daily to each restaurant. By internalizing this operation, the chain is able to sell excellent quality beef at casual dining prices. When asked why vertical integration is necessary, the restaurant says it would not be able to control the practices of an outside butcher as effectively as those of a butcher in-house. Since the quality and freshness of the meat is a critical part of the organization's strategy, exercising effective control is essential to meet performance goals. Interestingly, the chain's geographical reach is somewhat constrained by the driving time from the Dallas butchering facility. Albuquerque, New Mexico, is within an acceptable driving distance, but opening a restaurant in Denver, Colorado, is infeasible unless a new butchering operation is built to serve the new region, a new strategic problem. It is worth noting that in this case vertical integration clearly improves the firm's value offered more than it reduces cost.

Control over Access to Information

This problem involves control over who has access to valuable information. Two types of information in the supply relationship affect a firm's performance. First, the firm may gain from having information about a supplier's business; second, the firm may suffer from the spread of information about its own business from the supplier to the firm's competitors.

In the first case, information about the supplier, especially its costs, may give the firm insights that an uninformed competitor would lack. The government often recognizes this potential source of advantage as anticompetitive and tries to prevent it through threatening antitrust litigation. For example, the Regional Bell operating companies (RBOCs) must have a lawyer present at most meetings involving the marketing and transmission sides of their business to ensure that local resellers are not disadvantaged. This information may refer to valuable technologies, pricing, marketing plans and practices, or key aspects of the company's future direction.

In the second case, a credible promise of confidentiality can be a key selling point for a supplier. For instance, 3M makes the sticky tape on disposable diapers for both Kimberly Clark and Procter & Gamble. Needless to say, without sticky tape, disposable diapers lose a significant part of their usefulness. 3M must reassure these head-to-head competitors that it will not breach the wall of security that separates their individual accounts within its operations. Without this reassurance, the trade-off between (1) the advantage of 3M's superior technology and (2) the disadvantage of having strategic information potentially exposed to a rival might tip against the supplier and force one or both firms to find another source or bring the technology in-house, if technologically possible.

Strategy and Relative Capability[11]

A theory of vertical integration based on problems of control assumes that the organization that benefits the most from performing an activity is also the most competent. But, as we have suggested, this is not always the case. Even though control over decision making can provide a benefit to the firm, the firm may lack the ability to execute its own decisions capably. In the 3M example above, Procter & Gamble benefits when 3M protects its strategic information from Kimberly-Clark. But it is unlikely that Procter & Gamble could replicate 3M's production processes successfully.

Thus, in analyzing make or buy decisions, we need to compare the relative production costs or competence of the firm and its supplier in addition to looking at transaction costs or problems of control. In theory, the supplier always has lower production costs than the firm. However, this difference declines as the supplier's operations become more specialized to the firm's requirements. The reason is that specialization leads to lower volume levels

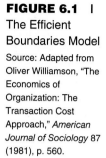

FIGURE 6.1 |

The Efficient
Boundaries Model

Source: Adapted from
Oliver Williamson, "The
Economics of
Organization: The
Transaction Cost
Approach," *American
Journal of Sociology* 87
(1981), p. 560.

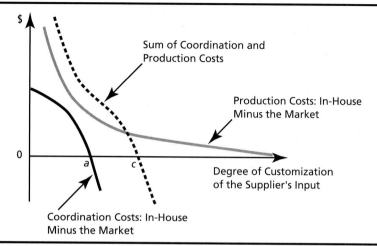

since the supplier is increasingly unable to sell the good or service to other firms, and as volume declines, the supplier's economies of scale in production are reduced, raising costs. This relationship is captured in Figure 6.1, which shows Oliver Williamson's "efficient boundaries model." The model indicates that a firm should consider the sum of transaction *and* production costs together in making its decision whether to bring an activity in-house.[12]

Note that in Figure 6.1, when specialization is low, in-house transaction costs are higher than transaction costs in the market. This simply means that for commodities organizations are inherently expensive to manage compared with the market. But as the input becomes more customized, the difference between coordination in-house and coordination with a market supplier plummets until at point *a* on the customization line, the comparison favors performing the activity inside the firm. If vertical integration were only a function of the improved coordination offered by the employment relation and asset ownership, the buyer at this point would bring the activity in-house. But there are production cost considerations as well. Because market suppliers typically maintain a production cost advantage due to economies of scale in the noncustom parts of the input, the sum of the coordination and production cost difference between in-house and market supply continues to favor keeping the activity outside the firm. However, as the input becomes even more specialized to the customer, the sum of the two types of cost becomes negative at point *c*. Here, the firm has a clear economic incentive to bring the operation in-house.

A classic example of the efficient boundaries model is the vertical integration of shareholder services in the mutual fund industry in the late 1980s. These services involve the important task of responding to shareholder telephone inquiries. If the responses to customer queries are executed poorly because of inadequate information about the fund's characteristics or procedures, customers may redeem their shares and switch to a competitor. As mutual funds proliferated in the 1980s and 1990s, customer retention became a key isolating mechanism. So shareholder services became a strategically important activity, raising the salience of control over hiring and training service personnel. Unfortunately, many suppliers had designed their businesses for a high volume of calls using cheap labor. These firms hired service representatives with a relatively low level of education, paid them close to minimum wage, and trained them to handle calls for many funds. These policies were successful for those funds whose strategies were based on low expenses but not for those funds whose strategies were based on customer retention through expert service. For this latter group, the unwillingness of suppliers to invest in better educated and trained personnel was unacceptable. They therefore brought shareholder services in-house to increase control over service personnel, sometimes with remarkably positive results. Interestingly, since integrating the computer systems that supported shareholder services was in most cases very expensive, these systems remained in the hands of suppliers.

In this example, the costs of suppliers were virtually always lower than the costs of mutual fund companies, consistent with the efficient boundaries model in Figure 6.1. But disagreements with suppliers about the way shareholder services should be designed and operated drove the buyers to bring the activity in-house. Even though supplier production costs were lower, the vertically integrated firms had higher quality service, a key value driver. Thus, you get what you pay for.

Sometimes, however, a firm will vertically integrate an activity to gain control over investment decisions and actually achieve lower costs than the supplier. For example, in the 1920s Ford Motor began to absorb many component suppliers so that its production lines could be integrated with its newly designed mass assembly line operations. The suppliers resisted the request that they invest in mass production, which would have aligned their production volumes and schedules with those of Ford. Their resistance, of course, made economic sense since they also delivered components to other car companies whose production lines were less automated than Ford's and who required smaller production volumes at less regular intervals. The only way Ford could achieve the high levels of efficiency inherent in its mass-production line was to vertically integrate into component supply. In this example, therefore, component production was actually cheaper inside Ford than in the supplier's facility, contrary to the economies of scale argument in the efficient boundaries model. But note that it was cheaper because the manufacturing process inside Ford was different from that in supplier firms.

A key point here is that, in both the mutual funds and Ford examples, in-house operations were quite unlike those of suppliers. In both cases, the difference between the firm's strategy and the supplier's strategy was revealed in conflict over investment decisions. When the firm gained control over these decisions through vertical integration, it developed a new process in-house that was substantially different from that of the supplier, either raising production costs in the case of mutual fund families, or reducing them in the case of Ford. The comparison of production costs between a firm and its supplier is therefore partially dependent on the technologies each has invested in; these in turn are determined by the strategies of each company.

The Strategic Sourcing Framework

It is easy to move from analyzing relative production costs to an assessment of the firm's relative competence to perform the activity. In addition to cost, competence includes achieving higher value such as product quality, superior technical features of the product, flexibility in production scheduling, ability to integrate with adjacent activities, and responsiveness to changes in customer requirements. Any of these aspects of competence could be critical for the firm strategically.

The importance of both control needs and relative competence suggests the simple framework shown in Figure 6.2 called the **strategic sourcing framework**.[13] The framework is useful for analyzing decisions for specific activities, such as distribution as in the case of Dell Computer, component fabrication as in the case of Ford, or butchering beef as in the case of Texas Land & Cattle. Activities vary in their strategic value to the firm, which determines how much control the firm feels it needs to exercise over them. Higher value to the firm leads to greater control needs, as in the property rights approach.

A firm's capability or competence compared to outside suppliers can obviously vary across activities, too. As we have discussed, the series of investments a firm makes over time will determine to a large extent its level of expertise. For example, if investments in information technology lag behind

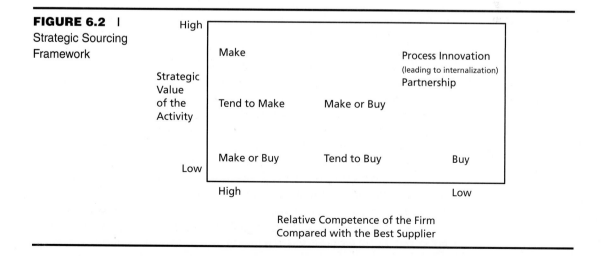

FIGURE 6.2 I
Strategic Sourcing
Framework

the industry trend, then it is possible that the firm will find itself with a low level of capability in IT and be forced to consider an outside supplier. Alternatively, a firm might lead the industry in investing in a particular activity, as Dell did in direct sales and distribution, and find itself ahead of rivals, like Hewlett-Packard, that are trying to catch up.

The strategic sourcing framework shows two conditions where a firm's control needs and capabilities coincide. One would expect that a strategically valuable activity would be one the firm was willing to invest in to raise its capability above other firms. Such an activity would clearly be performed in-house—a make decision (see the upper-left corner of Figure 6.2). Alternatively, a less valuable activity requires virtually no control over the supplier. Since suppliers have superior capabilities in producing standard goods, the activity would obviously be performed in the market—a buy decision (see the lower-right corner of Figure 6.2).

Strategic needs for control and the capabilities to perform an activity develop along different paths and often at different rates. When technologies and markets change, a firm's strategy and capabilities may become inconsistent. New market trends may force a firm to change its strategy and its needs for control over certain activities. Alternatively, a firm's relative competence may decline as new firms with superior capabilities enter the industry or existing competitors develop innovative practices. So, as discussed above, a higher strategic value need not mean that a firm is more capable than its suppliers in performing an activity. Likewise, it is possible, but rather uncommon, for a firm to execute an activity very capably but not value it strategically.[14]

Explaining Vertical Integration

The strategic sourcing framework can be used to explain two general patterns of vertical integration. The first pattern starts with the purchase of a standard good or service from a market supplier, as represented in the lower-right corner of the strategic sourcing box. When the strategic value of the input increases over time, the buyer desires more control in the relationship. This moves the activity from the lower-right corner of the box to the upper right. As it gives the firm some control, the supplier begins to specialize the input to the firm's needs.

The question at this point in the supply relationship is whether the supplier can cooperate with the firm as much as the firm wants. If so, then a stable partnership develops. Since supplier partnerships have become prevalent throughout the world economy over the past 20 years and involve a number of interesting issues, we will postpone a discussion of them until Chapter 7.

As circumstances change, however, cooperation often breaks down between the firm and its partner. When the partner cannot maintain the level of cooperation the firm requires, and the knowledge and resources needed to perform the activity are available to develop the in-house capability, the firm may vertically integrate. If investing in the capability is not feasible, the firm either can accept the costs of coordinating with the recalcitrant supplier, which reduces the effectiveness of the firm's strategy execution, or the firm can decrease its control needs by changing its strategy.

In the second pattern of vertical integration, the firm internalizes an activity that is not strategically important but for which the firm has a superior competence. In the strategic sourcing framework, the firm moves from the lower-right corner to the lower-left corner. Here the strategic value of the activity and the firm's competence to perform it are *not* aligned. The firm integrates because it *can,* not because it *should.* This misalignment involves some risk that the proliferation of in-house activities with low strategic value will increase the complexity and therefore the cost of managing the business, but without providing a strategic benefit. Nonstrategic activities performed in-house are deadweight when the organization competes with more focused firms.

Explaining Outsourcing

Outsourcing simply means the vertical deintegration of an activity. Outsourcing is one of the most important economic trends in the last 20 years and can be explained using the strategic sourcing framework. The framework highlights the two general patterns behind this trend.

The first pattern involves the deterioration of the firm's relative capability, either through (1) poor investment decisions, (2) the entry of a competitor with stronger capabilities, or (3) the appearance of a strong supplier. In spite of this deterioration, however, the strategic importance of the activity and therefore the firm's need to control it may remain high. In this case, the decision is to move from the upper-left corner to the upper-right corner in strategic sourcing framework.

When strategic value is high but relative competence is low, the firm has high control needs but cannot perform the activity in-house because it is too costly. The firm's high control needs mean it must find a supplier that is willing to give it the power to make strategically important decisions for the activity. These requirements might be, for example, control over quality, scheduling delivery, choosing technological features or design, locating facilities, or setting service levels. The supplier thus becomes a partner, allowing the firm greater discretion over the performance of the activity than would normally be allowed in a market relationship.

To bring the activity back in-house the firm must develop new process technologies to perform the activity at a level that is at least comparable to the best outside supplier. This investment is the first option in the upper-right corner of the strategic sourcing framework in Figure 6.2. The sidebar on Xerox provides an early example of a firm following this pattern.

The second pattern entails a shift in the strategy, not in the competence, of the firm. In this case, the firm's control needs decrease, even though the firm's capability to perform the activity remains higher than its supplier's.[15] Here, the firm moves from the upper left to the lower left in Figure 6.2.

Outsourcing at Xerox in the Early 1980s

There are many examples of firms that outsource strategically important activities in the interest of lowering costs. One of the best known is Xerox Corporation in the late 1970s and early 1980s. Xerox was the dominant maker of copiers until Canon entered the U.S. market in the 1970s. Canon initially sold small copiers, and its costs were much lower than Xerox's. As Canon began to introduce larger, higher-priced products, Xerox began to lose market share and, given its high fixed costs, to lose money. One of the steps Xerox took to reorganize its operations was to outsource the production of many of its components. Many of these components were strategically important, so the company had to maintain a significant degree of control over how the components were designed and produced. To gain this control, Xerox developed a number of innovations in the process of choosing and managing suppliers. First, it reduced the number of vendors from about 2,000 to 200, greatly increasing the amount of time that could be spent with any supplier. The 200 remaining were obviously the best in the pack, or "best in breed," based on Xerox's assessment of their capabilities compared with their competitors. Second, Xerox reorganized its purchasing organization to focus on specific commodities and assigned talented, experienced managers to deal with the chosen suppliers. Third, it brought these suppliers into the early stages of product development so that the components could be designed to lower costs in Xerox's assembly processes. Last, it typically assigned one supplier to each product, a practice called "single sourcing," so that the team of managers responsible for the component could work more intensely with one firm. These innovations produced a remarkable improvement in three key indicators of performance—cost, quality, and delivery—for the components included in the strategic sourcing program.

At the same time, Xerox introduced a number of process innovations in the manufacturing operations that remained in-house. These operations were benchmarked against the best outside suppliers and, in order not to be outsourced, had to perform at least as well as these suppliers on cost and quality. These internal operations began to act more like independent units that could lose the business of their internal customers if an outside supplier performed more effectively.

This process of holding internal units more accountable opened up a set of options for Xerox regarding its small set of high-performing market suppliers. With a more effective set of monitoring and evaluation tools, the firm was able to reassess whether the operations it had outsourced in distress could now be more economically produced in-house. Several of these components subsequently were reintegrated, but into a much leaner and more tightly run manufacturing division.

In this outsourcing pattern, where the strategic importance of the activity is low but it is more than competently performed relative to potential suppliers, the activity will most likely be kept in-house for a while. However, as the activity becomes less salient, investments in it are reduced, leading to a loss of its relative advantage over the market. As the firm's competence in the activity drops, the attractiveness of outsourcing rises. In this case, the organization's disinvestment in the activity relative to competitors leads to outsourcing, not the entry of innovators with stronger capabilities.

This second outsourcing pattern occurs primarily as an organization changes its strategic direction. In some cases, the strategic shift may be nothing more than a realization that much that was idiosyncratic in the organization's processes was not really valuable. Here the firm can turn effectively to suppliers with less customized inputs. A great deal of the outsourcing wave of the late 1980s and the 1990s involves shifting the in-house production of specialized, but low value-added, activities to market suppliers producing standardized goods and services.

Examples of this type of boundary decision abound in the outsourcing of parts of a firm's infrastructure. For example, PPG, a glass and specialty chemicals company, not only supplies its products to customers but provides services for its customers' downstream operations to which its products are major inputs. These services are necessary for these operations and were previously performed by the customer itself. By outsourcing these services to PPG, PPG's customers are freed to focus on more strategic activities. A second example is the emergence of a market for systems integration. Systems integrators take on the responsibility of assembling the parts of an information system for one or more of a firm's IT projects. This assembly task has traditionally been performed by the firm; by outsourcing the task it can direct its attention to more important tasks.

Outsourcing to China

Perhaps the most discussed outsourcing phenomenon in the last decade is the powerful rise of Chinese companies as suppliers of manufactured goods worldwide, but especially to the United States. Chinese imports to the U.S. just about doubled over the five years from 2000 ($100 billion) to the end of 2004 (a bit less than $200 billion). There are three possible reasons for this extraordinary rise in China-U.S. trade. One, China could have a country advantage in rapidly growing industries. Second, American firms could be replacing independent, non-Chinese suppliers, in the U.S. or elsewhere, with Chinese companies. Third, American firms could be outsourcing their production activities to China. As we will see below, all these reasons are to some extent valid.

Table 6.1 shows the dollar amounts of the 10 industries that account for about 60 percent of the total exports China sends to the United States. Providing some support for the first reason for China-U.S. trade, three of these industries appear to be fast growing: computer parts (e.g., DVD players), televisions (using DLP and LCD technologies), and perhaps certain kinds of telecom equipment. It should be noted that the Chinese advantage in these industries is not based on technological innovation, since the underlying technologies are sourced from companies in other countries (e.g., Samsung, Sharp, Texas Instruments). Instead, China is superior to other countries because of its low cost of production. The rest of the industries (apparel, toys, and so on) in Table 6.1 are clearly in the mature stage of the industry life cycle and have little, if any, sophisticated engineering content.

Teasing out clear answers to the other two reasons is not so easy. To see why this is so, let's look first at a large U.S. toy company, Hasbro. At the end of 1999, Hasbro began a restructuring program to eliminate in-house manufacturing and

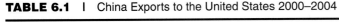

TABLE 6.1 I China Exports to the United States 2000–2004

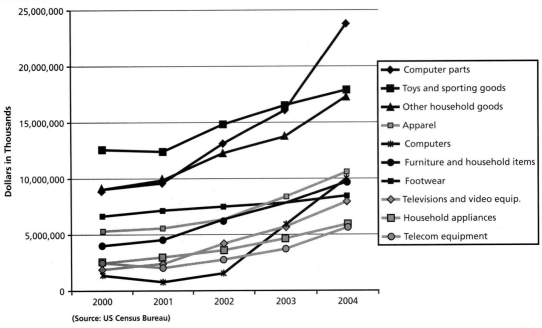

(Source: US Census Bureau)

shift production to independent Chinese firms, whose quality was controlled through a Hong Kong company. This is a clear case of outsourcing to low-cost Chinese suppliers. Now let's examine sourcing practices in the apparel industry. By the late 1990s the apparel industry already had a long history of using outside firms for clothing production. Here, the rise of China, as exemplified by the remarkable expansion of Luen Thai, a Chinese company in Dongguan that makes clothes for Polo, is not due to outsourcing from an internal unit as in the case of Hasbro. Rather, apparel companies switched from a non-Chinese to a Chinese supplier. So both reasons two and three may be valid depending on the firm and the industry.

Given China's superior competence based on low input costs, what control issues between customer and supplier might complicate this trend towards buying from Chinese companies? There are two ways to consider this problem. First, let's look again at the top 10 industries. What kind of control problems do they suggest? We cannot be absolutely sure. But because these industries are generally discrete commodities, such as furniture and clothes, there is little indication that a highly specialized relationship between buyer and supplier might emerge. In these industries, supplier processes in operations and logistics to assure superior quality and on-time delivery, for example, are standardized, and not specific to a particular customer. Second, remember that the cost advantage of Chinese firms is due to being in China itself. This means that the customer can find other Chinese suppliers with the same high levels of efficiency. Such strong competition in the supplier market induces the firm's current vendor to cooperate and therefore lowers the risk that control problems will become significant.

The causes and consequences of the Chinese outsourcing phenomenon are thus not at all surprising. They are based on the low costs of a developing country whose economy is growing very rapidly and whose labor force is very capable. Further, extensive competition among Chinese suppliers forces them to behave cooperatively in their supply relationships. Applying the strategic sourcing framework, then, we can say that U.S. firms outsource to China in order to move to a more competent (more efficient) supply base without incurring markedly higher transaction costs.

Additional Issues

Differences among Types of Uncertainty

These patterns of vertical integration and outsourcing are complicated somewhat by the firm's response to uncertainty. As discussed above, coupled with asset specificity, greater uncertainty over aspects of the supply relationship increases the relative advantage of in-house production. However, different types of uncertainty do not have the same effect on a firm's vertical integration decision. For example, it seems natural to ask why a firm would want to increase uncertainty in its own operations by vertically integrating a volatile activity, as opposed to remaining flexible by continuing to buy in the market.

As we mentioned above, two types of uncertainty have been frequently found to affect vertical integration decisions: volume uncertainty and technological uncertainty. Volume uncertainty concerns the volatility in the firm's demand for the supplier's input. Technological uncertainty involves the rate of change in the technologies used to produce the input.

Volume uncertainty is related to control over production scheduling decisions. The need for this kind of control increases as volume levels become more difficult to specify. Since both stock outs and high inventory costs can be strategically expensive when delivery is a key value driver, it is not surprising that empirical research generally has found that high volume uncertainty is associated with vertical integration, especially when supplier markets are not competitive.[16]

The research results for technological uncertainty are quite different. Several studies have shown that firms tend to outsource rather than vertically integrate when technological uncertainty is high and supplier markets are competitive.[17] The reason is that companies prefer to avoid investing in a technology when its viability is uncertain and when suppliers are willing to make these investments. As technological requirements shift, the firm makes the switch from the old to the new technology by changing suppliers. Thus, unlike changes in volume requirements, technological change alters the value offered by a supplier. A shift in technology neutralizes the value of customization by the old supplier, so the firm suffers lower switching costs.

This effect of technological uncertainty applies to those technologies in which a firm has little or no proprietary interest. When there are proprietary concerns, the need to control the transfer of technological information reduces the tendency to shift uncertainty onto the market. In this case, the firm makes a trade-off between the strategic advantage of controlling the unique path of the technology through in-house production and the advantage of technological flexibility through sourcing the technology from market suppliers.

The Problem of Consistency

How a firm manages its boundaries has an indirect but potentially significant effect on its ability to execute its strategy across all activities. Organizations perform more effectively when their activities fit together to form a consistent whole rather than a set of fragmented parts (see Chapter 5). Establishing and maintaining consistency requires the joint coordination and control of a group of activities, each of which becomes increasingly specialized to the others. How much the organization gains from this interdependence determines how much control is required over the relationships among the activities. The greater the benefit, the greater the control, and the more likely the organization will internalize the activities that are complementary.

Industry Dynamics

The dominant theory about how industry development affects vertical integration decisions is based on the stages of industry evolution. In the early stages of industry development, the volume required by a start-up firm is too small to justify an investment by potential suppliers. Consequently, start-ups produce for their own needs through vertical integration. As the industry grows and start-ups increase their volume, markets emerge for some inputs since the needs of several start-ups can be served together at lower cost. After the industry experiences a shakeout and passes through maturity into decline, the survivors will bring the production of inputs back in-house, since suppliers will not be able to aggregate demand efficiently.[18]

These arguments apply primarily to industries whose inputs are sufficiently specialized that firms in adjacent industries cannot profitably shift production into supplying the start-up firms at low volume. But the technologies of most new industries are not this distinct. Most start-ups buy some of their inputs from suppliers that also serve older industries since the suppliers have lower costs through economies of scope.

Make or Buy for Applications Software: An Extended Example[19]

One of the most important and difficult problems firms face is the management of their software infrastructure. Companies that can afford to maintain large information service departments develop a substantial amount of software for internal use. But there has been a very strong trend toward reducing the size of these departments to lower corporate costs. Correspondingly there has been a marked rise in the number of software vendors selling standardized solutions to problems that firms have been treating as nonstandard, such as manufacturing systems, human resource systems, and logistics systems. The market for software development, software packages, and implementation has thus jumped substantially in size, especially as firms outsource to India. The underlying economic principles of this industry can be understood in large part using the vertical integration and sourcing models discussed above. The key is to focus on relative technical competence on the one hand and the need to control investment in learning on the other.

Consider Southwest Airlines' attempt to vertically integrate its reservation system. For many years Southwest sourced the design and operation of this system from SABRE, which originally was the information services arm of American Airlines. Southwest's arrangement with SABRE worked reasonably well since the service to Southwest was kept distinct from SABRE's main reservation operation. As Southwest grew and its passengers began to demand a more sophisticated system, Southwest decided to build its own, forsaking SABRE's offer to build the new system for a fee. Unfortunately, Southwest's initial estimate of its own technical competence to build the system in-house fell short. So many problems arose in testing the new system that Southwest was forced to return to SABRE for an interim solution. This is a clear case of an attempt to vertically integrate an important activity that failed, at least initially, because of problems in technical competence. These problems prevented Southwest from fully controlling its reservations process directly and therefore inhibited it from innovating to improve value and lower cost.

Changing the Business Process

Firms that decide to modify or update their software-enabled business processes start by asking, "Do we want this process to be best practice in our industry or do we want it to be strategic?" If the answer is "best practice," then the answer seems to be: Find a software package. However, a suitable package is not always available. And, even if a package is available, it is not clear whether the package needs to be customized, who should tailor the software, if necessary, and who should manage any related organizational changes that may be required.

Firms that want to make their business processes strategic face similar difficulties. A key choice here is between building an internal capability through greater control over and involvement in the project, or exploiting the capabilities of an outside partner with broad experience of the business process or the underlying technologies. Most firms do not have all the technical skills they would like to have, much less all the process knowledge.

FIGURE 6.3 | Make or Buy for Software

	A. Business Process Change		B. The Software Sourcing Decision	
	New Business Process		**New Business Process**	
	Unique	Standard	Unique	Standard
Unique	**SpeedCo** The process was and will continue to be distinctive, unique, and maybe strategic.	**DistCo** A set of different processes will become "best practice."	**SpeedCo** Package not an option. Close control of both development and rollout deemed desirable.	**DistCo** Package selected. Vendor lead on rollout deemed desirable.
Standard	**NetCo** An old process will become innovative, but will not remain unique for long.	**WaterCo** The process was and will continue to be "best practice."	**NetCo** Package used for base code. Close collaboration with vendor.	**WaterCo** Package selected. Implementation managed internally but with strict performance expectations.

Old Business Process label appears at the left, spanning the Unique/Standard rows.

The key to these sourcing decisions is having a clear grasp of whether the current business process is unique or standard and whether the future business process will be unique or standard (see Figure 6.3). These two questions shape the knowledge management problem presented by the software application project.

A *standard* process is the same as processes in other firms. Processes become standard because they are shaped by accounting principles, industry rules, customer expectations, supplier practices, or regulatory pressures. Standard processes are easy for outsiders to grasp. For example, one would expect an experienced consultant to be able to sketch out the data model of a standard process (e.g., general ledger).

On the other hand, a *unique* process is distinctive in some important way compared to processes used by rivals. A firm's process may be distinct relative to its competitors because the firm offers different products or services, because the firm's structure is more centralized or decentralized than others, because its customers are larger or smaller or more regulated, or because its suppliers have different competencies. Processes may be unique by design, or by accident. They also may be distinct because the firm is either a leader or laggard in product or process innovation.

The current business process can therefore be either standard or unique, and the new process can be standard or unique. These four alternative situations are shown in Figure 6.3, part A.

1. Unique to standard   The most common situation is found in this cell: Here a firm with a process that is relatively unique wants to make the process standard, or "best practice." For example, a distribution firm, which we will call DistCo, grew from a regional to a national firm in the previous decade, primarily by acquisition. As it expanded, DistCo's core process, order fulfillment, began to vary across the facilities it acquired, since their processes were typically based on home-grown software. This variation presented a number of business problems for DistCo and its customers, so DistCo decided to standardize its order fulfillment processes throughout the firm with a package that had been widely adopted in the industry. The company did not consider this process to be a source of its competitive advantage—the firm simply wanted to achieve parity with its competitors.

2. Unique to unique   In contrast to DistCo, some firms value being unique in a particular activity. SpeedCo, a regional service firm specializing in customer service, also had an order fulfillment process that was unlike those of its competitors. At SpeedCo, this uniqueness was enabled by home-grown software, but by design, not accident. SpeedCo's entire company culture was unique in its industry—everything about the employees, from their attire to their actions, said "speed" to the company's customers. The purpose of the new order fulfillment process was to make the firm's services even more effective. The company thus believed this new process would be a key value driver and enhance its competitive position. The new process required new client-server technology, and hence new enabling software, which the firm assumed would have to be significantly, if not completely, customized to its requirements.

3. Standard to unique   The most compelling reason for a firm to shift from a standard to a unique process is that the firm has a new idea of how to design and execute it. A good example is NetCo, a firm that wanted a cross-functional process for managing its extensive telecommunications network. The new process would combine asset management, an accounting activity, with network management, an operations activity. Both the existing asset management and network management processes were "standard." The asset management process was shaped mainly by accounting principles and the network management process by professional convention. In the new process, network operators would have complete responsibility for managing the network as well as maintaining the firm's complex asset management records. The new approach would offer some operating economies but would not differentiate NetCo's service offerings to its customers. However, while the process envisioned would be unique in the industry, NetCo believed that after a while other firms would want to adopt a similar approach. Thus in the short run, the new process would be unique, but in the long run it would become standard.

4. Standard to standard   Finally, some firms have processes that have always been standard, and they would like to keep them this way. But process requirements are altered as products, customers, and underlying technology change. Our example here is the human resources department of a utility, WaterCo. Its existing process for maintaining employee records was common in the industry. Its enabling software, custom developed for WaterCo nearly two decades before by a consulting firm, included most features recommended by industry experts at that time. But current "best practice" in human resources was to shift record maintenance to employees. WaterCo wanted to maintain competitive parity by achieving the efficiencies promised by this new design.

Sourcing Decisions

These firms had to decide whether to purchase existing software or packages or build the software themselves. If appropriate codified knowledge is available and competitively priced, it is likely that a software package will be purchased. But it is important to control the developer's knowledge of the firm's business process and the software. Figure 6.3, part B, summarizes the sourcing decisions made in the four cases.

1. Unique to standard   DistCo selected a well-known package (e.g., SAP) to enable its order fulfillment process. This package embodied most of the technical and process knowledge that the firm needed. DistCo hired a consulting firm to provide parameterization and integration services, expecting to leverage its accumulated experience with the implementation of the software. DistCo discouraged learning on the part of the consultants and minimized the degree to which the software or processes would be tailored. The price DistCo paid for this choice was a difficult and painful implementation since the consultants did not know all of DistCo's old processes well enough to train the various users well or to persuade them that the new standard process was better. Considerable disruption and turnover ensued.

2. Unique to unique   SpeedCo never seriously considered any packages. It carefully evaluated bids from several large consulting firms. SpeedCo believed that it lacked some necessary technical know-how and thought at first that consulting firms might be better at designing the new process than it would. But in the end SpeedCo decided for several reasons to design the new process and develop the new software internally. First, it believed that the consultants would push them toward a more standard, less distinctive process; it worried that the consultants would not be willing to acquire much new specific knowledge about SpeedCo and its processes. Second, it was concerned that it might eventually have a conflict of interest with the consultants who could not be controlled by noncompete clauses in a contract. SpeedCo did not want knowledge about the sources of its competitive distinctiveness to leak out. Third, it concluded that the consultants did not have better project management and change management skills than it did. To get access to the particular technical and management skills SpeedCo felt it needed, the company hired contract workers and then phased them out as their skills were transferred to internal staff.

3. Standard to unique   NetCo purchased a package as a starting point for its application and hired a consultant to build the rest of its application around the package. The consultant worked in close cooperation with internal staff. NetCo exercised considerable influence over staffing assignments and methods. NetCo managers believed the supplier had invested far more effort in the project than contracted for, perhaps several times over their estimates. NetCo had not made an effort to form a royalty agreement with the supplier, but it agreed that the software being developed for the company would certainly be attractive to other firms.

4. Standard to standard   WaterCo selected a dominant package in the market for human resource applications (e.g., PeopleSoft). While the company used a consulting firm's knowledge to complete the design of the new process, it elected to manage the rest of the project internally with fairly specific specifications and performance outcomes. WaterCo received competitive bids from suppliers but was an early implementer of this package, and thus faced a situation where too few consulting firms were trying to serve too many purchasers, essentially not a very competitive situation.

To summarize, a firm trying to move from a unique process to a process enabled by a package will find rollout easier if, by virtue of some earlier engagement with the firm, suppliers are familiar with its processes. Those firms whose current processes are standard, or at least easy for the consulting firms to understand, will find implementing a package less painful. Firms moving from standard processes to unique ones will sometimes want temporary rather than long-term uniqueness. For that reason, their situation is appropriate for collaboration with a software vendor in a shared risk–shared reward arrangement leading to commercial exploitation. Such an agreement might provide royalties from future sales or future engagements to the innovating firm.

Firms that want long-term uniqueness in their processes will usually need to control the vendor's use of the knowledge acquired in the project. This is accomplished more easily by segmenting and restricting the breadth and depth of vendor knowledge than it is by contractual agreement. Controlling the flow of information unique to the firm is difficult, but controlling the flow of codified knowledge, such as that in a software project, can be nearly impossible.

Summary

In this chapter we have examined a range of approaches to vertical integration and outsourcing. First, the differences between relations with employees and relations with suppliers need to be recognized in terms of their implications for the firm's control over decision making. Simply put, suppliers have greater discretion in their actions and so are harder to control. Second, who owns an asset should be guided by who benefits most from owning it. Third, an asset from which the firm derives a significant benefit is obviously strategic if it lowers the firm's costs or raises value to the customer. So strategic assets are typically vertically integrated, and nonstrategic assets are bought from suppliers.

In addition to control issues, firms vary in their competence to execute activities. In some cases, control needs are high and so is the firm's competence in performing the activity; the logical consequence is vertical integration. Likewise, when control needs are low (e.g., for a commodity) and the firm's competence low, the input is bought from a supplier. Both the efficient boundaries model and the strategic sourcing framework, described in the chapter, outline the range of sourcing possibilities. The strategic sourcing framework in particular illustrates the dynamics of vertical integration and outsourcing as the firm's control needs and competence change over time.

Summary Points

- Decisions regarding a firm's boundaries can be critical to a firm's strategy and economic performance.

- Employees are different from suppliers in that they give up control, within legal and socially acceptable bounds, over those aspects of work that cannot be specified in adequate detail.

- An organization draws its boundaries around those activities that it can derive a higher value from controlling compared with suppliers.

- The attractiveness of vertical integration over buying from a supplier increases under two conditions: uncertainty and asset specialization.

- Specialization is a necessary but not sufficient condition for higher economic value.

- The strategic value of an asset correlates highly with the benefits from controlling the decisions necessary to sustain and develop it.

- A firm shifts its boundary either when its strategy changes and therefore its need for control over an activity increases or decreases, or when a supplier stops ceding the degree of control the firm requires.

- The three control problems that have motivated vertical integration decisions involve (1) the economic return to the supply relationship, (2) supplier investments in assets and human resources, and (3) a supplier's handling of strategic information about its own operations and about the firm.

- Even though a firm would benefit from controlling an activity, it may lack basic competencies to perform it.

- The efficient boundaries model argues that a firm should consider the sum of transaction *and* production costs together in making its decision to bring an activity in-house.

- The strategic sourcing framework shows the importance of both control needs and a firm's relative competence in performing an activity.

- Vertical integration usually occurs because of control problems with the supplier over strategically important decisions.

- Outsourcing occurs either when a firm loses its competence to perform an activity or when the activity ceases to be strategically important.

- Firms typically vertically integrate when volume uncertainty is high, but they may remain deintegrated when technological uncertainty is high, given a competitive supply base.

- Efforts to remain consistent within a firm may determine boundary decisions.

- The extent of vertical integration may be influenced by the industry life cycle.

Questions for Practice

Think how you would answer these questions for your current company, your previous place of work, or a business you are studying:

1. How does your firm handle relationships with suppliers that have assets specialized to your needs?

2. If your firm faces technological uncertainty, how does this uncertainty affect your make or buy decisions?

3. If your firm faces volume uncertainty, how does this uncertainty affect your make or buy decisions?

4. How often has your firm brought supplier activities in-house in response to high transaction costs?

5. How has your firm traded off transaction and production costs in its relationships with key suppliers?

6. What are the key aspects of control your firm requires over supplier decisions?

7. What are the key competencies your firm lacks that keep it tied to noncooperative suppliers?

8. How does your firm structure its strategic sourcing relationships to improve cooperation with suppliers?

9. How often has your firm outsourced an activity because suppliers were more competent?

10. What constraints does consistency among your firm's activities put on its make or buy decisions?

End Notes

1. The nature of the employment relation is a venerable topic of discussion and research in economics and organization. A central reference is H. Simon, *Models of Man* (New York: John Wiley, 1957); see also Oliver Williamson, Michael Wachter, and Jeffrey Harris, "Understanding the Employment Relation: The Analysis of Idiosyncratic Exchange," *Bell Journal of Economics* 6 (1975), pp. 270–78.

2. See Scott Masten, "A Legal Basis for the Firm," *Journal of Law, Economics, and Organization* 4 (1988), pp. 181–98.

3. The transaction cost theory of vertical integration is based on Ronald Coase's insights in "The Nature of the Firm," *Economica* 4 (1937), pp. 386–405. The theory has been developed primarily by Oliver Williamson. His seminal books are *Markets and Hierarchies* (New York: Free Press, 1975) and *The Economic Institutions of Capitalism* (New York: Free Press, 1985); see also Armen A. Alchian and Harold Demsetz, "Production, Information Costs, and Economic Organization," *American Economic Review* 62 (1972), pp. 772–95; and Benjamin Klein, Robert G. Crawford, and Armen Alchian, "Vertical Integration, Appropriable Rents, and the Competitive Contracting Process," *Journal of Law and Economics* 21, no. 2 (1978), pp. 297–326. For key empirical studies on transaction cost theory, see Gordon Walker and David Weber, "The Transaction Cost Approach to Vertical Integration," *Administrative Science Quarterly* 29 (1984), pp. 373–91; Gordon Walker and Laura Poppo, "Profit Centers, Single Source Suppliers and Transaction Costs," *Administrative Science Quarterly* 36 (1991), pp. 66–88; Scott Masten, James Meehan, and Edward Snyder, "The Costs of Organization," *Journal of Law, Economics, and Organization* 7 (Spring 1991); Scott Masten, "The Organization of Production: Evidence from the Aerospace Industry," *Journal of Law and Economics* 27 (1984), pp. 403–17; Erin Anderson and David Schmittlein, "Integration of the Sales Force: An Empirical Examination," *RAND Journal of Economics* 15 (1984), pp. 385–95.

4. Paul Joskow, "Contract Duration and Relationship-Specific Investments," *American Economic Review* 77 (1987), pp. 168–85.

5. For a test of the importance of vertical integration decisions on firm performance, see Jack Nickerson and Brian Silverman, "Why Firms Want to Organize Efficiently and What Keeps Them from Doing So: Inappropriate Governance, Performance and Adaptation in a Deregulated Industry," *Administrative Science Quarterly* 48 (2003), pp. 433–65.

6. The central works that lay out the property rights theory of vertical integration are Sanford Grossman and Oliver Hart, "The Costs and Benefits of Ownership: A Theory of Vertical and Lateral Integration," *Journal of Political Economy* 94 (1986), pp. 691–719; Oliver Hart and John Moore, "Property Rights and the Nature of the Firm," *Journal of Political Economy* 98 (1990), pp. 1119–58; and Oliver Hart, *Firms, Contracts and Financial Structure* (New York: Clarendon Press, 1995).

7. For a reasonable test of the property rights approach, see George P. Baker and Thomas N. Hubbard, "Make versus Buy in Trucking: Asset Ownership, Job Design and Information," *American Economic Review* 93 (2003), pp. 551–72.

8. For an interesting perspective on alternating governance, see Jack A. Nickerson and Todd R. Zenger, "Being Efficiently Fickle: A Dynamic Theory of Organizational Choice," *Organization Science* 13 (2002), pp. 547–66.

9. For a similar list of control dimensions, see Martin Perry, "Vertical Integration: Determinants and Effects," in *Handbook of Industrial Organization*, R. Willig and R. Schmalensee, eds. (Amsterdam: North Holland, 1988), Chap. 4.

10. George P. Baker and Thomas Hubbard, "Make versus Buy in Trucking: Asset Ownership, Job Design and Information," *American Economic Review* 93 (2003), pp. 551–72.

11. See Richard Langlois, "Transaction-cost Economics in Real Time," *Industrial and Corporate Change* 1 (1992), pp. 99–127; Richard Langlois, "Transaction Costs, Production Costs and the Passage of Time," in *Coasean Economics: Law and Economics and the New Institutional Economics,* Steven G. Medema, ed. (Dordrecht: Kluwer Academic Publishers, 1997), pp. 1–21.

12. See Oliver Williamson, "The Economics of Organization: The Transaction Cost Approach," *American Journal of Sociology* 87 (1981), pp. 548–77.

13. For an early version of this approach, see Gordon Walker, "Strategic Sourcing, Vertical Integration and Transaction Costs," *Interfaces* 18 (1988), pp. 62–93.

14. For an interesting model describing how transaction costs and capabilities interact over time, see Michael Jacobides and Sidney Winter, "The Co-Evolution of Capabilities and Transaction Costs: Explaining the Institutional Structure of Production," *Strategic Management Journal* 26 (2005), pp. 395–413.

15. See Ravi Venkatesan, "Strategic Sourcing: To Make or Not to Make," *Harvard Business Review*, November–December (1992), pp. 98–107.

16. See Marvin Lieberman, "Determinants of Vertical Integration: An Empirical Test," *Journal of Industrial Economics* 39 (1991) pp. 451–66; Dennis Carlton, "Vertical Integration in Competitive Markets under Uncertainty," *Journal of Industrial Economics* 27 (1979), pp. 189–209; Gordon Walker and David Weber, "Supplier Competition, Uncertainty and Make or Buy Decisions," *Academy of Management Journal* 30 (1987), pp. 589–96.

17. See Gordon Walker and David Weber, "Supplier Competition, Uncertainty and Make or Buy Decisions," *Academy of Management Journal* 30 (1987), pp. 589–96; and Srinivasan Balakrishnan and Birger Wernerfelt, "Technical Change, Competition and Vertical Integration," *Strategic Management Journal* 7 (1986), pp. 347–59.

18. See G. Stigler, "The Division of Labor Is Limited by the Extent of the Market," *Journal of Political Economy* 59 (1951), pp. 185–93.

19. This example is based on Cynthia Beath and Gordon Walker, "Outsourcing of Applications Software: A Knowledge Management Perspective," *Proceedings of the Thirty First Annual Hawaii International Conference on Systems Sciences* VI (1998), pp. 666–74.

CHAPTER 7

Partnering

Roadmap

In Chapter 6 on strategic boundaries, we analyzed the conditions under which firms vertically integrate or outsource a specific activity. We left for this chapter a discussion of partnerships. Firms become partners when they share control of an activity in order to achieve benefits they would not be able to attain from acting individually. The strategic value of the activity therefore has to be high, and each firm's competence to perform the activity alone should be low.

Although partnering in business is an ancient practice, in the past 20 years awareness of its potential benefits has increased tremendously. The trend in partnership formation has accelerated throughout the economies of advanced industrialized nations. In this chapter we will examine the reasons for the rise in partnership activity as well as its costs and benefits. The chapter is structured as follows:

- Recent Trends in Partnership Formation
  - Global Integration
  - The Diffusion of Japanese Partnership Practices
  - The Diffusion of Supplier Partnerships
  - The Outsourcing Wave in Services
  - The Rise of Supply Chain Management Practices
  - The Growth of Technology-Intensive Industries
  - The Emergence of Cooperation in Regional Networks
- Motivations behind Partnerships
  - Technology Transfer and Development
  - Market Access
  - Cost Reduction
  - Risk Reduction
  - Change in Industry Structure

Recent Trends in Partnership Formation

Partnering is not a recent phenomenon. For instance, in the early 1900s, many U.S. organizations formed joint ventures with non-U.S. firms to enter their home country markets. The U.S. company typically supplied the product, and the host country firm provided marketing and distribution. Joint ventures in global extractive industries are another example. Firms in industries such as oil and aluminum have partnered for many years for reasons of cost and risk reduction. The motivations behind these early partnerships remain relevant today.

However, over the past 20 years, partnerships have become much more frequent. To show how diverse partnerships have become and how significant they can be for a firm's strategy, it is useful to lay out the origins of this trend and its implications. We will briefly examine seven underlying reasons for recent partnering activity.

- The global integration of manufacturing and service industries.
- The diffusion of Japanese partnership practices.
- The diffusion of partnerships with suppliers.
- The rise of outsourcing as an accepted practice.
- The rise of supply chain management practices.
- The growth of technology-intensive industries.
- The emergence of regional networks of cooperating firms.

These developments are distinct. Each has specific implications for the increasing emphasis firms are placing on partnerships, and together they represent a broad movement toward increased interfirm cooperation.

Global Integration[1]

The first development is an increase in the global integration of manufacturing and service industries. As noted above, partnering has always been a preferred method of entering a foreign market. As more nations shift their political systems and economic policies to some form of democratic capitalism, opportunities are created for companies to enter these new markets and to produce inputs locally or buy them from local firms. The expansion of international markets makes it necessary for global firms to form partnerships across national boundaries in order to exercise control over up- or downstream activities performed locally. Examples of partnerships formed to penetrate international markets abound in such industries as airlines, telecommunications, semiconductors, manufactured goods, professional services, and media.

The Diffusion of Japanese Partnership Practices[2]

Japanese firms have led this globalization trend in a broad array of industries. These firms have extensive expertise in supplier partnerships at home and have exported this knowledge to markets in the United States and Europe. Since the early 1950s, with the success of the Toyota model and the reconstitution of large industrial groups such as Fuyo, Mitsubishi, Mitsui, and Sumitomo, Japanese firms have demonstrated that interfirm cooperation brings high benefits.

The origin of the Japanese subcontracting system is complex, based on a combination of prewar national policies and postwar economic opportunities. However, after Japanese managers described the system to numerous visitors who then conveyed the model to their U.S. counterparts, it was easy for non-Japanese companies to appreciate its virtues. Adoption of the model, with its emphasis on partnerships with a small group of competent suppliers, has since been widespread.

The Diffusion of Supplier Partnerships[3]

U.S. manufacturing firms had difficulty in responding to Japanese competition in the late 1970s and early 1980s and faced pressures from capital and consumer markets to improve performance by reducing costs and increasing quality. Many U.S. firms recognized that their production costs were too high for many strategically important components and were forced to outsource them to more efficient suppliers. Since the importance of these inputs required ongoing control over their design and production, these firms selected their new suppliers partly because they were willing to cooperate over the long term. As a result, both the buyer and supplier manufacturing communities experienced significant changes in their contracting and relationship management practices. In two well-known cases, Xerox and Ford, the companies learned the details of successful supplier partnerships from their Japanese joint venture partners, Fuji-Xerox and Mazda, respectively. The supplier partnership programs of both these companies were instrumental for the turnaround of these firms and led to a stream of visitors from other U.S. companies who subsequently implemented their own supplier management innovations.[4]

The Outsourcing Wave in Services[5]

In association with the need for cost reduction in manufacturing industries, a broad emphasis on outsourcing emerged first in the United States and subsequently in other countries, particularly in Europe. This trend involved primarily corporate services such as information technology, logistics, and human resources. Suppliers in industries specializing in these activities shifted their business practices to offer customers lower costs and at the same time greater control than was normally available in more arm's-length market relationships. Although in many cases the benefits expected from outsourcing have not been fully realized, firms continue to trade off higher control in-house for lower costs in the market as suppliers specializing in outsourcing expand. Partnership activity has increased not only because firms have an incentive to outsource, but also because there are more firms selling alliances as a viable type of supply relationship.

The Rise of Supply Chain Management Practices

Another area where partnership practices have diffused extensively is in supply chain management. There has been a remarkable rise in cooperation between buyers and suppliers to reduce cost and improve delivery time in the supply chain both domestically and globally. Supply chain management involves the establishment of close relationships both between a producer and its distributor and between a producer and its suppliers of materials and components. Often, these partnership systems involve logistics providers, such as Federal Express or UPS, as well as trucking and rail firms. The relationship between Procter & Gamble and Wal-Mart is a good example of this kind of closely coordinated alliance.

The Growth of Technology-Intensive Industries[6]

Over the past 20 years, partnering has also emerged with the considerable expansion of new industries based on innovative product and process technologies. The firms in these industries have grown and prospered to an unprecedented degree through interfirm partnerships. Biotechnology, semiconductors, software, and advanced materials are examples of industries following this powerful trend. The rapid growth in the number of firms in these industries has led to a proliferation of partnerships both between large firms to transfer complementary technologies and between large incumbents and small start-ups with potentially valuable technical innovations. As we will see below, the motivations behind the partnership activity in these industries are numerous and strategically very important.

The Emergence of Cooperation in Regional Networks

Finally, a number of observers have described the cooperative arrangements of small firms clustered densely together in small- and medium-sized communities within geographical regions. These clusters of firms specialize in the production of manufactured goods such as textiles, rugs, and ceramics. The firms share capital, information, technology, and inputs from local suppliers to which they are tightly connected. They also take advantage of a common pool of labor that has expertise in the technologies required for these businesses. Silicon Valley south of San Francisco in northern California is an excellent example of such a region.[7]

Motivations behind Partnerships

These seven trends have increased the salience of partnering. In addition to lowering the costs or risks associated with an activity, a partnership offers the firm some control over important dimensions of the supply or co-investment relationship that would not be available in a market contract. What do firms want to control? What are the strategic stimuli that spur firms to enter into a partnership? Below we will discuss five motivations:

- Technology transfer and development.
- Market access.
- Cost reduction.
- Risk reduction.
- Change in industry structure.

From a strategic perspective, the first four of these are sufficient for establishing a partnership.[8] But the last motivation—forming a partnership to affect industry structure—is usually not enough by itself to create an alliance. A change in industry structure influences the partners' market positions indirectly, making it hard to predict and observe. But because it may have a long-term positive impact on the firms' performance, industry change is a valid rationale for partnering when coupled with other motivations whose benefits are easier to assess.

Technology Transfer and Development

A common reason for a partnership is the transfer or joint development of innovative technology. Although large incumbent firms may have the resources to invest in new technologies (IBM, for example, has a tradition of excellent in-house R&D), technological change makes it difficult to keep up with the pace of development. So many incumbents are forced to partner with innovative start-ups.

The high rate of innovation in almost all industries where technology plays a key role is driven by new companies. The entrepreneurs are frequently former employees of an incumbent firm that failed to support their technological ideas. Start-up and incumbent managers often exploit their earlier connection by forming a partnership. Complementing the incumbent firm's need to access the entrepreneur's technology, the start-up often needs the large firm's capabilities, such as marketing skills and distribution, which are offered in exchange for exposure to the start-up's technological expertise.[9]

However, technology development partnerships are formed only among incumbents and start-ups. Large firms with complementary technologies have often formed partnerships for joint product development. Corning Glass, before its transformation into an optical components company, was legendary as an exploiter of joint venture opportunities. It formed alliances with a range of companies, including Dow Chemical, Asahi, Siemens, Mitsubishi, PPG, and Samsung.

Large firm partnerships are also common when there is competition within an industry for the dominant standard in a technology. Alliances of this sort have been common in the semiconductor industry in all stages of its history. The current battle over high definition DVD technology between Sony (Blu-ray) and Toshiba (HD-DVD) involves a host of partners on each side.

Large firms also establish partnerships in order to share knowledge about complementary technologies. For example, Motorola and Toshiba formed an alliance in the 1980s in part to share design and production technologies for memory and microprocessor chips. Toshiba had become a leader in the memory business because of lower costs, whereas Motorola had a strong capability in developing and manufacturing microprocessors. The memory and microprocessor businesses had traditionally benefited from communicating with each other. Memory engineers learned from the product innovations developed by microprocessor units, while microprocessor engineers learned from the process innovations in memory chip design and production. With the loss of the memory business to the Japanese and Koreans in the mid-1980s, U.S. microprocessor firms like Intel and Motorola were unable to exploit the cross-chip relationship in-house. Motorola's alliance with Toshiba, through the Nippon-Motorola subsidiary in Tokyo, was an attempt to recreate the benefit of cross-fertilization between the technologies.

A third type of large firm partnership focuses on interfirm learning of process innovations. The NUMMI joint venture between General Motors and Toyota in Fremont, California, established to produce General Motors cars with Toyota managerial and operations technology, is an example of such an alliance. In this case, General Motors attempted to learn Toyota's more effective managerial techniques and more efficient production techniques, while Toyota gained from learning about building small cars in the United States and from accessing valuable strategic information about a major U.S. competitor.[10] Many joint ventures and partnerships between U.S. firms and their Japanese counterparts in the 1980s, when competition with Japan was particularly intense, were motivated by the necessity of learning Japanese practices in a broad range of activities such as procurement, operations, logistics, human resource management, and technology development.

A final type of technological interdependence motivating large firm partnerships is patent sharing. This reason for partnering is especially prevalent in the semiconductor industry, where established firms hold large libraries of patents, many of which lie outside the current investment paths of their owners but are valuable for developing related technologies in other firms. Under these conditions, a partnership between two firms whose libraries contain sets of complementary patents clearly benefits both companies.[11]

Market Access

Gaining access to a new geographic market is one of the most common reasons for partnership formation. Such alliances are frequent in cases of international expansion where the costs of entry for a foreign firm can be prohibitively high. Entry costs can be raised either by regulatory restrictions or by difficulties in acquiring the knowledge or assets necessary to compete.[12]

In some countries, the partnership may be with a government monopoly, such as a telecommunications or energy agency, which has sole access to the local market. As countries deregulate their markets, however, the benefit of such a partnership shifts from market access to becoming an incumbent in a newly competitive industry. Incumbency can have either positive or negative effects on economic performance after deregulation, as discussed in Chapter 4.

When markets are not run by government monopolies but are highly concentrated, partnerships may be the only way for nondomestic firms to enter. For example, the major U.S. airlines have partnered with almost every non-U.S. airline to build global networks of alliances. These alliances substitute for direct entry into foreign markets. Each of these global alliance networks provides its customers with more efficient access to a larger number of airports worldwide. American Airlines' Oneworld alliance with British Airways, Canadair, Cathay Pacific, and others is an example of such a consortium. It gives customers of American Airlines access to the systems of the airline's partners as an extension of American's routes. United Airlines competes with American's consortium through partnerships with Air Canada, SAS, Lufthansa, All Nippon Airways, and others, a system called the Star Alliance. Delta Airlines has its own set of partners, and so on.

Another factor limiting market access is local content restrictions. In many countries, the finished goods of foreign firms are required to include a nontrivial percentage of locally produced components. But firms in the host country may be unable to achieve acceptable quality levels or provide adequate technical support. Local content restrictions may thus force a foreign company to form partnerships with domestic firms in order to transfer the technology necessary for high-quality production and service.

A final motivation for partnering to achieve market access occurs in alliances with local distributors. If a market has few distribution alternatives, the dominant distributor will have high market power. This firm has the ability to present the producer's goods to the end user in a way that may be consistent with the distributor's goals but not with the producer's business strategy.[13] Some foreign producers, however, may be large enough to create incentives for the distributor to form an alliance. A partnership may then be formed so that the producer has more control over how its products are presented.

Cost Reduction

Another major reason to form a strategic alliance is cost reduction. Costs can be reduced by combining the partners' activities, strengthening the learning curve based on higher cumulative volume, or coordinating the product flow between two partners. Each of these three sources of lower cost creates a different type of alliance.

An example of partnerships formed to achieve lower cost through shared activities is a consortium of health care companies. Health care organizations join together to reduce operating costs, especially in procurement. By building multihospital systems or allying with a service company, such as VHA, hospitals are able to lower their purchasing costs substantially. Service companies also provide other products at a discount to their member hospitals, such as information systems and financial and strategic planning consulting. The rise of such aggregate purchasing organizations has greatly changed the shape of hospital products and pharmaceutical markets by forcing price reductions.

Large-scale operations developed over time through joint ventures can provide increased learning benefits. When a large facility comes on line with new technology, an opportunity exists to achieve larger cost reductions through an enhanced experience curve. Such alliances are frequent in the semiconductor industry. For example, in 1992, IBM, Siemens, and Toshiba formed an alliance to develop and manufacture a 256-million-bit dynamic random access memory chip. RAM technology commonly benefits from steep learning curve effects.

Note that achieving low costs through process innovation requires the establishment of a separate administrative entity. It is generally not possible for size-based benefits to be achieved without establishing a separate unit from the partners, both physically and administratively. Although the venture may be adjacent to one of the partner's other facilities, the independence of the unit is important for scale-based learning to occur.

The relative independence of the venture is likely to be less important in an alliance initiated to reduce costs through improved interfirm coordination. These alliances are frequently **strategic sourcing** arrangements designed for more effective supply chain management. They are unlikely to involve equity investments, outside of Japan, or the establishment of a separate unit to administer the relationship. This type of partnership has diffused widely throughout manufacturing and service industries in the United States and other nations. A major focus of these alliances is cost reduction through the following:

1. Lower inventories produced by faster and more frequent delivery.
2. Product design practices focused on manufacturing efficiencies.
3. More effective higher-level planning to coordinate investment and production decisions.

Cost-based supply partnerships can occur between large buyers and small suppliers, which have unequal market power, or between a large buyer and a large supplier, each of which has substantial leverage over the other in the relationship. The well-known alliance between Wal-Mart and Procter & Gamble is an example.

The key practices for the buyer in a strategic sourcing relationship in manufacturing are the following:

1. Choose a limited number of competent suppliers, perhaps only one or two for each product, commodity, or component.
2. Establish an expectation of a long-term relationship based on joint innovation, planning, and sharing of cost improvements.
3. Coordinate closely with the supplier from the product design phase through prototype testing to full-scale manufacturing.
4. Build a strong purchasing organization run by high-profile management and linked through product teams to engineering and manufacturing.

These practices have typically been found in the outsourcing programs of large assemblers and their suppliers of services and components in the United States, Europe, and Asia and have diffused backward in the value chain through component producers to their materials suppliers.[14]

Suppliers that are competent in strategic sourcing relationships often promote these partnerships to new customers by convincing them that the lower costs of closer coordination are worth the investment. As the benefits from these relationships are realized, the customer's switching costs are raised, leading to a more stable customer base for the supplier. The supplier therefore has lower marketing costs in addition to the efficiencies of improved coordination with the customer over time.

Risk Reduction

Firms in industries with high rates of expansion or innovation typically invest in large portfolios of projects, many of which have uncertain cash flow projections. High uncertainty, coupled with limited resources, can constrain a firm's investment decisions, leading potentially to underinvestment in larger projects that are strategically important. Alliances can overcome this constraint, albeit at the cost of losing some control to the partner. Sharing the costs of the venture with one or more partners lowers the financial exposure of each firm.

Influence on Industry Structure

Alliance formation within an industry separates competitors into clusters that compete against each other. The organizations in each cluster have a common investment focus, which is too large to be covered by a single firm. Examples of such large-scale investments are a proprietary software or hardware standard, an airline route structure, a set of global telecommunications capabilities, or a commitment to serving a single large firm's market.

In some cases, an alliance can change the industry's structure. Sematech is a good example of an alliance centered on product and process innovation in the semiconductor industry. The motivation behind the partnership was to develop semiconductor technology in the United States to compete with Japanese firms. The original Sematech partners were almost all the major firms in the industry, except for IBM, and were strong competitors. However, once the firms demonstrated to each other that they could benefit from cooperation, the alliance endured. A consequence of this partnership was an increasing acceptance of cooperation among industry competitors in semiconductors.

The Disadvantages of Partnering

Almost all the reasons for partnering discussed above are based on the assumption that partners cannot go it alone. Nonetheless, alliances should always be examined as an alternative to executing a project in-house. An alliance entails giving up control over a project in order to combine resources with another firm. This loss of control can present real disadvantages. In most cases, if a firm has adequate resources to engage in a project without an alliance, *including the ability to assume the associated risk,* it is likely that the project would be vertically integrated. Below we discuss four problems caused by partnerships:

- Reduced control over decision making.
- Strategic inflexibility.
- Weaker organizational identity.
- Antitrust issues.

Reduced Control over Decision Making

Returning to the types of control over decision making that motivate vertical integration (see Chapter 6), partnerships imply less power for both partners over decisions of every type—financial, investment, and information diffusion. Control is reduced no matter what motivates the partnership or what form it takes. Decisions are made bilaterally or multilaterally between firms, not unilaterally, as would occur within a firm. The potential for conflict is therefore higher in a partnership than under vertical integration.

Strategic Inflexibility

Reduced control over decision making also leads to less flexibility in changing strategic direction. Partnerships and coalitions are notoriously poor at altering their investment paths in response to a shift in their environment. The Organization of Petroleum Exporting Countries (OPEC) has a reputation for continuous squabbling among its members when the level of oil production must be raised or lowered. Partners have objectives that overlap with the goals of the partnership but are not completely consistent with them. Since conflict over decision making grows when a firm's competitive conditions shift, industry change creates discord in an alliance and takes time and resources to deal with effectively.

A second kind of strategic inflexibility concerns the commitment of each partner to the resources of the other. Strategic sourcing agreements tie buyers to the technological capabilities of their suppliers, which are inevitably limited. In the same way, suppliers are tied to the advantages and disadvantages of their customers' market positions. Further, both buyers and suppliers are likely to be committed to each other because of the costs they have incurred in relationship-specific investments. Commitment to these investments will cause the relationship to persist beyond the point where a standard market relationship would be terminated. The relationship's persistence may create short-term losses because the value of the supplier's technology has declined in its partner's downstream market. Longer-term losses are possible if the partner's competitors build stronger market positions by introducing products with better technologies.

Weaker Organizational Identity

Among the many problems start-up firms face is the need to establish a coherent organizational identity. A coherent identity adds value to the firm as a focal point for building both employee ties to the organization and customer confidence in the organization's reliability. An organization builds its identity through the development of resources and well-defined capabilities that improve performance consistently.

But, in order to grow, start-ups frequently must form partnerships with larger firms to gain access to capital, complementary technologies, and distribution channels. In these partnerships, a start-up may lose control over investment and other types of decisions, lowering organizational coherence. A start-up with many partnerships thus must forge its identity over a longer period of time. The process will depend on which partners have been chosen and how effectively these partnerships have been managed.

Antitrust Issues

Partnerships, especially among competitors in concentrated industries, may raise antitrust concerns. But since the mid-1980s in the United States, regulators have come to believe that alliances benefit innovation and in some cases increase efficiency. Even so, when dominant competitors in an industry cannot show that their proposed alliance produces these benefits, weaker rivals may argue that the partnership will decrease competition, and an investigation can be initiated.

To alleviate antitrust concerns, the firms entering into a partnership need to show that any or all of the following characteristics are expected benefits:

- Greater efficiency in the alliance relative to the harm it poses to the competition.
- A partnership design that promotes competition, such as the development of an open standard.
- A forecast of a continuous stream of new technologies from the partnership.
- An increase in U.S. economic growth and global competitiveness.

The last attribute was a major selling point of Sematech, since the consortium was formed to develop technologies that were supposed to slow the penetration of U.S. markets by Japanese firms.

Partner Selection

There is probably no more important task in forming an alliance than choosing a partner. Frequently, organizations will speak of their partnerships as marriages, an analogy that has some relevance for partner selection: It is useful, for example, to reflect on how much time and thought often go into choosing a mate and how disastrous the consequences can be when casual acquaintances, with little knowledge of each other, marry spontaneously. We discuss below three key criteria:

- The potential partner's current capabilities.
- The partner's expected future capabilities.
- The number and quality of current and future partnering alternatives.

The Partner's Current Capabilities

To be selected as a partner, a firm must demonstrate competence in three key areas. First, it must show that it has the resources and capabilities necessary for the partnership's success. For example, in a technology alliance, the firm should have competence in the relevant technology. Similarly, in a partnership to reduce costs, the firm should have the necessary cost drivers in the targeted activity.[15] Second, a potential partner should be competent to manage its current operations effectively and to grow these operations at a rate consistent with the partnership's goals. Last, the potential partner should be able to manage its role in the alliance effectively. If the firm does not have the skills to cooperate, its other capabilities are irrelevant.[16]

The Partner's Future Capabilities

Just as important as the partner's current capabilities are what it can offer the alliance in the future. Future capabilities are particularly critical in technology alliances in which frequent technological innovation can make a partner's capabilities obsolete. Also essential is the partner's ability to grow with the relationship and make the necessary transition from entrepreneurial to general management, if the firm is a start-up.

Alternative Partners

Finally, any checklist for choosing a partner needs to include an assessment of alternative firms, not just for the relationship being considered, but for future relationships. This assessment is inevitably affected by the stage of industry development. If all potential partners were available at one time and their capabilities were observable, the matching process would be relatively straightforward. But in most industries firms enter the market for partnering over time rather than all at once. Further, the capabilities of potential partners are frequently not initially observable. Therefore, the time at which firms enter the industry and the reliability with which their resources and capabilities can be assessed affect which alliances are possible.

Even if firms could observe the capabilities of all potential partners, the problem of achieving effective cooperation remains. The reason is that effective cooperation is achieved in part through the evolving network of partnerships in the industry. That is, the ability of firms to cooperate becomes apparent only as the network of partnerships develops.

There are two views on why some firms are more able to cooperate effectively than others. In one view, cooperation is a capability that firms have independent of their position in the network. The alternative is that cooperation is affected by the structure of the network surrounding a firm. A dense network around a firm increases its incentives to limit self-interested behavior. The reason is that stories about a firm's behavior diffuse more quickly to other firms when they are all connected to each other. This system-level effect is called "social capital." Organizations that are embedded in denser clusters of interfirm relationships have higher social capital, experience greater constraint on their self-interest, and therefore exhibit greater cooperation. In a sense this concept of why firms cooperate is like the old adage in politics, "don't see no one nobody sent." That is, if the person is not close to you in the network already, you can't count on how he or she will behave.

But constraints on a firm's cooperative behavior emerge only as the industry evolves. Therefore, choosing a partner for its ability to cooperate successfully must in part be a function of the evolution of industry structure. If the social capital view is correct, early entrants to the network are at an advantage in choosing a partner on the basis of its capabilities but are at a relative disadvantage in choosing partners for their ability to cooperate. This trade-off shifts as the industry evolves. In the later stages of industry development, there are fewer capable firms to partner with, but the increasing constraint of the network raises the likelihood of effective cooperation.[17]

Partnership Form

Partnerships can take a number of forms that depend primarily on the reasons the alliance is established. We have outlined above four major reasons for partnerships: technology transfer and development, market access, cost reduction, and risk reduction. Alliances based on these motivations may be structured in several ways as discussed below.

Technology Transfer and Development[18]

The form of a partnership is determined to a large degree by what motivates it. This is especially true in technology-based relationships between established firms and start-ups. The motivation behind an alliance determines how much the partners invest to acquire information and build capabilities. As a technology's potential increases, a partner may shift or increase its investment. Or, if the size of the market for the partnership's output is found to be small and the market's prospects poor, the firm may choose to move on to other projects.

The first and most basic reason for partnering is the development of a window onto an emerging technology. An established firm with a **window strategy** forms a large number of low-cost relationships with start-ups. Each relationship provides information about a new technology but does not help build a path for the technology's development within the firm. Even though a technology is embryonic and its long-term potential highly uncertain, an established firm may find it necessary to learn about it. Partnering with a young entrepreneurial company is frequently an effective means of monitoring the technology's progress.

The second reason an incumbent might form an alliance with a start-up is to learn enough about a new technology to be able to plan for the development of projects based on it. Called an **options strategy,** this approach allows the established firm to make a small, low-risk investment lower than the amount required to develop the new technology to scale. This investment is, however, more than would be made under the window strategy. The firm might never develop the technology but has the ability to make an additional investment if the expected value of the project increases.

The third motivation for establishing an alliance is based on a plan to position the established firm in the emerging technology. A **positioning strategy** reflects a stronger commitment to the technology than an options strategy. In this case, the incumbent puts more financial, technical, and managerial resources into the alliance in order to build a viable business, either with the start-up as a partner or later with a wholly owned unit.

As a firm's motivation shifts from window to option to positioning, the degree of control the firm exercises in the relationship increases. Its competence as a potential competitor in the start-up's industry also rises. The increase in the control and competence of the established firm is due to its increasing investment in the partnership.

Four types of technology partnership, which are not mutually exclusive, indicate the established firm's level of investment:

- Research grant
- R&D contract
- License
- Joint venture

In addition, the firm may acquire equity in the start-up to improve the quality and amount of information received about the technology and perhaps to gain financially if the start-up becomes successful.

The four types intersect with the three motivations for forming the partnership. The research grant typically gives the incumbent rights to learn about technological developments but few proprietary rights over commercialization.

This form of alliance therefore fits the window strategy well. The R&D contract is more focused on specific start-up projects and can range from the right to observe developments to technology transfer and product commercialization arrangements. This type of alliance gives the established firm more control over the relationship and may be appropriate for both window and options strategies. A licensing arrangement between a start-up and an incumbent firm is formed to combine the entrant's technological expertise and the incumbent's capabilities in marketing and distribution. Because the established firm is not involved in technology development, there is little opportunity for technology transfer. However, the large firm has rights regarding product commercialization and has the opportunity to position itself in the product market as it emerges. Finally, the incumbent and start-up may enter into a joint venture that entails setting up a separate unit to develop the technology and possibly to commercialize it. The existence of a separate administrative entity in which both the start-up and the incumbent share responsibilities increases the opportunity to transfer technology and control technology development. Joint ventures apply therefore to window, options, and positioning strategies.

Many technology alliances involve an equity investment by the large firm in its start-up partner. This does not mean that the large firm can easily access the start-up's expertise, however, since there is typically a substantial disparity in the two firms' technological skills. An equity position may thus increase the incumbent firm's control over decision making but not lead to effective technology transfer. Without the ability to develop and commercialize the technology, the incumbent can only execute window and options strategies.

Cost and Risk Reduction

Alliances to achieve economies of scale or lower risk are almost always joint ventures. Partnerships of this type, whether they involve two or more firms, are analogous to bilateral or multilateral governed franchising schemes where the combination of resources or activities in the partnership provides each firm with greater efficiencies. In many cases, these ventures make the expansion, profitability, and perhaps even the survival of the partners possible.

Joint ventures in extractive industries are good examples of alliances to combine partners' activities. For instance, the Aramco consortium among U.S. energy companies was formed to explore for and produce oil and gas in Saudi Arabia and the Persian Gulf States at lower cost (and lower risk), given the scale of the venture, than any firm would have incurred individually. Likewise, aluminum companies have frequently established joint ventures, especially involving Alcoa and PUK, to build larger processing plants near bauxite deposits, thereby achieving lower costs. These ventures were formed to achieve efficiencies primarily in operations and logistics.[19]

Managing Partnerships

In any partnership three elements are essential to successful cooperation in managing the exploitation of complementary assets.[20] The first condition is the **convergence of purpose** between the two firms. This condition is rarely achieved in full but can be approximated as conflicts are resolved over time. The second condition is the **consistency of position** of the partnership in each firm's administrative structure. Since the partnership is only one of many projects in each firm, changes in each partner's project portfolio are likely to shift managerial interest toward or away from it, causing instability in the resources allocated to it. The more similar the positions occupied by liaison personnel in each partnering organization, the higher the consistency of position. Third, **management of the interface** between the partners frequently involves several levels of governance. The expectations of managers are likely to vary across these levels, causing problems in planning, coordination, and evaluation.

Convergence of Purpose

No partnership can be effective without a high degree of understanding between the partners. First and most important is a mutual belief that the partnership adds sufficient economic value to both firms to justify continuing the relationship. This value is easier to assess when uncertainty is low. Lower uncertainty makes it easier to calculate the returns to the partnership and to agree on their distribution.

Uncertainty surrounding these returns increases when innovation or the entry of new firms shifts the structure of competition in the industry. Partnerships in industries with high uncertainty are therefore difficult to maintain. Paradoxically, partnerships appear frequently when uncertainty is high precisely because most firms are unable to bear the uncertainty alone. Without the ability to develop or buy the resources and capabilities they need to compete, firms are forced to forge partnerships with each other. Because of the difficulties in forecasting returns reliably, standard market contracts are out of the question. These alliances therefore follow a long and frequently hard road of conflict and adjustment due to the joint need of the firms for control over decisions that cannot be specified in advance.

Handling the uncertainty within a partnership requires substantial managerial capability and experience. One way partners deal with this uncertainty is to order the issues they confront according to how well they can be managed successfully. For example, in many technology-based alliances the technical fit between the partners can easily provide a basis for cooperation. However, the strategic benefits of sharing technologies may differ substantially for each firm. For one firm, its partner's technology may represent a key component of a new product line in which the company is investing relatively large resources. For the other firm, the technology transferred may be an important but not critical addition to an already full set of offerings. So while the technical integration of the two firms is relatively straightforward, the lack of strategic fit complicates how investment decisions should be managed.

Cultural differences can also complicate the establishment of understanding between the partners.[21] These differences are anchored in different national or organizational management styles. Variation in national cultures has frequently been tied to misunderstandings in cross-border partnerships. For example, many U.S. companies found that partnering with Japanese firms in the 1980s produced surprises regarding technology transfer and the relevant time horizon for financial returns. With experience, national differences can be planned for and included in the calculation of costs and benefits associated with a partnership.

Organizational culture can also be a potent influence on the expectations that partners bring to the relationship. Highly bureaucratic organizations may attempt to impose strong reporting and control systems on the partnership. More informally organized firms resist these systems. Thus the partnership becomes both an opportunity for change and a constant challenge to established procedures.

Consistency of Position

The difficulties of establishing convergence of purpose are compounded by problems associated with different views of the partnership within each firm. Managers at different levels in each organization will vary in the value they place on the partnership and in the expectations they have for it. Top management frequently sees a partnership primarily as a strategic investment and has secondary knowledge of its technological and operating details. Middle management has primary knowledge of these details and is less involved in the development of corporate strategy. Technical personnel in turn have their own interests, typically involving the gathering of new knowledge related to enhancing professional reputation. Finally, corporate and business-level staff can have unique perspectives on the value of interunit coordination, in which the partnership can often become enmeshed.

For these constituencies to be managed effectively, each must relate consistently to the partnership over its history. When any position becomes involved in the partnership more frequently or intensely, that position may exert its preferences more strongly and the procedures set up to manage the relationship may become unstable. Each position, from top management to technical staff, has an important role to play over the partnership's life cycle. However, these roles should contribute to achieving the partnership's goals and not be allowed to intervene arbitrarily.

Managing the Interface

Managing a partnership is in many ways like managing a new venture. Like a new venture, a partnership requires the development of new practices and routines to achieve a unique set of objectives. Neither a venture nor a partnership is independent of the parent organizations since their resources are necessary for its success. The design and management of the interface between the organizations determine how effective the project will be.

Interface design is obviously determined by how the partnership is organized. At one extreme, the partnership is a joint venture formed by two firms to achieve economies of scale in activities such as operations, marketing, or distribution and is an independent administrative unit. Although the partners own the venture, a separate management runs it and is responsible for planning and executing the unit's strategy. The interface between this management team and the partners can frequently involve conflict over performance evaluation, resource allocation, and planning for future investment.

At the other extreme is a partnership without a separate administrative organization, involving only the efforts of both firms to coordinate their activities more effectively. An obvious example, which we have discussed at some length, is a strategic sourcing relationship. The key activities in the interface between buyer and supplier for this type of relationship are operations, logistics, procurement, and engineering. In addition, finance and planning can play important roles. If one or more of these functions questions the value of increased cooperation, the success of the relationship will be more difficult to achieve.

An example midway between a wholly independent joint venture and a strategic sourcing relationship is a partnership aimed at lowering logistics and inventory costs in distribution and mass market sales. In this case, the alliance is likely to have a dedicated management to organize and coordinate the relationship on a daily basis. This management will include personnel from both partners and focuses on the success of the relationship, not of the partners independently. This independence is beneficial assuming the strategies of both firms continue to be consistent with the partnership's goals. Under these circumstances, the managers of the partnership are likely to control closely the interface between the partners.

Alliance Dynamics

What causes alliances to end and new alliances to be formed? What are the causes of volatility in alliances? The discussion below focuses on three influences: the planned life of the project, shifts in the alliance's markets, and the dynamics of governing the relationship itself.

Life of the Project

One source of a partnership's longevity is the planned life of the project. For example, joint ventures among aluminum companies for the development of bauxite mines and adjacent aluminum production are planned to remain active until the bauxite has been depleted. The global network of these ventures is therefore quite stable, as the mines are quite large. Partnerships among global oil firms last long for the same reason. Alternatively, the histories of some projects in high-technology industries—for example, semiconductors or information processing—are as short or long as the life spans of the technologies involved. In many cases one or both partners may learn that the technology on which their partnership is based has a dimmer future than the initial estimate that motivated the alliance. In this case, even though the technological life cycle has not matured, the partnership is terminated since it can no longer be justified.[22]

Market Forces

The activity around which a partnership is built belongs to a market, which determines its value. When the activity is valued highly, the alliance endures. However, when the market becomes more competitive and alternatives to the activity are more available, the partnership can become less viable. For example, at some point in the history of a technology-based alliance a competitor may enter the market with a superior platform. The value of the alliance therefore begins to decline and the likelihood that it will be terminated increases. The partners may decide to leverage their relationship to switch to the new technology, but this would be a new project involving a new contract and new investments. Another example is the effect of deregulation on alliances formed to provide access when the market was closed. For instance, as European airline markets are deregulated, the alliances between non-European and European airlines for market access are made obsolete.

A second market force that affects the life of an alliance is industry performance. Some joint ventures can be viewed as options to expand a market position in an industry, as discussed above. When the growth in volume of a joint venture's industry increases over its historical trend, it becomes more likely that one partner will purchase the other's interest in the venture. When the industry's volume declines, however, joint ventures typically are not dissolved. The implication is that high volatility in industry performance will shorten the duration of partnerships, assuming an option to acquire the joint venture is contractually specified.[23]

Dynamics within the Relationship

Every alliance is based in part on each firm's knowledge and expectations of the other. At the outset, knowledge is imperfect, and each company learns about its partner, for better or worse, over time. How this learning progresses has important implications for how long the partnership lasts.

An analysis of auditor–client relationships, for example, shows that the failure rate of relationships falls, then rises, then falls with its age. Early problems in the relationship are discounted as part of necessary learning, forming a honeymoon period during which clients forgive poor performance that in other circumstances would cause the relationship to fail. In the middle phase, however, the tendency to forgive diminishes, and the likelihood of failure increases. As the relationship endures, the hazard rate falls again as the partners adapt to each other's idiosyncrasies, and the costs of switching to another auditing firm increase. The likelihood of vertical integration in the auditor–client relationship is zero, but in most types of cooperative relationships partners are not so constrained. A general version of this life-cycle approach to a buyer–supplier relationship might therefore be consistent with transaction cost reasoning regarding vertical integration discussed in Chapter 6.[24]

Age-related cooperative dynamics suggest that learning in the relationship is roughly symmetric, as each side becomes specialized to the other. With this mutual specialization comes an opportunity for joint learning. It has been observed that the written contract between two partners can act as a "repository of knowledge" generated over time as the firms deepen their understanding of each other's capabilities and requirements. [25] In some cases, however, one partner may cooperate with the primary aim of learning the capabilities of the other and breach the terms of the contract when the education is completed. This pattern of behavior has been attributed to Japanese companies that acquired technological expertise by partnering with non-Japanese firms, then terminated the agreement when the partner's capabilities had been learned.[26]

Summary

There is no question that partnering is one of the most prevalent and fastest growing business practices in developed countries. Why is this so? To answer this question we started the chapter by examining the underlying trends behind the rise of partnerships and the general motivations of alliance formation. The several disadvantages of cooperative arrangements, especially for smaller and newer firms, were then discussed. We also looked at how firms should go about selecting partners and how alliances are managed. Finally, the dynamics of alliances were laid out, showing how forces both inside and outside the cooperative arrangement can affect its performance. Each of these issues captures an essential part of our understanding of how partnerships arise and then either succeed or fail.

Summary Points

- When the strategic value of an activity is high but the firm's competence to perform the activity is low, the firm has two options: (1) improve its competence and bring the activity in-house, or (2) try to find another firm, a partner, that is willing to give up some control over aspects of the activity so that its strategic value can be realized.

- There are seven trends in partnership activity:
  - the global integration of manufacturing and service industries
  - the diffusion of Japanese partnership practices
  - the diffusion of partnerships with suppliers
  - the rise of outsourcing as an accepted practice
  - the rise of supply chain management practices
  - the growth of technology-intensive industries
  - the emergence of regional networks of cooperating firms.
- There are five motivations for partnership formation:
  - technology transfer and development
  - market access
  - cost reduction
  - risk reduction
  - change in industry structure.
- Partnerships should always be examined as an alternative to executing a project in-house.
- The major disadvantages of partnerships are:
  - reduced control over decision making
  - strategic inflexibility
  - weaker organizational identity
  - antitrust issues.
- In selecting a partner, a firm uses three key decision criteria:
  - the potential partner's current capabilities
  - its expected future capabilities
  - the number and quality of current and future alternatives.
- The form of a partnership is determined to a large degree by the motivations for its existence, especially in technology-based relationships.
- An established firm may have one of three motivations for forming an alliance with a start-up technology firm:
  - a window strategy
  - an options strategy
  - a positioning strategy.
- There are five types of technology-based relationship ordered by the large firm's control over the alliance:
  - research grant
  - R&D contract
  - license

- joint venture
- partial ownership
- Alliances to achieve economies of scale are almost always joint ventures combining specific resources from each partner.
- Once the partnership is in place three conditions are necessary for its effective governance:
  - convergence of purpose
  - consistency of position
  - effective management of the interface between the partners.
- There are three influences on alliance dynamics:
  - the planned life of the project the alliance is designed for
  - shifts in the markets for the activities the partnership involves
  - the dynamics of governing the relationship itself.

Questions for Practice

Think how you would answer these questions for your current company, your previous place of work, or a business you are studying:

1. What partnerships is your firm currently engaged in?
2. Why did it enter into these partnerships?
3. Did it compare the benefits of partnering with vertical integration?
4. How were the partners selected in each instance?
5. Was there evidence of partner expertise in cooperating with other firms?
6. How has your firm avoided or mitigated the disadvantages of partnering?
7. How does the form of each partnership match the reason motivating it?
8. How convergent are your firm's purposes in each alliance with those of the partner?
9. How well does your firm manage the interface with each partner?
10. How has your firm learned to become more effective in cooperating with each partner?

End Notes

1. See Bruce Kogut, Gordon Walker, and Wei-jian Shan, "Knowledge in the Network and the Network as Knowledge: The Structure of the Biotechnology and Semiconductor Industries," in *The Embedded Firm: On the Socioeconomics of Industrial Networks,* Gernot Grabher, ed. (London: Routledge, 1993).

2. See, for example, Xavier Martin, Will Mitchell, and Anand Swaminathan, "Recreating and Extending Japanese Automobile Buyer–Supplier Links in North America," *Strategic Management Journal* 16 (1995), pp. 589–620; Martin Kenney and Richard Florida, *Beyond Mass Production: The Japanese System and Its Transfer to the United States* (New York: Oxford University Press, 1993).

3. See Susan Helper and David Levine, "Long-Term Supplier Relations and Product Market Structure," *Journal of Law, Economics, and Organization* 8 (1992), pp. 561–81.

4. See Jeffrey Dyer, "Specialized Supplier Networks as a Source of Competitive Advantage: Evidence from the Auto Industry," *Strategic Management Journal* 17 (1996), pp. 271–91.

5. See Laura Poppo and Todd Zenger, "Do Formal Contracts and Relational Governance Function as Substitutes or Complements," *Strategic Management Journal* 23 (2002), pp. 707–26.

6. For a broad set of readings on the growth of technology-based industries, see Stephen P. Bradley, Jerry A. Hausman, and Richard L. Nolan, *Globalization, Technology and Competition* (Cambridge, MA: Harvard Business School Press, 1993).

7. For a description of the rise of partnership networks in Silicon Valley, see AnnaLee Saxenian, "The Origins and Dynamics of Production Networks in Silicon Valley," *Research Policy* 20 (1991), pp. 423–37.

8. See Kathryn Harrigan, *Strategies for Joint Ventures* (Lexington, MA: Lexington Books, 1985).

9. See, for example, Frank Rothaermel, "Incumbent's Advantage through Exploiting Complementary Assets via Interfirm Cooperation," *Strategic Management Journal* 22 (2001) pp. 687–99; Ashish Arora and Alfono Gambardello, "Complementarity and External Linkages: The Strategies of Large Firms in the Biotechnology Industry," *Journal of Industrial Economics* 4 (1990), pp. 361–79.

10. See, for example, Paul Adler, Barbara Goldoftas, and David I. Levine, "Stability and Change at NUMMI," in Robert Boyer, Elsie Charron, Ulrich Jürgens, and Steven Tolliday, eds., *Between Imitation and Innovation: The Transfer and Hybridization of Productive Models in the International Automobile Industry* (New York: Oxford University Press, 1998), pp. 128–60.

11. See Bronwyn Hall and Rosemarie Ham Ziedonis, "The Determinants of Patenting in the U.S. Semiconductor Industry, 1980–1994," *Rand Journal of Economics* 32 (2001), pp. 101–28.

12. See Witold J. Henisz and Bennet A. Zelner, "Political Risk Management: A Strategic Perspective," working paper, The Wharton School, University of Pennsylvania, 2002.

13. See Gordon Walker, "Strategic Sourcing, Vertical Integration and Transaction Costs," *Interfaces* 18, no. 3 (1988), pp. 62–73.

14. John Paul MacDuffie and Susan Helper, "Creating Lean Suppliers: Diffusing Lean Production throughout the Supply Chain," in Paul Adler, Mark Fruin, and Jeffrey Liker, eds., *Remade in America: Transforming and Transplanting Japanese Management Systems* (New York: Oxford University Press, 1999).

15. See Toby E. Stuart and Joel M. Podolny, "Local Search and the Evolution of Technological Capabilities," *Strategic Management Journal* 17 (Summer special issue, 1996), pp. 21–38.

16. See Jeffrey H. Dyer and Harbir Singh, "The Relational View: Cooperative Strategy and Sources of Interorganizational Competitive Advantage," *Academy of Management Review* 23 (1998), pp. 660–80; Akbar Zaheer and N. Venkatraman, "Relational Governance as an Interorganizational Strategy: An Empirical Test of the Role of Trust in Economic Exchange," *Strategic Management Journal* 16 (1995), pp. 373–93.

17. See Gordon Walker, Bruce Kogut, and Wei-jian Shan, "Social Capital and Structural Holes and the Formation of an Industry Network," *Organization Science* 8 (1985), pp. 109–25.

18. See William Hamilton, "Corporate Strategies for Managing Emerging Technologies," *Technology in Society* 7 (1985), pp. 197–212.

19. See John Stuckey, *Vertical Integration and Joint Ventures in the Aluminum Industry* (Cambridge, MA: Harvard University Press, 1983).

20. See Yves Doz, "Technology Partnerships between Larger and Smaller Firms: Some Critical Issues," in F. J. Contractor and P. Lorange, eds., *Cooperative Strategies in International Business* (Lexington, MA: Lexington Books, 1988).

21. See Arvind Parkhe, "Interfirm Diversity, Organizational Learning, and Longevity in Global Strategic Alliances," *Journal of International Business* 22 (1991), pp. 555–78.

22. See Gordon Walker, "Strategy and Network Formation," in *Advances in Strategic Management,* J. Baum and H. Rao, eds. (Greenwich, CT: JAI Press, 1988).

23. See Bruce Kogut, "Joint Ventures and the Option to Expand," *Management Science* 37 (1991), pp. 19–33.

24. See Dan Levinthal and Mark Fichman, "Dynamics of Interorganizational Attachments: Auditor–Client Relationships," *Administrative Science Quarterly* 33 (1988), pp. 345–69.

25. See Kyle Mayer and Nicholas Argyres, "Learning to Contract: Evidence from the Personal Computer Industry," *Organization Science* 15 (2004), pp. 394–410; also, Jeffrey Reuer, Maurizio Zollo, and Harbir Singh, "Post-formation Dynamics in Strategic Alliances," *Strategic Management Journal* 23 (2002), pp. 135–51.

26. For an interesting discussion of how the distribution of benefits affects partnering behavior over time, see Tarun Khanna, Ranjay Gulati, and Nitin Nohria, "The Dynamics of Learning Alliances: Competition, Cooperation, and Relative Scope," *Strategic Management Journal* 19 (1998), pp. 193–210.

Expanding the Scope of the Firm

CHAPTER 8

Competing in Global Markets

Roadmap

Over the past 30 years, a casual observer of competition across a broad range of industries would have seen an increasing trend toward the global integration of markets and technologies.[1] The number of companies whose brands have become solidly international over this time period is astonishing. In addition to the large U.S. and European companies whose businesses have been traditionally global such as Citibank, Ford, IBM, DaimlerChrysler, and Philips, we can add McDonald's, Nike, Intel, Microsoft, Disney, Gap, Sony, Panasonic, Toshiba, and a host of others. Not only do consumers worldwide buy similar products made by global firms, but these firms develop their ideas and manufacture their products wherever the results are best, in California, China, Ireland, or Mexico.[2]

Global markets present opportunities for growth and financial performance. They also place significant pressures on domestic industries to compete more intensely. A firm can experience these opportunities and pressures together, making participation in global markets necessary and strenuous.

For the firm to perform effectively within its worldwide market position, the financial and operating nuances of global competition must be learned. This experience can be costly and almost always increases the complexity of strategic decision making. Yet it is disastrous for a firm to avoid global trends in its industry. Avoidance inevitably produces a weakened market position as the firm's customer base switches to global competitors that are able to leverage their worldwide scope to lower cost or spur innovation.

In this chapter we will discuss the underlying principles of global competition. First, we will examine the basic theories of regional and country advantage. Our focus will be on why regions within countries are differentiated, and then why countries matter.

Second, we will look at how firms use and, in some instances, overcome country differences to build successful global businesses. Global firms typically vary in where they locate their activities across countries. In some industries this variation contributes strongly to performance differences; in other industries the contribution may not be so great.

Third, global competition entails the entry and exit of firms into and out of geographical regions. The dynamics of interregional entry and exit are important because they determine in part how firms locate their activities worldwide. Understanding these dynamics helps to explain how firms balance the costs incurred when a firm enters a country and the costs incurred when it exits, especially the sacrifice of goodwill and other sunk investments.

Fourth, it is important to look at how firms organize their activities to compete globally. Initially, companies whose international sales are a small proportion of total revenues will assign responsibility for their global business to a separate administrative unit. Later, as international sales grow, responsibility for them becomes integrated with the rest of the organization.

The chapter is structured as follows:

- Overview

- Why Do Regions Matter?

  - Labor Pooling

  - Specialized Local Suppliers

  - Technological Spillovers

- Why Do Countries Matter?

  - Laws and Regulations

  - National Cultures

  - Natural Resources and Geography

- Porter's Diamond Model

- A Framework for Global Competition

  - Nationally Segmented Industries

  - Industries Vertically Integrated across Countries

  - Horizontally Integrated Industries

  - Vertically and Horizontally Integrated Industries

  - The Global Configuration of Firms

  - Change in Configuration

- Modes of Entering Foreign Markets

- Organizing for Global Competition

- Summary

- Questions for Practice

Why Do Regions Matter?

Before we can understand how differences among nations affect the strategies of firms, we need to discuss why geographical regions, frequently quite small in size, emerge as centers of production for specific industries. A facile explanation for regional advantage is that resources are not equally distributed geographically. Some regions are well endowed while others are less fortunate. But this explanation does not help us to understand the economic geographies of industries whose major inputs are intangible, or that do not need to locate near raw material sources. Silicon Valley is not a hub of high technology because it has a lode of silicon. Consequently, we need a broader perspective on why managers locate their activities in one region rather than another.

In his classic exposition of economic theory, Alfred Marshall laid out a careful and strikingly current set of arguments explaining why the firms in many industries tend to cluster together geographically, often within a few miles of each other.[3] Marshall suggested that there were three reasons why geographical clusters appear: (1) the advantages of pooling a common labor force; (2) the gains from specialized local suppliers; and (3) the benefits from technological spillovers in the region.[4]

Labor Pooling

One obvious reason firms locate in a region is to benefit from a pool of workers whose skills are specific to the firm. But it is important to understand when labor pooling adds value. The key factor is the predictability of the firm's needs. If a firm's labor requirements are easily forecasted, then it can plan to attract workers to wherever it finds favorable market conditions. Here global workforce planning substitutes for local labor pooling. However, if a firm experiences some uncertainty in its need for workers, locating where there is additional labor to fill unexpected demand is valuable since it lowers the cost of finding qualified workers quickly.

Specialized Local Suppliers

When many firms in an industry locate in the same region, they can create a potential market for local suppliers specialized to the firms' requirements. Two conditions lead to the emergence of these vendors.

First, the firms and their suppliers must concentrate their operations in the region at about the same pace. As local demand for their output rises, suppliers increase their production, and the number of suppliers goes up. But locating near customers in one region may restrict a supplier's ability to set up facilities close to buyers in other regions. So how suppliers trade off satisfying customers inside and outside their region has an impact on regional development.

The second condition concerns the specialization of supplier inputs to local customers. The more specialized these inputs, the more closely coordinated the relationship between buyer and supplier needs to be. Colocation generally makes close coordination of input design and production more efficient. As suppliers' inputs become more specialized to local buyers, they become less able to sell outside the region. The local supplier base therefore grows.

Technological Spillovers

One of the most obvious reasons firms in the same industry concentrate in the same region is the benefit they receive from sharing technological information.[5] Even though the firms are competitors, location in the same region offers opportunities for mutual observation that are more frequent and intensive than would be available at a distance. But these opportunities give the firms an economic benefit only as long as the region is a source of major innovations and no firms outside the region have strong early-mover advantages.

Both product and process innovations diffuse more quickly within a region than between regions for a variety of reasons. First, managers and workers are connected through interpersonal networks outside of work. These networks, in addition to contacts through regional industry associations, facilitate the flow of technical and other types of information. The strength of these flows obviously depends on how effectively an innovating firm protects its ideas and inventions. The greater the protection, the weaker the flows from that firm.

An obvious but significant example of a region that has benefited from information diffusion is Silicon Valley. One explanation of its success as a center for high-technology industries is the relative openness of incumbent firms to partnering with start-ups. An interesting comparison is the region around Boston centered on the two beltways, Route 128 and Interstate 495. In the 1970s and 1980s Boston also had a large concentration of high-technology firms but did not grow at the same rate as Silicon Valley. AnnaLee Saxenian has proposed that the hierarchical and highly controlled system of interfirm relationships in the Boston area, with Digital Equipment at its head, was not as conducive for technology spillovers as the more decentralized and less controlled network that developed in northern California.[6] Saxenian's insight is that the key to achieving a regional advantage due to technological spillovers is the policies, some formal, some ad hoc, in powerful, central firms that inhibit or promote the spread of innovative ideas. Digital Equipment in Boston was simply less interested in building a regional technology base than the core firms, such as Hewlett-Packard, in Silicon Valley.

The second reason technology spillovers occur is the transfer of managers and professionals across firms in the region. There are two obvious types of transfer. The first involves start-ups by former employees of incumbents, and the second involves mobility among existing firms. An active entrepreneurial sector increases the number of new ideas that will be developed, shared, and commercialized. Employee transfer between incumbents is an obvious extension of the benefits of labor pooling. Although managers are typically enjoined from sharing technical information developed during their previous employment, the skills they learned are portable and can be applied to new projects. Generalized templates of innovations can be transferred to other firms, as occurred in Japanese manufacturing industries during the 1960s and 1970s.

Third, regional associations, which meet to match people to jobs and resources, are essential for increasing the geographical concentration of the industry, both through growing incumbents and developing start-ups. Meeting face-to-face helps entrepreneurs, venture capitalists, managers, engineers, and marketing professionals build relationships. The association thus is a forum in which technological spillovers can occur.

Finally, the location of firms in a region presents opportunities for informal communication on technological issues. As managers from different firms associate outside of work, they often talk about common problems in dealing with suppliers, customers, and regulators. Sharing information in this way may not directly produce technological innovation. However, there may be indirect effects as new information frames issues in novel ways, raises questions that had not been asked before, and stimulates a search for answers to problems that were seen as intractable.

The development of technological spillovers from regional colocation thus ultimately depends on the repeated exchange of ideas across firms.[7] Achieving an effective rate of exchange requires the recognition that more cooperation among firms in the region leads to greater returns. Obviously, there are limits on the degree to which competitors can share information directly. In many cases, sharing of this kind is simply impossible, given the importance of protecting proprietary technology. Managing the tension between competition to increase firm growth and cooperation for regional growth is therefore a critical challenge. No region can succeed as a hub of industry activity without balancing these two forces well.

Why Do Countries Matter?

Laws and Regulations

We typically describe global competition as rivalry among firms in different countries. It is common to think about a nation as a discrete economic entity, whatever the regional clustering of industries within it. As sovereign states, nations regulate economic behavior through legal sanctions. In general, competitive markets cannot be developed without a strong rule of law within which disputes are resolved fairly and constructively. National laws and regulations significantly influence investment, the shape and scale of demand for products and services, and trade. But laws are malleable, and so firms and their agents target governments in order to influence the substance and trends of policies.

Governments frequently intervene in industries and markets to shape the intensity and direction of investment behavior. Investment may be encouraged through government subsidies to promote innovation or lower costs. Or it may be discouraged through high taxes or lengthy and arduous certification procedures.

Government policy can also influence demand by raising or lowering taxes on final and intermediate goods. Demand and investment behavior can

The Global Pharmaceutical Industry

Price controls in the pharmaceutical industry can take many forms. National regulation may impose a cap on the manufacturer's price or on the amount national health insurance programs pay for the drug. Regulators may also refer to the prices charged in other countries as benchmarks. Table 8.1 shows how broadly price control policies vary across countries:

TABLE 8.1 | Price Regulation of the Pharmaceutical Industry in 15 Countries

Y = regulation of drug prices through this policy	Austria	Belgium	Denmark	Finland	France	Germany	Greece	Ireland	Italy	Netherlands	Norway	Spain	Sweden	UK	US
Control of manufacturer price		Y		Y			Y	Y			Y	Y			
Control of reimbursement price	Y	Y	Y	Y	Y		Y	Y	Y	Y	Y	Y	Y		
Cross-country comparisons	Y	Y	Y	Y	Y		Y	Y	Y	Y	Y	Y	Y		
Reference pricing			Y			Y					Y	Y		Y	
Payback required if volume exceeds target	Y	Y			Y			Y	Y			Y	Y	Y	
Profit control												Y		Y	
Promotional spending control		Y			Y							Y		Y	
Pharmacoeconomic evidence recommended				Y						Y	Y	Y			
Fixed wholesale margin	Y	Y			Y	Y	Y	Y	Y			Y			
Fixed pharmacy margin	Y	Y	Y	Y	Y	Y	Y	Y	Y		Y	Y	Y	Y	Y
Patient copayment	Y	Y	Y	Y	Y	Y	Y	Y	Y			Y	Y	Y	Y
Control of OTC price		Y					Y								
Control of hospital price		Y					Y	Y	Y			Y			

Source: Adapted from Margaret Kyle, "Pharmaceutical Price Controls and Entry Strategies," forthcoming in *Review of Economics and Statistics,* 2005.

Price regulation has a number of important consequences. First, drug companies are less likely to launch their products in countries with stringent price controls since prices there are lower. A low price early in the rollout of the drug depresses later pricing, since countries set their prices through benchmarking on the first market entered. Long-term revenues from the drug are therefore reduced. Second, pharmaceutical companies that are headquartered in highly regulated countries tend not to launch their drugs in other countries. This means that heavy price controls in a country tend to create home-grown drug industries, since firms outside the country tend not to enter and domestic firms tend not to expand internationally.[8]

also be affected by macroeconomic policy in industry regulation and the management of interest rates by central banks. The sidebar on price regulation in the global pharmaceutical industry shows how important government policy can be in affecting the behavior of firms across countries.

Finally, governments vary substantially in their trade policies. Some countries remain highly protectionist for some industries, while others have moved strongly toward free trade. Protectionism can take a number of forms, including high tariffs on imported goods, restrictions on certain kinds of imports, regulatory barriers to certification, laws precluding the procurement of nondomestic goods and services, and the regulation of industries, such as wholesale distribution, which raises the costs of foreign entrants. Trade policy is commonly designed to help domestic firms compete. The growth of domestic firms in the home economy can strengthen their cost structures and ability to innovate, thereby increasing their competitiveness internationally. However, agriculture, unquestionably the most widely protected industry worldwide, is not uncommonly defended from international competition for political reasons.

National Cultures

Nations have unique cultural traits determined by their geography, climate, languages, religions, martial history and orientation, arts, political systems, family and social traditions, and economic mores. These factors significantly affect the opportunities for growth and profitability of indigenous firms and foreign entrants. Differences in consumer tastes across countries are frequently attributed to cultural differences rooted in a complex of traditions regarding how goods and services are consumed or used. Examples of these cultural differences extend across a spectrum of markets from food and clothing products to medical care, entertainment, and transportation. The sidebar on drug purchasing patterns shows the power of national differences in behavior.

In addition to its contribution to national differences in buying habits, culture has a powerful influence on the competitive strength of firms across industrial sectors. Some nations have developed orientations toward work that differentiate its quality or efficiency from work in other countries. Whether these differences are due to social, cognitive, affective, or physical factors is never completely clear.[9]

Hugh Whittaker's study of the introduction of advanced numerical machine tool technology in Great Britain and Japan provides an instructive example.[10] He shows that the approaches of British and Japanese workers to the same technology are quite dissimilar. British workers interpret the problems posed by the technology as primarily hardware based, while Japanese see the problems originating in software. This difference is primarily due to the contrast between the Japanese emphasis on software programming as essential for manufacturing and the British focus on traditional craft skills.

TABLE 8.2 | Percent of Revenues in 12 Developed Nations by Type of Drug

Type of Drug	Country											
	U.S.	Japan	Germany	France	Italy	UK	Canada	Spain	Brazil	Mexico	Argentina	Aust/NZ
Cardiovascular	17.51%	19.19%	23.45%	24.95%	24.26%	22.94%	23.77%	22.74%	14.63%	8.03%	16.42%	23.73%
Central nervous system	21.76	6.05	12.94	15.23	11.67	18.13	19.01	17.56	13.82	11.76	15.28	16.74
Alimentary	14.71	15.69	16.13	14.96	14.45	16.09	14.54	15.05	16.55	18.94	17.59	16.04
Anti-infective	9.62	11.50	8.58	10.25	11.70	4.71	6.28	7.88	8.62	17.49	9.94	6.18
Respiratory	10.13	6.93	8.81	9.15	8.48	13.09	8.20	10.74	10.13	11.17	7.63	11.65
Musculoskeletal	5.50	6.72	4.62	4.73	5.80	5.23	6.12	5.29	8.34	7.54	7.83	5.05
Genitourinary	7.02	2.06	6.06	6.05	6.00	5.99	5.70	4.99	10.75	6.97	7.54	4.49
Cytostatics	2.68	6.53	5.12	2.65	4.53	3.05	3.51	4.18	0.45	0.53	1.49	3.16
Dermatologicals	3.60	2.73	3.72	3.42	3.27	4.04	4.54	3.67	7.63	5.97	6.28	5.41
Blood agents	1.61	7.13	2.93	2.63	4.06	1.35	1.88	2.93	1.36	1.47	1.69	1.37
Sensory organs	1.83	3.17	1.52	1.89	2.17	1.79	2.23	2.06	2.81	2.14	3.16	2.42
Diagnostic agents	1.30	3.59	2.24	1.48	1.26	1.34	1.81	0.04	0.12	0.14	0.64	0.81
Hormones	1.18	2.26	2.14	1.72	1.79	1.34	0.76	2.74	2.25	1.75	2.51	0.49
Parisitology	0.15	0.01	0.15	0.22	0.07	0.39	0.18	0.04	1.34	0.92	0.47	0.49
Total Revenues in Millions of $US	$97,385	$51,434	$14,424	$13,283	$9,035	$8,888	$5,524	$5,290	$5,153	$4,905	$3,422	$2,849

Source: Adapted from Margaret Kyle, "Entry in Pharmaceutical Markets," working paper, Duke University, 2002.

Drug Purchasing Patterns

Table 8.2 shows the frequencies with which different types of drugs are bought in 12 developed countries. Ten of the countries have quite similar purchasing patterns. Japan and Mexico are the exceptions. Compared to other countries, Japanese tend to buy fewer drugs that have to do with the central nervous system (CNS) or with genital or urinary problems. However, they buy more blood agents, which are primarily anticoagulants. Mexicans in turn purchase a higher percentage of anti-infective drugs but a lower percentage of drugs involving heart disease (cardiological). Do these patterns reflect cultural differences? For example, compared to other countries, are the Japanese less troubled by mental disorders or less confident that CNS drugs are effective? An analysis of disease trends would possibly answer this kind of question but perhaps not completely. These differences in purchasing frequencies are clearly tied to country specific factors that influence drug company R&D and marketing programs and therefore have important effects on firm strategy.

Although both perspectives are valid, these national differences have obvious and important consequences for how the problems are solved and future innovations are developed.

Natural Resources and Geography

The last, and perhaps most obvious, factors that create national advantages in an industry are the country's natural resources and geographical location. Many countries are rich in natural resources—such as oil, minerals, and arable land—while others lack them to a significant degree. Further, some nations have been lucky enough to be located on major trade routes, offering opportunities to build mercantile experience. Others are off the beaten path.

Are natural resources necessary for national wealth? The obvious answer is no. Countries with few natural resources have built strong economies with many multinational firms while other nations with abundant resource stocks lag behind their neighbors. Japan is one the best examples of the former case. It has almost no oil or minerals and must import raw materials from other countries for its needs. At the same time, it has the second largest economy in the world. In contrast, Russia has tremendous energy and mineral reserves. But these resources are just beginning to be developed, and there are significant political and organizational impediments to this effort. Thus, although natural resources are undoubtedly a potential advantage for a country, they are not always managed effectively. Poor management decreases the benefit a country receives from its endowments and perhaps lowers potential future benefits as competing resources are discovered in other countries with more effective economic systems.

FIGURE 8.1 |

Porter's Diamond Model

Source: Michael Porter, *The Competitive Advantage of Nations* (New York: Free Press, 1990), p. 72.

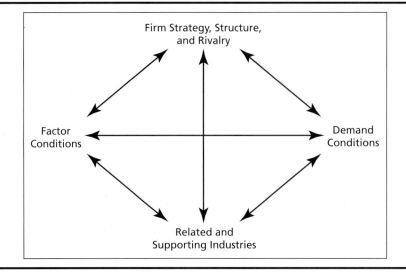

Porter's Diamond Model

Michael Porter has argued that differences among countries regarding the international competitiveness of their industries can be distilled to four major factors:

• Factor conditions, including supplier markets.

• Customer characteristics.

• Industry competitive dynamics.

• Trends in firm strategy and structure.

Figure 8.1 shows Porter's Diamond Model of national advantage.[11]

As we have discussed, factor conditions such as natural resources and geographical location are a traditional source of country-specific advantage. Porter makes the important point that although these may provide a favorable baseline, they are neither necessary nor sufficient to establish a home firm's competitive advantage, especially when specialized knowledge is critical for product commercialization.

The importance of related and supporting industries reflects the clustering of buyers and suppliers in the same region. Again the key is the effectiveness of specialized relationships between firms. These relationships are developed to create benefits through information sharing, improved coordination of product flows and service, and the joint development of projects designed to improve performance, especially in cost and quality. For example, the Japanese automobile industry benefits substantially from its large network of specialized suppliers, which has been built up over many decades.

The Diamond Model's third element involves common modes of competition in a country. Competitive practices become pervasive among firms in a country as innovations diffuse throughout the economy, and national cultural and legal boundaries constrain their international transfer. Over time, of course, these practices may transcend country boundaries. But initially, domestic firms benefit from being early movers. National advantages based on these innovations are thus a form of spillover that pertains to strategy and organization.

An excellent example here is the rise of an emphasis on quality in manufactured goods in Japan, beginning in the 1950s with W. Edwards Deming's introduction of statistical procedures to Japanese firms. The Deming Award for quality excellence became a highly desired and recognized achievement among Japanese companies. Winners built small shrines outside their corporate headquarters commemorating the honor. But the major benefit to Japanese industry was the intensity with which firms competed for the prize. This competition produced a remarkable range of process innovations in almost every activity in the value chain. As a national movement, the "quality revolution" in Japan reflected a form of competition that raised the country's industrial expertise to world prominence.

Finally, a nation may have a distinctive set of customer preferences that force firms in an industry to develop specific strategies and structures. The more demanding customers are in a firm's home country, the stronger the firm's practices must be for it to succeed domestically. If the firm can use these practices to compete internationally, it will have an advantage over companies from other countries where customer demands are not as stringent.

Again, one of the best examples of country-specific demand characteristics is Japan. As the Japanese economy grew in the 1950s and 1960s, businesses and consumers became notoriously picky about quality and did not like to pay more for higher-quality goods. These buying practices forced Japanese firms to learn how to be more efficient at producing goods that were more functional and durable. Developing these value and cost drivers was almost intuitive since the firms were run by Japanese managers and workers who understood their customers well. When firms began to export and then produce their goods overseas, they found that customers outside Japan were hungry for the type of products Japanese customers had become used to. Consequently, Japanese firms increased their worldwide market shares in a variety of consumer and industrial durable goods industries. Their market positions were sustainable since it took some time for non-Japanese companies to imitate their practices.

Without a doubt, the most discussed country today as a global competitor is China, with India a close second. While we have discussed how Japanese firms gained from being in Japan, we can ask what benefits Chinese companies receive from being in China. The sidebar addresses this question.

The China Advantage

China has had one of the most powerful runs of growth in recent history, as shown in the chart below.[12]

motivations could be thought of as exploiting an intrinsic Chinese resource or capability.

	2000	2001	2002	2003	2004
GDP per head (US$ at purchase price parity)	3,960	4,330	4,720	5,230	5,810
GDP change (%)	8	7.5	8	9.3	9.5
Government consumption of GDP (%)	13.1	13.4	13.2	12.6	11.8
Labor costs per hour in US$	0.58	0.67	0.77	0.87	0.99
Recorded unemployment (%)	8.2	9.3	9.7	10.3	9.9
Forex reserves (US$m)	168,278	215,605	291,128	408,151	731,427
Foreign direct investment inflow ($USb)	42.1	48.8	55	53.5	60.6

But how do Chinese firms benefit internationally from being based in China? The chart shows that labor costs in China are very low. The cheap labor undoubtedly helps Chinese exports as we showed in Chapter 6. However, labor costs are not at all the whole story behind China's ability to build a country advantage over the long term.

Although it may not be apparent to non-Chinese observers, Chinese firms generally focus on competing in China not on competing globally. In a recent survey, 91 percent of the Chinese firms polled stated that their main target was the Chinese market. Moreover, Chinese companies generally see each other as their major competitors, not foreign firms. They view rivalry within China as their greatest threat, since it puts significant downward pressure on their prices.

When Chinese firms do expand internationally, they usually have one of three motivations, none of which have to do with low Chinese labor costs. One, a Chinese company may be seeking a steady supply of energy, as seen in CNOOC's purchase of Indonesian oil and gas reserves. Two, the firm may be fleeing an industry that is highly mature in China such as consumer electronics. TCL's joint venture with Thomson and TI in flat panel TVs is a good example here. Or three, the firm may be searching for a more upscale brand, as illustrated by Lenovo's purchase of IBM's PC business. None of these

Moreover, Chinese companies don't always have an easy time competing overseas. They often encounter stricter rules regarding property rights than they are used to at home, as Huawei discovered in the United States. Also, investment analysts in Europe and the United States are impatient with the low transparency that Chinese firms have become used to at home. Only a handful of Chinese international competitors, such as Haier, have adapted effectively to these new demands.

Finally, Chinese executives perceive their workers as insufficiently innovative. There is little apparent drive in the workforce to improve operations through continuous improvement in processes. So at this point, there seems to be not much impetus among Chinese firms to develop management or operating practices that will create a country advantage in international competition.

It would be foolish, however, to make too many assumptions about how Chinese companies may one day compete internationally. China is an enormous market that is highly competitive. As Chinese consumers increase their already substantial taste for quality and brand, Chinese firms will improve their practices and overcome many of the challenges they face today. The sheer scale of the economy in China, coupled with the ambition of Chinese firms for growth, should produce a number of world-class competitors.

A Framework for Global Competition

If global competition were only a matter of firms competing against each other on the basis of their countries of origin, we could reduce it to a comparison of national resources, economic policies, and cultures. Indeed, there has been much debate about whether the global success of Japanese firms over the past 20 years is due to their location in Japan or to their strategic acumen. The truth is undoubtedly a combination of both these factors. Honda, Mitsubishi, and Sony are truly global companies, producing and selling their products around the world. Their success is due both to the advantages of starting off in Japan and to their expertise at global competition.

Global strategy is thus more than simply leveraging the benefits of the firm's country of origin. It also means leveraging the firm's resources and capabilities across national markets. Many firms have been quite successful at building strong positions in markets outside their home countries through the worldwide coordination of value chain activities including R&D, operations, logistics, procurement, and brand management.

Competing successfully as a global firm means achieving higher economic performance than indigenous rivals. To do so repeatedly requires establishing and defending a superior market position over local firms. Companies with successful global strategies extend their domestic positions to international markets and compete effectively both at home and abroad.

Bruce Kogut distinguishes between two types of advantage: country-specific (or comparative) advantage, which derives from a firm's home country; and firm-specific (or competitive) advantage, which is due to the capabilities of the firm itself (see Table 8.3).[13] Comparative advantage based on country characteristics has been discussed earlier in the chapter. Competitive advantage in global markets is produced when a firm aggregates one or more activities to achieve a stronger position, than local competitors.[14] The global firm's

TABLE 8.3 | Global Strategy Framework

		Country-specific Advantage	
		Low	**High**
	Low	Nationally segmented industry	Vertically integrated industry across borders
Firm-specific Advantage			
	High	Horizontally integrated industry across borders	Horizontally and vertically integrated industry across borders

Source: Adapted from Bruce Kogut, "Designing Global Strategies: Comparative and Competitive Value Chains," *Sloan Management Review*, 1985.

superior market position may arise from a range of value drivers, such as superior technology, geographical scope, breadth of line, and brand. The resources and capabilities producing this value are specific to the firm and protected from rivals. Similarly, a firm's dominant cost position, controlling for value, may be due to

- Economies of scale in one or more activities, such as operations, procurement, or technology development.
- Economies of scope from products sold across multiple markets.
- The diffusion of superior practices from the home country to satellite units in regional markets.
- An accelerated learning curve from aggregating the experiences of regional units.

These cost drivers can make global firms more efficient in local markets compared to their nonglobal rivals.

To understand how country- and firm-specific advantage are related to each other, it is useful first to think of them as applying to industries rather than firms. Table 8.3 outlines how this works for four types of industry. Each type represents a highly stylized but helpful way to think about competition in local and global markets.

Nationally Segmented Industries

The first type of industry is isolated within each country, for all countries worldwide. No country has a special advantage over any other in providing critical resources, so there is nothing for a firm to leverage across borders. Further, no firm has a special advantage over any other firm across borders in the resources and capabilities that produce superior value or cost drivers. Kogut calls this type of industry "nationally segmented."

What kind of industry might this be? First, there can be no firm-specific value advantage cross-border. So either each country is distinct in the kind of value customers want or all firms can deliver about the same value no matter where it is delivered. The average barbershop might be an example of the latter. Further, firms cannot develop superior cost drivers from aggregating activities across countries. So the minimum efficient scale in each activity must be small enough that local firms can be competitive. Also, whatever economies of scope are available should be attainable by local as well as global competitors. Last, since no country has a comparative advantage over any other, there are no learning benefits for firms competing across national markets. In other words, there is no economic basis for firms in one country to dominate worldwide markets nor is there an opportunity to establish a global franchise.

In the present era of extensive global competition by firms in almost all markets, it is hard to find examples of nationally segmented industries. Until the late 1970s, however, it was common for professional service industries, such as law firms and advertising firms, to be local rather than global. There were several obvious reasons for this international segmentation. First, professional service firms have very low fixed costs, leading to few, if any, scale or scope economies in everyday business activities. Also, as they grow, this type of firm typically becomes increasingly fragmented internally, making it difficult to transfer specialized service innovations across units in different countries. Since professional service firms make their money by selling know-how, the absence of an ability to transfer innovations effectively across national boundaries is a major impediment to globalization. Third, these firms typically provide services that are specialized to specific customer needs, which are tied to national regulations and market idiosyncrasies. The pervasiveness of specialized services makes it easier for local firms to compete on the basis of their knowledge of the regional or national market.

These technological and market barriers to globalization became clear when Maurice and Charles Saatchi of Great Britain tried to globalize the advertising industry in the 1980s. Since there were no available scope economies from combining the acquired companies in Europe and the United States, the brothers' initial attempt failed as costs outstripped revenues. It soon became evident, however, that the Saatchis had focused on the wrong model for internationalizing the industry.

The Saatchi brothers' failure had to do with their timing as well as with their execution. Once global customers understood that it would be possible to buy advertising services in more than one country from a single agency, the door opened for new attempts at establishing multinational advertising firms. Many of these, such as Omnicom, JWT, EuroRSCG, and Grey, are in existence today. These firms focus on serving a global customer base rather than competing with local advertising firms for local business. Although the latter can be a significant part of their business, it is not the economic rationale behind their multinational organization. Rather, their ability to offer one account to a multinational customer and to coordinate advertising across markets differentiates them from local firms and adds value when the customer's worldwide marketing strategy requires such coordination. Higher value due to geographic scope, not lower cost, provides the rationale for the global professional service firm.

It would be wrong, however, to assume that there were *no* international professional service firms prior to 1980. McKinsey, the management consulting firm, has had a global practice since the early part of the 20th century. In many countries, McKinsey established an early mover advantage as a highly differentiated consultancy. It overcame the difficulties of transferring specialized knowledge across borders by hiring innovative, energetic professionals with a high capacity for learning. The network of these consultants was more cohesive than that of other firms and enabled the diffusion of new administrative practices, such as the multidivisional form, to industrialized nations worldwide. It is likely that McKinsey benefited substantially from being American since the United States, at the time McKinsey began to expand internationally, was a hub of administrative innovation.

Industries Vertically Integrated across Countries

The second kind of industry in Kogut's scheme is vertically integrated across countries. In this case, one country possesses resources that are relatively unique and valuable, leading to intercountry trade. If there is a benefit to coordinating upstream operations in one country and downstream marketing in another country, firms are likely to own operations both in the nation that has rich resources and in the nations where customers buy the end products. This pattern of international integration is typical of extractive industries such as aluminum, oil and gas, and copper. There is little advantage, however, from combining activities, such as technology development, procurement, or operations, across countries to achieve economies of scale or scope.

Note that again we encounter the question of how different stages in the value chain should be governed. In this case, the two stages of interest are the one dedicated to exploiting the rich resources of one country and the one dedicated to selling in other countries the products based on the resources. Why should one firm own both these activities? The answer is that there are economic advantages to controlling them both, based on the logic regarding organizational boundaries that was presented in Chapter 6. However, here there is a special twist to that logic. In Chapter 6 we discussed how firms might differ in their competence to execute an activity. But in international competition the competence needed to produce the upstream input is tied to a country-specific endowment—a natural resource. So joining up- and downstream stages under the governance of a single firm must be due to control issues alone. If there are no coordination benefits to joint ownership, then there is no vertical integration.

Horizontally Integrated Industries

The third type of industry in Kogut's framework is horizontally integrated in one or more activities across countries. Firms integrate their activities across countries to achieve lower costs through economies of scale or scope. For example, it may be less costly to centralize production in a single location and to export to local markets worldwide. This location may be chosen more for its closeness to global distribution channels or to other activities in the firm, like R&D, than because of an inherent country-specific advantage.

Which activities should be centralized to improve worldwide performance? In some industries, centralized technology development brings substantial productivity benefits. For example, global pharmaceutical companies have tended to locate R&D activities in a few facilities to increase innovation rates. If R&D professionals were dispersed in smaller units throughout the world, their interaction would be less frequent and they would probably be less productive. In other industries, the key activity to centralize may be operations in order to lower costs. This policy is especially evident in industries that have been traditionally decentralized by country as a result of company growth strategies, as is typical in European durable goods. For example, during the 1970s and 1980s, as customers across local European markets became more similar in their tastes and needs, companies in consumer products industries (e.g., Procter & Gamble) began to centralize the production of their goods. This trend continued as an increasing number of products could be sold with only a little alteration for local language and customs.

A last activity that might be centralized to improve performance is marketing. In this case, firms in an industry might develop worldwide marketing strategies to direct the local strategies of country managers. Centralized marketing has become prevalent in the soft drink industry, especially as Coca-Cola and Pepsi-Cola compete globally for worldwide market penetration and share.

Vertically and Horizontally Integrated Industries

The fourth kind of industry is one where both country- and firm-specific advantages are important. Country differences influence the location of business activities, whereas differences among firms are reflected in the relative strengths of their global market positions. As consumers are exposed to the same media advertising for a core set of goods worldwide, the benefit from aggregating activities increases relative to locating country by country. It is rare in fact for an industry not to have some firms whose activities are globally centralized. Further, the benefits of locating activities, especially technology development, in highly productive regions have become clearly recognized. Thus, firms in many industries compete by exploiting both comparative and competitive advantage simultaneously.

The Global Configuration of Firms

A firm's location of activities to exploit aggregation and regional benefits can be called its "configuration." Any firm that competes in more than one country has a configuration that represents where the activities in its value chain are located. Moreover, firms in the same global industry may have different configurations. There are four reasons for these differences.

First, firms in the same industry may differ because of the comparative advantage associated with their **country of origin.** A firm originating in a country with a strong advantage in one or more value chain activities, such as operations or R&D, is likely to keep the activity located at home rather than dispersing it to host nations. A good example of this phenomenon is the use of Japan as a hub of operations by firms producing consumer and industrial durables in the late 20th century. However, one must consider the effect of industry structure and stage of evolution in the firm's home country. Firms whose home industries are more mature and therefore more concentrated tend to have a greater degree of foreign direct investment, especially in R&D.[15]

One notable case is Komatsu, a producer of earthmoving equipment. Komatsu was originally a weak, second-tier firm in Japan. Threatened by the entry of Caterpillar, the dominant global firm, into the Japanese market in the late 1960s, Komatsu struggled to become more competitive by improving its cost structure as well as its product quality and technology. During this period, Japanese manufacturing firms developed a range of innovations in operations, procurement, R&D, logistics, and human resource management; Komatsu benefited from this wave of innovation substantially. Also, labor, materials, and capital costs in Japan were quite a bit lower than costs in other industrialized countries. These country-specific advantages motivated Komatsu to keep operations, particularly component fabrication and the assembly of the firm's products, at home.

The relevant comparison is Caterpillar. Caterpillar was the primary earthmoving equipment contractor for the United States during World War II. When the war ended, its equipment was strewn around the globe and used for rebuilding the physical infrastructures of the nations where the battles had been fought. Caterpillar therefore maintained local sales and distribution dealerships to serve national markets. It also set up decentralized production facilities in many countries to economize on transportation costs and shifts in exchange rates, since there was no inherent cost advantage to keeping operations within the United States.

In the 1970s Komatsu began to export to less-developed countries and the Eastern bloc. These markets did not require local service, which could be best provided by local dealers, allowing Komatsu to invest more in building its centralized manufacturing capability. Over time, Komatsu succeeded in producing a broader product line whose quality was roughly equal to Caterpillar and whose cost was substantially lower. Only when it entered the U.S. and European markets aggressively was Komatsu forced to consider decentralizing some of its operations and to build local dealer networks. Even with this shift in configuration, however, its operations remained much more centered in Japan than Caterpillar's in the United States.

Second, firms will differ in their configurations because they occupy different **strategic positions** in the world market. Global firms competing in local markets will be positioned differently on the dimensions that customers use to value products. For example, in certain markets some firms will emphasize delivery, while others will focus on technology or quality. Whatever market position a firm has chosen constrains where and how it locates its activities. A global firm that competes on price against local and global rivals typically configures its activities to achieve economies of scale by centralizing in the locations with the lowest input cost or most efficient practices. Alternatively, a firm that competes on value through advanced design or functionality is likely to locate its technology development in a region where the most current expertise is generated. In contrast, a firm that sells customized products will locate its activities locally to coordinate design and production more efficiently with local customers. Further, a firm that sells to global customers will be likely to centralize marketing to improve the coordination of sales to large accounts.

Third, configuration is determined by the firm's **size.** Smaller firms are less able to build local businesses that are large enough to achieve economies of scale in key activities and so are forced to centralize globally. For example,

Ford is about one-third the size of General Motors in sales and yet competes against GM in all world markets. Because of its large size, GM has traditionally had almost completely independent units in Europe and North America since each geographical unit has sufficient volume to achieve economies of scale in design and production. Ford, because of its smaller size, does not have these economies and so is forced to construct "world cars" such as the Mondeo. These cars are designed in one location, Europe or Michigan, and built in plants around the world. GM's cars in Europe and the United States, however, are very different.

Fourth, firms will differ in their configurations because of the **entry opportunities** available to them when they expand into the world market. The example of Caterpillar after World War II is apt here. Caterpillar's opportunity at that time was incomparably greater than that experienced by any other firm since. Komatsu took advantage of Japan's rise to world prominence in manufactured goods, but the firm's global dealer network has remained much smaller than Caterpillar's because of Cat's extensive early market penetration. Thus, one reason Komatsu's marketing and distribution remains more centralized than Caterpillar's is the difference in opportunities each firm faced when it began to sell overseas.

Another example is Citibank, part of Citigroup. Beginning in the early 20th century, Citibank (in its previous incarnation as First National City Bank of New York) expanded its global operations to serve U.S. firms that were investing in other countries. The network of branches grew over time so that the bank could serve clients in almost every industry in almost every part of the globe. This network itself constituted a significant entry barrier to other banks, such as Deutsche Bank and HSBC, which strove to expand their global presence.

In both the Caterpillar and Citibank examples, the opportunities in the initial stages of industry globalization allowed the development of a more extensive configuration. Late entrants into the global market are generally unable to match the geographical reach of firms that entered earlier. Of course, as we discussed in Chapter 4, this entry barrier remains powerful only if there has been no significant innovation that older firms cannot match. Such an innovation by late entrants would change the way firms compete and open markets to innovators.

Change in Configuration

As market forces change, so do the configurations of firms. These shifts in structure and location are due to (1) changes in country-specific advantages, such as the remarkable rise of India in software and China in manufacturing; (2) to broad technological and administrative innovations, such as the Internet and Web services; and (3) changes in strategy, as firms shift their value and cost drivers. If a firm can access or develop new resources and capabilities only by entering new countries, it must change its configuration. For example, in the 1980s and 1990s a number of non-U.S. companies, such as Sony, Matsushita, and Vivendi, were attracted by the talent, innovation, and global presence of the

U.S. entertainment industry. Those firms believed that their business units could leverage the resources of the movie studios to great effect. The results however, have been disappointing because of the inherent difficulties of managing these assets.

The key point here is that a firm's configuration is an important element of global strategy execution. Firms within the same market position but with different configurations compete on the basis of how their activities are organized and located across the world. The sustainability of a firm's market position depends on how well it has configured these activities compared to competitors. When innovations alter the benefits of particular locations or centralized structure, firms will be forced to reconfigure how their activities are organized in order to remain economically viable. (See the sidebar on Viacom for an example of how this framework can be used to explain expansion in global markets.)

Modes of Entering Foreign Markets

Firms commonly enter nondomestic markets with low levels of investment and build their presence as demand for their goods or services increases. Initially, it is usual for a firm to export its product or to license its technology to a host country firm. As demand for the product rises, the firm typically increases its level of investment in the new market. For example, a licensing agreement may be changed to a joint venture, and over time a joint venture may be acquired. Or, after selling through export, a firm may set up production facilities in a foreign market to meet the specialized needs of large local customers.

This process of increasing control over international operations is typically called **internalization**.[16] The theory of internalization is not very different from the theory of managing firm boundaries we examined in Chapter 6. A firm raises its level of investment when it can realize economic returns to specialized activities more efficiently than the host country supplier. This supplier, whether of production, sales, or distribution, may be extracting higher economic returns from the relationship than the firm can accept. So the firm replaces the supplier by vertically integrating into the activities it performs.

There are several key points to recognize about an internalization decision. First, such a decision is viable only if the firm is able to perform the supplier's activity effectively. The competence of the firm is critical, just as it is for vertical integration decisions in general. Second, in the case of international expansion, a firm may be able to increase its competence by leveraging experience it has developed elsewhere in the world. Once a firm has established an integrated business in one country, it may find it easier to establish an integrated business in other countries.

A second entry path involves large-scale investments, such as telecommunications infrastructure, energy plants, or exploration facilities. In this case, especially if the investment is made in a country whose political and economic institutions are developing, there may be substantial political risk.[17] The firm is more vulnerable to a breach of contract after the facility is built and the

Viacom's Global Challenges

How can country- and firm-specific advantage be used to shed light on the strategic challenges of global companies? We can show its usefulness by analyzing the global product lines of Viacom, a large media conglomerate. Among its many media businesses, Viacom has three major international units: Paramount (movie and TV production), MTV (the global music TV channel), and Nickelodeon (the global children's programming channel). Viacom units benefit from the corporation's size and diversity in selling to distributors overseas (e.g., satellite and cable firms), which value purchasing a broad array of media content. The elements of a complete media platform include entertainment, sports, news, children's programming, music, premium movies, and other specialty content. Viacom has first-tier units in movies and TV shows, children's programming, and music.

However, Viacom's three units have very different strategic positions in the global market. Paramount's movies and television shows are attractive to distributors primarily because of their U.S. style and content and not any competitive advantage of Paramount. Paramount's very strong position in global media markets is therefore based on the comparative advantage of Hollywood. Nickelodeon and MTV have rather similar positions that are different from Paramount's. In many country markets both units face substantial local competition and do not benefit from being American. Further, each local Nickelodeon and MTV show must be customized substantially to local tastes, reducing the possibility of leveraging cross-country skills. So it is not clear whether the programming and production capabilities of Nickelodeon or MTV can be used to establish superior positions in a local country market, even if they offer local content. These two units are therefore struggling with the challenge of building competitive advantage globally, a very different strategic task from that faced by Paramount, which simply produces more hit movies and shows to be sold worldwide. Viacom's major thrust into global markets thus has been to use Paramount as a lead unit in negotiations with non-U.S. distributors and to bundle Nickelodeon and MTV with it, thereby smoothing their expansion.[18]

investment is sunk. Political risk threatens the returns a firm receives from its investment through (1) the potential governmental appropriation of the firm's assets; (2) removal of price guarantees; (3) removal of guarantees regarding shifts in currency or exchange rates; or (4) favoritism toward competitors. In general, these threats are lower when

- The firm is large and well connected both within the host country and internationally, increasing its bargaining power.
- The regulating institution in the host country stretches across economic sectors and is well established, decreasing its vulnerability to attack by political entrepreneurs.
- Powerful interests within the country benefit from trade liberalization, providing the firm with political allies.
- The firm's investment is not associated with a notable redistribution of wealth or value in the host country, lowering the chance to be attacked politically.

Organizing for Global Competition

Doing business in more than one country clearly complicates how a firm is organized. Competing abroad usually means more specialized geographical units are developed at higher levels in the organization. The reason for the high salience of international units is that they require top management oversight if they are to grow effectively. Why might this be so?

Single business firms, such as we are concerned with here, are usually organized according to functions, as discussed in Chapter 5. When international expansion begins, with low levels of investment, global business is frequently organized either under marketing or in a staff unit. But as investment in international operations grows and the firm brings more of its nondomestic business under its direct control, resource allocation decisions become more complex and more integrated with the rest of the organization. At this point the firm has three options for organizing its global and domestic business.

The first option is the formation of an international division in addition to the existing functional units of marketing, operations, and R&D. The advantage of this option is that it allows managers to focus on increasing international growth. Typically, the international division is comprised of units based on the firm's global regions. The disadvantage of this structure is that responsibility for international competition is separated from the core line organization. Top management must therefore coordinate international and domestic operations, assisted by liaison personnel between the units.

A second option is to subordinate international operations to the functions themselves. In this case, the functions may be organized geographically so that marketing, for example, contains a separate unit for each region where the firm competes. This option allows each function to coordinate its investments globally. Worldwide coordination within functions may be especially important when the firm sells to global customers, as is common in service industries such as financial services and telecommunications, or when the firm competes against global competitors whose strategies are multiregional, as in products industries such as soft drinks and soap. However, this option creates problems for coordinating activities across the value chain (e.g., between marketing and operations) since conflicts between functions within a region must again be resolved at the top of the firm.

A third option is organizing first on the basis of the global regions and second on the functions that make up the business. Here regional managers, rather than functional managers, control how the firm competes in particular geographical areas. Each regional manager acts virtually as an independent general manager, responding to local opportunities and constraints. Clearly, this way of organizing for global competition is appropriate when the regions are sufficiently different in their competitive characteristics that the advantages of local control over the firm's activities are greater than the advantages of global centralization. One benefit of regional control is the ability to compete more effectively for local customers with special requirements. In general, the more specialized the local needs, the more likely the firm is to give greater control to regional managers.

Fourth, many firms adopt a combination of these options, centralizing some activities globally and decentralizing others by region. For example, technology development may be centralized in a region, such as Silicon Valley for semiconductor design or southern California for automobile design. Operations and marketing, however, may be decentralized by region, so that the basic designs created centrally are modified, built into products, and sold according to the needs of local customers.

A second form of hybrid structure is the elevation of one or more countries in a firm's hierarchy alongside a functional structure in which the other global regions are subordinated. In this case the country is an important and specialized market which requires top management attention. U.S. firms have frequently positioned Japan in this way in their organization, and it is likely they will give China a similar importance.

Finally, the use of hybrid structures has led in some organizations to create more complex networks among worldwide units. The flows within the network consist of people, components, resources, and information, and are managed by a central hub through intricate rules and coordination mechanisms. These rules are focused on building worldwide competitiveness by exploiting either comparative or competitive advantage or both, depending on the needs of the business. Christopher Bartlett and Sumantra Ghoshal have called the network form a **transnational**.[19] Table 8.4 shows centralized, decentralized, and transnational organizational structures for global firms.

The transition to the transnational can occur whether the firm is initially centralized or geographically decentralized. For example, Bartlett and Ghoshal describe how in the 1980s Matsushita, the giant Japanese conglomerate, operating from its powerful Japanese base, slowly decentralized authority to its regional

TABLE 8.4 | Types of Organizational Structure of Global Firms

	Global	Multidomestic	Transnational
Configuration of assets and resources	Centralized by function	Decentralized by geography	Dispersed, interdependent, and specialized
Role of overseas operations	Implement parent company strategies	Sensing and exploiting local opportunities	Differentiated contributions by local units to worldwide operations
Development and diffusion of knowledge	Knowledge developed and retained at the center	Knowledge developed and retained locally	Knowledge developed across regions and shared globally

Source: Adapted from Christopher Bartlett and Sumantra Ghoshal, *Managing across Borders: The Transnational Solution* (Cambridge, MA: Harvard Business School Press, 1989), p. 65.

units and linked them through Japanese headquarters to create a worldwide network for improved strategy execution. Thomas Malnight has shown how Citibank, initially highly decentralized geographically, built a powerful network of information and resource transfers among its national units in order to compete more effectively against competitors entering its core global commercial banking business.[20]

The transnational form is a worldwide control and coordination system. As such it poses significant challenges for other elements of strategy execution such as the construction of consistent global activity systems, the development of a strong culture within the firm, and the design of effective incentives throughout the organization. The complexities of execution in the transnational thus surpass those of the simpler centralized or decentralized forms. The benefits from the network can be fully realized only as the firm invents novel processes to manage these complexities effectively.

Summary

In this chapter we have discussed why geography is an important part of a firm's strategy. Global competition is a pervasive, growing force that can either improve or constrain a firm's opportunities for gain. Firms benefit from clustering in regions because of three factors: labor pooling, specialized suppliers, and technology spillovers. Countries overlay regions with laws, regulations, location, endowments, and the many aspects of national culture. To understand how firms compete in this context, we need to separate the benefit due to belonging to a region and country—called comparative advantage—from the benefit a firm receives from its own resources and capabilities—called firm or competitive advantage. Global rivalry is most complex when these two benefits are combined. Expansion into new geographical markets is driven by a logic that is remarkably close to that of vertical integration—based on control and competence. Further, the challenges of managing a global business reflects the full range of issues involved in strategy execution.

Summary Points

- Global markets present opportunities for growth and increased performance as well as place significant pressures on domestic firms to compete more intensely.
- Marshall suggested that there were three reasons why geographical clusters appear: (1) the advantages of pooling a common labor force by firms in the industry; (2) the gains from inputs from local specialized suppliers; and (3) the benefits from technological spillovers in the region.

- Regional markets for technological innovation are highly imperfect; they are structured around a set of core firms, mostly large incumbents; and they are dependent on the policies of these firms regarding how technological innovation should diffuse throughout the region.

- Saxenian's insight is that the key to achieving a regional advantage due to technological spillovers is a set of policies, some formal, some ad hoc, in powerful, central firms that promote the spread of innovative ideas among firms in the region.

- Start-up activity can be especially critical for regional growth within an industry sector when there is a high rate of technological innovation that stretches the capabilities of incumbents.

- In addition to their governing role as makers of policies and regulations to guide economic behavior, nations are also geographical locations with identifiable cultural traits and orientations.

- Porter's Diamond Model includes resource arguments for comparative advantage, the value of having leading edge customers, the competitive dynamics of an industry within a country, and the norms of organization building.

- Kogut distinguishes between two types of advantage: comparative advantage, which is associated with benefits due to a firm's home country; and competitive advantage, which is due to the capabilities of the firm itself.

- Nationally segmented industries are those where no country has a special advantage over any other in providing critical resources to the industry and no firm has a special advantage in value or cost drivers that can be used to compete across borders.

- Competing successfully as a global firm means achieving economic performance that is higher than that of indigenous competitors in each local market.

- Industries are vertically integrated across countries when there is a benefit to coordinating upstream operations in a resource-rich country and downstream marketing in another country.

- In horizontally integrated industries, firms integrate their activities across countries to achieve lower costs.

- Vertically and horizontally integrated industries are those where both comparative and competitive advantage are important.

- Kogut calls a firm's location of activities, both locally and globally, to take advantage of aggregation and regional benefits *configuration*.

- The process of increasing control over international operations is typically called *internalization*.

- The organization of global firms depends on the relative importance of functional and geographical determinants of economic performance.

- Firms that build and support global networks of managers to enhance worldwide coordination are called transnationals.

Questions for Practice

Think of an industry in which you are working or have worked or that you are researching to answer the following questions.

1. What are the major global trends your industry faces?
2. How has your firm responded to these trends?
3. How have your competitors responded to them?
4. If your firm competes globally, what forces led you to expand from your home country?
5. What path has your firm taken to grow globally? Has it been effective?
6. What country factors has your firm exploited to improve its positions in its global markets?
7. What are the sources of your firm's competitive advantage in global markets, if any?
8. How is your firm organized to compete globally? Is this form of organization effective?
9. How are your firm's competitors configured globally? How do these configurations affect the level of competition in the industry?
10. What are the five key initiatives that will improve your firm's global competitiveness?

End Notes

1. See UNCTAD, *World Investment Report 2004* (Geneva and New York: UN, 2004).
2. Thomas L. Friedman, *The World Is Flat* (New York: Farrar, Straus, and Giroux, 2005).
3. Alfred Marshall, *Principles of Economics* (London: Macmillan, 1920), 8th ed.
4. For a cogent presentation of these arguments, see Paul Krugman, *Geography and Trade* (Cambridge, MA: MIT Press, 1991).
5. For a classic study of this phenomenon using patent data, see Adam Jaffe, Manuel Trachtenberg, and Rebecca Henderson, "Geographical Localization of Knowledge Spillovers: Evidence from Patent Citations," *Quarterly Journal of Economics* 108 (1993), pp. 177–98.
6. AnnaLee Saxenian, *Regional Advantage: Culture and Competition in Silicon Valley and Route 128* (Cambridge, MA: Harvard University Press, 1994).
7. See Olav Sorensen and Pino G. Audia, "The Social Structure of Entrepreneurial Activity: Geographic Concentration of Footwear Production in the United States, 1940–1989," *American Journal of Sociology* 106 (2000), pp. 424–62.
8. Margaret Kyle, "Pharmaceutical Price Controls and Country Strategies," forthcoming, *Review of Economics and Statistics.*

9. For an influential approach to national differences in managerial style, see Geert Hofstede, *Cultures and Organization: Software of the Mind* (London: McGraw-Hill, 1991).

10. D. Hugh Whittaker, "New Technology and the Organization of Work: British and Japanese Factories," in *Country Competitiveness,* Bruce Kogut, ed. (New York: Oxford University Press, 1993).

11. Michael Porter, *The Competitive Advantage of Nations* (New York: Free Press, 1990).

12. The Economist Intelligence Unit, *Domestic Companies in China: Taking on the Competition*, 2005.

13. Bruce Kogut, "Designing Global Strategies: Comparative and Competitive Value-Added Chains," *Sloan Management Review,* Fall (1985), pp. 15–27.

14. See Jaideep Anand and Bruce Kogut, "Technological Capabilities of Countries, Firm Rivalry and Foreign Direct Investment," *Journal of Business Studies* 28 (1997), pp. 445–66.

15. See Raymond Vernon, "International Investment and International Trade in the Product Life Cycle," *Quarterly Journal of Economics* 80 (1996), pp. 190–207; Louis Wells, ed., *The Product Life Cycle and International Business* (Cambridge, MA: Graduate School of Business, Harvard University), 1972.

16. See for example, Peter J. Buckley and Mark C. Casson, "Analyzing Foreign Market Entry Strategies: Extending the Internalization Approach," *Journal of International Business Studies* 29 (1998), pp. 529–63.

17. For a useful account of the political risks of large infrastructure investments, see Witold J. Henisz and Bennet A. Zelner, "Legitimacy, Interest Group Pressures and Institutional Change: The Case of Foreign Investors and Host Country Governments," working paper, Wharton School, University of Pennsylvania, 2003. See also Stephen Kobrin, "Political Risk: A Review and Reconsideration," *Journal of International Business Studies* 10 (1979), pp. 67–80.

18. See Joseph Bower and Thomas Eisenmann, *Viacom, Inc: Carpe Diem,* Case number 9-396-250, Cambridge, MA: Harvard Business School Publishing, 1996.

19. Christopher Bartlett and Sumantra Ghoshal, *Managing across Borders: The Transnational Solution* (Cambridge, MA: Harvard Business School Press, 1989).

20. Thomas Malnight, "The Transition from Decentralized to Network-Based MNC Structures: An Evolutionary Perspective," *Journal of International Business Studies* 27 (1996), pp. 43–66.

CHAPTER 9

New Business Development

Roadmap

Almost all firms begin as a single business, competing in one industry with a single product line. For example, Intel, which has developed the world's standard microprocessor for personal computers, originally produced memory chips. Dupont, one of the largest chemical and plastics companies in the world, began as a gunpowder company. IBM, the world's largest computer firm, started as an adding machine company. General Electric (GE), perhaps the world's most successful diversified company, began as a producer of lightbulbs. The list of large dominant firms currently in a major business that is a significant variant or radical departure from the firm's initial enterprise is very long.

What motivated these firms to diversify? Intel's core business had become highly competitive and it needed a new source of revenues and earnings. IBM diversified in response to an emerging market that threatened the core business. Dupont had underutilized assets (plant capacity) that it could use to produce a new product (paints) in a new market. These motivations are only a few of the many reasons new business development is so prevalent among firms worldwide.

The new ventures of these three firms eventually achieved their goals. However, there is no guarantee that diversification will succeed. Many large firms now primarily in one business (e.g., General Motors, Coca-Cola, Kodak) have historically been diversified more broadly, with poor results.

Diversification occurs only when a firm develops a new independent unit with its own strategy and activities, not when a new product extends a current product line. Each business unit competes in its own product market, both helped and hindered by the parent company's resources and capabilities. When these are enabling, the parent contributes value to the business unit. When they are constraining, the parent takes value away.

When it adds a new business, a firm faces a distinct set of new strategic challenges. To succeed in its market, a new business relies on the parent firm for key assets. At the same time, existing businesses can benefit from the new venture. Managing this tension between what the parent company adds to the new business unit and what the business unit provides the company is central to achieving high performance as a diversified firm.

This chapter is structured as follows:

- The Process of New Business Development

- Motivations for Diversification

  - Contributions of the Venture to the Corporation

  - Making the New Business Successful

- New Market Chacteristics

- Managing New Ventures

  - Differentiation and Integration

  - New Venture Governance

- Diversification in Different Nations

- Summary

- Questions for Practice

The Process of New Business Development

How do firms plan and launch new ventures? This process occurs in the context of an established, viable, perhaps dominant, business or set of businesses that defines the firm's strategy. In many cases, firms resist introducing a new business because of commitments to existing investments. In most firms, the current strategy is the lens through which proposals for new investments are assessed (see Figure 9.1).[1]

FIGURE 9.1 | The Process of New Business Development

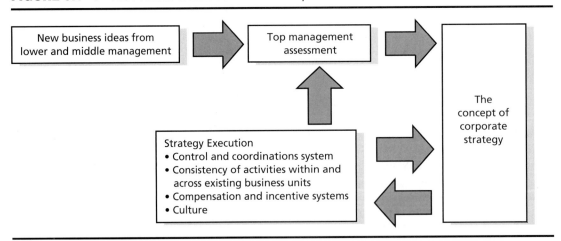

Source: Adapted from Robert Burgelman, "A Model of the Interaction of Strategic Behavior, Corporate Context and the Concept of Strategy," *Academy of Management Review* 8 (1983), pp. 61–70.

Most new business ideas originate outside the normal operations of the corporation. These ideas are typically initiated by managers whose views of markets and technologies are not dominated by the ongoing necessities of competing in the firm's core business. Thus, the development of innovative ideas is separate from the firm's traditional strategy.

But not all the innovations proposed are valuable or practical. Each proposal must be assessed in terms of its match to the company's technological, organizational, and political systems. Upper-level managers play a key role in making this assessment since they know the firm's current strategy well but also are detached enough from it to appreciate its limitations. These executives thus act as a filter through which new ideas are passed.

New ideas accepted by the firm's top managers are investigated further and evaluated as potential investment decisions. These proposals determine which markets the firm will compete in and how it will compete over the next planning cycle. If no new proposals are agreed to, the firm's strategy remains unchanged. On the other hand, if new projects are accepted, the firm's strategy will shift and a new strategic concept of the firm will emerge.

Top management decides on new business proposals even as it executes the firm's current strategy daily. No firm can expand or change successfully without a solid, stable core of earnings. So, alongside the nonroutinized process of producing and filtering innovative concepts exists the routinized process of effectively executing the current strategy. How the firm relates the nonroutine and routine processes is critical to its ability to adapt to change in its markets.

As shown in Figure 9.1, the concept of the firm's strategy is the central reference for both processes. New concepts for business diversification arise throughout the organization and are fed to senior management for review. Those concepts that are accepted change the current strategy as new businesses are added to the firm. Senior management's assessment of new business ideas is influenced by its involvement in executing the current strategy. As the firm's strategy changes though diversification, so do the elements of strategy execution. These changes alter the roles of top managers and create new criteria for assessing new ventures. The process of diversification through internal development then goes forward.

Motivations for Diversification

As managers begin to think about diversification, they typically ask two questions:

- What is the new business going to do for the firm?
- What is the firm going to do for the new business?

The first question pertains to the ways in which the new venture contributes to the firm's financial performance and to the other businesses in the firm. There are three contributions the venture can make:

- Reduction in earnings volatility.

- Growth in revenues or earnings.
- Favorable repositioning of current businesses.

The second question takes the reverse perspective—what does the firm add to the new venture? Given that the new business must compete effectively to produce targeted financial returns, what resources and capabilities can the firm give it to strengthen its market position and increase its performance over time? This question focuses on leveraging the assets of the firm as it grows through new business development.

Contributions of the Venture to the Corporation

Risk Reduction   One reason for diversifying is to reduce earnings volatility. This financial motivation is not sufficient for diversification however. The reason is that, by diversifying risk through adding new businesses, managers take on a function that shareholders can perform more efficiently. Stockholders typically diversify the risk in their portfolios through owning shares in companies whose returns are relatively uncorrelated. Since the costs of diversification would normally be much larger than the costs of adjusting a stock portfolio, it seems clear that adding new businesses to lower the corporation's financial risk is a poor use of resources.[2] Risk reduction should be subordinated to improving returns in each business unit, which can only occur when the corporation builds strong ventures or develops ventures that strengthen current businesses.

Corporate Growth in Revenues and Earnings   It almost goes without saying that new businesses are developed with the intention to increase the parent firm's revenues and earnings, especially when the growth of core units has slowed. A firm that starts or buys new businesses to improve its financial performance may be successful if it consistently has superior information relative to competitors with similar growth strategies.[3] However, greater and perhaps more sustainable value is achieved by effectively leveraging the firm's resources and capabilities into the new business.[4] Although increasing corporate performance, as a goal, determines which new businesses are most attractive, goals do not achieve themselves.

Repositioning Existing Businesses   New business development can also be motivated by the need to reposition one or more of the firm's existing businesses. In this case, the new business adds resources or capabilities that improve the economic performance of core business units. For example, global media companies, such as Fox, Disney, AOL Time Warner, and Viacom, commonly expand through the development or acquisition of content or distribution businesses. Fox's development of Fox Kids allowed Rupert Murdoch to offer a more complete bundle of programming to distributors in international markets, thus increasing the value of his existing entertainment units.

There are three major risks in repositioning attempts. First, the benefit from the new business may be lower than expected, as AOL has discovered in its acquisition of Time Warner. Second, the isolating mechanisms protecting the new business's contribution to the diversified firm may be weak, so competitors can copy or design around it. Third, the diversifying firm may not be able to sustain the new business's market position so that it declines over time, reducing its benefit to the firm. These three risks become less significant the more the company contributes to improving the new business and increasing its success in its market.[5]

Making the New Business Successful

There are in general five types of contribution the corporation can make to the new business:

1. Financial capital
2. Resources
3. Capabilities
4. Entrepreneurial management skills
5. General management skills

Financial Capital as a Corporate Input   When corporations allocate funds to business units, they substitute for external sources of capital. A corporation is therefore frequently viewed as having an "internal" capital market. How well can an internal capital market function compared to the "external" capital market composed of trading and lending activities? The answer is that *on average* corporations cannot be more efficient than the external markets they replace. Therefore, just having the capital to invest in a new venture is not a sufficient reason for a firm to diversify.

However, there may be cases where the firm is the more effective source of funds for a new business. When the firm's business units have common activities, the firm's overall market value may be greater than the total average values of the industries its units compete in.[6] Also, the firm may increase its performance by investing in those businesses that would have difficulty finding financing in the external capital market.[7] In general, these units are relatively small and have high growth potential. We will discuss these issues in more detail in the next chapter.

Leveraging Resources   Perhaps the most straightforward rationale for diversification is the exploitation of excess capacity—either current or prospective—in some part of a firm's resource base. Examples of this type of diversification are legion. They range from Dupont's move from gunpowder into paints in the early 1920s—based on excess operating capacity after the end of World War I—to Amazon.com's introduction in 1999 of toy and electronics merchandising, based on its central electronic commerce channel for books and music.[8] In Dupont's case, the resource is empty plant floor space; in Amazon's case, the resources are primarily its large customer base and the brand equity of its website as a marketing channel.

We can use these two examples to understand how leveraging resources enables new business development. Dupont primarily leveraged its plant operations, and Amazon primarily its marketing. So operations tied together the old and new businesses at Dupont and the marketing channel linked the old and new businesses at Amazon. Generally, the greater the number of activities shared by the existing businesses and the new venture, the closer they are in the way they compete in their product markets.

Since every diversification event involves entry into a new industry, the key question the firm must ask is: How much do the resources leveraged from the old business improve the new venture's market position? Every business is positioned on a set of value and cost drivers that determines its economic contribution. The resources the firm leverages to support the new venture tie it to a particular market position and determine how the venture will compete. If the firm's resources do not give the new business a superior market position compared to competitors, then any returns to the venture will be driven more by industry factors, such as high growth or weak buyers and suppliers, than by competitive advantage.

An important way to think about leveraging resources across business units from a cost perspective is **economies of scope.**[9] As a cost driver within a diversified firm, scope economies increase the efficiency of two or more businesses through combining the resources they have in common. Without economies of scope, there is no cost reduction from sharing and therefore no motivation to leverage resources.

An example of how a shared resource benefits a firm from a value perspective is the price premium attached to a corporation's brand. For example, the GE brand has value independent of any other GE asset or activity. It is a shared resource among GE businesses. An illustration of the brand's worth is the GE water heater, a product that is produced by a private label manufacturer and sold through Home Depot, which initiated the product concept. GE merely brands the product and receives a percentage of the sale price.

Remember that the parent company's resources may not be more valuable for the venture than the resources it could purchase elsewhere or develop independently of the parent. For example, Amazon's online electronics store leverages its parent's website. To the extent Internet electronics businesses have higher margins and faster growth than non-Internet competitors, the new unit benefits from simply being online. It is unclear whether Amazon's brand and customer base contribute more to the venture's performance than those of other Internet companies. The important point here is that when Amazon as a brand or source of Internet customers does not increase the venture's value or lower its cost *compared to rivals,* the venture may as well source its Web portal from any Internet supplier.

It should be obvious that Dupont's excess capacity in operations was probably not a critical resource for the new paint business. This business, standing on its own, independent of Dupont, would have been able to find a facility somewhere that substituted for the empty factory. So Dupont's use of its excess capacity added little or nothing strategically to the new business. For the paint business to succeed, other resources or capabilities from the core business were necessary. Unfortunately, these contributions were hard to come by, and the business underperformed the market consistently until new senior management was installed at Dupont in 1923 and reorganized the whole corporation.

All inputs of the parent to its businesses can thus be seen as alternatives to inputs offered in the market. Both the business and parent must ask themselves whether the shared or transferred resource is superior as a source of economic gain to competing market alternatives and can be protected from imitation. If so, then leveraging the resource makes economic sense. If not, then other rationales for diversification must be found.

Leveraging Capabilities in Activities   The third type of contribution a firm may make to a new business is a capability. For example, the firm may have become expert at flexible manufacturing systems in its original business, at building and managing partnerships with suppliers of key components, or at marketing a line of technologically complex products to business customers.

The potential for leveraging capabilities raises two questions. First, how does the capability add value to the new business? Like a resource, the expertise must add or enhance a value or cost driver and thereby improve the market position of the venture against competitors. Second, how can the capability be transferred to the new business? Assuming that the new venture's value chain is separated from the firm's other businesses, the firm must find a way of adding the capability to the new unit.

The paradox of transferring a key capability is that the more beneficial it is to the firm and may be to the venture, the less transferable it is likely to be. Transferring a capability is easier when it can be codified and its elements taught and communicated.[10] But codified capabilities are in general less protected from imitation and so are less valuable. The chance of at least partial imitation by rivals is increased when the capability's observable qualities are exposed, reducing its contribution to the performance of the venture over time.

This problem is especially acute for firms making their first diversification attempt. Although a single business has experience applying its capabilities in its original market, it obviously has no experience in generalizing these practices to other businesses. So it cannot know what can be transferred effectively. Moreover, in creating templates to capture the firm's capabilities, the firm exposes what has been hidden in the informal expertise of its personnel. How the firm manages the tension between the need to codify capabilities in order to transfer them and the need to protect them from imitation determines to some extent its ability to grow through diversification.

Leveraging Entrepreneurial Capabilities   Resources and capabilities are not the only assets a firm can transfer from an old to a new business. In many instances the firm has previous experience managing rapid growth in other start-ups. If this experience produces valuable practices, the management team can be said to have a capability for growing a business across major increments in size. This management skill is critical for business unit growth over the industry life cycle.

Growing a new business requires expanding capacity in all activities with an eye to trends both in demand and in competitors' responses. Successful businesses in the growth stage develop scalable value and cost drivers to penetrate the market. In addition, boundary decisions must be made for strategically important activities. Some activities will be performed by the business, some by other units within the parent corporation, and some by outside suppliers through partnering arrangements.

Thus, capacity expansion, process innovation, and boundary choices are ongoing challenges as a business expands. Knowing when and how to make appropriate investments can improve the performance of the venture. For example, during the 1999 Christmas season, Amazon.com had fewer stockouts in its online toy store than its major rivals, toysrus.com and etoys.com. Due to its greater experience in large-scale holiday purchasing through the Internet, Amazon was able to predict demand and manage logistics requirements more effectively. Management experience within the parent company is thus a potentially valuable capability for the venture's expansion.

Clearly, if the growth demands of the venture differ from the parent's existing businesses, management's experience will be less applicable. The risk of failure therefore increases when a firm starts ventures in industries whose technologies or customers have characteristics that are radically different from the core of the enterprise.

Core Competence   One of the most important concepts introduced over the past 20 years for understanding successful product diversification is **core competence.** The idea of a competence is broadly used by managers to denote a type of capability. However, the original meaning of the term "core competence" is much more complex and far-reaching.[11]

The central idea of core competence is that multibusiness firms may have one or more technological resources or capabilities that can serve as a foundation for new business development. These capabilities are shared and developed jointly by more than one business unit so that economies of scope are achieved in the growth of the technology platform. However, the scale and complexity are much greater than simple diversification, adding one new business at a time.

Core competence implies both a technology platform shared across business units and the ability to develop new businesses based on that platform. The development of new business units that build on and feed back into the technology platform strengthens the firm's growth path. The novel technological applications on which new businesses are based, when shared with other business units within the corporation, stimulate further innovation, which in turn leads to more entrepreneurial activity. The entrepreneurial dimension of core competence is therefore critical for understanding the concept's power for corporate growth.

Core competence thus combines two types of corporate contribution to the business: technological capability and entrepreneurial skill. Both of these are necessary and neither is sufficient for technology-based diversification. Sustaining such an expansion path is a key issue for diversified firms, especially as technology platforms change in value over time and new business opportunities appear.

One of the best examples of a firm that has developed and exploited a core competence is 3M. 3M is known for the enormous number of innovations it has developed in advanced materials, especially adhesives. Post-it notes is perhaps the most notable example of the corporation's diversification into unusual and unusually successful applications of adhesives technology. But it is just the tip of an enormous iceberg of innovation. The combination of 3M's highly generative technology base in materials and its promotion of new businesses tied to this base has been a major source of growth for the firm over the past 20 years.

Leveraging Capabilities in a Type of Strategy   In addition to entrepreneurial skills, a second type of management capability that can be transferred to a new venture is expertise in designing and implementing a particular strategy. The benefits of firmwide specialization in a particular market position are (1) managers across businesses can share a common set of practices for building and sustaining competitive advantage; and (2) corporate executives have a more homogeneous and therefore more comparable set of investment proposals. Investing in one type of strategy over time also increases the firm's ability to identify promising business opportunities compared to corporations whose pool of proposals is more diverse.

A firm that manages a portfolio of businesses that emphasize cost advantage is Emerson Electric. Emerson manufactures consumer and industrial durable goods, primarily with engine or motor components, and competes through low costs with consistent success. By leveraging cost management expertise in new ventures and applying stringent performance criteria to each business, the corporation grows revenues and earnings.

In comparison, Johnson & Johnson has traditionally specialized in increasing the value of its products and services to health care professionals. This emphasis has been challenged by increasing price competition in health care products markets over the last two decades. In response, Johnson & Johnson has tried to lower the costs of its businesses while maintaining to a large extent the decentralized structure that promotes new venture generation and growth.

New Market Characteristics

Every diversification decision is an entry decision. The new market should be enough like the firm's core business to allow a productive transfer or sharing of existing resources or capabilities. The transfer is productive when the existing assets contribute in an important way to establishing and maintaining a competitive advantage for the firm in the new market.[12]

What constitutes an attractive market opportunity for the diversifying firm? First, the **ultimate size** of the new market must be large enough that the firm's long-term goals for the new business are achieved. Managers often overlook this condition when they diversify into fast-growing markets whose ultimate size is only moderate. Second, the **growth rate** of the market should be sufficient to allow the new business to innovate. It is difficult for a venture to establish long-term viability against incumbents battling for a dwindling number of customers. Last, the venture should be favorably positioned in the **future industry structure.** The trend in industry structure, in terms of the strength of competition, substitutes, ease of entry, and buyer and supplier power, should provide an opportunity for the venture to achieve competitive advantage. The venture's growth strategy should be directed at achieving a future market position that is both stable and large enough to support continued investment. Exploiting this opportunity is a major task of diversifying firms.[13]

Managing New Ventures

Differentiation and Integration

Once a new business has been initiated, the parent firm must both manage the venture's growth and continue to expand the more mature businesses in the firm's portfolio. There are two major challenges for the firm in this process. The first, called **differentiation,** involves separating the new venture from the existing businesses. The second challenge, called **integration,** concerns linking the firm's resources and capabilities to the venture so that they can improve its market position.[14]

The degree of differentiation depends on two questions: (1) How well can the venture realize its goals when it is nested in the firm's existing business systems? (2) How should the venture leverage the activities it shares with other corporate units in order to meet its goals? A common answer to the first question is that a nested venture does poorly, while an answer to the second question depends on how the relationship between the venture and the existing businesses is coordinated.

A classic instance of a mismatch between new and incumbent businesses involves ventures developing disruptive technologies, as discussed in Chapter 4. The strategic significance of these ventures can be very high. Even so, these ventures are typically underfunded and poorly managed. There are two reasons: (1) they are focused on markets that are peripheral to the corporation's traditional customer base; and (2) they forecast initial performance levels that are too low to be considered significant in the business unit portfolio.

Therefore, the key issue for the governance of a new venture within the larger firm is how to emulate the advantages of starting up a company in the market while enabling the venture to tap into the parent firm's resources and capabilities. The more alien the new market in terms of its competitive requirements and initial size, the less support the venture is likely to get from the firm. But if the venture is strategically important, these tendencies to underfund and undermanage it need to be corrected.

New Venture Governance

There are four key tasks in new venture governance:

- Establishing multiple methods for unit valuation.
- Using alternative resource allocation mechanisms.
- Implementing life-cycle based managerial incentives.
- Developing alternative coordination and control mechanisms.

Establishing **multiple valuation methods** for old and new business units is necessary since ventures require performance metrics tailored to their markets and strategic goals. Growth may need to be subsidized to build scale, for example. Developing metrics to match the venture's strategic challenges adds to those used by the firm's more mature business units.

The second governance task is the use of alternative **resource allocation mechanisms.** Because the venture faces market uncertainty, its economic performance is hard to forecast. But an adequate level of funding will be critical for the unit's success. Therefore, a different set of rules for allocating resources needs to be developed. These rules should impose resource constraints on the venture in line with its strategic importance, including estimates of both the upside potential of success and downside risks of failure.

The third governance task concerns implementing life-cycle based **managerial incentives.** Firms facing substantial change need a stable cadre of entrepreneurially oriented managers. Without such a group, the firm will be reduced to managing mature, low-margin businesses with low prospects for growth. However, many managers are loathe to start up new ventures because early payoffs are virtually nonexistent and later payoffs, however large, are fraught with risk. Clear models indicating the personal benefits of entrepreneurial success within the firm therefore need to be developed. For example, William L. McKnight, a former chairman of the board at 3M, said, "Management that is destructively critical when mistakes are made kills initiative. It's essential that we have many people with initiative if we are to grow."[15]

The fourth task involves developing alternative mechanisms for **interunit coordination and control.** Transfers between the venture and other units may be governed as a market or through the management hierarchy. At the market end of the governance spectrum, the venture buys goods and services from other in-house businesses using prices often set by comparison with external transactions. This arrangement differentiates the venture from the other businesses but reduces the benefits of incubating it within the parent. At the hierarchical end of the spectrum, the venture may be located within an existing business unit and is subject to its administrative procedures and constraints. The parent organization may provide the venture with significant resources, for example, shared production facilities, but entrepreneurial incentives are dulled.

Most multibusiness firms, therefore, adopt coordination and control mechanisms somewhere in the middle of the spectrum—combining both market and hierarchical arrangements. We will discuss these mechanisms in detail in the next chapter.

Carve-outs

One way to maintain entrepreneurial incentives within the firm, as well as provide a means for valuing the venture, is to offer equity in the unit to buyers outside the firm. Venture managers who are vested in the unit's stock may gain substantially when it goes public, in amounts similar to those possible if the venture had been independent. The firm also benefits from holding stock in the venture. Corporate managers therefore are more receptive to new venture ideas that have a high potential for economic performance as valued by public equity markets. Thermoelectron pursued this strategy successfully in the early phases of its diversification history.[16]

Diversification in Different Nations

We have emphasized the contributions existing businesses make to the new venture. Without these contributions, there is simply no reason for the venture to exist within the parent firm. One might ask whether this connection between a firm's core businesses and its new ventures produces a single, deterministic path of expansion from one industry into another. For example, oil companies have diversified virtually en masse into petrochemicals, primarily to take advantage of economies of supply and logistics and the management expertise in operating large-scale processing facilities. Do we find that this kind of lockstep industry-to-industry expansion path is followed by all industries in every country?

The answer is no: Industry-to-industry diversification patterns vary substantially across nations. These differences exist even though in each country the businesses in the diversifying firms are related through sharing resources or capabilities.[17]

The reason for such differences is that the opportunities for diversification in each country are to a large extent determined by institutional factors, and the strength and character of these factors are specific to each nation. Forces such as regulation, industry associations, labor involvement in the governance of firms (as found in Germany), and relationships among owners of incumbent firms, are powerful for some industries and weaker for others depending on the country. Variation in these forces across nations will therefore skew the opportunities available to any firm attempting to grow through diversification. Different opportunity sets create different country-specific expansion paths for firms in the same original industry.

It is important then not to assume that diversification patterns will be uniform around the world. Nor is it sensible to assume that there is only one industry into which a firm must diversify to achieve economies of scope in combining activities across businesses. Which new industries are chosen is in part a function of the structure of opportunities presented by nation-specific institutions.

Summary

In this chapter we have examined why and how firms diversify into new industries. We have looked at where ideas for new ventures come from and how they are evaluated. In addition, we considered the various reasons firms are motivated to diversify and the mechanisms for managing new ventures. Finally, we saw that diversification paths can vary across countries because of differences in national institutions.

But how successful is diversification as a means of improving overall firm performance? In general, the risks are high. As we will see in the next chapter, the share prices of unrelated diversified firms tend to trade at a discount compared to their more focused competitors. We will see that this diversification discount constitutes a failure in execution and look at the various remedies firms have tried to overcome it.

Summary Points

- Every diversification event involves entry into a new industry.

- The contribution of a firm's resources and capabilities to a new venture is central for achieving and defending its competitive advantage.

- When the potential of its initial business wanes, a firm begins to search for other markets to apply the skills and resources it has developed.

- There are three general types of new market opportunity: one that involves a new technology, a new set of customers, or both of these.

- Establishing new businesses rarely solves a firm's economic problems in its core business.

- As a firm begins to think about diversification, it can ask two questions: What is the new business going to do for the firm? What is the firm going to do for the new business?

- There are in general five types of contribution the corporation can make to the new business: financial capital; resources, such as distribution channels or brand equity; capabilities in activities such as marketing or operations; entrepreneurial management skills in growing or revitalizing businesses; general management skills in managing larger businesses.

- All inputs of the firm to its businesses can be seen as alternatives to inputs offered in the market.

- An important way to think about leveraging resources between business units and benchmarking these resources against market alternatives is *economies of scope.* Economies of scope are achieved when a firm is effective at coordinating the joint execution of specialized activities shared by both the firm's incumbent business and its new venture.

- A corporation has a core competence when its business units share a generative technology platform and develop innovations that create new business opportunities.

- An attractive market opportunity has a high ultimate size, high future growth rate, and a future market structure that favors the new business.

- In most firms, the current strategy is the lens through which all proposals for new investments are assessed.

- The two major challenges for the firm in managing the new venture development process are differentiation and integration.

- Industry-to-industry diversification patterns vary substantially across countries because of differences in institutional factors that determine market opportunities.

Questions for Practice

Think of an industry in which you are working or have worked or that you are researching to answer the following questions.

1. What are primary reasons your firm has diversified into new industries?

2. How successful have your efforts to diversify been?

3. What are the reasons for your successful efforts? The reasons for your failures?

4. What managerial capabilities—entrepreneurial or general management—do your business units share?

5. Does your firm focus on one type of market position—for example, low cost or high value?

6. What are key resources and capabilities that are transferred or shared among the business units in your firm?

7. How do these resources and capabilities enhance the value and cost drivers of the business units?

8. How might they detract from the units' value and cost drivers?

9. How does your firm manage the differentiation and integration of new ventures?

10. How does your firm find new ventures opportunities?

End Notes

1. Robert A. Burgelman, "A Process Model of Internal Corporate Venturing in the Diversified Major Firm," *Administrative Science Quarterly* 28 (1983), pp. 223–44.

2. Yakov Amihud and Baruch Lev, "Risk Reduction as a Managerial Motive for Conglomerate Mergers," *Bell Journal of Economics,* Autumn 1981, pp. 605–17; Peter Lane, Albert Canella, and Michael Lubatkin, "Agency Problems as Antecedents to Unrelated Mergers and Acquisitions: Amihud and Lev Reconsidered," *Strategic Management Journal* 19 (1998), pp. 558–78.

3. Jay Barney, "Strategic Factor Markets: Expectations, Luck and Business Strategy," *Management Science* 32 (1986), pp. 1231–41.

4. Richard Makadok, "Towards a Synthesis of the Resource-Based and Dynamic Capabilities Based Views of Rent Creation," *Strategic Management Journal* 22 (2001), pp. 387–402; for empirical support of this argument, see Laurence Capron, "The Long-Term Performance of Horizontal Acquisitions," *Strategic Management Journal* 20 (1999), pp. 987–1018.

5. For an examination of the relative advantages of receiving value from the new unit as opposed to giving value to it, see Capron, "The Long-Term Performance of Horizontal Acquisitions," pp. 987–1018.

6. Belen Villalonga, "Diversification Discount or Premium? Evidence from the BITS Establishment-Level Data," *The Journal of Finance* 59 (2004), pp. 479–506.

7. Matthew Billet and David Mauer, "Cross-Subsidies, Internal Financing Constraints and the Contribution of the Internal Capital Market to Firm Value," working paper, Cox School of Business, Southern Methodist University, 2003.

8. For a detailed description of Dupont's diversification into paints, see Alfred D. Chandler, *Strategy and Structure* (Cambridge, MA: MIT Press, 1962). Chandler's book remains a classic text on the management of diversification.

9.   David Teece, "Economies of Scope and the Scope of the Enterprise," *Journal of Economic Behavior and Organization* (1980), pp. 223–47.

10. Udo Zander and Bruce Kogut, "Knowledge and the Speed of the Transfer and Imitation of Organizational Capabilities: An Empirical Test," *Organization Science* 6 (1995), pp. 76–92; Gabriel Szulanski, "Exploring Internal Stickiness: Impediments to the Transfer of Best Practice within the Firm," *Strategic Management Journal* 17, (1996), pp. 27–44; Gabriel Szulanski and Sidney Winter, "Knowledge Transfer within the Firm: A Replication Perspective on Stickiness," working paper, Reginald Jones Center, Wharton School, University of Pennsylvania, 2000.

11. C. K. Prahalad and Gary Hamel, "The Core Competence of the Corporation," *Harvard Business Review* (May 1990), pp. 79–91.

12. Birger Wernerfelt and Cynthia Montgomery, "What Is an Attractive Industry?" *Management Science* 32 (1986), pp. 1223–30; Birger Wernerfelt and Cynthia Montgomery, "Tobin's q and the Importance of Focus in Firm Performance," *American Economic Review* 78 (1988), pp. 246–50; Lois Shelton, "Strategic Business Fits and Corporate Acquisition: Empirical Evidence," *Strategic Management Journal* 9 (1988), pp. 279–87.

13. Henry Christensen and Cynthia Montgomery, "Corporate Economic Performance: Diversification Strategy versus Market Structure," *Strategic Management Journal* 2 (1981), pp. 327–43.

14. Yves Doz, Reinhard Angelmar, and C. K. Prahalad, "Technological Innovation and Interdependence: A Challenge for the Large, Complex Firm," *Technology in Society* 2/3 (1985), pp. 105–25.

15. *A Century of Innovation: The 3M Story,* St. Paul, MN: 3M Company (2002), p. 9.

16. Jeffrey Allen, "Capital Markets and Corporate Structure: The Equity Carve-Outs of Thermoelectron," *Journal of Financial Economics* 48 (1998), pp. 99–124.

17. See Bruce Kogut, Gordon Walker, and Jai-deep Anand, "Agency and Institutions: National Divergences in Diversification Behavior," *Organization Science* 13 (March/April 2002), pp. 162–78.

CHAPTER 10

Managing the Multibusiness Firm

Roadmap

When a firm has diversified into more than one line of business, it faces a new set of strategic challenges. Its primary objective is to achieve higher financial performance than its units would attain if they were independent. No public firm that fails notably in this objective can survive for long in an economy with an efficient capital market. Extreme failures are bought by entrepreneurs and broken up or reorganized.

The concept of the multibusiness organization became widely accepted during the early 1900s when diversified firms in the United States realized they could not manage a portfolio of businesses using an administrative system based on functional activities. Alfred Chandler, in his classic book *Strategy and Structure,*[1] describes the rationale and process of shifting from functional or geographic divisions to a product structure. The rationale had two parts: (1) putting functional activities under a product division manager would lower coordination costs within each product line, and (2) a larger, more powerful general office at the corporate level would allocate resources more effectively. As firms in other countries recognized these benefits, the multidivisional structure diffused throughout the developed world.

The multidivisional form solved some but by no means all of the problems faced by diversified firms. A firm must continuously analyze the advantages and disadvantages its units receive from being jointly owned. Capital must be reallocated efficiently across business units to take advantage of profitable growth opportunities. Also, the interunit flow of goods and services must be managed to meet market needs. Finally, activities must be combined across units to increase productivity. Through these actions, the firm substitutes for external markets in which its business units might otherwise buy capital or goods and services. How these problems should be addressed is the topic of this chapter, which is structured as follows:

- Managing the Internal Capital Market

- Managing the Portfolio of Businesses

Managing the Internal Capital Market

An obvious and central contribution the corporation makes to its business units is financial. In a diversified organization the firm substitutes for external capital markets by allocating financial resources to its business units. However, a singular focus by management on this financial contribution has received serious criticism.

Examples of diversified firms that were solely financially driven and failed to manage their business units well are legion. In the late 1960s a number of U.S. firms (e.g., Transamerica, LTV, and ITT) followed a strategy of high growth through diversification into businesses whose value chains were unrelated to each other. Three problems emerged. First, there was no enduring economic rationale at the level of operations for a business unit to belong to the corporation (e.g., lower cost inputs or access to valuable proprietary assets). Second, the businesses were managed to support short-term corporate financial goals, frequently leading to an erosion of market position. Third, the complexity of the corporate structure exceeded the management capability of corporate executives. These three problems compounded over time led to a decline in corporate performance and either the eventual failure of the corporation or its reorganization through spinning off businesses.

Multibusiness firms whose units are linked only through financial cross-subsidization are therefore generally viewed as having a poor system of governance. In more efficient financial markets, such firms usually trade at a discount to the market value of their business units. This kind of undervaluation, called the **diversification discount,** occurs because investors cannot perceive what a conglomerate adds to its business units to justify the costs of corporate management, which are allocated to the units as overhead.[2] Moreover, there is a general belief that corporate management cannot effectively invest in the best opportunities because of political biases within the resource allocation system.[3] Thus, it is not clear why the business units would not be better off as publicly traded entities, sourcing whatever corporate services are provided by the parent from external suppliers. In this way, shareholders would be able to perceive the economic potential of each business directly as opposed to through the veil of corporate reporting.

This logical alternative to conglomeration has hardly prevented managers from rebuilding conglomerates in waves throughout the modern capitalist era. Why is this so? How can corporate management add value to a firm's business units in the absence of operating synergies? There are a variety of answers to this question.

First, the firm may believe it has developed novel corporate management policies. For example, Hanson Trust under Lord Hanson and Gordon White bought dominant businesses in mature low-technology industries (cement, liquor, trucking) that were undermanaged financially. Hanson then improved the financial performance of these businesses using small teams of specialists. In general, aside from these specialists, corporate management was very lean, keeping the allocation for overhead quite low. The incumbent management of the revived unit was given incentives to keep costs down without losing the unit's dominant position. In a sense, Hanson was building a portfolio of cash cows. If the structure of competition became more complex, requiring significant investment to maintain the unit's market position, the business was sold. Hanson was simply not in the business of investing in complicated strategic situations. During the 1970s and 1980s, the number of businesses that fit Hanson's target profile was sufficient to allow a string of acquisitions, leading to substantial growth in corporate revenues and earnings and therefore to a higher share price. However, as the availability of targets waned, there was little to justify Hanson's ownership of the now-healthy units. Consequently, the corporation divested the bulk of its portfolio of businesses and is now focused on building materials.

A second reason for a moderation or reversal of the diversification discount is the way the internal capital market is used to allocate resources across businesses. There are two necessary conditions to improve a conglomerate's value. First, internally generated financial resources should flow to those businesses that have significant growth opportunities, as indicated by a high industry market-to-book ratio, for example. Second, growth businesses that receive funds from the corporation should have difficulty raising money in external capital markets.[4] That is, a firm with an internal capital market that favors investments in financially constrained units with high growth potential will suffer a lower diversification penalty.

An example of a firm that is likely to have achieved a diversification **premium,** rather than a discount, is General Electric. In 2004, GE had the second highest capital market value in the world. Although it is difficult to assess the worth of many GE units as independent businesses, GE's remarkable valuation as a corporation suggests strongly that it contributes significantly to its businesses. GE grows by adding new businesses to its vast array of successful enterprises, but it also focuses intensely on the value it adds as a corporation to its current units. The corporation constantly develops new policies for managing its existing businesses so that the benefit from belonging to GE increases. (Later in this chapter we will discuss GE's policies of sharing process innovations across business units.) If the benefits from being part of the corporation begin to drop below those offered by market sources, the relative performance of GE's units decreases as competitors become better positioned and build stronger resources and capabilities. GE therefore is careful to divest those businesses to which it can add little value and to keep and support those businesses that it can help succeed.

Managing the Portfolio of Businesses

A major, necessary task of corporate management is managing its set of business units to increase overall economic performance relative to other investment opportunities. A well-known, but flawed, tool for this task is the growth-share matrix. This framework highlights many of the problems in managing a business-unit portfolio. Developed in the 1960s by the Boston Consulting Group, this method compares business units along two dimensions: the business unit's industry growth rate and the unit's relative market share within the industry. Units within the firm are related to each other solely through cash transfers.

A simplified version of the growth-share matrix is shown in Figure 10.1. The matrix has 4 quadrants. In the lower-left is a large business unit with a dominant market share in a low growth market; this type of unit is commonly called a *cash cow*. (There may be more than one.) In the lower right there are several units that have low market shares in low growth markets; these businesses are pejoratively called *dogs*. In the upper-right quadrant are a number of businesses with low market shares in high growth markets; these units are *question marks*. And finally in the upper left are units that have achieved high market share in fast-growing markets; call these businesses *stars*. Top management uses cash from cash cows to invest in question marks, which have greater growth potential. Through these investments, question marks develop into stars, which dominate their markets. As its industry matures, a star maintains its dominant position and becomes a new cash cow that in turn supports the growth of new question marks. Figure 10.1 shows this process for a typical star and question mark.

Why doesn't this rather intuitive process work? To understand why it is broken, we need to understand the premises that underlie it.

The model's primary assumptions are the following:

1. A cash cow has cash because it has the lowest costs compared to competitors, based on its greater experience associated with higher cumulative volume.

FIGURE 10.1 |
Boston Consulting
Group Growth-Share
Matrix

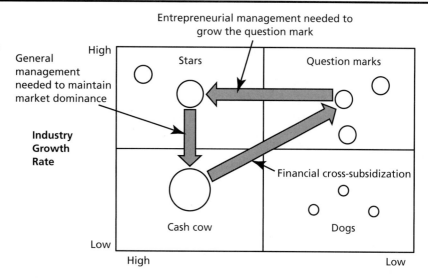

2. Compared to other units in the firm, a cash cow generates higher cash flows but, because its market is growing slowly, faces fewer investment opportunities. It therefore has more cash than it needs to sustain its market position.

3. The excess cash that a cash cow produces should be invested in new businesses (question marks) so they can grow to achieve dominant market shares in their high growth markets.

These three assumptions—which imply that acquiring market share is an effective business strategy and that internally generated funds should be used to subsidize new business development—are key elements of the growth-share model.

Implicit in the model, moreover, are three more assumptions that highlight the tasks of managing the portfolio of business units over time:

- A firm must have the entrepreneurial capability to grow new businesses to dominance in their markets, while the markets continue to grow. This capability produces superior positioning and execution at every stage of business unit growth.

- The firm should have the necessary general management capabilities to retain the value of each business through the shakeout and mature phases of its industry's life cycle. No business unit approaching cash cow status can afford to lose its dominance.

- Third, maturing business units must be sufficiently large to spin off enough cash to support the generation of new businesses. As demand

and margins in traditional markets decline, new cash cows need to carry the internal funding requirements of the firm. (See the box on IBM.)

Meeting all of these assumptions is necessary for the successful application of the growth-share matrix. Inadequate attention to any of them can lead to missing growth targets and insufficient capital for future expansion through new business development. For example, the low-cost–market share model applies poorly to multibusiness firms whose businesses are primarily value driven with strong sustainable market positions, as Johnson & Johnson was before the 1980s. Further, market share may not represent the presence of lower costs but instead be the outcome of other sources of competitive advantage such as superior technological innovation, as in the case of Intel; excellent customer service and retention, as in the case of Cisco; or a broad, well-positioned product line, as in the case of Accenture.

However, although the assumptions of the growth-share matrix render it inappropriate for most multibusiness firms, the problems it tries to solve are generic. The challenges of developing an economically viable portfolio of businesses are pervasive. New businesses must be nurtured and developed to maturity, while failures, including cash cows that have lost their usefulness, must be sold or shut down. Without such an ongoing dynamic, the multibusiness firm cannot add value to its businesses as a whole.

In addition to relative market share and industry growth rate, a firm's businesses commonly vary on other important dimensions that complicate the problem of portfolio assessment. These dimensions can be broken into industry and business unit characteristics:

1. Industry characteristics:
   - Growth rate in revenues and units.
   - Rate of change in the growth rate.
   - Average profitability.
   - Trend in average profitability.
   - Key value and cost drivers across firms.
   - Structure and dynamics of competition.
   - Regulatory pressure.
   - Entry barriers.
   - Buyer and supplier power.
   - Trend in viability of substitutes.
   - Trend in viability of complements.
2. Unit characteristics:
   - Key value drivers.
   - Key cost drivers, in addition to the learning curve.

IBM Global Services: The Emerging Cash Cow or Star?

With the rise of the PC in the early 1990s, IBM confronted a difficult situation regarding future growth of internally generated funds. The company's Hardware segment, consisting of mainframes, minicomputers, and PCs, was projected to grow at less than its traditional rate of expansion, in both revenues and profitability. The Software segment, composed primarily of middleware such as Lotus Notes, was also forecasted to expand slowly. Although these two segments together would produce annual revenue in the range of $45 to $50 billion over the decade, neither was growing sufficiently to increase earnings at IBM's historical rate (see Figure 10.2). The company's share price would therefore suffer without an additional and much more aggressive contributor to growth.

The Global Services segment filled this role. From 1994 to 1999, Global Services revenue grew at an average annual rate of about 28 percent compared with a little over 2 percent for both

Hardware and Software. Further, Global Services' gross profit grew by an average 38 percent, with a major boost in 1998 as it absorbed part of the Global Finance unit. Software profits increased by 8 percent, and Hardware actually declined by 8 percent. Interestingly, Software remained by far the most profitable segment in the corporation both in terms of gross margin and percentage contribution to the corporate bottom line (see Figure 10.2.c).

So we observe that IBM's revenue explosion in Global Services has substituted for the declining Hardware segment in the portfolio. However, the margins of Global Services were close to Hardware's margins, so IBM did not receive an explosion in net income. The far right column of the charts shows that this pattern has persisted until 2004. Why has this been so?

One possibility is that Global Services reinvested its profits to continue its growth; that is,

FIGURE 10.2 | The Contributions of Segments to Corporate Revenues, Profits, and Margins at IBM

A. Segment Annual Revenues and Contributions to IBM Corporate Revenue

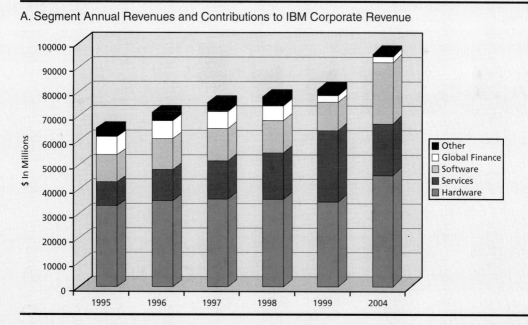

B. Segment Annual Gross Profits and Contributions to IBM Gross Profit

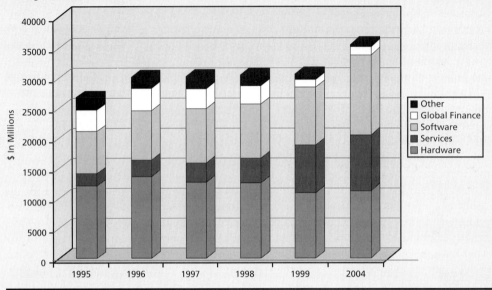

the line of business remains a "star" in the Boston Consulting Group's terminology. Another, less favorable, interpretation is that large services businesses are inherently expensive and will become even more so when their growth slows. If this turns out to be the case, contrary to the reinvestment explanation, IBM will ultimately be forced to find a new source of earnings growth.

C. Segment Annual Gross Margins and Contribution to IBM Corporate Gross Margin

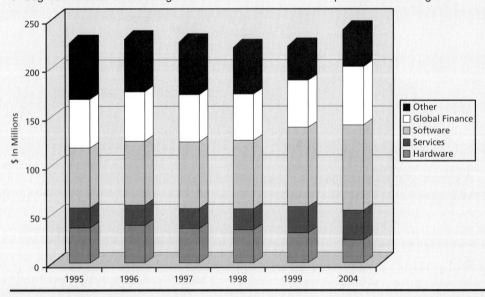

- Defendability of unit resources and capabilities.
- Interdependence of the unit with other units in the firm.

Portfolio analysis tools typically locate units along two dimensions. The first characterizes the attractiveness of the industry in which a business competes while the second dimension denotes the strength of the business's position within the industry. These dimensions capture the two powerful predictors of business economic performance—industry factors and market positioning—as introduced at the beginning of this book.

The metrics used for these dimensions of the portfolio analysis tool should map onto the way the units compete. To the extent that the units compete on achieving a defendable cost advantage based on scale economies or the learning curve, the growth-share matrix may be appropriate. But portfolios of businesses with more complex strategies require customized arrays to allow a more useful comparison. The industry and business unit dimensions listed above, combined with the tabular format of the growth-share matrix, provide a good starting point for developing such tools.

Relationships among the Business Units: Transfers and Centralization

Careful allocation of capital and effective portfolio management are necessary but not sufficient to produce sustainable performance for a multibusiness firm. As important, if not more so, are shared resources and capabilities across the businesses. Interunit transfers and shared resources in centralized activities are key elements of multibusiness strategy.

Interunit Transfers of Goods and Services

One of the most observable and important types of contributions business units can make to each other within a firm is the transfer of goods and services. These transfers are akin to inputs from the outside market and are frequently benchmarked against external suppliers. Interunit transfers in a multibusiness firm typically occur between profit centers, each of which also competes in an external product market. Because each unit is evaluated in terms of profitability, conflicts may arise between serving internal versus external customers, or between buying from internal versus external suppliers. These conflicts raise a host of questions regarding the value the corporation adds to its business units, especially when competitors face different organizational constraints that enable better strategy execution.

In examining these questions here, we will adopt the perspective of the internal buyer, the business unit receiving the goods or services. From this unit's viewpoint, sourcing from a division inside the firm is justified if it adds more to the unit's performance than relationships with outside vendors would contribute. But an internal supplier may exploit its relationship with the internal buyer through raising the cost the buyer incurs or lowering the value it receives. The reason is that the internal supplier may need to improve its performance in its outside markets and, to do so, shaves its investment levels within the firm. In this case, the parent firm that owns both units must make a trade-off between serving the interests of the internal customer and competing effectively in the internal supplier's outside markets.

To understand this trade-off, it is useful to think again about the control dimensions that pertain to buyer-supplier relationships. Buyers, whether inside or outside the firm, want control over three types of supplier decisions: (1) pricing, (2) investment in resources and capabilities that influence quality, technology, and other important value drivers, and (3) the management of sensitive information. We argued that gaining control over a supplier's decisions was more efficiently accomplished within a single organization, since the economic interests of the buyer and supplier were aligned. But this argument is complicated by the shift from a single to multibusiness firm where both units are profit centers.

This complexity is illustrated well by the issues of interunit pricing. Prices between units are logically called transfer prices and may be mandated or negotiated. In an extensive study of transfer pricing practices, Robert Eccles identifies four types: mandated market price, mandated full cost, exchange autonomy, and dual pricing.[5]

1. *Mandated market price.* In this case, there is a corporate policy tying the in-house buyer to the in-house supplier, and the supplier, not the buyer, is clearly dominant in the relationship. The supplier has the same price for both internal and external sales. The buyer cannot buy the good or service outside the parent corporation although the supplier may sell to external customers. Since there is no relative cost advantage for the buyer based on input prices, it is hard to justify this type of transfer price if the buyer's market position is based on lower costs. That is, under a mandated market price the buyer must receive a benefit from coordinating investments in value drivers, rather than through lower cost inputs.

   The internal buyer's position in its market might be based, for example, on value drivers such as customization, speed of delivery, or technology. In the case of customization, the market-based transfer price would be cost plus whatever markup the internal supplier would charge for specialized goods in the market. In the case of delivery, the internal relationship assures a source of supply for the internal buyer, which may be important if there is significant volume uncertainty in the market for the input. The internal relationship may also give the buyer access to critical technology developed by the supplier.

2. *Mandated full cost.* Here too the buyer and supplier are locked together through a corporate policy of vertical integration. But the buyer now dominates. The supplier sells to the buyer at full cost (actual or

standard) as opposed to market price. Eccles found only a few firms that transferred their products internally at variable cost, in contrast with economic theory which advocates marginal cost transfers. Unlike market-based transfer prices, full-cost prices can be used to support a buyer strategy of cost leadership. We might ask why the supplier isn't merged with the buyer unit. The common reason is that scale economies that cannot be achieved within the buyer can be accomplished by a separate unit that sells to the buyer and (at market price) to external buyers. The supplier thus has the problem of balancing its internal sales at cost and its external sales at market price. The tension in this balancing act may well degrade the level of cooperation the supplier offers the buyer when changes in the relationship are necessary.

3.   *Dual pricing.* Dual pricing involves two transfer prices: full cost to the buyer and market price to the supplier. Although this policy seems to solve the conflicts presented by both cost- and market-based methods, it is inherently unstable. The reason is that it undermines the integrity of the corporation's management control systems. In some situations the buyer and supplier can both report profits while the corporation as a whole is losing money. The method is useful when only a few key transactions require special attention within the firm. These transactions may be critical for entering a market quickly, challenging a major competitor in important accounts, or preventing entry by strong rivals.

4.   *Exchange autonomy.* This pricing scheme applies when transactions between the internal buyer and supplier are not mandated—that is, there is no policy of vertical integration. In general, the volume of such transactions is low, and neither buyer nor supplier has a clear strategic rationale to engage in the transaction. The price in a particular transaction could be based on cost or the market depending on the characteristics of the good or service. It is rare for this type of internal supply relationship to be systematic; more often it is used to handle ad hoc transactions.

The trade-offs associated with these four types of transfer price indicate that there is no dominant solution to the internal pricing problem within a multibusiness firm. The strategies of both the in-house supplier and buyer must be considered when the transfer price is set. Also important is the availability of external market prices as benchmarks for internal transactions.

It should be clear that any relationship between a buyer and supplier within a firm should be benchmarked against possible alternative arrangements, such as partnerships with external firms. If competitors of the internal buyer are able to achieve control over important investment decisions of their market partners—and receive a lower price at the same time—then the advantages of vertical integration have disappeared. For many years this was the case for deintegrated Japanese manufacturing companies such as Toyota and Canon that competed successfully against traditionally more vertically integrated U.S. rivals such as General Motors and Xerox. The response of the U.S. rivals varied from denial (GM) to adoption of Japanese outsourcing methods (Xerox). Thus, vertical integration, when represented by transactions between profit centers, is not necessarily superior to all other forms of supplier governance.

The Centralization of Activities

The centralization of activities within a corporation is like vertical integration in many ways. The problems of buyer control over the supplier are the same in that buyers compare internal prices (or allocations) and performance levels to those available from external suppliers. However, there are also significant differences.

Centralized activities are typically structured to improve either unit cost or value. But the most common rationale for centralizing an activity such as procurement or distribution is to reduce costs. A business unit that requires special inputs for strategy execution typically experiences conflict with the centralized activity, which is oriented toward standardization to raise efficiency. This conflict can be resolved if the unit changes its strategy to accommodate the standard policies. Corporate management must judge whether the repositioning of the business unit in its market produces a higher economic gain than allowing the unit to use another supplier. By forcing businesses to use inputs from the centralized activity, management favors those strategies that are consistent with the centralized standard. Only units with especially strong positions in their markets and substantial contributions to corporate revenues and earnings will be able to resist this trend.

Forced compliance with a centralized activity thus implies the emergence of a single business strategy. It can also imply the transformation of the multibusiness firm back into a single business. As more activities are centralized, the trade-off between operating as one business through a functional structure, with the businesses subordinated to activities, and a multibusiness structure, with the functional activities subordinated to the businesses, becomes increasingly apparent.

This trade-off between a single and multibusiness model may be muted when centralized activities are formed as profit centers and forced to compete in external markets in addition to delivering goods and services to internal customers. Such a shift in governance has the benefit of forcing the central unit to focus on market positioning and to invest in resources and capabilities that lead to a superior economic contribution. To the extent the activity's investments are consistent with the strategies of internal businesses, conflict surrounding the value of internal transactions should be reduced. If, however, the centralized unit positions itself in external markets in ways that are at odds with internal businesses, conflict will increase.

Centralizing Technology Development   To illustrate the issues that arise in centralizing an activity, consider technology development. In general, there are three reasons for centralizing it in a multibusiness firm.

- Scale economies in research and development.
- Scope economies in research and development.
- Shared process innovation.

Scale economies can occur when similar R&D activities with high fixed costs are combined in a single unit. Also, by aggregating these activities the corporation can focus its research efforts on projects that appear the most promising. Some of these projects may not have been economically feasible when R&D was decentralized because the smaller units could not support the investments required.

Scope economies are realized when a range of applications from one technology platform are pursued within a single corporate unit. Lower costs are achieved through the sharing of management and research personnel, facilities, and equipment. As each application is developed, it can be spun off as the basis of a new business unit. This type of centralized technology development is strongly related to Hamel and Prahalad's concept of core competence.[6]

Gains from centralized process innovation are produced when corporate management directs the type and rate of process improvement in the business units, (as we will see in a discussion of GE below). Top-down initiatives are effective when they generalize easily and create measurable benefits to a large proportion of the business units. Adoption should be mandated, since exceptions undermine the legitimacy of corporate management's role in introducing new techniques. The next section on GE's top-down initiatives under Jack Welch illustrates the range of innovations that can be developed.

Top Down Initiatives: Centralized Process Innovation at GE

General Electric is widely regarded as one of the best-managed multibusiness firms in the world. Its stock price premium over the combined market value of its business units is generally viewed as substantial. Yet its units share relatively few, if any, activities in their value chains. The Aircraft Engines unit is radically different from Engineered Materials, which is different from NBC, which is different from Appliances, and so on. So the argument that closely related businesses are necessary for a successful multibusiness firm is not supported here. Why not?

One explanation is corporate leadership. From his first months as chairman and CEO in 1981 until his retirement in 2001, Jack Welch initiated a series of organizationwide innovations in strategy and operations. Innovations were applied to all business units and withdrawn only when a unit could show that it received no benefit. Strategic initiatives had been made in the 1970s by GE's top management under Reginald Jones and even earlier, but Welch took the practice to a much higher level. In addition to a massive restructuring of the portfolio of businesses, Welch introduced a wide variety of corporate mandates. These mandates, in order of their introduction during Welch's tenure, were the following:

1. Reduce bureaucratic behavior.
2. Define markets globally.
3. Develop managers as leaders.
4. Promote sharing across business units.
5. Set very aggressive goals.
6. Build service businesses.
7. Implement Six Sigma quality programs.
8. Identify and remove managers who are underperforming compared to their peers.
9. Force all business units to implement e-commerce strategies.

These initiatives can be separated into three categories: (1) directions for growth, (2) management development, and (3) process innovation within and across units. Of these, perhaps the most novel is the mechanism for sharing innovations among the businesses.

GE induces sharing process innovations across units by rewarding it, punishing resistance to it, and simplifying the mechanisms through which sharing occurs. GE corporate management argues that all its businesses, however disparate their technologies and product markets, essentially follow a common template (see Figure 10.3).[7]

The processes in this template were targets for developing innovations that can be shared across the corporation. For example, a business unit that had developed a highly effective system for customer service referred its innovation to a central GE clearinghouse to assess whether the process was valuable

FIGURE 10.3 |
The Common
Business Template

Inputs	⟶	Throughput	⟶	Outputs
Processes				*Processes*
• People				• Marketing
• Money				• Pricing
• Energy				• Billing
• Space				• Quality Control
• Supplies				• Customer Service

Source: Adapted from Steven Kerr, personal communication, March 2000.

FIGURE 10.4 |

Quality Matrix

	Goals			
Key Factors	**1**	**2**	**3**	**4**
Quality leadership				
Supplier management				
Process operation control and improvement				
Quality information management				
Problem-solving techniques				
People commitment				
Customer satisfaction				
New product technology/ service introduction				
Change capability				

Rating scale: 1 = No current activity

2 = Ongoing efforts

3 = Competent

4 = Best practice

5 = Confirmed best practice

Source: Adapted from Steven Kerr, personal communication, March 2000.

enough, and sufficiently codifiable, to warrant transferring it to other GE business units. These units had to have excellent reasons for not adopting a process that passed this test.

The Quality Matrix was an example of a template that GE diffused throughout its units. The units used the matrix to assess their progress toward the production of very high quality outputs (see Figure 10.4). Each business unit was rated on the factors associated with specific goals and worked toward the highest ranking—confirmed best practice—in each factor over time. Welch stated that managers not trained in the Six Sigma quality process would be neither promoted nor ultimately employed at GE. So the quality process template was a critical managerial tool.

This kind of template could be developed for any of the other processes in Figure 10.3, as well as for throughput activities. The critical tasks were (1) to identify the key factors that contribute to meeting the activity's goals, and (2) to describe the best practice for each factor. How effectively these tasks were performed determined whether a state-of-the-art practice was created.

Process innovation sharing at GE achieved economies of scope by combining the ideas of business units in different industries. The scale and diversity of GE's business portfolio provided an almost ideal laboratory for experimentation in those processes common to all units. Identifying these processes and enforcing cross-unit transfer partially overcame the disadvantage of the corporation's unrelated form of diversification.

Developing Corporate Infrastructure

The last problem in managing multibusiness firms concerns the development of a corporate infrastructure to support the business unit strategies. The most intuitive framework for this infrastructure consists of the elements of strategy execution. Just as line managers must execute effectively within their business units, corporate executives are responsible for developing organizationwide policies to control, compensate, and focus the overall firm.

Control and Coordination

In the past 40 years, multibusiness firms worldwide have developed two innovations to the multidivisional form. The first of these is the strategic business unit, and the second—for global firms—is the worldwide product structure. Each was created to improve corporate infrastructure as a tool for achieving competitive advantage.

Strategic business units (SBUs) were initially developed at GE in the late 1960s to carve out discrete businesses from a larger product structure that had ceased to reflect the underlying economics of the corporation. GE's revenues were growing faster than its profits, suggesting a lack of strategic focus. The SBUs were designed to reestablish this focus by pulling together under one manager the assets and decision-making authority necessary to compete in a distinct product market. The SBU managers were also responsible for developing their strategies and submitting strategic plans to the corporate office for review. These plans sharpened management's analysis of investment decisions and enabled the formulation of more effective plans for the organization as a whole. The corporate infrastructure was thus enhanced, and the overall firm's performance improved. Since GE's initiation of the SBU concept, many companies have adopted something like SBUs to intensify managerial focus on achieving competitive advantage.

The worldwide product structure emerged for different reasons. Global multibusiness firms competed both across product lines and across countries. U.S. and Japanese firms first diversified in home markets that were large enough to allow the development of domestic product divisions along with an international division for nondomestic operations. In contrast, European firms did not have large enough home markets to allow the development of domestic product structures and so, as these firms expanded internationally, they created country divisions, each of which had its own product divisions. Over time, in both the U.S.-Japanese and the European models, the tension between domestic and nondomestic business units rose, creating the need for either greater integration, as in the transnational structure described in Chapter 8, or a clearer hierarchy. Facing this problem, many firms shifted to a worldwide product structure with the geographical units reporting to global product managers. The emergence of this structure was based on the assumption that worldwide competitive advantage would be achieved more effectively through the value and cost drivers that overlapped across regions as opposed to those that were regionally unique. The worldwide corporate infrastructure was thus adjusted to increase its contribution to product line performance.

Compensation and Incentives

Corporate incentives are commonly designed to promote interbusiness sharing of innovation, reduce conflict in transfers, and improve the acceptance of centralized resources. Multibusiness firms use broad-based metrics to reduce distortion in the same way they are used at the business level. Incentive schemes that reward unit managers based on corporate performance induce them to cooperate, thereby increasing the business units' contributions to each other. Without this inducement, market mechanisms within the firm would limit the effective transfer of resources and capabilities that is essential to overall firm viability.

At the same time, because business units are profit centers competing against at least some single business firms, performance metrics must reflect the economic constraints faced by an independent company. There should consequently be a recognition of the cost of capital that independent firms incur.

There are three major objectives in choosing a performance metric for divisional reporting:[8]

- It should enable effective decision making by the unit manager.
- It should allow effective management performance appraisal.
- When followed, it should lead to an improvement in corporate economic performance.

There are also several secondary objectives:

- It should be communicable in simple yet flexible language.
- It should be usable to compare divisions against competitors.
- It should be applicable to any investment situation.

The two best known and used performance metrics are (1) return on investment (ROI) and (2) residual income. ROI is measured as the division's net income over total capital invested in operations, both current and fixed. Four benefits to ROI have been noted:[9]

- It is comprehensive in that anything that affects financial statements is reflected in the ratio.

- It is easy to understand and calculate.
- It is a method that can be applied to any unit that makes a profit.
- It can be used to evaluate and compare the performance of competitors.

These benefits, however, are not enough to overcome the major problem with ROI: It induces managers to make decisions that are not in the interest of shareholders, as Figure 10.5 shows.

Suppose a manager was going to invest in the projects shown in Figure 10.5 and could select more than one. Which would he or she choose? If improving ROI were most important, the manager would choose only Project 1, since Projects 2 and 3 would reduce average ROI, *even though they increased profitability*. If improving earnings were most important, the manager would choose all three projects, but this decision would lower both average ROI and the return to shareholders. If improving shareholder returns were most important, the manager would choose Projects 1 and 2, lowering ROI, but raising the benefit to shareholders.

On which performance measure should the manager base his decision? According to all accounting and finance texts, the answer is improving shareholder value, since shareholder returns are in theory the best long-term predictors of the market value of the firm. Projects 1 and 2 should therefore be chosen, not just Project 1. Thus, using ROI alone to measure division performance can reduce shareholder value.

To correct for the problems with ROI, GE in the 1960s developed the concept of residual income. Business unit managers should invest in a project only

FIGURE 10.5 | Project Choice

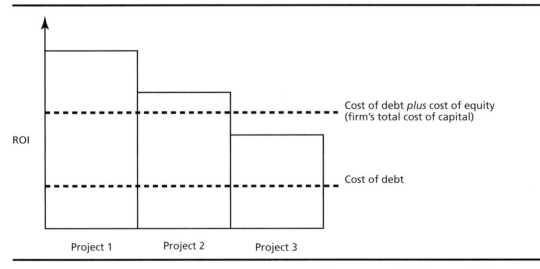

Source: Adapted from Sudhakar Balachandran, "How Does Residual Income Affect Investment? The Role of Prior Performance Measures," *Management Science,* forthcoming, 2006.

if its residual income is positive. It is computed as the net income generated by a project minus a capital charge, typically the weighted average cost of capital (WACC) as a percentage times the capital invested.[10]

Why is correcting for the cost of capital or a capital charge important? An answer is shown in the following comparison of two projects:

FIGURE 10.6 |
Comparison of ROI
and Residual
Income

	Project A	Project B
Capital invested	$1,000	$5,000
Net annual return	$200	$750
ROI	20%	15%
Residual income: Excess of earnings over capital charge		
at 12%	$80	$150
14%	$60	$50
17.5%	$25	$−125

Here the ROI of Project A is higher than Project B. But at a cost of capital of 12 percent, Project B produces higher residual income. This advantage decreases, however, as the cost of capital increases. Project B's return becomes negative when the cost of capital exceeds 15 percent, its ROI. Because residual income is based on the cost of capital, it ties project valuation to the opportunity costs associated with investment and thus to market forces. ROI has no such linkage.

Culture

The effect of corporate leadership on the organization's culture is generally appreciated but at the same time vaguely understood.[11] Nonetheless, two important attributes of an effective culture should be noted: willingness to take risk and to learn openly. These two outcomes are essential for long-term competitive advantage in each business unit. To the extent top management develops a strong culture that promotes risk taking and open-loop learning, the corporate infrastructure can contribute markedly to economic performance.

Summary

This chapter has focused on how a multibusiness firm can add value to its business units. By managing its portfolio of businesses (and its balance sheet) effectively, the firm lowers its low cost of capital, thereby allowing the businesses to invest in a broader range of projects. By organizing and managing relationships among its units, the corporation increases the value they add to each other, strengthening their market positions. Corporate earnings thereby increase, raising the stock price and lowering the cost of capital further. Through centralizing activities in which scale and scope economies can be achieved, corporate management improves productivity while limiting the discretion of business unit managers as their market positions overlap. Top managers can also play a strong role in inducing business units to adopt state-of-the-art processes in all activities, which will improve economic performance. Finally, the corporation's infrastructure should reflect and reinforce the strategies of the business units. Firms that design their corporate policies to support business unit market positions will have stronger results.

Summary Points

- The primary objective of the multibusiness firm is achieving higher financial performance than the firm's units would achieve if they were independent.

- As an innovation, the multidivisional form is necessary to allow business units in a corporation sufficient control over their decisions to compete effectively in their particular product markets.

- The economic rationale behind the corporation's financial contributions to the business units, where the firm acts solely as a substitute for the capital market, has received serious criticism.

- In more efficient financial markets, conglomerate firms usually trade at a discount to the value of their business units, a phenomenon called the diversification discount.

- There are two necessary conditions to improve the conglomerate's value:
  - internally generated financial resources should flow to those businesses that have significant growth opportunities, as indicated by a high industry market to book ratio;
  - the growth businesses that receive funds from the corporation should be unable to find a source with a lower cost of capital in the external capital markets.

- Perhaps the best-known framework for characterizing relationships among the business units in a corporation is the BCG growth-share matrix.

- All portfolio analysis tools typically locate units along two dimensions, one characterizing the attractiveness of the industry in which a business competes, and the other dimension denoting the strength of the business's position within the industry.

- Because each unit is evaluated in terms of profitability targets, as opposed to budgetary constraints, conflicts may arise between serving internal versus external customers, and between buying from internal versus external suppliers.

- From the internal customer's viewpoint, the internal supply relationship is justified economically if it contributes more to the customer's performance than competing suppliers in the market would if they were delivering the goods and services.

- In an extensive study of transfer pricing practice, Eccles identified four types of transfer price: mandated market price, mandated full cost, exchange autonomy, and dual pricing.

- The strategies of both the in-house supplier and buyer must be taken into account when the transfer price is set, especially regarding long-term market positioning and volume requirements.

- The centralization of an activity, because it is typically focused on standardizing the capabilities of that activity across all business units, implies the partial emergence of a single business strategy within the corporation.

- If the centralized unit positions itself in external markets in ways that are at odds with internal businesses, conflict will increase.

- The task of aligning the firm's infrastructure with business unit strategies reflects the same elements of strategy execution found within the units themselves.

Questions for Practice

Think of an industry in which you are working or have worked or that you are researching to answer the following questions.

1. What methodologies does your corporation use for evaluating its portfolio of businesses? How are they linked to financial performance and to business strategy?

2. What methods does your organization use to allocate resources to the business units? How are they tied to market forces?

3. What are the critical transfers that occur between businesses in your firm?

4. How are these transfers managed to increase the performance of the internal buyer and supplier?

5. What activities has your company centralized to gain economies of scale and scope?

6. How are these activities managed to increase business unit performance?

7. What are the most important top-down initiatives in your company? How have they contributed to the success of the business units?

8. How is your company structured? How does this structure affect the ability of the business units to improve their performance?

9. What are the key corporatewide compensation and incentive schemes in your company? How are they related to market forces?

10. Has your company developed a culture that affects business unit performance positively? If so, what are the culture's key elements?

End Notes

1. Alfred D. Chandler, *Strategy and Structure* (Cambridge, MA: MIT Press, 1962).

2. See P. G. Berger and E. Ofek, "Diversification's Effect on Firm Value," *Journal of Financial Economics* 37 (1995), pp. 39–65; Belen Villalonga, "Diversification Discount or Premium? New Evidence from BITS Establishment-level Data," *Journal of Finance* 59 (2004), pp. 479–506; Matthew Billet and David Mauer, "Cross-Subsidies, External Financing Constraints, and the Contribution of the Internal Capital Market to Firm Value," *The Review of Financial Studies* 16 (2003), pp. 1167–70.

3. See Paul Milgrom and John Roberts, "An Economic Approach to Influence Activities in Organizations," *American Journal of Sociology* 94 (1988), pp. S154–S179; R. Rajan, H. Servaes, and L. Zingales, "The Cost of Diversity: The Diversification Discount and Inefficient Investment," *Journal of Finance* 55 (2000), pp. 35–80; Julie Wulf, "Influence and Inefficiency in the Internal Capital Market: Theory and Evidence," Department of Management, Wharton School, University of Pennsylvania, working paper (2002).

4. See Matthew Billet and David Mauer, "Cross-Subsidies, External Financing Constraints, and the Contribution of the Internal Capital Market to Firm Value," *The Review of Financial Studies* 16 (2003), pp. 1167–70.

5. Robert Eccles, *The Transfer Pricing Problem* (Lexington, MA: Lexington Books, 1985).

6. Gary Hamel and C.K. Prahalad, "The Core Competence of the Corporation," *Harvard Business Review* (1990), pp. 79–91.

7. I am indebted to Steve Kerr for sharing this template.

8. David Solomons, *Divisional Performance: Measurement and Control,* 2nd ed. (New York: Markus Weiner Publishing, 1985).

9. Robert N. Anthony and Vijay Govindarajan, *Management Control Systems,* 9th ed. (Burr Ridge, IL: Irwin/McGraw-Hill, 1998).

10. Residual income is related to EVA®, a valuation methodology developed by Stern Stewart, a financial consulting firm. EVA® is calculated in the same way as residual income except that it adjusts accounting profits to reflect economic as opposed to accounting gains or losses. It is defined as the (adjusted) net operating profit after tax (NOPAT) minus a capital charge that reflects the firm's cost of capital. See Joel Stern, and John Shiely, *The EVA Challenge; Implementing Value-added Change in an Organization* (New York: John Wiley, 2001).

11. See for example, John Kotter, *Leading Change* (Cambridge, MA: Harvard University Press, 1996).

Governing the Firm

CHAPTER 11

Corporate Governance

Roadmap

Corporate governance has become a topic of international concern. A number of unexpected, major corporate bankruptcies and near failures in the United States and Europe have been related directly to governance failures. Severe financial irregularities at companies such as Enron, Worldcom, Global Crossing, and Tyco have led to huge equity losses, enraging shareholders who have blamed the companies' boards of directors and top management. In addition, the excessive compensation of numerous CEOs, primarily in the United States, in the late 1980s and especially in the 1990s, has led regulators, investors, and the general public to question how compensation decisions are made. CEO compensation in the United States has far outstripped that of lower-level workers with apparently little relationship to shareholder return. Serious questions have thus been raised about board and top management competence and accountability.

Because of these trends, most of the attention in the United States over the past several years has been on the design of accounting and financial reporting rules and on conformance to them. This emphasis on reporting is critical, since full and accurate reporting of financial information underlies the effective functioning of capital markets. However, the ongoing function of corporate governance is much broader and encompasses an extensive array of other practices, such as consultation on financial and managerial innovations outside the firm, advising on legal and regulatory issues, and oversight of strategic planning. These governance practices can have a profound impact on how well the firm performs.

How should firms be governed in modern capitalist economies? What are effective roles for the board of directors and top management? What are their legal obligations and liabilities? How do developed countries differ in their laws and practices regarding the governance of firms? This chapter is structured as follows:

- What Is Corporate Governance?

- Agency Theory

- The Board of Directors

  - The Legal Duties of the Board

What Is Corporate Governance?

A broad view of corporate governance is that it comprises the institutions and mechanisms that design and monitor the rules used to make decisions that involve compliance with legal, accounting, or governmental regulations. Compliance is a critical task in all organizations since it bears directly on exposure to regulatory risks. Stronger rules for compliance within a firm lower the probability of illegal, illegitimate, or dangerous employee behavior. For example, many organizations in heavy industry, such as Chaparral Steel, try to achieve a perfect record on worker safety, reducing the organization's potential liability and raising employee morale and commitment.

Effective governance also involves designing decision-making rules that improve the firm's performance. Governance focuses on ensuring that the firm performs at or close to its economic potential, consistent with the expectations of the firm's owners. Governance and the development of the firm's strategy are thus strongly linked.

Agency Theory

The dominant approach to understanding the governance of a firm is called agency theory.[1] The basis of agency theory is the relationship between a principal, for example, the owner of a firm, and an agent, the firm's manager. The owner wants the manager to make decisions that conform to the owner's interests, primarily economic. The manager gets paid to make these decisions and the owner monitors the manager's behavior to make sure compliance is achieved. But the manager's desires may conflict with those of the owners. For example, the manager may want to invest in projects that increase his or her own wealth at the owner's expense. In an effectively designed principal–agent relationship, however, the manager's own preferences are suppressed due to the way he or she is compensated and monitored by the owner.

How does this framework apply to corporate governance? In 1932 Adolf Berle and Gardiner Means argued that the control of modern corporations had passed from their owners to professional managers.[2] Berle and Means suggested that the shift occurred because ownership became dispersed among many individuals and institutions at the beginning of the 20th century, making effective owner control of the firm very difficult. Weakened owner control allowed managers to make decisions in a context of much looser oversight and monitoring.

The change in control had potential important consequences for the division of a firm's profits. As managers became more powerful, they gained greater control over decision making and therefore over how much of the firm's profits were to be allocated to owners, to current and future projects, and, importantly, to themselves. Assuming managers are interested in increasing their own wealth, the increase in their power meant that their compensation rose at the owners' expense. Further, managers may invest in assets, such as corporate jets and elegant hotel suites, which benefit them more than the firm.

But there is an alternative view of this shift in control over decision making in the firm. First, when shareholders diversify their holdings over a number of firms, generally they lower the overall riskiness of their investments, a good outcome. So the reduced scrutiny over managerial decision making must be weighed against the lower risk associated with a more diversified investment portfolio. Second, if management appears to be behaving in its self-interest at the expense of the firm's owners, the shareholders can simply divest their holdings and buy shares in a better managed company, driving down the stock price of the poorly managed firm. Third, giving managers greater discretion may improve decision quality since they are likely to have better information about the firm's markets and operations than owners. However, the problem remains of ensuring that these decisions are in the owners' interest.

So how do the many shareholders that own the firm control and monitor the few managers that make the firm's strategic decisions? The answer commonly given is that shareholders act through the board of directors. All incorporated organizations are required to have a board of directors that represents shareholder interests. Coupled with capital market evaluation of managerial decision making, the internal control of managerial behavior through the board and its procedures can steer the organization toward higher performance.[3]

A useful framework for understanding how the board and management allocate control over decision making is shown in Figure 11.1.[4] To involve the board of directors, projects must clearly be of substantial scale and importance. For example, the board typically considers the start up of new businesses through acquisition or internal development, divestitures, major process innovations such as those in information technology, capacity expansion projects, top management hiring decisions, changes in accounting and financial reporting, as well as the ongoing performance of the firm's products and lines of business. Decisions regarding smaller, less complex projects are delegated to management.

The degree of project detail received by the board depends on the firm's size and complexity. For example, whereas the board of a start-up firm would

FIGURE 11.1 | The Decision Process under the Separation of Ownership and Control

Top Management	The Board of Directors
Project Initiation: Generates proposals for allocating resources and structuring contracts	*Project Ratification:* Chooses among the proposals to be implemented
Project Implementation: Executes the proposals chosen by the board	*Project Monitoring:* Measures and rewards project and firm performance

probably have discussions about the firm's relationships with major customers and suppliers, the board of a large Fortune 50 company such as IBM or GE would be much less likely to get this level of information given the firm's large number of businesses and product lines.

We turn now to the duties of the board and the public scrutiny they have received.

The Board of Directors

Without question, a firm's board of directors has the primary responsibility for corporate governance. The board represents shareholder interests by ensuring that the firm makes those strategic decisions that contribute most to shareholder value, whether in major transactions such as acquisitions or divestments, or in the company's strategic plan. Also, the board selects and compensates the CEO and, in many organizations, other members of the top management team. Further, the board is responsible for the firm's financial reporting and manages the relationship between the firm and its outside auditor. Finally, the board advises the CEO and his or her team on critical issues faced by the firm, such as financial and managerial issues and innovations, changes in markets and technologies, and shifts in regulation.[5]

The members of a board of directors are either insiders, such as the CEO and other members of top management, or outsiders from other institutions. If the firm is a member of a major stock exchange, the board of directors is required to have at least three committees: an audit, a compensation, and a nominating committee, each composed of outside directors (see the New York Stock Exchange rules in the appendix to this chapter). The American Law Institute Corporate Governance Project also recommends this structure.[6] Firms vary in board structure, depending on their governance needs, beyond these core three committees. Some firms may add a finance committee to monitor and advise on key financial projects. Many firms also have an executive committee to handle the board's business. Finally, some firms have established the role of lead director, who serves as a supernumerary in managing board tasks.

The Legal Duties of the Board

There are two fundamental director duties recognized in corporate law: (1) the duty of care and (2) the duty of loyalty.[7] These two important guides of director behavior, in conjunction with what is called the business judgment rule, underpin the legal liability of directors. In addition to these explicit and necessary duties, directors may also advise management on a range of strategic problems, including regulatory, financial, technological, and human resource issues. This advice can be a crucial contribution of the board of directors to top management, as we will see below.

Duty of Care   The American Law Institute defines a board director's duty of care as "the care that an ordinarily prudent person would reasonably be expected to exercise in a like position and under similar circumstances."[8] The absence of care is negligence. So shareholders angry about the poor performance of a firm must show that the directors were negligent in their board activities.

This duty carries with it a requirement to develop knowledge related to the firm's business. To demonstrate care, as well as increase his or her contribution to the firm as an advisor, a director should become familiar with the business fundamentals of the firm. For example, directors of steel firms might be knowledgeable about planning and budgeting for large capital projects, international trade, metallurgy, contracting with unionized labor, and managing large customer accounts. In contrast, the directors of a start-up software firm might know about software development practices, trends in hardware and software operating systems, sources of venture capital, and marketing to emerging customer segments. Also, directors are considered to have shown greater care when they use in-house and external experts and consultants, such as accountants, lawyers, and investment bankers, as advisors to evaluate projects and reports.

Implicit in the duty of care are the director's duties to inquire into and remain informed about the firm's ongoing activities. Obviously, a board's constant search for better information about the company reduces the potential for management misbehavior. Courts have judged directors that have not made inquiries or remained informed in violation of their legal obligations.

How directors search for information is up to them. Specifically, directors do not have to "presume rascality" by management.[9] Obviously, however, once management's behavior raises red flags that signal potential problems, a focused investigation is warranted.[10]

The Duty of Loyalty   A second explicit duty of corporate directors is the duty of loyalty, which is defined as a "duty in good faith to act in the best interests of the corporation."[11] More generally, the director must act in a way that is "fair" to the corporation. When there is a conflict between the director's own benefit and that of the firm, the law is clear that the firm's interest dominates. What is the firm's interest? Generally, it is congruent with but not identical to that of the shareholders.[12] Other constituencies may have a claim to a director's loyalty, such as local communities, labor, and suppliers, depending on the jurisdiction. These constituencies are often called stakeholders.[13]

The Business Judgment Rule   Underlying the duty of care is the business judgment rule. This rule is used as a "safe harbor" or protection when a director's duty of care is being questioned. This means that when managers make poor business decisions, but the board has adhered to the duty of care guidelines, directors are less likely to be sued successfully by shareholders for not representing their interests.[14] The following statement by the American Law Institute is worth noting:

> The fact is that liability is rarely imposed upon corporate directors or officers simply for bad judgment and this reluctance to impose liability for unsuccessful business decisions has been doctrinally labeled the business judgment rule . . . For efficiency reasons, corporate decisionmakers should be permitted to act decisively and with relative freedom from a judge's or jury's subsequent second-guessing. It is desirable to encourage directors and officers to enter new markets, develop new products, innovate, and take other business risks.[15]

The American Law Institute defines the business judgment rule as follows:

> A director or officer who makes a business judgment in good faith fulfills the [duty of care] if the director or officer:
>
> (1)   is not interested in the subject of his business judgment [in the sense of having a pecuniary or other form of self-interest];
>
> (2)   is informed with respect to the subject of the business judgment to the extent the director or officer reasonably believes to be appropriate under the circumstances; and
>
> (3)   rationally believes that the business judgment is in the best interests of the corporation.[16]

So directors are not likely to be liable for poor company performance when they

1. Abide by the duty of care through remaining informed and asking management probing questions.
2. Uphold the duty of loyalty by dealing fairly with the firm in their judgments.
3. Follow the business judgment rule by making decisions that they believe are best for the firm.

How effective is this legal framework in governing corporations? On average, the answer is: very effective. But there are always exceptions. Consider the notorious case of Enron and its bankruptcy in December 2001, as described in the sidebar.

The Fall of Enron

Starting in early 1999, management behavior at Enron began to raise a number of red flags. Should the board have responded more aggressively to management's actions as these red flags appeared?

Enron

No business failure in recent years has stimulated more discussion about corporate governance than that of Enron in December, 2001. Enron's bankruptcy resulted from a string of policies and investment decisions, each of which alone would not have brought the company down. But in combination they were disastrous.

To understand Enron's fall, we need to look at its origins. The firm began as a merger of natural gas pipeline companies in 1985. As the U.S. Federal Energy Regulatory Commission (FERC) steadily deregulated the price of natural gas from 1985 to 1992, Enron expanded to exploit new opportunities. In 1988 it opened a subsidiary in the United Kingdom to take advantage of the privatization of the British power industry and in 1989 launched GasBank, a gas trading operation.

Throughout the 1990s Enron expanded rapidly into international markets. Enron also diversified into new trading businesses, making markets in commodities such as electricity, paper, pulp, coal, and broadband. The company bought an electric utility in the United States in 1997, formed Enron Energy Services in 1997, and acquired Wessex Water in the United Kingdom in 1998 as the platform for its water subsidiary, Azurix. Finally, in 1999 Enron introduced EnronOnline, which quickly became the largest e-business website in the world.

This aggressive growth pattern matched a steady increase in Enron's share price, consistent with the bull market of the 1990s (see Figure 11.2). As the decade ended, it became clear that Enron's traditional pipeline business had become much less relevant for its earnings growth than the aggressive pursuit of new businesses and the company's dominant presence in Web-based energy trading. Correspondingly, in late 1998,

FIGURE 11.2 | Percentage Change in Enron Share Price Compared to the NASDAQ and Dow Jones Index from 1990 until Enron Bankruptcy in late 2001

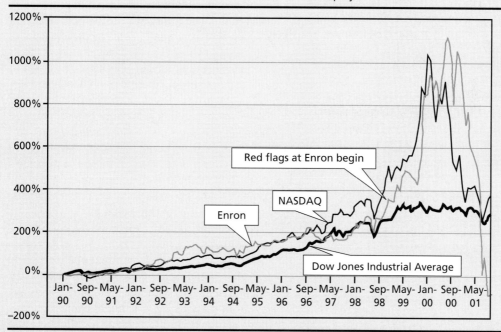

the company's share price began to track the technology-heavy NASDAQ index much more closely than the staid Dow Jones index. It is natural that Enron's management had a strong interest in maintaining the firm's high valuation, and the key was to meet consistently market expectations of the company's earnings.

But there were some severe encumbrances to achieving this goal:

1. The power plants and pipelines Enron owned and operated worldwide did not grow earnings quickly.

2. Many of these plants and pipelines were in countries with unstable economies and substantial political risk.

3. Enron's trading businesses made their money on volume and frequently involved commodities that would not be delivered until far into the future.

To solve these problems, Enron executives adopted two practices whose extensive use was innovative but questionable:

- First, to remove high-risk projects from the balance sheet, Enron formed special purpose entities (SPEs).[17] For example, Enron's investment in Rhythms NetConnection, an Internet start-up with high initial losses, was bought by an SPE called LJM. Andrew Fastow was the general partner in LJM, a potential conflict of interest, since Fastow was Enron's CFO. LJM was followed by other SPEs: notably LJM II, LJM III, and the Raptors. The Raptors were to play a major role in the company's downfall.

- Second, Enron booked revenues from its energy trading and service operations as profit at the time a trade or deal was made, even though the actual dollars from the transaction would not be received until the contract was fully executed, perhaps many years in the future. This practice, called mark-to-market accounting, had been approved for Enron by the FERC in 1991.

Both SPEs and mark-to-market accounting had been used in the energy industry and other industries for many years. But critical questions emerged about Enron's use of them:

First, the SPEs at Enron were designed, not for a legitimate economic purpose, but to "accomplish favorable financial statement results" through keeping debt off Enron's books and hiding losses in the company's merchant investments.[18] Many of the SPEs involved the exchange of Enron stock for cash. Further, the credit capacities of four SPEs, called the Raptors, established in 2000 and 2001, were preserved through derivatives based on Enron's stock. Through the use of these SPEs, Enron was able to report earnings, from third quarter 2000 to third quarter 2001, that were roughly $1B higher than they would have been had the assets the Raptors owned been consolidated on the company's balance sheet. As Enron's stock declined in value, the Raptors had to be dissolved and the company's earnings had to be restated, causing a further drop in the stock and eventually bankruptcy.[19]

Second, mark-to-market accounting greatly confused the relationship between profits and cash flow.[20] The company's profits were large, but its cash flow was small.[21] This inconsistency was aggravated by Enron's role as the dominant trader in many energy-related markets. Because of Enron's dominance, there was no adequate market to determine prices other than Enron itself. Moreover, maintaining earnings growth required booking new projects at an increasing rate, primarily through investing in riskier projects. Since the early returns of many of these risky projects were likely to be negative, their assets had to be kept off the balance sheet: hence, Enron's increasing use of special purpose entities.

How was the firm governed during Enron's extraordinary period of growth? The Enron board of directors was composed of experienced executives and academics, many of whom had been associated with the company since the 1980s or early 1990s. The board had a high proportion of outside directors, who staffed its audit and compensation committees. The board met five times a year, and the minutes of its meetings showed a reasonable attention to detail.[22]

In its investigation of the board's role in the Enron bankruptcy, however, the Senate Committee on Governmental Affairs identified 16 red flags the board should have reacted to from January 1999 until October 2001. These red flags were a mix of signals regarding managerial conflict of interest, high risk taking, outsized transactions or financial results, unexpected business failure, and management incompetence. They began roughly at the time Enron's stock began to take off with the NASDAQ and leave the Dow Jones Industrial Average behind (see Figure 11.2). Starting in 1999, the rise in Enron's share price made it a more attractive source of collateral in the special purpose entities.[23] So about the time the red flags started to appear, the company was entering an unprecedented era of growth in its market value, as the Internet boom took hold.

The answer of the Senate subcommittee investigating the board's role in Enron's bankruptcy was a strong yes. Over the vociferous objections of the board members, the Senate subcommittee came to the following conclusions:[24]

1. The Enron Board of Directors failed to safeguard Enron shareholders . . . by allowing Enron to engage in high-risk accounting, inappropriate conflict of interest transactions, extensive undisclosed off-the-books activities, and excessive executive compensation . . .

2. The Enron board of directors knowingly allowed Enron to engage in high-risk accounting practices.

3. Despite clear conflicts of interest, the Enron board of directors approved an unprecedented arrangement allowing Enron's chief financial officer to establish and operate the LJM private equity funds that transacted business with Enron and profited at Enron's expense. . .

4. The Enron board of directors knowingly allowed Enron to conduct billions of dollars in off-the-books activity to make its financial condition appear better than it was and failed to ensure adequate public disclosure of material off-the-books liabilities that contributed to the company's collapse.

5. The Enron board of directors approved excessive compensation for company executives, failed to monitor the cumulative cash drain caused by Enron's 2000 annual bonus and performance unit plans, and failed to monitor or halt abuse by board chairman Ken Lay of a company-financed multimillion dollar, personal credit line.

6. The independence of the Enron board of directors was compromised by financial ties between the company and certain board members. The board also failed to ensure the independence of the company's auditor, allowing Arthur Andersen to provide internal audit and consulting services while serving as Enron's outside auditor.[25]

The last point made by the Senate subcommittee reflected a groundswell of comment regarding Andersen's involvement with Enron, eventually leading to Andersen's failure as an accounting firm. Enron's board complained that they were misled by both Andersen and Enron's managers.[26] More generally, the responsibility of boards to assess the credibility of "gatekeepers," such as accountants, lawyers, stock analysts, and investment bankers, has become the topic of an important debate.[27]

In hindsight, it is easy to argue that Enron's board of directors should have taken a more conservative approach. But in the heat of the moment, with the notoriety and market success of the company, as well as the affirmation of outside counsel and accountants, the firm's policies may have appeared acceptable. How can boards in the future not fall into this trap?

The Response to the Collapse of Enron

Enron is a cautionary tale of greed, incompetence, and poor corporate governance. What makes the company interesting is that it appeared to be an innovator in a new industry—one that the firm itself was developing. Its board was composed of savvy businessmen and academics, but the directors did not understand the brave new world of Enron Online, the stock market bubble, arcane structured finance, and the growth implications of mark-to-market accounting for long-term contracts. Moreover, they were clearly poor judges of character and ability when it came to Enron's management. The reader can decide whether the board exercised sufficient care and abided by the business judgment rule.

The public response to Enron's collapse was angry and loud. Congress investigated and subsequently passed the Sarbanes-Oxley Act in January 2002. To ensure that accounting firms act more effectively as gatekeepers, the act specified stricter conditions for auditor independence and established the Public Company Accounting Oversight Board to oversee accounting practices. The act also assigned additional responsibility for the accuracy of corporate financial documents to a firm's chief executive and chief financial officers, who are required to sign off on the reports submitted to the SEC. These officers face criminal penalties for certifying a report with the knowledge that it has inaccuracies. The act required a firm's management to attest to the effectiveness of the corporation's internal controls and the firm's auditor to sign on to management's assessment (see the sidebar on rule 404). Finally, explicit rules were laid down for the firm's audit committee, including the independence of its members and its responsibility for the firm's auditor. These new rules were seen as tightening the firm's governance requirements, primarily regarding financial reporting.

Also in response to Enron and the rash of other financial reporting scandals in 2000 and 2001, the major stock exchanges in the United States redesigned their own rules for the corporate governance of listed companies. Notable among these were the new prescriptions of the New York Stock Exchange (NYSE). On August 1, 2002, the NYSE Board of Governors approved a new and more extensive set of governance standards, which were subsequently submitted to the SEC for review and approval (see the appendix at the end of the chapter).

Rule 404

No part of the Sarbanes-Oxley Act has stimulated more of a reaction than Rule 404. This rule requires a firm and its accountants certify that its internal controls are sufficient to preclude more than a remote chance that its reported finances would have to be materially restated. What exactly does this mean?

To adhere to 404, a company has to inspect *every one* of its processes that has an effect on financial reporting. If there is a problem in the design or reliability of a process, it must be fixed. Obviously, the larger the company, the more processes there are, sometimes running into the tens of thousands. Even in relatively simple firms, the number of processes to be inspected can be substantial.

The most severe type of problem that can be found in a process is called a material weakness, defined as a defect that could lead to a material restatement of the firm's finances. Although Rule 404 does not specify what materiality means precisely, companies and their accountants have used a rule of thumb of 5 percent or more of net profits (pretax). All material weaknesses that are not remediated are required to be made public in the firm's annual report, an embarrassing and potentially damaging announcement.

About 10 percent of the roughly 6,100 companies filing annual reports in the first six months of 2005 declared a material weakness. Shareholders tended to punish these companies by selling their shares. The most harmful types of weakness, in terms of the drop in share price compared to market over 60 days, were problems in tax accounting (-5.77 percent), in documentation (-5.29 percent), and in personnel (-4.8 percent).[28]

This task of inspecting the firm's processes is daunting for companies that are not normally subject to regulatory oversight or are lean on accounting staff. Several surveys of moderately large companies ($15 to $18 billion in revenues) found that the costs of compliance with rule 404 in 2004 were in the range of $4.4 million to $7.8 million per firm. These costs were expected to decline in 2005. Yet, there was no consensus among these firms that the compliance exercise forced by Rule 404 yielded any real benefits other than increasing the public's confidence in business behavior, still an important outcome.[29]

These reforms were directed almost exclusively at improving a company's reporting system and shaping board composition and structure. In general, the reforms did not address the quality of the advice and counsel the board gives to top management. Board management relations are guided by the business judgment rule, as described above in the section on the legal duties of the board. We now turn to the issue of board effectiveness.

Board of Directors' Effectiveness

While the recent reforms are likely to improve the accuracy of financial reporting, will they also improve the contribution of corporate governance to shareholder value? Before we attempt to answer this question, we need to ask whether there is any contribution to begin with.

One way of looking at the importance of good governance is to examine how its opposite, bad governance, destroys the market value of the firm. What might bad governance mean? A simple but powerful characterization is the number of provisions a company puts into its bylaws and committee charters to prevent being taken over by another firm. The more provisions there are, the greater the difficulty of being acquired, which insulates the board and management from shareholder complaints. In contrast, having fewer provisions opens the company to potential pressure from outside bidders, forcing the board to act in the shareholders' interest.

Antitakeover defenses fall into four major categories. The most prevalent types of defense are listed below:

Tactics for delaying hostile bidders:
- *Blank check:* the board can issue preferred stock without shareholder approval.
- *Staggered board:* directors are elected in cohorts, so that a majority cannot be elected at one time.
- *Special meeting:* shareholders cannot request a meeting of the board.
- *Written consent:* shareholders must submit written requests to the board.

Board and management protection:
- *Compensation plan:* for example, rabbi trusts that are triggered by a change of control.
- *Golden parachutes:* provisions that specify large payouts to the board or management when control changes.
- *Liability and indemnification:* typically insurance policies, paid for by the company, that protect the board and management from shareholder suits.

Voting rules:
- *Supermajority voting:* a takeover can only be approved by a supermajority of the board and a majority of shareholders, or a majority of the board and a supermajority of shareholders.

Other:
- *Fair price:* bidders must pay all shareholders the same price.
- *Poison pill:* the board may declare for existing stockholders a dividend, which gives them the right to buy one share for each of their existing shares, when a bidder's holdings have exceeded a certain percentage of the company's equity, say 15 percent.

What do these provisions imply for the valuation of the company?

The answer is: They have a significant effect. Paul Gompers and colleagues have studied the impact of takeover defenses by looking at two groups of firms.[30] One group, called "democracies," has the lowest number of provisions (five or less), and the second group, called "dictatorships," has the highest number (roughly 14). Gompers shows that if a shareholder bought "democracies" and sold "dictatorships" short, his or her return would be about 8.5 percent per year, a truly remarkable amount. The moral here is that protection provisions, however

TABLE 11.1 | Effects of Board Independence and Size on Firm Performance

	Effect on Operating Performance	Effect on Shareholder Value	Occurrence of Significant Events Affecting Performance
Higher percentage of independent directors on board	Operating performance lower when proportion of outsiders increases[31]	Share price decreases when insiders selected, unless they have high stock ownership[32]	• Poison pill less likely[33] • Resignation of poor performing CEO more likely[34] • Selection of outside CEO more likely[35] • Fewer shareholder lawsuits[36] • Resistance to greenmail[37] • Golden parachutes more likely when outsiders join after CEO[38]
Higher percentage of independent directors on finance committee	Operating performance increases[39]	Share price increases[40]	
Board interlocks with other firms			• Poison pill more likely when interlocked firms have one[41] • Acquisitions more likely when interlocked firms do them[42] • More likely to adopt multidivisional form when interlocked firms do[43]
Smaller board size	Higher operating performance in small firms[44]	Higher share price performance[45]	

Note: The numbered footnotes in the table body refer to sources in the End Notes.

comforting they may be to a company's board and officers, are not at all in the interest of shareholders.

In addition to governance provisions, board characteristics have been found to influence firm performance, but the nature of the effect depends on what performance means. Table 11.1 shows what we know. To summarize:

1. There is no guarantee that firms will achieve higher operating performance when they add more independent board members.

2. Shareholders benefit when independent directors have power (e.g., membership on the finance committee).

3. With more outsiders, the board makes decisions that in general but not always preserve the shareholders' interest (e.g., they are more likely to replace a poor performing CEO and resist greenmail, but also provide more golden parachutes).

4. Independent directors act as conduits of innovations to the firm, some potentially harmful (e.g., knowledge of antitakeover defenses, acquisition practices).

The benefit of outside directors thus depends on what outcome we are focused on. Why are these results not more consistent with the idea of separating ownership and control?

One simple explanation of why increasing governance by outsiders does not improve a firm's economic performance is the following: Ineffective firms add independent directors, but the new board itself cannot overcome the firm's poor market position and the mobility barriers in the industry. Remember that the board ratifies but does not propose strategic decisions. Strategy making begins with the CEO and his or her team.

The role of the board therefore needs to be examined in conjunction with the CEO for its effectiveness to be assessed. The board of directors cannot turn a company around or improve its performance; only the CEO can do that. The board can, however, fire a poor performing CEO, as outsider dominated boards are more likely to do (see Table 11.1). Returning to the Enron story, perhaps the board's close relationship with top management damaged its ability to ferret out key problems and see the red flags for what they were.

CEO Compensation

The chief executive officer plays a primary role in designing and executing the firm's strategy. When the firm consistently performs well, the CEO normally receives some of the praise. Likewise, when the firm does badly, the CEO takes the blame. Given that pay and performance should be aligned in order to provide the correct feedback to decision makers, we can ask the following question: How does the performance of the firm affect how much the CEO makes in the various components of compensation, such as salary, bonus, stock options, and perquisites, as well as compensation in total?

There are three points of view on this question. The first is that CEO compensation depends primarily on the scale of the task, captured in the firm's size in revenues.[46] Since managing larger firms in general requires more effort and ability, CEOs of bigger organizations are likely to be paid more.

Second, top management compensation should reflect higher returns to shareholders.[47] This argument is based on the principal–agent model. Shareholders, again, are the principal and attempt to control the behavior of the agent—the firm's CEO—through appropriate incentives designed by the board of directors.[48]

The third point of view involves the board's composition and CEO reactions to it.[49] As a company's board becomes more independent, the CEO may attempt to gain favor with board members and induce them to accept proposals, including those regarding compensation. CEO ingratiation and persuasion behavior with the board can thus determine higher pay.

What do we know about the effects of size, performance, and CEO ingratiation on compensation? Interestingly, firm size is the dominant factor predicting CEO compensation, consistent with the analysis in the next section on the small business health insurance industry.[50] Then, controlling for size, compensation is weakly related to changes in shareholder returns.[51] The strength of this relationship increases when stock awards and stock options are included in the compensation package and when the firm's stock price volatility is low.[52] Last, even considering the effects of firm size and performance, the ingratiation of the CEO with the board can increase his or her compensation.[53] So all three points of view have some validity.

How do CEOs in the same industry compare in their compensation? How much do size and performance determine different kinds of compensation, such as salary, bonus, and other types such as stock grants and options, within the same industry? How stable are compensation patterns over time? These questions are answered for a reasonably representative industry—the individual/small group health insurance industry—in the next section.

Trends in CEO Compensation in the Health Insurance Industry

Studying a single industry can illustrate how firm performance and types of CEO compensation are related over time. The industry chosen here is comprised of 20 midsized and larger firms selling individual and small group health insurance between 1998 and 2001. Most of these firms are direct competitors for the same customers.

We predict four types of CEO compensation:

1. Salary
2. Bonus.
3. Other compensation (e.g., stock grants, options, reimbursed travel and housing expenses).
4. Total compensation.

These are examined separately in 1999, 2000, and 2001. Table 11.2 shows the average and median change in these types of compensation over the three years. There are two obvious trends: an outsized rise in "other" compensation from 1999 to 2000 and a reduction in the growth of all types of compensation from 2000 to 2001. CEO compensation over time, even within a single industry, thus hardly follows a smooth pattern.

Five indicators of a firm's scale and performance are used to predict CEO compensation. These measures are revenues (scale), market capitalization (capital market performance), market-to-book ratio (capital market performance), return on equity (accounting performance), and earnings per share (accounting performance). Each of these is measured in the year when the CEO's compensation was determined, since we can assume that what the compensation committee decides reflects how well the CEO has done in the current

TABLE 11.2 I Trends in CEO Compensation—All Firms, 1999 to 2001

	Change, 1999–2000 (%)				Change, 2000–2001 (%)			
	Salary	**Bonus**	**Other**	**Total**	**Salary**	**Bonus**	**Other**	**Total**
Average change	19%	18%	168%	69%	5%	4%	106%	14%
Median change	8	11	high	29	4	0	2	1

TABLE 11.3 | What Predicts CEO Compensation?

Types of CEO Compensation	Five Factors Predicting CEO Compensation					Variation in Compensation Explained by the Five Factors (%)
	Revenues	Market Cap	Market/ Book	ROE	EPS	
Salary	40.85*	16.13	17229	181278	19840	76%
Bonus	123.13*	6.45	126855	781409	10861	58
Other: Stock options, stock grants, etc.	49.33*	−57.96	49149	728420	−56672	16
Total Comp	213.32*	−35.36	193228	1691136	−18439	59

*The coefficients with an asterisk have a statistically significant effect of the factor on the types of compensation.

year as opposed to how well he or she will do in the next year. For example, the committee decided on 1999 CEO compensation in late 1998. The level of remuneration reflects the board's approval or disapproval of performance during 1998, not the CEO's performance in the year to come.

These five factors predict four separate elements of the compensation package: (1) CEO salary, (2) bonus, (3) other compensation, and (4) total compensation. The levels of these elements are estimated using regression analysis on all 20 firms combined across the three years, adjusting for potential industrywide yearly differences. The analysis estimates the effects of firm scale and performance on compensation levels for all the firms together. It should be noted that the actual metrics that the board uses to make compensation decisions in any firm are unknown, but in many cases the scale and performance factors do quite a good job of predicting what compensation levels are chosen.

Table 11.3 shows a summary of the results. The entries in the table are regression coefficients. For present purposes, we are interested in whether a factor, such as revenues or market capitalization, predicts compensation with statistical significance, as indicated by an asterisk.

The analysis shows that revenues are the best predictor of CEO compensation in the industry and that the factors overall predict a relatively high percentage of the variation in all compensation components except "other," for which the model has little predictive value (see the last column in the table). These results are consistent with research showing the effect of scale on CEO compensation in other industries, as discussed above.

We can also use this analysis to benchmark the CEO compensation of each firm in the industry. First, we estimate what one would expect a CEO's compensation to be, given the size and performance of his or her firm. Second, we can compare this estimated value to the CEO's actual compensation. If the estimated value is higher, one could argue that the CEO is paid less than the firm's characteristics would predict; if the estimated value is lower, the CEO is paid more than normal.

TABLE 11.4 I How Many Firms Were Consistently Above or Below the Norm?

Patterns of Compensation over the Three Years	Number of Firms
Never above industry trend	8
Above industry trend for one year	5
Above industry trend for two years	3
Above industry trend for all three years	3

Looking only at total compensation, the following patterns emerge from the benchmarking (see Table 11.4). Six firms are consistently above the industry trend for two or three years, while 13 firms are consistently below it—twice as many. Thus, in this industry the CEOs of a few firms are "overpaid" while the CEOs of the other firms are "underpaid." So it is much too simple to say that CEOs in general make too much money. Just ask those in the underpaid group whether this is their experience.

Governance in Different Countries

In this chapter, we have discussed primarily the role of owners, boards of directors, and CEOs in shaping a firm's governance agenda and decisions. This point of view (called the Anglo-American model) has been developed in the United States and Great Britain over many centuries and has become one of the major parts of the modern capitalist economy. The expectation of effective governance associated with this model reduces the risk faced by a supplier of capital to corporations. Without available capital, managers could not invest in new projects and entrepreneurs would not start new businesses.

Yet this model is not the only one that has developed in capitalist countries (see Table 11.5 for a comparison of the five largest capitalist nations). In some countries, governance may be strongly influenced by other factors such as government intervention and networks of firms in addition to boards of directors. In Japan and France the government bureaucracy is powerful and diligently monitors firm behavior. Further, in Japan groups of large companies are tied together in *keiretsu,* with a central firm and a bank at its hub, unlike the more dispersed ownership and management systems in the United States and parts of Europe.[54] In contrast, the relationship between German shareholders and the companies in which they own shares is mediated by large banks, such as Deutsche Bank and Commerzbank. These banks, as well as other large financial institutions including Allianz, the mammoth German insurance firm, have substantial influence over corporate governance in large German companies.[55] To build a comprehensive framework of corporate governance, then, we need to include government intervention, the legal system, and interfirm networks with boards of directors and owners.

How do these separate factors contribute to effective governance? We have seen that in the United States, boards of directors have some influence but not as much as we might have expected. Directors are not tightly controlled

TABLE 11.5 | Institutional Environments of Large Firms by Country[56]

	France	Germany	Japan	United Kingdom	United States
Owners	Public, Families	Public, corporations, financial institutions, families	Public corporations	Public, financial institutions	Public, financial institutions
Boards of directors	Limited power	Strong: bank representation; labor/ management codetermination	Weak boards; strong insiders	Relatively powerful; shareholder influence	Relatively powerful; institutional shareholder influence
Interfirm networks	Two investment banks central; social elites	Financial institutions central; no industrial groups	Banks central; industrial groups; social elites	Weak structure; some social ties	Weak structure; institutional investors central
Government intervention	Variable	Low; noninterventionist	Strong bureaucracy	Increasing deregulation	Increasing deregulation

by the legal system in terms of legal liability, and so pursue their duties more in the spirit of following norms of proper governance than in fear of shareholder suits.[57] At the same time, a company's managers are constrained by competitive pressures in the product market to make effective investments and are compensated for growing the firm. This combination of weak boards and strong managers in the United States contrasts with stronger owners and weaker managers in Germany.[58] Thus, it is the combination of the full range of governance factors in each country that determines how well firms are governed and how able they are to compete locally and in international markets. Advanced capitalist countries, including those listed in Table 11.5, have developed effective combinations of key governance elements that together force entrepreneurs to respect the demands of their sources of capital. These combinations evolve in response to breakdowns in the governance system. The responses to the current governance problems in the United States, with which this chapter began, are examples of this adjustment process.

Summary

In this chapter we have covered the broad and enduring topic of corporate governance. Effective governance begins with a strong, knowledgeable board of directors that is willing to limit the number of takeover defenses to a minimum. An effective board assists the CEO in compliance matters and in making strategic decisions.

In response to Enron's failure, new compliance rules were established in the United States to create a higher standard of financial reporting. But these new rules probably cannot assure better strategic judgment by boards. There is little evidence that firm performance improves as outsiders are added.

Finally, corporate governance is fundamentally driven by a range of institutions within a society, such as the legal system, government regulation and intervention, and the connections among the owners of firms. Major capitalist countries vary substantially in these characteristics. International comparisons of firm strategy should account for these differences, as societal institutions supplant or substitute for each other across countries to produce governance practices that may or may not be equally effective.

Summary Points

- A broad view is that governance comprises the institutions and mechanisms that design and monitor the rules used to make decisions in the firm, especially those decisions that involve compliance with legal, accounting, or governmental regulations.

- Effective governance also involves designing decision-making rules that improve the firm's performance.

- Governance focuses on ensuring that the firm is performing at or close to its economic potential, consistent with the expectations of the firm's owners.

- The dominant approach to understanding the governance of the firm is called agency theory.

- Through the board of directors, shareholders that own the firm control and monitor the managers that make the firm's strategic decisions.

- If the firm is a member of a major stock exchange, the board of directors is required to have at least three committees: an audit, a compensation, and a nominating committee, each composed of outside directors.

- Two fundamental director duties recognized in corporate law are the duty of care and the duty of loyalty, which in conjunction with what is called the business judgment rule, underpin the legal liability of directors.

- The reforms in response to Enron's failure were directed almost exclusively at improving the financial reporting system and the shape of board composition and structure, but did not address the quality of the advice and counsel the board gives to top management.

- There is no guarantee that firms will achieve higher operating performance when they add more independent board members.

- Shareholders benefit when independent directors have power (membership on the finance committee).

- With more outsiders, the board makes decisions that in general but not always preserve the shareholder's interest.

- Independent directors act as conduits of innovations to the firm (knowledge of antitakeover defenses, acquisition practices).
- The role of the board therefore needs to be examined in conjunction with that of the CEO for its effectiveness to be assessed.
- CEO compensation is tied primarily to firm size, higher returns to shareholders, and CEO ingratiation and persuasion behavior with the board.
- It is important to recognize that in some countries, governance may be strongly influenced by other factors, such as government intervention and networks of firms, in addition to boards of directors.
- To build a comprehensive framework of corporate governance, we need to include government intervention, the legal system, and interfirm networks to boards of directors and owners. The number of takeover defenses in a firm's bylaws and charters reduces its market value.

Questions for Practice

Think of an industry in which you are working or have worked or that you are researching to answer the following questions.

1. What is your board's committee structure? Is it effective?
2. What is the proportion of insiders to outsiders on the board? How effective are outside directors in bringing an objective perspective to board issues?
3. How effectively does your board interact with management in discussing key issues confronting the company? Is there a full and open discussion that leads to effective decisions?
4. How has your company responded to Sarbanes-Oxley requirements? Has it benefited operationally from its response?
5. What are the key provisions your company has put in place to control its interaction with shareholders?
6. How effectively does your board involve itself in strategic issues facing the company?
7. How effectively does the board address management succession?
8. How effectively does the board deal with executive compensation issues?
9. Has your company developed and published a comprehensive set of corporate governance guidelines?
10. What are the key institutional factors within your country that influence the way your company is governed?

NYSE Rules for Board Structure and Composition (excerpts)

The New York Stock Exchange Corporate Governance Rule Proposals:

1. The boards of listed companies must have a majority of independent directors.

2. No director qualifies as independent unless the board of directors determines that the director has no material relationship with the listed company; has not been an employee of the company for five years; has not been affiliated with or employed by an auditor, present or former, of the company for five years; has not for five years been part of an interlocking directorate in which an executive officer of the company serves or on a compensation committee of another company that employs the director; does not have family members that have been in these categories in the past five years.

3. Nonmanagement directors must meet at regularly scheduled meetings without management.

4. Companies must have a nominating/corporate governance committee composed entirely of independent directors. This committee must have a written charter that addresses the committee's purpose, its goals and responsibilities, and an annual performance evaluation of the committee.

5. Companies must have a compensation committee composed entirely of independent directors. The compensation committee must have a written charter that addresses:
   a. The committee's purpose
   b. Its duties and responsibilities, including
      - A review and approval of corporate goals and objectives relevant to CEO compensation.
      - An evaluation of the CEO's performance in the light of these objectives.
      - The setting of the CEO's compensation based on this evaluation.
      - Recommendations to the board regarding incentive compensation and equity-based plans.
      - An annual performance evaluation of the compensation committee.

6. Each company must have an audit committee composed of a minimum of three persons and completely of independent directors. Director's fees are the only compensation audit committee members may receive.

7. The audit committee's authority and responsibilities are increased, including the sole authority to hire and fire independent auditors and approve significant nonaudit relationships with the independent auditors. Also, the audit committee must have a written charter that addresses:

   a. The committee's purpose—which at a minimum must be to:
   - Assist board oversight of:
     - The financial integrity of the company's financial statements.
     - The company's compliance with legal and regulatory requirements.
     - The independent auditor's qualifications and independence.
     - The performance of the company's internal audit function and of the independent auditors.
   - Prepare the report that SEC rules require be included in the company's annual proxy statement.
   - The duties and responsibilities of the audit committee—which at a minimum must be to:
     - Retain and terminate the company's independent auditors (subject, if applicable, to shareholder ratification).
     - At least annually obtain and review a report by the independent auditor describing the firm's internal quality control procedures and any material issues raised by the most recent quality control review or peer review of the firm.
     - Discuss the audited annual financial statements and quarterly financial statements with management and the independent auditor.
     - Discuss earnings press releases, other financial information, and earnings guidance provided to analysts and rating agencies.
     - As appropriate, obtain advice and assistance from outside legal, accounting, or other advisors.
     - Discuss policies regarding risk assessment and risk management.
     - Meet separately, periodically, with management, the internal auditors, and independent auditors.
     - Review with the independent auditor any audit problems or difficulties and management's response.
     - Set clear hiring policies for employees or former employees of the independent auditors.
     - Report regularly to the board of directors.
     - Perform an annual performance evaluation of the audit committee.

   b. Each company must have an internal audit function.

8. Shareholders must be given the opportunity to vote on all equity—compensation plans, except inducement options, plans regarding mergers or acquisitions, and tax qualified and excess benefit plans.

9. Listed companies must adopt and disclose corporate governance guidelines, including:
    a. Director qualification standards.
    b. Director responsibilities.
    c. Director access to management and, as necessary and appropriate, independent advisors.
    d. Director compensation.
    e. Director orientation and continuing education.
    f. Management succession.
    g. Annual performance evaluation of the board.

10. Companies must adopt and disclose a code of business conduct and ethics for directors, officers, and employees and promptly disclose any waivers of the code for directors or executive officers. The following topics should be addressed:
    a. Conflicts of interest.
    b. Exploitation of opportunities offered by employment at the company.
    c. Confidentiality.
    d. Fair dealing.
    e. Protection and proper use of company assets.
    f. Compliance with laws, rules, and regulations.
    g. Encouraging the reporting of any illegal or unethical behavior.

11. Listed foreign private issuers must disclose any significant ways in which their corporate governance practices differ from those followed by domestic companies under NYSE listing standards.

12. Each listed company CEO must satisfy to the NYSE each year that he or she is not aware of any violation by the company of NYSE corporate governance listing standards.

13. The NYSE may issue a public reprimand letter to any listed company that violates a NYSE standard.

End Notes

1. For the seminal reference on the application of agency theory to the governance of firms, see Michael C. Jensen and William H. Meckling, "Theory of the Firm: Managerial Behavior, Agency Costs and Ownership Structure," *Journal of Financial Economics* 3 (1976), pp. 305–60.

2. Adolf Berle and Gardiner C. Means, *The Modern Corporation and Private Property* (New York: Macmillan, 1932).

3. For an extensive review of both internal and external controls on managerial decision making, see James Walsh and James Seward, "On the Efficiency of Internal and External Corporate Control Mechanisms," *Academy of Management Review* 15, no. 3 (1990), pp. 421–58.

4. See Eugene F. Fama and Michael C. Jensen, "Separation of Ownership and Control," *Journal of Law and Economics* 26 (1983), pp. 301–25.

5. For a cogent list of the duties of the board, see the Business Roundtable, *Principles of Corporate Governance,* May 2002.

6. The American Law Institute Corporate Governance Project is the most authoritative source in the legal community regarding corporate governance. See Douglas Branson, *Corporate Governance* (Charlottesville, VA: The Michie Co., 1993), p. 228.

7. See Branson, *Corporate Governance,* chaps. 6, 7, and 8.

8. American Law Institute Corporate Governance Project, section 4.01 (a), cited in Branson, *Corporate Governance,* p. 264.

9. *Briggs v. Spaulding,* 141 U.S. 132, 1981.

10. Branson, *Corporate Governance,* p. 273.

11. Ibid., p. 394.

12. Ibid., p. 396.

13. R. Edward Freeman, *Strategic Management: A Stakeholder Approach,* Boston: Pitman, 1984.

14. Ibid., p. 342.

15. American Law Institute, *Principles of Corporate Governance,* § 4.01 (c) comment, (1994), p. 174.

16. American Law Institute Corporate Governance Project, section 4.01 (c), cited in Branson, *Corporate Governance,* p. 328.

17. A special purpose entity is a business designed solely to control a particular activity or asset, such as an aircraft electric power plant, or pipeline. Typically, a firm that has built the pipeline, for example, finds outside partners to invest in it and thereby take some of the risk associated with its profits and losses. If these partners own 3 or more percent of the entity, the firm doesn't have to consolidate the asset on its balance sheet, thereby avoiding accounting for its profits or losses. Also, the firm cannot control the asset; it must be controlled by the special purpose entity.

18. *Report of Investigation by the Special Investigative Committee of the Board of Directors of Enron Corporation,* William C. Powers, Jr., chair, February 1, 2002. This report was called the Powers report after the committee's chairman.

19. The problems involved how much of the special purpose entity Enron's partners owned and how much Enron controlled the entity. Andrew Fastow, Enron's CFO, and Michael Kopper, one of his assistants, were subsequently charged by the federal government for fraud related to their roles in setting up and managing these entities.

20. See Andrew Hill, Joshua Chaffin, and Stephen Fidler, "Enron: Virtual Company, Virtual Profits," *Financial Times,* February 3, 2002.

21. See Gretchen Morgenstern, "How 287 Turned Into 7: Lessons in Fuzzy Math," *New York Times,* January 20, 2002.

22. U.S. Senate Committee on Governmental Affairs, Permanent Subcommittee of Investigations, *The Role of the Board of Directors in Enron's Collapse,* 107th Cong., 2nd sess., May 7, 2002.

23. Ibid., p. 262.

24. Ibid., pp. 717–50.

25. Ibid., July 8, 2002, p. 3

26. See note 22 above.

27. See John C. Coffee, "Understanding Enron: It's about the Gatekeepers, Stupid," Columbia Law & Economics working paper no. 207, July 30, 2002.

28. Don Durfee, " The 411 on 404," *CFO magazine,* September 1, 2005.

29. *FDIC Outlook*, Fall 2005, pp. 11–14.

30. Paul Gompers, Joy Ishii, and Andrew Metrick, "Corporate Governance and Equity Prices," *Quarterly Journal of Economics,* February (2003), pp. 107–55.

31. Sanjai Bhagat and Bernard Black, "The Non-Correlation between Board Independence and Long Term Performance," *Journal of Corporation Law,* Winter 2002.

32. Stuart Rosenstein and Jeffrey Wyatt, "Inside Directors, Board Effectiveness, and Shareholder Wealth," *Journal of Financial Economics* 44 (1997), pp. 229–52.

33. Gerald F. Davis, "Agents without Principles? The Spread of the Poison Pill through the Intercorporate Network," *Administrative Science Quarterly* 36 (1991), pp. 583–613.

34. Michael S. Weisbach, "Outside Directors and CEO Turnover," *Journal of Financial Economics* 20 (1988), pp. 267–91.

35. Kenneth Borokhovich, Robert Parrino, and Teresa Trapani, "Outside Directors and CEO Selection," *Journal of Financial and Quantitative Analysis* 31 (1996), pp. 337–55.

36. Idalene F. Kesner and Roy B. Johnson, "An Investigation of the Relationship between Board Composition and Shareholder Suits," *Strategic Management Journal* 11 (1990), pp. 327–37.

37. Rita D. Kosnik, "Greenmail: A Study of Board Performance in Corporate Governance," *Administrative Science Quarterly* 32 (1987), pp. 163–86. Greenmail is a stock price premium paid to a firm attempting a hostile takeover to stop the takeover attempt.

38. Harbir Singh and Farid Harianto, "Management–Board Relationships, Takeover Risk, and the Adoption of Golden Parachutes," *Academy of Management Journal* 32 (1989), pp. 7–24; James Wade, Charles O'Reilly, and Ike Chandratat, "Golden Parachutes: CEOs and the Exercise of Social Influence," *Administrative Science Quarterly* 35 (1990), pp. 587–604. A golden parachute is a severance package for a top executive, typically triggered by a change in control of the firm, that according to the IRS exceeds three times the manager's average annual compensation over the previous five years.

39. April Klein, "Firm Performance and Board Committee Structure," *Journal of Law and Economics* 41 (1998), pp. 275–303.

40. See note 37.

41. Gerald F. Davis, "Agents without Principles? The Spread of the Poison Pill through the Intercorporate Network," *Administrative Science Quarterly* 36 (1991), pp. 583–613.

42. Pamela Haunschild and Christine Beckman, "When Do Interlocks Matter? Alternative Sources of Information and Interlock Influence," *Administrative Science Quarterly* 43 (1998), pp. 815–44.

43. Donald Palmer, P. Devereaux Jennings, and Xueguang Zhou, "Late Adoption of the Multidivisional Form by Large U.S. Corporations: Institutional, Political and Economic Accounts," *Administrative Science Quarterly* 38 (1993), pp. 100–32.

44. Theodore Eisenberg, Stefan Sundgren, and Martin T. Wells, "Larger Board Size and Decreasing Firm Value in Small Firms," *Journal of Financial Economics* 48 (1998), pp. 35–55.

45. David Yermack, "Higher Market Valuation of Companies with a Small Board of Directors," *Journal of Financial Economics* 40 (1996), pp. 185–202.

46. See David Ciscel and Thomas Carroll, "Determinants of Executives Salaries: An Econometric Survey," *Review of Economics and Statistics* 62 (1980), pp. 7–13. Sydney Finkelstein and Brian Boyd, "How Much Does the CEO Matter? The Role of Managerial Discretion in the Setting of CEO Compensation," *Academy of Management Journal* 41 (1998), pp. 179–90.

47. See, for example, Rajesh Aggarwal and Andrew Samwick, "The Other Side of the Tradeoff: The Impact of Risk on Executive Compensation," *Journal of Political Economy* 107 (1999), pp. 65–105; Ciscel and Carroll, "Determinants of Executives' Salaries: An Econometric Survey," pp. 7–13; John Garen, "Executive Compensation and Principal–Agent Theory," *Journal of Political Economy* 102 (1994), pp. 1175–99; Brian Hall and Jeffrey Liebman, "Are CEO's Really Paid Like Bureaucrats?" *Quarterly Journal of Economics* 111 (1998), pp. 653–91; Joseph Haubrich, "Risk Aversion, Performance Pay and the Principal–Agent Problem," *Journal of Political Economy* 102 (1994), pp. 258–76; and especially, Michael Jensen and Kevin Murphy, "Performance Pay and Top Management Incentives," *Journal of Political Economy* 98 (1990), pp. 225–64.

48. Aggarwal and Samwick, "The Other Side of the Tradeoff," pp. 65–105; Garen, "Executive Compensation and Principal–Agent Theory," pp. 1175–99; Hall and Liebman, "Are CEOs Really Paid Like Bureaucrats?" pp. 653–91; Haubrich, "Risk Aversion, Performance Pay and the Principal–Agent Problem," pp. 258–76; Christopher Ittner, David Larcker, and Marshall Meyer, "Performance, Compensation and the Balanced Scorecard," working paper, The Wharton School, University of Pennsylvania, 1997.

49. James Westphal, "Board Games: How CEOs Adapt to Structural Board Independence from Management," *Administrative Science Quarterly* 43 (1998), p. 511.

50. Ciscel and Carroll, "Determinants of Executives Salaries," pp. 7–13.

51. Kevin Murphy, "Corporate Performance and Managerial Remuneration: An Empirical Analysis," *Journal of Accounting and Economics* 7 (1985), pp. 11–42.

52. Hall and Liebman, "Are CEO's Really Paid Like Bureaucrats?" pp. 653–91; Aggarwal and Samwick, "The Other Side of the Tradeoff," pp. 65–105.

53. See note 48.

54. For a discussion of business groups in general, see Tarun Khanna, "Business Groups and Social Welfare in Emerging Markets: Existing Evidence and Unanswered Questions," *European Economic Review* 44, nos. 4–6 (May 2000), pp. 748–61.

55. See Bruce Kogut and Gordon Walker, "The Small World of German Ownership: National Networks of Ownership," *American Sociological Review* 66 (2002), pp. 317–35.

56. Adapted from Bruce Kogut, Gordon Walker, and Jaideep Anand, "Agency and Institutions: Organizational Form and National Divergences in Diversification Behavior," *Organization Science* 13 (2002), pp. 162–78.

57. See Donald C. Langevoort, "The Human Nature of Corporate Boards: Law, Norms and the Unintended Consequences of Independence and Accountability," *Georgetown Law Journal* 89 (2001).

58. See Mark Roe, *Strong Managers, Weak Owners: The Political Roots of American Corporate Finance* (Princeton, NJ: Princeton University Press, 1994).

CHAPTER 12

Strategic Planning and Decision Making

Roadmap

Throughout this book we have focused on the factors that determine a firm's economic performance. Our primary interest has been in how a business achieves a competitive advantage through establishing and defending a superior market position in domestic or global markets. Once established in its core business, the firm may diversify into new industries. Its performance will then depend on improving the profits of all its business units and increasing the productivity of corporate activities.

How should managers make the resource allocation decisions that lead to competitive advantage? What decision-making process should managers follow to define the firm's strategy and the elements of its execution? This final chapter addresses these questions by discussing the strategy-making process, especially strategic planning, at the level of the single business unit and the corporate level of the multibusiness firm. The chapter is structured as follows:

- What Is Strategic Planning?

- Planning in a Single Business

  - Statement of Intent and Business Scope: Vision and Mission

  - Analysis of Industry Structure and Trends

  - Statement of Financial Goals and Related Metrics

  - Development of Strategic Initiatives

  - Programs to Implement Strategic Initiatives

- Planning in Multibusiness Firms

  - Resource Allocation

  - Portfolio Management

  - Interbusiness Relationships

  - Centralization of Activities

What Is Strategic Planning?

Strategic planning is fundamentally a line management, not a staff, activity. Planning forces line managers to evaluate investments in terms of their contribution to financial goals, which in turn are set in the context of industry trends and the behavior of competitors. Without such a plan, managers have at best a sketchy roadmap for increasing the firm's performance and therefore can make no convincing promises to investors about the firm's future value.

Strategic planning extends top management leadership and power. No firmwide planning system can succeed without the support and involvement of the CEO. The substance of an effective plan includes top management's concept of how to make the firm more successful and shows how this vision leads to superior economic performance.

As a decision-making process, an effective planning exercise is designed to neutralize as much as possible the common biases in managerial choice (see the sidebar). Planning presents an opportunity for management to surface a range of innovations that would otherwise remain buried by incremental control systems such as standard budgeting. In many companies, the major benefit from strategic planning is not the written plan but the new ideas, management commitment, and consensus that are stimulated by open discussions in the planning process. In fact, it is safe to say that planning without problem solving is a sterile exercise.

Strategic decision making thus overcomes organizational drift.[1] A firm that ceases to innovate experiences either inertia, which reflects a rigid commitment to traditional practices, or ineffective change, which fails to match shifting market conditions. These rigidities lower economic performance as the firm's resources and capabilities lose their competitiveness against more innovative rivals. As the life cycle continues through shakeout into maturity, and possibly disruption, the benefits from strategic planning can only increase.

Expertise in strategic planning often constitutes a capability that contributes to economic performance. Firms that are more able planners make investment decisions that are better aligned with current and future market conditions than firms whose resource allocation decisions are ad hoc. For example, the business units within GE benefited substantially from the design and implementation of its strategic planning system in the late 1960s and 1970s.

It is common for managers in companies with volatile markets to reject strategic planning as too restrictive for effective decision making. The argument is that by the time the plan is finished, the assumptions behind it have changed. However, this is rarely true.[2] Very often, enduring industry conditions underlie the volatility that managers perceive. A start-up firm, for example, is typically

Decision-Making Biases

Management decision making is plagued by influences, primarily psychological, that create distortions in judgment. These influences range from a bias toward the short term (myopia) to a tendency to weight losses more strongly than gains.[3] A range of decision-making biases is presented below.

Myopia

When cash flows are discounted, money received in the short term is necessarily worth more than money received farther out in time. However, there is strong evidence that many managers implicitly weight the short term even more by applying a higher discount rate to longer-term returns. Myopia of this kind favors projects whose profits are realized early rather than late in the project's history, even though the value of these projects might be lower than alternatives, when assessed at a constant discount rate. Obviously, firms that continually choose projects that have high shorter-term returns but a lower overall value will underperform competitors that are not myopic.[4]

Sunk Costs

It has long been recognized that projects should be evaluated on how much they will earn, not on how much has been spent on them. Yet managers have a tendency to continue investing in poor projects in order to "get their money out." This "sunk cost fallacy" is pervasive in industries with large capital investments whose payouts are meager. An interesting variation on the role of sunk costs in strategic decision making is found in the exit decisions of firms in volatile geographical markets. When the market declines, firms with valuable sunk investments, such as a brand or distribution network, resist exiting because these resources would be very expensive to rebuild upon reentry, when the market picks up.[5]

Framing in Gains or Losses[6]

Another source of bias in decision making, the effect of framing of decisions in terms of gains or losses, is articulated by prospect theory. According to prospect theory, decision makers tend to be risk seeking regarding losses but risk averse regarding gains. This means, on the one hand, that we tend to accept unfavorable gambles in an attempt to avoid a loss that is certain. On the other hand, we avoid favorable gambles in order to receive a guaranteed gain. The intuition is that the pain caused by negative outcomes is greater than the pleasure produced by positive returns. So we try to avoid our losses through gambling, even though we could lose more. However, once we are guaranteed a gain, we lock it in rather than gamble to get a higher amount.

Information Availability[7]

Decision makers tend to weight information that is already present or salient over absent or more mundane information, however important the latter might be objectively for an effective outcome. Such a bias may arise because management has been recently exposed to the information, a "recency" bias, or because the information has high visceral content that creates a lingering impression, a "vividness" bias. Thus, the decision is skewed by the heavier use of more available information with a stronger emotional impact. For example, a firm that has recently lost an important customer may be particularly sensitive to decisions that pertain to retention even though these decisions may be less profitable than alternatives.

Information Anchoring[8]

Information anchoring is similar to availability but refers to the order in which information is received. All information used in decision making is presented and processed sequentially.

What is presented and perceived first in the information flow acts as an anchor that provides a reference point for the rest of the information stream, skewing the decision-making process toward choices in which early information plays a stronger role. For example, if a firm is planning on growing internationally, it may explore country opportunities sequentially. The countries early in the sequence may create an anchoring effect as the managers expand their analysis. This effect endures even as all the opportunities are examined together.

unable to receive funding from investors without a comprehensive scan of the industry and a description of its product's expected market position. The business plan that entrepreneurs create for their investors has many elements in common with the strategic plan of a more mature company.

The distinction between strategic and tactical obscures the importance of small actions that are essential for establishing and defending competitive advantage. Any activity controlled by the firm that affects its market position is strategic, no matter how small the expense or number of persons involved. In many cases, the major benefit of planning is not identifying what the firm is currently doing well, but what it needs to do, however small in scope, to increase its performance.

Thus, strategic planning is not strategy execution. But planning makes execution more effective. To reiterate from Chapter 5, there are four elements of execution that affect the firm's capabilities:

- Incentives and compensation.
- Consistency among activities.
- Control and coordination systems.
- People, culture, and learning.

Each of these elements should be clearly addressed in the planning process to ensure that the desired capabilities are being developed, whether within a single business or across the units of a multibusiness firm. For example, in a single business, aligning incentives to support strategy execution always constitutes a key program. In a multibusiness firm with strategically interdependent units, additional incentive programs may be included in the corporate plan. These programs might apply to centralized activities, or to parts of the corporate infrastructure, such as information technology. Consistency between the business unit plans and the corporate plan reduces nonproductive conflict and improves unit performance.

Planning in a Single Business

To compete in its markets, a business with a single product line, whether it is an independent firm or a unit within a larger multibusiness firm, makes resource allocation decisions that are combined in an annual budget. Strategic planning overlays and informs the financial reporting system by detailing the logic behind the cash flow forecasts. Moreover, an effective plan moves the business closer to choosing the best set of projects for improving performance, given the business's current market position and the constraints of competition.

A strategic plan at the business level should have the following elements:

- A mission statement that defines the business's scope of business and strategic intent.
- An analysis of the business's industry and market position relative to competitors and a statement of assumptions regarding the competitive environment.
- The business's financial and operating goals.
- The strategic initiatives necessary to achieve these goals.
- The specific programs necessary to achieve each strategic initiative.

The strategic planning process should also

- Act as a tool for management decision making.
- Communicate the organization's strategy without jargon and in a format that is conceptually coherent.
- Generate commitment from employees and motivate their actions.
- Motivate the organization's systems of financial and operating control, including its metrics.
- Be reviewed regularly and in response to unexpected and significant market changes.

Statement of Intent and Business Scope: Vision and Mission

A strategic plan should begin with a statement that describes the scope of the business in terms of its product line and markets served. Frequently called a **mission statement,** this section of the plan puts a boundary around the types of investments that are consistent with the identity of the business. The mission statement should typically be no longer than several sentences. Longer statements tend to lose their impact when communicated within the organization or to customers, suppliers, or investors.

The plan sometimes contains a separate statement on the general goals of the firm. This **vision statement** is usually quite short and captures the firm's aspirations and strategic direction. For example, the business may target market dominance in a value driver such as service, product quality, or brand awareness. Or the vision may focus on achieving the lowest costs in the industry.

The distinction between mission and vision statements is not fixed in practice. Some firms have only a mission statement, combining business scope and intent in one message. Other firms, such as GE, have developed an additional set of core values, which communicate expectations about employee behavior and signal the overall style of the organization in its business conduct. Sometimes a presentation of the firm's values is contained in the mission statement itself (see Starbucks and eBay in the sidebar on page 312).

The Mission and Vision Statements of Notable Firms in 2002

Archer-Daniels-Midland

Mission: To unlock the potential of nature to improve the quality of life.

Dell Computer

Vision: There is a difference at Dell. It's the way we do business. It's the way we interact with the community. It's the way we interpret the world around us, our customer's needs, the future of technology and the global business climate. Whatever changes the future may bring, our vision, Dell vision, will be our guiding force.

Mission: Dell's mission is to be the most successful computer company in the world at delivering the best customer experience in markets we serve. Dell will meet customer expectations of highest quality, leading technology, competitive pricing, individual and company accountability, best in class customer service and support, flexible customization capability, superior corporate citizenship, financial stability.

PepsiCo

Mission: Our mission is to be the world's premier consumer products company focused on convenience foods and beverages. We seek to produce healthy financial rewards to investors as we provide opportunities for growth and enrichment to our employees, our business partners, and the communities in which we operate. And in everything we do, we strive for honesty, fairness, and integrity.

Starbucks

Mission: Establish Starbucks as the premier purveyor of the finest coffee in the world while maintaining our uncompromising principles as we grow. The following five guiding principles will help us measure the appropriateness of our decisions:

1. Provide a great work environment and treat each other with respect and dignity.

2. Apply the highest standards of excellence to the purchasing, roasting, and fresh delivery of our coffee.

3. Develop enthusiastically satisfied customers all of the time.

4. Contribute positively to our communities and our environment.

5. Recognize that profitability is essential to our future success.

eBay

Mission: We help people trade practically anything on earth. eBay was founded with the belief that people are basically good. We believe that each of our customers, whether a buyer or a seller, is an individual who deserves to be treated with respect. We will continue to enhance the online trading experiences of all—collectors, hobbyists, dealers, small business, unique item seekers, bargain hunters, opportunistic sellers, and browsers. The growth of the eBay community comes from meeting and exceeding the expectations of these special people.

The success of the mission and vision depends less on their specific structure than on how well they communicate the firm's objectives and key resources and capabilities, real and desired. The mission and vision must articulate clearly and succinctly how the firm intends to compete. The benefit of developing such an effective statement can be significant and should not be underestimated.

Mission and vision statements have been used by many single and multibusiness firms as preambles and framing devices for the strategic plan as a whole. For example, Johnson & Johnson uses the mission statements in the strategic plans of its companies to establish distinct boundaries between them regarding their technologies and markets. J & J companies with clearly separate business definitions should have fewer conflicts with each other, reducing the need for corporate intervention.

Analysis of Industry Structure and Trends

No plan can be effective without a broad assessment of both industry trends and the firm's market position relative to competitors. A key planning task is identifying how much macroeconomic and industry factors contribute to the firm's economic performance. Isolating these factors allows the firm to distinguish its own contribution to profitability. Armed with this estimate, the firm can then figure out more clearly the payoffs to its strategic initiatives.

The firm's current market position provides a baseline for the firm's strategic direction. An analysis of the market position should include a detailed assessment of competitors' business strategies. The breadth and depth of this assessment can vary substantially across strategic plans depending on the rate of change in competitor strategies and in market structure.

Firms can be highly selective in how they perceive the competitive landscape.[9] But whatever lens is used to define the industry, a firm must obviously identify and analyze carefully those rivals that directly compete with it. At the same time, there may be competitors in management's peripheral vision whose products threaten the firm's future market position, as we have seen regarding disruptive technologies in Chapter 4. Trends in industries with complementary products also bear watching. A careful scan of industry conditions thus includes all forces and firms that currently influence or might influence the firm's economic performance (see Table 12.1).

Industry and competitor analysis typically deals with uncertainty and complexity in forecasting macroeconomic trends and industry forces such as the behavior of buyers, suppliers, and rivals. One technique that many companies have found useful is scenario analysis.[10] Using this method, managers build two or three discrete, complex, and internally consistent visions of the future. Typically, one scenario has negative implications for the company's performance, and another has positive implications. If a third is constructed, its implications lie between the other two. The scenarios can serve as reference points to test the robustness of the firm's strategy. Alternatively, they may lead to a radically different view of the future and therefore to a change in strategy, as happened at Royal Dutch Shell from the late 1960s through the 1970s. Based on its scenario analysis, Shell was the only oil firm to forecast the 1973 oil crisis and later to anticipate the glut of oil after the end of the Iran-Iraq War in 1981.[11]

Statement of Financial Goals and Related Metrics

Financial Goals   Goal setting focuses management attention and pushes the planning team to articulate in detail which investments are strategically

TABLE 12.1 I   The Elements of Competitor Analysis

The following questions are useful for analyzing industry forces:

- What are the key macroeconomic variables that affect profits in the industry?
- What are the current macroeconomic trends?
- What are the critical regulatory factors that influence performance in the industry?
- What are the key industry forces (e.g., powerful buyers, strong substitutes, ease of entry) affecting firm profitability?
- What are the trends in these forces?
- What are the entry and exit rates in the industry?
- What are the trends in these rates?
- Has the industry passed through a shakeout?
- Has the industry experienced significant disruption? If so, how have entrants competed against incumbents?
- If not, are there identifiable forces or products that could be disruptive to the industry?
- What are the key value and cost drivers in the industry?
- How is the industry structured into strategic groups based on these value and cost drivers?
- What is the trend in industry revenue?
- What are the key competitors the firm faces in its major markets?
- What are their strategies and performance levels?
- Which competitors are growing faster in revenue than the industry trend? Why?
- What is the trend in industry profitability?
- Which competitors are growing faster in profitability than the industry trend? Why?
- What new strategic initiatives and programs have key competitors developed, if any?
- How likely is it that these initiatives will improve the market positions of these competitors?
- How aggressive are these firms in growing their market positions?
- How aggressively do these firms defend their positions?
- Where is the firm located in this competitive landscape in terms of its value and cost drivers?
- How are the resources and capabilities underlying the value and cost drivers protected from imitation?

important. Without financial objectives, the strategic planning process has no logical connection to economic outcomes, and decisions made in the process have little or no strategic impact. Management therefore has difficulty arguing that these decisions are important and motivating commitment to them.

Setting financial goals forces management to be explicit about its expectations and assumptions. Conventional financial projections reflect the firm's capabilities for profitability and growth in the context of competitive constraints and general industry conditions. Goal setting in strategic planning exposes and in many cases challenges the assumptions behind these projections in order to accelerate improvement in performance.

There are three key questions in setting the business's financial goals: How many time periods should they be set for? What are the key financial metrics that capture economic performance? And, obviously, what should the goals be? The answers to these questions shape to a large degree the plan's scope and depth.

The Planning Period   The length of the financial planning period depends on the volatility of a firm's strategic situation. A reasonable time horizon in relatively stable markets is three years. The extended planning period forces management to articulate its view of how the firm will improve its performance as competition and other industry forces evolve. For example, what will drive the firm's sales: generic market or segment growth; increased market share based on superior value drivers; repeat sales based on the firm's value drivers and retention capabilities; or geographical expansion? Regarding profitability, managers must address questions regarding the costs to achieve high sales growth. Typical questions might be: How do costs respond to increased scale and scope? What new practices must be developed to increase efficiency? What capacity planning challenges does the firm face? Without a longer planning horizon, these issues are less likely to be addressed directly. As the rate of market change increases, the length of the planning period must obviously shorten. But whatever the degree of market volatility, there are substantial benefits to setting goals as far into the future as possible.

Many managers shy away from setting longer-term goals, not because their industries have greater instability, but because they are unwilling to identify the longer-term consequences of strategic decisions. These managers believe that current operations, expanded into the future, will be sufficient to support the firm's economic performance. In some cases such a belief may be true. But more often in competitive markets the assumption is false and induces organizational drift. Managerial resistance to long-term goal setting therefore makes the firm vulnerable to decline.

Financial and Operating Metrics   Firms typically set goals for those financial metrics that either indicate economic performance or act as key inputs to it. The most common performance metrics for single business planning are revenues, net profits, and return on investment. Firms focused on economic value added will set goals for return on equity, cost of capital, and perhaps the spread between them. Some businesses may also target growth rates in return on equity. Capital-intensive businesses may set targets for return on assets and the firm's degree of leverage. Scale-driven businesses in industries where larger firms can exert significant market power may track market share as a key metric. In any case, the metrics chosen and the goals set should be centrally related to the firm's economic performance in its product market over time.

Financial goals must be aligned with operating goals measured by the business metrics that guide the management of a firm. The interplay of financial and operating metrics is critical for setting robust objectives. Business metrics reflect the value and cost drivers that determine the firm's market position. For example, measures of quality, service levels, and time to delivery capture key aspects of value, while inventory turnover, administrative expense, and purchase price variance are important cost indicators. Business metrics also measure the sources of revenue growth. For example, revenue goals must be consistent with the number of salespeople and the average sale per person over the relevant time period. An aggressive revenue target may be reduced when its underlying assumptions about sales force growth and productivity are closely examined. Alternatively, weak revenue goals may be increased when an expanded sales force appears feasible.

Setting Goals   Confronted with setting financial goals, managers commonly rely on two benchmarks: the firm's historical performance and the performance of competitors. A firm is commonly aware of its own financial trend and sets goals to improve it. But benchmarking against rivals shows the extent to which this trend is based on industry- as opposed to firm-specific factors. If the firm's trend is below the industry average, then the long-term market position of the firm is vulnerable. More aggressive goals and the innovations to achieve them are required. If its trend tracks the industry average, the firm's performance is subject primarily to industry forces. In this case, goal setting hinges on whether the firm can develop a strategy to grow faster than competitors. Finally, if the trend is above the industry norm, the firm must focus on staying ahead.

Many firms advocate setting "stretch" goals, which push management to exceed expected performance targets based on firm or industry trends or to overcome difficult barriers to growth or profitability. Stretch goals represent the far edge of the possible. Their benefit lies in stimulating a level of innovation beyond what management has already imagined. In many cases, even though stretch goals are not achieved, the initiatives and programs developed to reach them would not have been conceived without the extra push these goals provide.

Development of Strategic Initiatives

The essence of the strategic plan is the strategic initiatives through which the business intends to improve and defend its market position. The initiatives define how the firm will compete in its market and achieve its performance targets. Together the initiatives should be consistent with the logic of creating and protecting a superior market position. They also represent the general categories to which programs are assigned for planning purposes.

General categories for initiatives are as follows:

1. Projects that directly improve the firm's value drivers consistent with competitive forces and customer preferences, for example:

    a. Improve quality

    b. Enhance service

    c. Advance product technology

    d. Increase product line breadth

    e. Support complements

    f. Increase brand awareness

2. Projects that directly improve the firm's cost drivers, consistent with the product's value.

3. Projects that raise customer retention including:

    a. Increasing service levels

    b. Broadening the scope of the customer relationship

    c. Increasing the customization of the product to the customer

4. Investments in growth through, for example:

    a. New sales channels

    b. New capacity

    c. New product development

    d. New research programs, if appropriate

    e. New geographical regions

5. Termination or turnaround of underperforming relationships and activities such as:

    a. Customers

    b. Products and projects

    c. Key assets, such as production facilities

    d. Regions

6. Development of risk management and compliance initiatives.

As a whole, strategic initiatives serve as an organizing framework for activities throughout the firm. This framework, when it includes the programs under each initiative, can be used to track the progress of the business over the planning period. Such a tool is particularly useful for assessing how well the plan is being executed.

Programs to Implement Strategic Initiatives

No plan can be effective without the development of operating programs.[12] Programs are the basic units through which the strategy is executed. They may be ongoing or created to achieve specific strategic initiatives. Developing programs in the planning process tests the feasibility of the plan's goals and the initiatives designed to accomplish them.

Program Accountability and Schedule   Each program should have an accountable manager and a specific time frame for its completion. Accountability and schedule make monitoring programs simpler and tie their implementation to the firm's compensation and incentive system. Without a lead manager and a set of milestones for each program, top management can lose its focus on executing the plan, increasing implementation costs substantially.

Program Valuation   The standard method for determining the economic value of a project is discounted cash flow analysis (DCF), in which the cash flows associated with a project are identified and then adjusted in each period using a discount rate, representing alternative uses of capital. The adjusted cash flows are then summed to determine the project's net present value (NPV). The overall value of the firm then is simply the sum of the values of the projects that comprise it. This methodology is important since it is tied to the firm's valuation in its capital markets: In theory the higher the NPVs of a firm's projects, the greater the firm's market value.

A second useful method for project valuation, especially for projects that are relatively uncertain and involve multiple decision points, is real options analysis. Real options analysis is an extension of the options models applied to financial instruments. Real options are commonly used to value investments such as new production capacity, technology projects, exploration projects such as oil or gas wells, and even joint ventures with other firms.[13] The sidebar compares NPV and real options as valuation methods.

No project with a negative NPV should be accepted. But this does not mean that a firm invests in all projects with a positive NPV over the planning period. Firms will vary in the projects they choose based in part on their degree of myopia, or short-term orientation. NPV reflects a project's net discounted cash flow, but it does not reflect when those cash flows occur. A more myopic firm might discount long-term cash flows more heavily, leading to a set of programs based heavily on short-term returns. Another firm, more risk neutral, may invest in more long-term projects.

Which of these choices is correct? The planning process itself does not answer this question. A firm's strategic decisions represent wagers on a variety of factors that influence long-term competitive advantage, including the rate of technological change, the growth rate of demand, trends in customer preferences, and the strength of isolating mechanisms. Each firm's plan thus reflects management's decision-making biases and its assumptions regarding long-term viability as the industry evolves. Although planning cannot directly correct for these tendencies, it can be very useful in surfacing them and analyzing their implications for firm performance.

Program costs are tied to the annual budget, while program performance is tied to the business metrics included in the goals of the strategic plan. For example, the performance of customer service programs can be measured by program-level metrics such as customer satisfaction and by the higher-level customer retention outcomes that satisfaction should influence. The economic value of customer service programs can then be calculated by analyzing the costs incurred to achieve a target level of service and the revenue received from repeat customers over time. The results of this

Net Present Value and Real Options

A simple example serves to show the differences between NPV and real options methods.[14] A firm is considering investing $800 in a manufacturing plant. It produces a product whose price in the first year will be $100, with the revenue delivered at the time of the investment. In the second year the price may be either $150 or $50, with equal probability, and will remain steady thereafter. For simplicity, assume that the only cost the firm incurs to produce the product is building the plant and that the plant produces only one product each year. The diagram for the product's price over time looks like this.

Year 1	Year 2	Year 3 and Beyond
Prob = .5 ↗	Price = $50 →	Price = $50
Price = $100		
Prob = .5 ↘	Price = $150 →	Price = $150

The net present value of this investment is the total cost plus the value of the revenues over the life of the project, discounted at a rate of say 10 percent, which represents the firm's opportunity costs of investing elsewhere. Since the firm receives a sure $100 in the first year and an expected value of $100 in every year thereafter:

$$\text{NPV of the plant} = -800 + \sum_{t=0}^{\infty} \frac{100}{(1.1)t} = -800 + 1,100 = 300$$

Using this method, the firm should invest in the plant and makes $300 over its life.

Applying the real options methodology to this problem requires two important assumptions. First, the investment in the plant must be irreversible—that is, once built, the plant has virtually no resale value. Otherwise, the $800 investment could be recouped if the market for the plant's products did not materialize. Second, there must be some uncertainty about the future price of the product, as there is in year 2 of the example. Without uncertainty, the concept of an option loses its meaning since there is no value to waiting for some future state of the market to materialize.

Given these assumptions, the key to applying the real options framework is to allow the possibility of waiting to make the investment until the future states are revealed. So, in the example the firm might wait to invest until the beginning of the second year in order to observe which direction prices moved. If the price shifts to $50, the discounted value of revenues is $500, which is below the $800 cost of the plant. In this case, the firm would clearly not make the investment. But if the price turns out to be $150, discounted revenues are $1,500, which produce a very good return. The value of waiting for further information is therefore obvious. The calculation of the NPV when the firm waits is the following:

$$\text{NPV} = (0.5)\left[\frac{-800}{1.1} + \sum_{t=1}^{\infty} \frac{150}{(1.1)t} \right] = \$386$$

319

The investment of $800 is discounted one period because it may not be made until year 2, and the cash flows are multiplied by .5 since there is only a fifty-fifty chance the price will be $150. The value of the project if the firm waits is $386.

How much is waiting worth to the firm? The simple answer is the difference between waiting, $386, and not waiting, $300, which is $86. This is the value of the option to postpone the decision until the uncertainty regarding future prices is resolved.

Now imagine two kinds of plant: one that is available only in the first year and must be built then for $800, and another that can be built either in the first year or the second. The price of the second plant is yet to be determined. We know that waiting is more profitable, so the firm should be willing to pay more for the flexibility inherent in the second plant, but how much more?

To find out, we assume that the firm would not wait to build a plant in the second year if the plant's cost was so high its NPV was less than that of the $800 plant built in the first year. So we need to calculate the cost of a plant that could be built later and whose NPV is at least equal to the value of investing in the first year:

$$300 = (0.5)\left[\frac{-C}{1.1} + \sum_{t=1}^{\infty} \frac{150}{(1.1)^t}\right]$$

where C is the unknown cost of the plant.

Solving for C shows that the firm would be willing to build a plant for $990, at most, in order to be able to wait until the second year. The value of being able to wait is thus $190. Flexible plants that cost less than $990 will have a greater return than inflexible plants that cost $800 or more.

The NPV and real options frameworks are thus very closely related but vary in their appropriateness depending on the characteristics of the project. Almost any investment can be viewed in real options terms. However, the analogy to financial options works best when the firm has a large investment that cannot be reversed and when uncertainty exists about long-term payoffs.

Also when the cost of the investment is below a certain threshold, the options approach ceases to be relevant.

Finally, how the payoffs are specified over time is crucial in applying the real options framework. For example, if there are significant scale-driven cost drivers, such as scale economies or the learning curve, a firm that invests early will ultimately have lower costs and higher returns than competitors that wait. In this case, the payoffs of early movers should be higher, decreasing the value of waiting. Alternatively, if all firms can take advantage of these cost drivers, the payoffs should be comparable and competitive forces do not affect investment timing.[15]

analysis can then be compared with the return from investing in acquiring new customers to estimate how much net economic value customer retention produces.

Table 12.2 shows a sample template for a set of programs under a strategic initiative in the strategic plan.

TABLE 12.2 | Sample Program Template: Strategic Initiative

Program	Accountable Executive	Begin Date	Finish Date	Status
Improve Customer Retention **(partial list of programs)**				
Completed				
1. Customer relations management attrition model	Ted Wilson		Completed	
Ongoing				
2. Customer service— staff retention	Mary L. Williams		Implemented	Ongoing
3. Customer service— staff training	Mary L. Williams		Implemented	Ongoing
4. Customer relations management monitor customer service	Lillian Armstrong		Implemented	Ongoing
To be Implemented				
5. Customer relationship management— develop strategy	Bill Evans		Strategy developed by 3/1/06	
6. Customer relations management— information capture	J. R. Morton		Developed by 4/1/06	
7. Customer service— formalize work management	Earl Powell		Assessment of vendors 3/1/06— Implement scheduling software 7/1/06	
8. Customer service— redesigned customer survey	Earl Powell		5/1/06	
9. Customer service— sales force survey	Earl Powell		5/1/06	
10. Customer service— sales training with customer service	Earl Powell	6/1/06		
11. Develop new tools for analyzing performance data	Earl Powell	Design by 3/1/06	Implement by 4/1/06	

Planning in Multibusiness Firms

In a multibusiness firm the corporate strategic plan should be the core document for managing the organization as a whole. The elements of the plan are best understood in terms of the key corporate level tasks:

- Allocate resources across business units through the internal capital market.
- Manage the portfolio of businesses for growth and profitability.

- Organize and manage relationships among the business units to increase value or reduce cost.
- Centralize activities across businesses to increase value or lower cost.
- Increase the economic contribution of the businesses through top-down initiatives.
- Develop corporate infrastructure that supports business unit value and cost drivers.

The corporate plan should include a section of each of these tasks, in addition to sections on each corporate staff unit—for example, legal, corporate development, human resources, information technology, communications, accounting, finance, and the office of the CEO. Much of the activity at the corporate level is necessarily routine as it meets ongoing regulatory requirements. However, in an age when both compliance and internal audit are increasingly important, the potential benefit of annual planning for the corporate office cannot be underestimated.

Resource Allocation

The goal of resource allocation is to invest in and support those businesses whose projects produce the highest economic return. The strategic plan of each business outlines the drivers of the unit's competitive position and the sources of its economic return. In conjunction with its knowledge of the businesses and their industries, corporate leadership uses this information to determine which units will make the most money and skews resources towards them.

A useful way of comparing unit performance information is the Marakon profitability matrix (see Figure 12.1).[16] This simple array charts each business in the corporation in terms of (1) its trend in market share—gaining or losing, and (2) the ratio of its return on equity (ROE) to the corporation's cost of

FIGURE 12.1   I   The Profitability Matrix

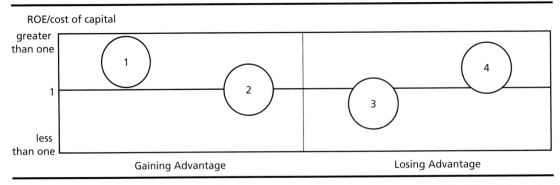

Source: Adapted from Michael Rabin, Uta Werner, and Jim McTaggart, "Beyond Performance Measurement: The Use and Misuse of Economic Profit," Marakon Associates, August 1, 1994.

capital. The best position is to gain share profitably (a ratio of ROE to the cost of capital greater than one); the worst is to lose share unprofitably.

The four sample business units in Figure 12.1 differ substantially in their profiles, which raises a number of questions. For example, why is unit 4 losing advantage and remaining highly profitable? Two quite different answers are: The business is not reinvesting its profits in projects to counter more aggressive competitors, or the average return on equity in its industry is high relative to the corporation's cost of capital. Which answer is true has important consequences for future resource allocation.

Portfolio Management

A firm cannot ignore the inevitable erosion of its core businesses due to industry maturation. The corporate plan should therefore always address the challenge of new business development. If technology is an important value driver for business units that share a common technology platform, the corporate plan should include a section on the development of core competence, as described in Chapter 9. This section should outline the development of the technology platform as new products or applications are introduced. An exception to including a section on managing the portfolio for growth might be when an organization is failing or bankrupt and therefore focusing exclusively on asset management.

Interbusiness Relationships

Chapter 10 outlined how multibusiness firms manage the transfers among the business units. An effective transfer policy aligns the value and cost drivers of the business units so that vertical integration improves their market positions. It is often the case that traditional transfer policies have become obsolete as business unit markets have changed, creating unproductive interunit conflict and underperformance. The planning process is one mechanism for resolving these issues.

Centralization of Activities

The corporate strategic plan in a multibusiness firm should also articulate how shared or centralized activities, such as marketing, logistics, or procurement, contribute to business unit performance. The assumptions behind centralization are critical for the strategic direction of the business units, since shared activities have a direct influence on value and cost drivers. The planning process presents an opportunity to assess how centralization affects business performance and to improve firm practices and policies.

Top-Down Initiatives

Top-down initiatives are a key contribution of corporate leadership to business unit performance. The planning process provides an opportunity to look at their impact and identify where new initiatives may be warranted. Particularly important are initiatives, such as quality and e-commerce programs, that influence business unit market positions directly.

Corporate Infrastructure

The functions of the corporate office—legal services, human resources, information technology, accounting, and finance—have both support and compliance roles regarding the business units. An overview of how these functions contribute to business unit strategies can be a useful part of the plan, especially if ad hoc problem solving that involves corporate and business policies has ceased to be effective. Including separate sections in the plan for each function can also be useful, as markets and regulatory requirements change.

Summary

In this chapter we have covered how firms, both single and multibusiness, develop strategic plans to improve performance. The best plans are a line management tool, not the result of a staff exercise. They arise from a spirited discussion of the opportunities and challenges the firm faces and incorporate new ideas based on openness and experimentation. The results of this discussion then constitute the firm's commitments, as initiatives and programs, to improve its market performance. Strategic planning is thus a key event in the annual cycle of organizational assessment and renewal.

Summary Points

- Strategic planning is fundamentally a line, not a staff, activity.
- Strategic planning extends top management's leadership and power.
- Strategic planning overcomes organizational drift.
- Strategic planning is not strategy execution but makes execution more effective.
- A strategic plan at the business level should have the following elements: mission statement, analysis of the industry, goal setting on financial and operating metrics, strategic initiatives, and operational programs.
- A strategic plan at the corporate level in a multibusiness firm should be the core document for managing the organization as a whole.
- The corporate plan should serve the following functions:
  - Allocate resources among the units.

- Stimulate the creation of new businesses.
- Organize and manage interunit relationships.
- Centralize activities across the business units.
- Develop top-down initiatives.
- Develop corporate infrastructure.

Questions for Practice

Think of an industry in which you are working or have worked or that you are researching to answer the following questions.

1. How does your organization use strategic planning to develop projects and allocate resources?
2. How effectively does your firm utilize a scan of the industry in its planning process?
3. How effectively does your company set financial and operating goals?
4. How has your firm used the strategic planning as a problem-solving process?
5. How has your company used strategic planning to expose and neutralize destructive cognitive biases in decision making?
6. In what ways does strategic planning help your firm in project evaluation?
7. What are the key strategic initiatives your company has taken and how are they linked to your strategic plan?
8. In what ways does your firm link program development to strategic planning?
9. How does your firm link strategic planning to the core elements of strategy execution?
10. How are the key financial tools your firm uses to make investment decisions tied to your strategic planning process?

End Notes

1. See Michael Hannan and John Freeman, "Structural Inertia and Organizational Change," *American Sociological Review* 92 (1984), pp. 149–64.
2. For an interesting discussion of strategy making in volatile markets, see Kathleen Eisenhardt and Donald Sull, "Strategy as Simple Rules," *Harvard Business Review* (January 2001), pp. 107–16.
3. For summaries and commentary on general psychological biases in managerial decision making, see J. Edward Russo and Paul Schoemaker, *Decision Traps* (New York: Simon and Schuster, 1989); Daniel Kahnemann and Amos Tversky, *Choices,*

Values and Frames (Cambridge: Cambridge University Press, 2000); Max Bazerman, *Judgment in Managerial Decision Making* (New York: John Wiley, 2001); James Walsh, "Managerial and Organizational Cognition: Notes from a Trip Down Memory Lane," *Organization Science* 6 (1995), pp. 280–321.

4. For a discussion of how myopic decision making in the United States may have hindered its global competitiveness, see Michael Porter, *Capital Choices* (Washington, DC: Council on Competitiveness, 1992); for a range of interesting studies on myopic behavior in general, see George Loewenstein, *Intertemporal Choice* (New York: Oxford University Press, 2002).

5. For a classic discussion of this phenomenon, see Avinash Dixit, "Entry and Exit Decisions under Uncertainty," *Journal of Political Economy* 97 (1989), pp. 620–38.

6. For the seminal article on framing in terms of gains and losses, see Daniel Kahnemann and Amos Tversky, 1979, "Prospect Theory: An Analysis of Decision under Risk," *Econometrica* 47 (1979), pp. 263–91.

7. See Amos Tversky and Daniel Kahnemann, "Availability: A Heuristic for Judging Frequency and Probability," *Cognitive Psychology* 5 (1973), pp. 207–32.

8. See Amos Tversky and Daniel Kahneman, "Judgment under Uncertainty: Heuristics and Biases," *Science* 185 (1974), pp. 1124–31; Paul Slovic and Sarah Lichtenstein, "Comparison of Bayesian and Regression Approaches to the Study of Information Processing in Judgment," *Organizational Behavior and Human Performance* 6 (1971), pp. 641–744.

9. There is a large literature on managerial cognition in strategic decision making; for biases in perceiving competitors, Edward J. Zajac and Max Bazerman, "Blind Spots in Industry and Competitor Analysis: The Implications of Interfirm (mis) Perceptions for Strategic Decisions," *Academy of Management Review* 16 (1991), pp. 37–56; Joe Porac and Howard Thomas, "Taxonomic Mental Models of Competitor Analysis," *Academy of Management Review* 15 (1990), pp. 224–40; Anne Huff (ed.), *Mapping Strategic Thought* (New York: John Wiley, 1990); Rhonda Reger and Anne Huff, "Strategic Groups: A Cognitive Perspective," *Strategic Management Journal* 14 (1993), pp. 103–24.

10. For seminal papers on scenario analysis, see Paul Schoemaker, "When and How to Use Scenario Planning," *Journal of Forecasting* 10 (1991), pp. 549–64; Paul Schoemaker, "Multiple Scenario Development: Its Conceptual and Behavioral Foundation," *Strategic Management Journal* 14 (1993), pp. 193–213.

11. See Pierre Wack, "Scenarios: Uncharted Waters Ahead," *Harvard Business Review* (September–October 1985), pp. 73–89.

12. For an insightful view of the importance of programs in a business's strategic plan, see Larry Bossidy and Ram Charan, *Execution* (New York: Crown, 2002), chaps. 7, 8, and 9.

13. See for example, James L. Paddock, Daniel R. Siegel, and James L. Smith, "Option Valuation of Claims on Real Assets: The Case of Offshore Petroleum Leases," *Quarterly Journal of Economics* 103 (1988), pp. 479–508; Charles H. Fine and Robert M. Freund, "Optimal Investment in Product-Flexible Manufacturing Capacity," *Management Science* 36 (1990), pp. 449–66; Timothy Folta and Kent D. Miller, "Real Options in Equity Partnerships," *Strategic Management Journal* 23 (2002), pp. 77–88.

14. The example here is adapted from Robert Pindyck, "Irreversibility, Uncertainty and Investment," *Journal of Economic Literature* 29 (1991), pp. 1110–48; see also Avinash Dixit and Robert Pindyck, *Investment under Uncertainty* (Princeton, NJ: Princeton University Press, 1994), chap. 2.

15. For a discussion of first-mover advantage in competing under uncertainty, see Birger Wernerfelt and Aneel Karnani, "Competitive Strategy under Uncertainty," *Strategic Management Journal* 8 (1987), pp. 187–94.

16. For a comprehensive discussion of portfolio models, see Arnaldo Hax and Nicolas Majluf, *The Strategy Concept and Process* (Upper Saddle River, NJ: Prentice Hall, 1996), chap. 17.

Glossary

A

absorptive capacity   The ability of the firm to adopt innovations developed by other organizations based on its prior experience with similar or related practices or technologies.

activity system   The set of identifiable activities, policies, and practices that comprise the key elements through which the firm operates.

agency theory (in corporate governance)   The theory of corporate governance that specifies management as the agent of shareholders and the board of directors as their representatives responsible for ensuring that management decision making adheres to their interests.

alignment problem in incentive systems   The problem caused by a disconnect between the task outcomes desired and the measures used to assess task performance.

antitakeover defense   A policy written into a company's bylaws or board charters that inhibits a potential acquirer from bidding for control of the company.

arms race   A type of competition in which two or more firms invest in product or process innovations at about the same rate and with about the same contribution to their market positions so that no firm gains an advantage over the other.

asset specificity   The specialization or customization of a supplier's assets or activities to the requirements of a buyer.

B

backward integration   A firm's vertical integration into an activity that is closer to the source of raw materials than to the customer, as when an assembly firm integrates a component fabrication activity.

balanced scorecard   A planning system focused primarily on goal setting and compensation.

BCG (Boston Consulting Group) matrix   A portfolio management method based on market growth and relative market share.

Bertrand competition   Competition on price.

blank check   A takeover defense that allows the board of directors to issue preferred stock to thwart a potential acquirer from gaining control of the company.

business judgment rule   A rule used as a "safe harbor," or protection, when a director's duty of care is being questioned.

buyer concentration   A high level of concentration in the industry the firm sells its product to.

buyer experience   The extent to which buyers have experience of the firm's product.

buyer power   The ability of the buyer to force the firm to lower its price without lowering the value offered, or raise its value without raising its price, or both.

buyer surplus   The difference between the value the buyer receives from a product and the price the firm charges for this value.

C

capability   The firm's ability to accomplish tasks that are linked to performance by increasing value, decreasing cost, or both, through the coordinated efforts of teams whose members may change even as the practices involved persist and improve.

capital asset pricing model (CAPM)   A model for valuing stocks by relating risk and expected return, based on the idea that investors demand additional expected return (called the risk premium) if asked to accept additional risk.

cartel   A group of firms in an industry that have agreed, either legally or illegally, to make decisions jointly in order to increase their profits.

carve-out   The partial spin-off of a business unit from a firm by offering some of the equity in the unit to the public.

cash cow   A business unit, in the portfolio of a diversified firm, that has a dominant market share in a low growth industry.

causal ambiguity   The difficulty competitors encounter in copying a rival's capability because they are unable to map out the policies and practices that underlie it.

centralization   The creation of a single higher-level activity (e.g., procurement or marketing) to replace disparate activities located in lower-level units.

coasting in an activity system   The continuation of an activity in the activity system without changes.

comparative advantage   The benefit that a country contributes to local firms, competing globally, through inputs such as capital, materials, labor, technology, and practices.

compensation system   The system within the firm used to reward managers and workers for task performance.

competitive advantage   The combination of a superior market position and the ability to defend this position from competitors.

complement or complementary product   A product in another industry whose pattern of demand is positively correlated with the firm's product or that increases the value of the firm's products (e.g., ski resorts and skis).

concentration ratio   The ratio of the aggregate volume of the top firms in an industry, typically the top four or eight, to total industry volume.

consistency in an activity system   The extent to which the activities in the system reinforce each other to improve the firm's execution of its strategy.

controllability problem in incentive systems   When managers are unable to identify how much performance is due to skill, effort, or luck.

core competence   The combination of a strong technology platform and entrepreneurial management skills, within a multibusiness firm, that leads to the creation of new businesses whose learning feeds back into and strengthens the platform.

core elements in an activity system   Key policies and activities that have a major impact on the firm's market position.

core rigidity   The inability of a firm to adapt to changing market or technological conditions because of its attachment to its core practices and customers.

corporate governance   The institutions and mechanisms for the design and monitoring of the rules used to make decisions that involve compliance with legal, accounting, or governmental regulations, and the rules that align the firm's performance with the expectations of its owners.

cost advantage   The extent to which one firm has lower costs than its rivals in selling to a customer.

cost leadership   The strategy of achieving the lowest costs in an industry.

cost of capital   The weighted average of (1) the firm's cost of equity, calculated either using CAPM or the dividend capitalization model, and (2) the cost of the firm's debt.

Cournot competition   Competing on volume.

crossing the chasm   The movement of a firm's customer base across the product life cycle from the early adopter market segment to the early majority segment.

customer-based organizational structure   A type of organizational structure in which customer industries are the primary mode of organizing activities.

D

dedicated asset   An asset external to the firm that is dedicated to the firm, such as a distribution channel or a supplier.

demand (volume) uncertainty   The extent to which the volume of the firm cannot be forecasted.

differentiation   The generic strategy associated with achieving a value advantage over competitors.

direct or explicit collusion   The coordination, through direct communication, of prices, production volume, or other decisions, by a group of firms in an industry in order to lower competition and increase profits.

disruptive technology   Christensen's term to describe a product based on a new technology, composed primarily of standard components, whose price and functionality are substantially lower than the incumbent product, which is not initially desired by customers in the core market, but which achieves rapid acceptance as customers switch to it and leave incumbent firms.

distinctive competence   Those resources and capabilities of a firm that produce critical value and cost drivers, leading to a superior market position.

distortion in incentive systems   The problem created by the underweighting of hard-to-measure activities and the overweighting of those that are easy to measure.

diversification   The firm's investment in a new business unit.

diversification discount   The empirical finding that multibusiness firms typically trade at a discount to a set of comparable single businesses.

dominant design   The culmination of a series of innovations, across firms and over the industry life cycle, in a product's components, architecture, and related value drivers, such as service, network externalities, complements, or breadth of line.

double-loop learning   Problem solving that extends outside the task's normal domain and raises questions about the task parameters themselves.

dual pricing   Transfer pricing that involves two prices: full cost to the buyer and market price to the supplier.

duopoly   Competition between two firms.

duty of care   A board director's duty to exercise the care that an ordinarily prudent person would reasonably be expected to exercise in a like position and under similar circumstances.

duty of loyalty   A board director's duty to act in good faith regarding the best interests of the corporation.

dynamic capability   The ability of a firm, as it grows, to build its innovative potential effectively.

dynamic growth cycle   The cycle of firm growth linking size, innovation, productivity, profitability, and capacity expansion.

E

early adopter customers   Customers who are attracted to a product early in its life cycle primarily because of the product's technology.

early majority customers   Customers who are attracted to a product in the stage in the life cycle after early adopters.

early mover advantage   That part of a firm's competitive advantage due to the firm's having entered an industry early in its history and made a series of investments in innovation and capacity.

economic contribution   The difference between the value offered by a product to a customer and the firm's cost to produce that value.

economies of scale   The decline in a firm's recurring average costs with higher volume over the long term, as fixed costs are spread across a larger number of units produced.

economies of scope   When a firm incurs a lower cost from producing two products using shared assets and practices compared to the cost of producing the products separately.

efficient boundaries model   The model developed by Oliver Williamson to describe the relationship between asset specificity, transaction costs, production costs, and vertical integration.

employment relationship   The rules that govern the relationship between the firm and an employee.

entry barriers   The factors that raise the costs of firms in entering an industry.

exchange autonomy   A transfer pricing scheme that applies when transactions between the internal buyer and supplier are not mandated—that is, there is no policy of vertical integration.

F

forward integration   Vertical integration into an activity that is closer to the customer (e.g., sales, distribution, or service).

functional structure   A type of organizational structure in which functions (e.g., marketing, operations) are the primary mode of organizing activities.

five forces   Michael Porter's framework for describing the five industry factors that influence firm performance—buyers, suppliers, competition, entry, and substitutes.

fixed costs   Those costs that remain relatively constant as volume changes.

G

generic strategy   Michael Porter's characterization of two market positions that may lead to superior profitability—cost leadership or differentiation.

geographical structure   A type of organizational structure in which geographical regions are the primary mode of organizing activities.

global configuration   The locations across countries where global firms have placed their activities.

golden parachute   A clause in an executive's employment contract specifying that he or she will receive large benefits if the company is acquired and the executive's employment is terminated.

H

hierarchical referral   The coordination mechanism in which managers refer a problem to superiors for resolution.

hypercompetition   The state of competition in which firms, typically in a mature industry, engage in both multipoint competition and an arms race.

I

incentive system   The reward system through which individuals and units are motivated to perform their tasks.

incomplete contracting   When all the contingencies that impinge on a contracting relationship between two parties cannot be specified at the time the contract is written.

industry evolution   The passing of an industry through three stages: growth, shakeout, and maturity.

information anchoring   The decision-making bias associated with the overuse of information that is received first in a sequence.

information availability   The decision-making bias associated with the overuse of information that is most available.

interdependency problem in incentive systems   When performance depends on the efforts of a team, making it difficult to identify individual contributions.

internal capital market   The allocation of financial capital to businesses within a multibusiness firm, substituting for the external capital market.

internalization in global strategy   The vertical integration of a global firm into activities performed in a host country, initially sales and distribution, and subsequently other functions.

isolating mechanisms   The factors that sustain a firm's market position by increasing customer retention or impeding imitation or countering.

J

joint venture   A business created by two firms so that they can pursue a common interest or complementary interests.

L

labor pooling   The sharing of a common labor force by firms in the same geographical region.

learning costs   The costs incurred by a firm or manager in learning a new practice.

learning curve   The steep reduction in an activity's costs through learning as volume increases.

limit pricing   The price firms in an industry may set to deter entry.

low-cost inputs   Inputs whose prices are lower than competitors' inputs due to sourcing either from a low-cost geographical region or from a highly efficient, dedicated supplier.

M

mandated full cost   A transfer price in which an internal supplier sells its product to an internal buyer at full cost.

mandated market price   A transfer price in which an internal supplier sells its product to an internal buyer at market price.

Marakon profitability matrix   A portfolio assessment method, developed by Marakon Associates, which assesses business units in terms of (1) whether they are gaining or losing competitive advantage and (2) their ratios of return on equity to the firm's cost of capital.

market position   The location of a firm in an industry defined by the level of value customers and the cost the firm incurs to produce that value.

matrix structure   A firm's reporting structure in which two dimensions (say, function and region) are equally weighted so that some managers have two superiors.

mission statement   The part of a strategic plan that describes the firm's business scope and intent.

mobility barrier   The costs of moving from one strategic group to another, typically understood to be imposed by the actions of firms in the target group.

monopoly   An industry structure in which one firm is the sole supplier to customers.

multidivisional (product) structure   The structure of a multibusiness firm in which the primary organizing dimension is the business unit or division.

multidomestic structure   The structure of a global firm in which the regions operate as separate businesses.

multipoint competition   Competition between firms, typically in a mature industry, in which they face off against each other with broad product lines across geographical regions or market segments.

N

network externalities   Economies of scale in demand, which means that the benefit each customer receives from a product increases as new customers are added.

niche market   A submarket, within an industry, whose customers have special preferences.

noise in incentive system   An incentive system attribute that makes it difficult to separate individual employee effort and skill from luck and the contribution of other employees.

noncooperative strategic interaction   Competition that ensues when firms in an oligopoly interact by observing each other and making decisions based on what the other does or may do, but without communicating.

O

oligopoly   A small group of firms that compete with each other and dominate rivalry in an industry.

options strategy in partnering   An approach to partnering that allows a firm to learn enough about a new technology to be able to plan for the development of projects based on it, through making a small, low-risk investment below the amount required to develop the new technology to scale.

organizational structure   Typically, the formal reporting structure of the firm, but it may also include the network of informal relationships.

outsourcing   The shifting of an activity from inside the firm to an outside supplier.

P

partnership   A relationship, almost always between a buyer and a supplier, that is closely coordinated in order to achieve joint gains.

patching in an activity system   The addition of a new core element to a firm's activity system.

path dependence   The tendency of a firm over time to invest in innovations that are upwardly compatible with each other, thereby creating a relatively unique path of product and process development.

perfect competition   The state of competition when no entrant to an industry can make more than its cost of capital.

piece rate compensation system   The compensation system in which workers are rewarded on the basis of their output.

poison pill   An antitakeover defense in which the board may declare for existing stockholders a dividend of the right to buy one share for each of their existing shares when a bidder's holdings have exceeded a certain percentage of the company's equity, say 15 percent.

portfolio management in a multibusiness firm   Corporate management of the set of businesses in a multibusiness firm.

positioning strategy in partnering   An approach to partnering in which the incumbent puts more financial, technical, and managerial resources into the alliance in order to build a viable business, either with the start-up as a partially independent partner or later with a wholly owned unit.

price competition   Competition based on the price of the product.

price leadership   An industry practice in which one firm takes the role of setting prices for the industry as a whole.

prisoner's dilemma   A game in which two players have two strategies, A and B, so that when they both play strategy A, each wins a little; and when one player plays A and the other B, the B player wins a lot and A player loses a lot; but when both play B, they both lose a little; with the outcome that, without communication, both play B and lose a little.

process innovation   An innovation in an activity to lower costs or improve value.

product innovation   The development of a new product, typically with higher technical functionality.

product life cycle   The passage of a product through three major stages: growth, maturity, and decline.

product line extension   The addition of new products to a firm's product line.

property rights   The legal rights assigned to the owner of a tangible or intangible asset that prevent others from copying its design, core attributes, or other characteristics.

property rights approach   The theory, first introduced by Sanford Grossman and Oliver Hart, whose core proposition is that the company internalizing an activity has the most to benefit from controlling investments in it.

Q

quantity competition   Competition through investments in volume.

R

real options   The extension of financial options models to nonfinancial investments such as new production capacity, technology projects, exploration projects such as oil or gas wells, and even joint ventures with other firms.

repository of knowledge (in a partnership)   The presence and availability in a partnership of the two firms' cumulative experience in dealing with each other over time.

residual income   A divisional performance measure that includes a charge for the firm's cost of capital.

resource complementarity   The extent to which the returns to two resources are positively correlated.

ROI (return on investment)   The ratio of a project's profit, adjusted for taxes and interest payments, to the investment in the project.

S

Sarbanes-Oxley Act   An act of the U.S. Congress in 2002 to establish a governing body for the monitoring of financial reporting and accounting firms (the Public Company Accounting Oversight Board), impose new

accountability for corporate executives concerning their firms' financial reports, and impose new standards for internal controls within firms.

scale-driven cost driver   A cost driver that becomes more effective as volume increases (e.g., scale economies, scope economies, and the learning curve).

scale-driven value driver   A value driver that becomes stronger as volume increases (e.g., network externalities, geographic scope, brand, breadth of line).

scenario analysis   A process in which managers identify possible future states of their business environment, commonly used in strategic planning.

search costs   The costs a firm or individual incurs in searching for a new product or supplier.

shakeout   The second stage in industry evolution in which the number of firms exiting the industry exceeds the number of firms entering.

staggered board   A corporate governance policy pertaining to the election of directors such that shareholders cannot replace a majority of the board in any year.

strategic alliance   A business relationship between two firms to pursue joint or complementary interests for gain.

strategic complementarity   A competitive situation in which a firm has a higher marginal return when it responds aggressively to an aggressive move by a competitor, or correspondingly, weakly to a weak move by a competitor.

strategic group   A group of firms in an industry that share a common market position, such as the low cost group in a domestic airline industry.

strategic initiatives   A part of a strategic plan that describes the overarching tasks, usually not more than five or six, that are necessary for achieving the firm's goals.

strategic planning   A process in which top management and unit heads define the direction of the company, its financial and operating goals, the major initiatives required to achieve those goals, and the underlying tasks necessary to accomplish the initiatives.

strategic pricing   Pricing at or below cost, typically in the growth stage of an industry, in order to build market share and in the expectation that costs will drop due to economies of scale or the learning curve.

strategic sourcing   A set of programs in procurement, operations, product design, and logistics that focuses on a small set of highly qualified suppliers so that control and coordination over the supply base is improved and input costs lowered.

strategic sourcing framework   A framework that combines two dimensions—the relative competence of the firm and the strategic importance of the activity—to explain the logic behind vertical integration and outsourcing decisions.

strategy execution   The combination of four elements—(1) control and coordination; (2) consistency among activities; (3) compensation and incentives; and (4) culture, people, and learning—that produce the capabilities underlying the firm's value and cost drivers.

strong organizational culture   A culture in which there is a robust consensus among employees about the values, norms, and decision rules of thumb in an organization.

stuck in the middle   A market position in which the firm has neither the highest nor lowest value offered and neither the highest nor lowest cost.

substitute product   A product that performs a similar function to that sold by the firm, but is in a different industry (e.g., a fan compared to an air conditioner).

sunk costs   Costs incurred as a result of a one-time investment in an asset or activity whose benefit continues afterward (e.g., the costs of software development or making a movie).

supplier power   The ability of a supplier to extract higher profits from its buyer either by raising prices, lowering the value delivered, or both.

supporting elements in an activity system   Activities that augment the benefit provided by core elements in the activity system.

sustaining technology   Christensen's definition of a new technology, introduced into an industry, to which incumbent firms can adapt.

switching costs   The costs incurred by a customer in switching from one product to another.

T

tacit collusion   The coordination, without direct communication, of prices, production volume, or other decisions by a group of firms in an industry in order to lower competition and increase profits.

technological substitution   The introduction of a new technology whose characteristics give it higher functionality than the existing technology.

technological uncertainty   The inability to forecast effectively which technology will be best suited for a particular product.

technology platform   The set of technical practices, skills, and assets within a firm that are necessary for the repeated development of variations on a core technological base (e.g., adhesives or LCD screens).

technology spillovers   The transfer of technological knowledge among firms in a geographical region.

thickening in an activity system   The addition of activities around a core element in a firm's activity system.

time compression diseconomy   The cost of trying to develop a capability in less time than the original firm.

transaction cost   The costs incurred by a buyer and its supplier in managing their relationship.

transaction cost theory   The theory, proposed by Oliver Williamson, that vertical integration occurs in response to high transaction costs in the supply relationship.

transfer price   The price of a product transferred between two business units in a multibusiness firm.

transition costs   The costs a buyer incurs in its production process when it removes one component (e.g., a piece of equipment) and replaces it with another.

transnational structure   A type of structure found in global firms that emphasizes both functions and regions through a network of managers.

trimming in an activity system   The deletion of a core element and the elements attached to it when they fail to fit the direction of the rest of the activity system.

V

value advantage   When a firm offers higher value to the customer than its competitors.

value chain   The set of activities that comprise a typical single business, as construed by Michael Porter.

value driver   A determinant of value offered by a firm to its customers.

value net   A framework, developed by Brandenberger and Nalebuff, that describes the ways in which interfirm cooperation can produce higher joint profitability.

vertical integration   The shifting of an activity from a market supplier to inside the firm.

vision statement   A part of a strategic plan that states succinctly the firm's ambitions.

W

willingness-to-pay   That price which a customer would be willing to pay for a product in the absence of competitors but in the presence of substitutes.

window strategy in partnering   A relationship that provides information about a new technology to an established firm but does not help to build a path for the technology's development within the firm.

Name Index

Subject Index